DESIRE, GIFT, AND RECOGNITION

Christology and Postmodern Philosophy

Jan-Olav Henriksen

William B. Eerdmans Publishing Company
Grand Rapids, Michigan / Cambridge, U.K.

Published 2009 by
Wm. B. Eerdmans Publishing Co.
2140 Oak Industrial Drive N.E., Grand Rapids, Michigan 49505 /
P.O. Box 163, Cambridge CB3 9PU U.K.
www.eerdmans.com

Printed in the United States of America

14 13 12 11 10 09   7 6 5 4 3 2 1

Library of Congress Cataloging-in-Publication Data

Henriksen, Jan-Olav.
Desire, gift, and recognition: christology and postmodern philosophy /
    Jan-Olav Henriksen.
       p.   cm.
    Includes bibliographical references.
    ISBN 978-0-8028-6371-3 (pbk.: alk. paper)
    1. Jesus Christ — Person and offices. 2. Postmodernism —
    Religious aspects — Christianity.   I. Title.

    BT203.H47 2009
    232 — dc22
                                        2008046515

The publication of this book was made possible through
a generous grant from the Research Council of Norway.

DESIRE, GIFT, AND RECOGNITION

Contents

Acknowledgments

There are good reasons to ask why there is a need for another book on Jesus. However, as I hope becomes clear in the Introduction, not much has been done to make an interpretation of the Jesus story by means of postmodern philosophy. My own work on this book has been encouraged by a host of people, and I need to thank the following for making the book possible, and for encouragement during the final stages of its finalization:

The members of the Center of Theological Inquiry in Princeton, 2006-2007, provided excellent opportunities for discussion and exchange. Some of the members, and others, have read, commented, and/or encouraged, including Graham Maddox (Armidale, Australia), Hermann Paul (Leiden, the Netherlands), and Christine Yoder (Columbia Theological Seminary, Decatur, GA). Thanks also to Wentzel van Huyssteen (Princeton), LeRon Shults (my new colleague in Kristiansand, Norway), Marius Mjaaland (Oslo), and Maud Laird Eriksen (Uppsala) for giving encouraging comments along the way. A special thanks to Kenneth Reynhout, Ph.D. student at Princeton Theological Seminary, who worked through the whole manuscript and improved my English significantly, in addition to discussing some substantial issues with me.

Thanks also to the staff of the CTI, especially Will Storrar and Kathi Morley, who made the winter of 2006-2007 a wonderful time for both my family and me. The chances they provided for doing concentrated research were indeed invaluable. It is a gift to look back at the writing period of a book like this and realize how much the writing has been accompanied by good memories of community with friends, colleagues, and family. I know from personal experience that this is not always the case.

I would like to thank the Norwegian School of Theology, Oslo, for providing me with the possibility for a long sabbatical during which this book could be written. Without the generous support from my employer this work would not have been possible. Thanks also to the Norwegian Research Council for a substantial publication grant.

Finally, I would like to thank W. B. Eerdmans publishers for embarking on yet another project with a Norwegian scholar, and for their professional handling of the process in making this a book. A special thanks to Bill Eerdmans, who was enthusiastic about the project even during the time of planning, and thereby made me believe that this was a book worth doing.

JAN-OLAV HENRIKSEN
Princeton, New Jersey,
and Oslo, Norway

Introduction:
Christ from Other Angles

Christology as the Impossible?

In many ways Christology — the doctrinal formulation of the identity and work of Jesus Christ — seems to express something impossible: that a human is also God, that he is resurrected from the dead, that he instigated a new world order and a reality different from the present one. Hence, it is also often rejected by non-believers as nonsense. In recent philosophy we can nevertheless see an emerging and increasing interest in phenomena that are part of the reports we have on the life of Jesus, especially in the Synoptic Gospels.[1] Having read some of this philosophy, I find it increasingly striking how relevant much of this philosophy seems for a possible understanding of what takes place in the history of Jesus. Despite these commonalities, I have not yet come across a book that makes the attempt to develop a more comprehensive understanding of the scattered insights

---

1. I rely mostly on the synoptic narratives of Jesus in the following — both because they are narratives, and thereby can be seen as opening up to other strategies of reflection than do the other New Testament literature, and because the access to concrete phenomena is easier in this material than in John and Paul. This does not imply, though, that I neglect other material totally. For others who adopt the same type of strategy, cf. e.g., John Macquarrie, *Christology Revisited* (London: SCM Press, 1998), pp. 26ff., and in New Testament scholarship, N. T. Wright, *Jesus and the Victory of God: Christian Origins and the Question of God,* vol. 2 (London: SPCK, 1996), and more recently Marcus J. Borg, *Jesus: Uncovering the Life, Teachings, and Relevance of a Religious Revolutionary,* 1st ed. (San Francisco: HarperSanFrancisco, 2006). The emphasis on the narratives as basic for the interpretation of Christology is also affirmed in the seminal work of Edward Schillebeeckx, *Jesus: An Experiment in Christology* (New York: Seabury Press, 1979), pp. 77ff.

1

into the different phenomena that philosophy now gives attention to by reading them from within the framework of Christology.[2] This book is an attempt to address that deficiency.

Impossibility faces us not only in Christology. What matters most to us is often what seems most impossible. The call from the other demands that we struggle for justice, but we cannot fulfill its demand, so justice is still wanting. We have a desire to love and be loved, but often we end up loving only ourselves. Can a gift be given? Can hospitality be offered without self-interest? Is desire only egotistic? These phenomena, phenomena through which human life, given the right circumstances, might flourish, are the very same phenomena that often appear as problematic or ambiguous: In recent philosophy there is a lot of talk about such phenomena, which I, for lack of a better name, call *phenomena of surplus*[3] — gift, forgiveness, love, desire, recognition, sacrifice, hospitality, excess, trust, and reconciliation, to name some. These phenomena give color to human life, but they constantly escape us as well, or deteriorate into the opposite of what their initially perceived goodness promises us. They also call us into a kind of endless hermeneutics, as they are never exhaustively grasped in our concepts.[4] This endless hermeneutics was initiated already in the New Tes-

---

2. There are, however, some exceptions from this generic statement, e.g., in David W. Odell-Scott, *A Post-Patriarchal Christology*, American Academy of Religion Academy Series, No. 78 (Atlanta: Scholars Press, 1991). His book is not related to the narratives, however, but to the conceptual formulations of later Christological doctrine, esp. Chalcedon. David Hadley Jensen, *In the Company of Others: A Dialogical Christology* (Cleveland: Pilgrim Press, 2001), deals mostly with inter-religious issues, and Hent de Vries, *Philosophy and the Turn to Religion* (Baltimore: Johns Hopkins University Press, 1999) deals extensively with postmodern philosophy in relation to religion, but not with more specific Christological themes.

3. Jean-Luc Marion calls these *saturated phenomena*, but this entails that he is using a purely phenomenological approach to them. That is not a route I follow consequently here, thus the different way of formulating these experiences.

4. This type of endless hermeneutics is well articulated in the work of Paul Ricoeur, cf. Richard Kearney, *On Paul Ricoeur: The Owl of Minerva, Transcending Boundaries in Theology and Philosophy* (Aldershot, UK: Ashgate, 2004), p. 5: "The central thesis of hermeneutics, he insists, is that interpretation remains an ongoing process which no one vision can totalize. This entails a belonging to meaning in and through distance. Or to put it in another way, hermeneutics endeavours to render near what is far — temporally, geographically, scientifically, culturally — by reappropriating those meanings that have been 'distantiated' from our consciousness. Once again, the textual paradigm proves exemplary. By exposing myself to the textual horizons of 'other' meanings, I transcend the familiar limits of subjective consciousness and open myself to possible new worlds. If then subjectivity continues to

tament, and has been carried out in every theological work since. Why? Because there is something excessive about such phenomena, a point presently noted by several philosophers that I will refer to in this book.[5] What can we learn of such phenomena when we approach them from a more Christological angle? What place can such phenomena have in Christology?[6] And what new angles can they offer us as new angles for understanding the issues around which Christology circles? These are the underlying questions of this book.

Systematic theology and philosophy of religion each suffer from a mutual condition of contemporary isolation. The split manifests itself in how systematic theology is largely carried out without taking much notice of what is taking place in post-metaphysical and postmodern philosophy of religion, which tries to develop an interpretation of religious issues without immediate recourse to conditions beyond history. Often, it instead develops its insights with reference to past philosophical positions and established church teaching.[7] On the other hand, much of postmodern philosophy, including postmodern philosophy of religion, seems to take little or no notice of the major elements that structure the content of the Christian traditions, and instead focuses on the abstract, formal, and/or metaphysical elements that these traditions have brought about. Can these two disciplines then be brought into a more fruitful relationship with each other, and if so, how? I think they can, and this book is an at-

---

exist for hermeneutics, it is as that 'self-as-another' attained only after our intersubjective detours of interpretation."

5. In addition to Marion, Derrida and Ricoeur are among the most prominent. Ricoeur also deals with it in an explicitly theological context, in Paul Ricoeur, *Figuring the Sacred: Religion, Narrative, and Imagination,* trans. David Pellauer (Minneapolis: Augsburg Fortress, 1995), esp. pp. 279ff. An extensive treatment of Derrida's and Marion's conceptions of gift can be found in Robyn Horner, *Rethinking God as Gift: Marion, Derrida, and the Limits of Phenomenology,* 1st ed., Perspectives in Continental Philosophy, No. 19 (New York: Fordham University Press, 2001).

6. Christology should here be understood in the wider sense suggested by J. Macquarrie, who holds that it is more than a historical study of the man Jesus from Nazareth. It is a *theological* enterprise that seeks to "put Jesus in the context of Christian faith, asking about his relation to God on the one hand and to the human race on the other, and asking how we must think of a person who can sustain these relations." Cf. John Macquarrie, *Jesus Christ in Modern Thought* (London and Philadelphia: SCM Press and Trinity Press International, 1990), p. 5.

7. There are, however, notable exceptions, of which I here only mention Dalferth and Kearney. For more on their work, see below.

tempt to make this happen. The major reason for doing this is that I remain convinced that the central content of the Christian tradition has much to gain from a close encounter with postmodern philosophy. By "the central content," I mean the story of Jesus Christ, and how he can justifiably be thought to reveal God (given that we later specify more extensively the understanding of "reveal" and "God").[8]

Christian faith in Jesus Christ holds the understanding of Jesus — and Jesus' understanding of God — to be the very center of its basis. But how can there be a relation between this core Christological concern and postmodern philosophy? One way to answer that question would be to say, simply, that there is no such relation. This book is written based on the conviction that there *could be* a link, but that it is not *necessary,* be it from a theological or from a philosophical point of view. *Could be* implies that there is *no necessity* in using postmodern philosophy to develop the content of Christology, just as there is no "hidden" Christology in postmodern philosophy. But postmodern philosophy might be interpreted on the basis of resources in Christology, just as Christology might find new ways of articulating itself by means of such philosophy. That is what I intend to attempt in this book.

To read Christological themes in light of postmodern philosophy means both that we have to select specific material, and that this light might illuminate a reading that expands understanding, where we are allowed to look at familiar things in new and different ways. Moreover, it means that we sometimes are able to see things in new and clearer ways that would in themselves have otherwise appeared complicated. At this point I need to clarify: I use the notion "postmodern" in a sense that sees the need for alternatives to mere rationalistic, humanistic, or idealistic forms of philosophy, alternatives that take account of the multiplicity of meanings and significance in the different phenomena of human life. It is used as a generic term for philosophies that allow us to disturb, deconstruct, and open up dimensions and experiences in human life in order to see them from more than one perspective, and to allow for a non-reductive

---

8. Hence, I do not try to develop an understanding of Jesus — and elements of Christology — that only focuses on cross and resurrection as the main themes. I admit that without resurrection there would be no Christology, but that is not to say that cross and resurrection are "constitutive for the identity of Jesus as the divine Son of God" (so Colin J. D. Greene, *Christology in Cultural Perspective: Marking Out the Horizons* [Grand Rapids: Eerdmans, 2004], p. 337).

description of them that also takes them seriously in their own historical context. Accordingly, even a philosopher like Hegel is one that I can include in this category, at least with regard to these concerns.

To my mind, to connect the two dimensions of understanding found in Christology and postmodern philosophy seems to presuppose two things: First, both are ways of dealing with, interpreting, or offering resources for orientation in the world we live in and experience. Both the Christological traditions and postmodern philosophy have bearings on how we interpret and relate to the world, and to basic elements and conditions in human life. Second, this implies that Christ and the message of Christ cannot be thought of as so unique that the content of Christology is without impact on ordinary human life — or as something totally different, something totally other than what can be experienced outside of the realm of faith and Christology. On the contrary, it is my contention that the reason *why* Christology still has something to say to contemporary believers is that what it struggles to formulate is something deeply rooted in the basic phenomena that guide and carry ordinary human experience.

The theological concerns that determine the argument of this book can be summarized thus:

- An attempt is made to maintain and articulate a Christology that does not compromise the church's traditional message about Christ, but nevertheless seeks to explore the concerns of the tradition from angles other than those usually engaged in systematic theology, and to formulate some of the experiential conditions for this doctrine.
- An attempt is made to develop a positive appropriation of postmodern philosophy by linking some of its insights to Christological issues.
- Consequently, an attempt is made to show how the reality revealed in the life of Jesus Christ can be understood and articulated from angles other than those traditionally privileged as sources in Christology (e.g., Bible and the creeds and confessions of the church).
- Furthermore, an attempt is made to explore different, perhaps even disturbing, ways to articulate the content of the Gospels. Thereby the study tries to make accessible the content of these traditions in a fashion other than the one now often regarded by many people in Western society as disconnected from their life-world. Thus I want to

create a possibility for overcoming the impression that the teaching of and about Christ is dated.

- The study is based on the conviction that all theology is an interpretation of experience (experience available also to philosophical analysis). Moreover, I want to suggest how theology can also open up to new experiences (by means of articulating the silenced, the not-articulated, the un-said, and the un-seen) in a manner that reveals the surplus of reality, a surplus flowing from the creative generosity of God.
- Finally, and ambitiously, the aim of the book is to disclose how the life, teaching, and practice of Jesus open up an understanding of God that might also be articulated from present philosophy, and thereby places the Christian understanding of God within a wider framework.

There are two deliberate choices at the basis of this enterprise: First, I do not start with linking "God" to postmodern philosophy. That has been done by many already, but too often in a manner that does not contribute anything but new modes of philosophical theology with a more or less contingent relation to the specific *Christological* content of this religious tradition.[9] When taking my point of departure in *Christ,* I address the specific Christian understanding of who God is by advancing the argument that the identity of God is most profoundly disclosed in the life, teaching, and practices of Jesus of Nazareth.

To discuss the concrete religion of Jesus — the theology of Jesus — in light of a postmodern and more or less distinctively apophatic or negative theology might seem confused or counterproductive. But it is neither. The way Jesus describes or even proclaims God opens up an understanding of God outside the established limits of thinking about God. The many parables disclose a God who represents a surplus compared to what is given in established conceptions of merit and reward, or virtue and vice. Hence, in the same manner that Jesus deconstructs a totally negative theology by means of his positive affirmations of God, he is nevertheless still easier to understand in light of an apophatic theology that affirms that

9. Examples of this are G. Vattimo, M. Heidegger, M. C. Taylor, C. Winquist, and to some extent also parts of the work of J.-L. Marion. A notable exception here, which demands serious attention, is John D. Caputo, *The Weakness of God: A Theology of the Event,* Indiana Series in the Philosophy of Religion (Bloomington: Indiana University Press, 2006).

God is more and other than what can be said. For example, the parables always hint at something more than what can be exhaustively said, something that is a surplus.[10] The parables constitute the possibility of realizing a surplus that cannot be grasped; Jesus' speech about God constitutes an expression of God in the discourse that represents a surplus compared with the ordinary speech of God as some"one" "within" a system of religious discourse, or, if you will, of onto-theology.

There is one advantage of going about things in this manner: This approach roots our discussion and analysis in a concrete religion, even more so by making use of its already-established conceptual resources. Therefore, we are able to ground our own reflections in a context that immediately can help us to discern the relevance of what we are doing. If these analyses are not linked to the context of a specific religion (Christianity), or make it appear in a recognizable and illuminating manner, then they are not helpful for that tradition and its understanding of itself.

These considerations *could* also be read as a limitation of the project: they seem to make the following a profoundly *Christian* enterprise. But that need not be the case. I readily admit that this project emerges out of my interest in understanding the Christian tradition, and my intention is to contribute to and communicate with it. But both the concrete elements analyzed and the philosophy used in order to do so can prove relevant for other religious traditions as well. In that sense, this is not a project aimed solely at disclosing the uniqueness of Christianity, but rather the opposite: I want to show how Christianity in its very roots is related to elements accessible to ordinary forms of human life that might have bearings on other types of religious self-reflection as well. To name just one example of what I am aiming at: In the story about Jesus meeting Bartimaeus in Mark 10, there is a lot to gain by interpreting this text in light of Hegel's understanding of what takes place in a process of mutual recognition of two parties who exist in an asymmetrical relationship. By reading the story in this light, we are able to develop an understanding of how Jesus appears in the Gospels that sheds light on his claim to be "The Son of Man," or as Paul interpreted him: the true image of God.

As mentioned, the main purpose of the following project is to make the contents of traditional, constructive Christology accessible by ap-

---

10. Cf. Borg, *Jesus: Uncovering the Life, Teachings, and Relevance of a Religious Revolutionary*, p. 152.

proaching it from *other* angles, i.e., angles provided partly by recent philosophical thinking. I am deeply aware of the temptation to reduce the contents of Christology to mere illustrations of theological (or philosophical) points and insights. However, the study will be carried out under the conviction that recent philosophy is discussing issues that could help open up, illuminate, and deepen our understanding of what is at stake in the *whole* history of Jesus Christ.

A postmodern approach to theology and Christology immediately also presents us with the question: *What in our present cultural situation makes it so important to stress the non-conclusive, the open and excessive, and the undecided elements in Christological thinking?* This approach is taken for granted, advocated and developed by many, but not many ask this meta-question. I think there are two primary explanations for the presence of this feature, one based more or less in contemporary theory, and the other in basic insights of Christology itself: First, the contemporary plurality and lack of clear and well-defined contexts for Christology shape the hesitancy against closure, as does the historical awareness of our own finitude. More politically, "the unprecedented rise in refugees, exiles, homeless and stateless peoples finds an echo in the growing popularity of ideas such as kenosis, emptying, exile and the nomadic among some postmodern philosophers."[11] Moreover, it is still a valid insight of Christology that Christ and his work are not defined properly and exhaustively by any of our concepts or conceptions.

A Sketch of the Main Constructive Elements to Be Used — and for What Purpose

From the *theological* point of view, the angles from which I propose to make an alternative approach to Christology are made up of two material components that will be developed throughout the book:

a) The understanding of God in the theology of Jesus. It is a central point behind this approach that Jesus' theology is *practiced* in his life, message, and ministry. His practice, based on his understanding of

11. Graham Ward, *Christ and Culture: Challenges in Contemporary Theology* (Oxford: Blackwell, 2005), p. 77.

God, is developed along lines of generosity and inclusiveness when he is confronted with people in need.[12] On the other hand, his proclamation of God provokes a response among his antagonists that creates new boundaries among people instead of dissolving them. This theology of Jesus is closely linked to his understanding of the kingdom of God. In general, what the approach from the theology of Jesus provides is an understanding of how Jesus, by making manifest what I will call *the surplus of creation,* reveals God in a surprising, non-calculable, unpredictable manner that simultaneously reveals Jesus himself as the true representative of this God. This leads internally to the second theological point of view:

b) The understanding of Jesus as the true image of God *(Imago Dei).* Building upon the understanding of the human being as *imago Dei,* I develop how Jesus is the true representative of the God he proclaims.[13] It is as such a representative that he reveals God. This interpretation makes it possible to gain insight into how Jesus can be understood as the true human person, thus providing an angle for understanding classical Christology's understanding of Jesus as *vere deus, vere homo.* This approach has profound bearings on the understanding of the *why* of the crucifixion of Jesus, and provides a new angle to the understanding of atonement and reconciliation. Moreover, seeing Jesus as the one who manifests and reveals the *surplus of creation* provides us with a new, and perhaps original, approach to understanding his resurrection.

---

12. That this practice is important to understand how Jesus understands God is underscored in several of the contributions in Markus N. A. Bockmuehl, *The Cambridge Companion to Jesus,* Cambridge Companions to Religion (Cambridge and New York: Cambridge University Press, 2001). Marianne Meye Thompson holds that "it is a mistake to limit our investigation of Jesus' understanding of God to the material of Jesus' teaching. The evidence provided by the shape of his life and practices, such as his prayer, exorcisms and his death, yields material that also illumines Jesus' convictions about God. It is the whole picture of Jesus' life and practices that gives depth to Jesus' teaching about God" (p. 43). Moreover, as becomes clear in the following, G. Stanton (*The Cambridge Companion to Jesus,* p. 71) focuses on how the "message, miracles and actions of actions of Jesus are all focused on the socially and religiously marginalised, for God's kingly rule belongs to them (Matt 5.3 par. Luke 6.20)."

13. I have described the central elements in the understanding of *imago Dei* in *Imago Dei — Den teologiske konstruksjonen av menneskets identitet [Imago Dei — The theological construction of human identity]* (Oslo: Gyldendal 2003; published in Norwegian only) and will build on that work in the present context.

From the above, it should be clear that I want to address the issues of Christology from angles that are internally related to the Christian traditions, and that serve as constructive resources for the work planned. However, these theological issues will be opened up and elaborated by using different "tools" and insights from recent theology, philosophy, and philosophy of religion. The content of this approach will be developed more extensively in the next part of this book. Before I do so, however, it is necessary to make clear how I see the task of philosophy in the context of the present project.

In general, most of the *philosophy* I will use in order to open up issues in Christology is related to the social level of human life (including the moral). At this level, phenomena as recognition, gift, and desire are presently discussed in manners that arguably are easy to relate to Christology. In addition, I also think there is a need for framing the present discussion of onto-theology[14] in a manner that relates it more directly to the theology of Jesus. One could say that I again install philosophy as the handmaid of theology, but if that turns out to be the case, then this handmaid will, metaphorically speaking, have a voice of her own as to how we can elaborate different understandings of the issues in question.

The underlying choice of elements from contemporary philosophy as a discussion partner for Christology is motivated by the conviction that there are central issues relevant to theology implied in some of the material that this philosophy provides. I am convinced that against that background the present project will be able to provide what it aims at: developing a Christology from other angles. However, this approach also underscores that the present study is not meant to supersede, or eliminate, traditional approaches to Christology, but rather to deepen our insights into its content in light of what we know and engage with today. Hence, the project has a *supplementary* and *exploratory* rather than a strictly doctrinal aim. My previous experience with this way of working suggests that for contemporary systematic theology, this is a fruitful approach.[15]

14. Cf. Merold Westphal, *Overcoming Onto-Theology: Toward a Postmodern Christian Faith*, 1st ed., Perspectives in Continental Philosophy, No. 21 (New York: Fordham University Press, 2001).

15. Stephen H. Webb illustrates the fruitfulness of this enterprise in his comment on excess, which could also count as relevant to other themes mentioned here. In fact, postmodernism does have a moral edge; it can be defined as an obsession with excess to the extent that excess upsets our metaphysical desires for control and disables our personal quests

From this material and the angles it provides, the challenge arises as to how to identify and describe the *specific character* of the content of the reality revealed in and by Jesus Christ, with special regard to presently acute issues in philosophy and philosophy of religion. If we see *revelation as a mode of reality we are made able to see, and as something we did not see earlier, or did not see in the same way,* such a view would be in accordance with the suggestions above on *phenomena of surplus.* It opens up our understanding to the presence of a reality that is already there, but previously not realized in a similar manner. Hence, it is a revelation of a reality, not only of a certain type of knowledge (although it also opens up to knowledge).

The critical question this project faces echoes the one stated above: Am I using Christology to make or illustrate some general philosophical points, or am I using philosophy to make Christological points? The answer is: both. The reason for this is that Christology articulates elements that are very specific to the identity of Christian faith, whereas these elements are nevertheless also anchored in our common reality — a reality that we also explore by means of philosophy.

---

for domination. Excess decenters the subject and thus makes room for new kinds of otherness. See Webb, *The Gifting God: A Trinitarian Ethics of Excess* (Oxford: Oxford University Press, 1996), pp. v-vi.

PART I

Angles for a Postmodern Christology

Post-Metaphysical Prologue:
On the Word "God" and Its Meaning for a
Christology Searching for Other Angles

In the Beginning Was the Word — and the Word Was "God"
(John 1:1)

Christianity breaks up Greek philosophy from within — deconstructs it, by insisting on logos as being incarnated. Thus, the incarnated logos is shaping problems, opening up ruptures and fissures in a world of closed metaphysics, announcing that there is something more behind and beyond the world as articulated in Greek metaphysics. This surplus or excess is necessitating the concept of incarnation. *In*carnation is the case in question. The *scandalon* is not only that the Word is incarnated, but that the Word incarnated is God. The identity of logos and God, and the presence of God in the world as incarnated, is to be explored.[1]

Hence, we start at the beginning — at John's beginning — and try to

1. Cf. Walter Lowe, "Christ and Salvation," in *The Cambridge Companion to Postmodern Theology*, ed. Kevin J. Vanhoozer (Cambridge: Cambridge University Press, 2003), p. 249: "It [the Christian Tradition] also holds that the presence [of God in Christ] is 'hidden' in the form of one who was rejected, reviled, and crucified. In thinking this twofold testimony to presence and hiddenness, the Derridean concept of presence may prove useful. It enables us (though Derrida himself might not encourage us) to make a distinction between something's being present, per se, and its *being present in the mode of 'presence.'*" As will become more apparent later, this makes the whole of Christ's ministry one of disturbance and rupture, more than an illustration of a system marked by closure. Hence, the road to "postmodern" Christology is not given, but is always marked by the fact that in the presence of Christ, God is hidden. God is, as E. Jüngel says, the secret of the world. A secret cannot be fully told, if it is to remain a secret — marked by something still to be, still to come, still not fully present.

see this start from another angle, although we still have to maintain that *this is the start*. But here it is a start that is different from the one usually invoked in the mind of a reader or a listener to John 1 — a start possible only after we have bracketed the Word's metaphysical status, to affirm that it has become flesh, has become post-metaphysical. The logos (meaning) of the logos (word) is the way it functions in the world, Wittgenstein tells us. Thus, we do not start with any metaphysics of pre-existence, but with the very word "God." When the word God becomes flesh, it means that it is inscribed in a certain situation and praxis, and this praxis makes the word understandable. In order to understand the word, exactly what the word "God" means, we have to look to the way it is practiced. This is a different angle to Christology. It is a different start, a different beginning. It is not what the author of John had in mind when he wrote his Gospel, but it might nevertheless be conveying some of the meanings he intended.[2]

In the beginning was the word — and the word was "God." This word, the word *God,* is there from the very beginning. By placing this word at the beginning, the author of John affirms that this very word makes all the difference. Or better — it generates a lot of differences. For a while we can postpone taking a stand concerning the *reference* of this word — we can defer the *existence* of what we call God — because the word itself allows for a lot of questions to emerge — but the word nevertheless opens up a different space. John lets Jesus appear in this space. Jesus appears in the space that God — the word God — opens up.

By stating it as the very beginning, the author of John's Gospel affirms how the word "God" is what matters most, and what generates everything else of significance. To say that there is or was something prior to God would be to say that God is not God — that this word has no meaning.[3] It is not only a point of departure — it is a decisive point of *orientation*.

Everything in the story about Jesus can be seen as generated by this

---

2. The attempt in the following is thus also different from the admirable task that J. Macquarrie takes up in *Jesus Christ in Modern Thought* (Philadelphia: Trinity Press International, 1991), pp. 105ff., to develop a modernized interpretation of the prologue to John. His contribution should nevertheless be mentioned as an attempt to make sense of that "metaphysical" prologue in a time when metaphysics is by many no longer considered the recommended philosophical way of theology.

3. Cf. Hugh Rayment-Pickard, *Impossible God: Derrida's Theology, Transcending Boundaries in Philosophy and Theology* (Aldershot, UK, and Burlington, VT: Ashgate, 2003), p. 3.

word: the narratives about Jesus — called the son of God — are impossible to understand without some reference to this word. Hence, how one relates to this word determines how one allows for one's own world to be generated, to appear, to be experienced, ordered, organized, and oriented. When the word "God" does not function as such a point of departure and orientation, it becomes an empty word, loses its significance, stops shaping the world. Then we also lose the narrative into which the beginning of the Gospel of John invites us.

What is implied in this is that the word "God" is not neutral, not without significance. More than this, it makes significance possible. In the previous paragraph, the words "one" and "we" are references to the contemporary readers of the word "God" — and "God" poses a challenge to us, the readers and users of this word. How we use, understand, and practice the word "God" is not given. The word itself opens an ambiguous space.

The prologue of John itself testifies to the ambiguity opened by the word "God": those who received the word had light — i.e., were able to see, while others did not. The question about the identity of Jesus Christ is linked to how and what he lets us see through and by the word "God" — and the other way around: how the word "God" allows us to see something specific in the human Jesus whom we call the Christ.

That is, provided that the word "God" is first. In the story John tells, the word God is in the beginning. This is no accident, no contingency, but based on the insight that if the word "God" is not the first word to be uttered in the story about Jesus, we somehow get another story. In this book I am trying to see Christ from other angles. However, the word "God" is the very first angle we can use to approach the question of what is first and last when we start speaking about Jesus and his relation to the world. If one does not start with the word "God" when one speaks of Jesus, one makes an angle in a world already established without God, the very principle required for understanding him. That is exactly what has to be avoided — and what postmodern philosophy helps us to achieve, by claiming that there is always a difference implied, something else and more to be said, something that points back to another beginning than the one given with the subject itself.

Beginning in "God" is thus not substitutable by anything else. It is either "God" or nothing in the case of speaking about Christ.[4] If one does

4. As Traugott Koch says in *Jesus von Nazareth, der Mensch Gottes* (Tübingen: Mohr

not start with "God" in the narrative about Christ, one does not only get another story — but also, in a specific sense, one loses the story that is worth telling about Christ. For what's the point of telling a story about Christ without using the word "God"? How can one even use the word "Christ" unless one implies the word "God"? Hence, in the beginning, the word "God" is the necessary word. It has to appear before any of the subsequent contingencies.

Why is the start important? The start itself is not important, but what and who is starting. The start oscillates between the Word and the human being Jesus. The Word (= God) opens up to an understanding of the human, and the other way around: this human, Jesus, opens up to another understanding of the word "God." As language opens us up to a world not accessible in the same way without that very language, the Word challenges us to find angles by which we can express the world in a manner appropriate to what the Word opens up. The interplay between the human Jesus and the word "God" starts at the very beginning — if at all. What is derived from this interplay is *Christ*. But this definitive derivation is at the same time indefinite, open, and possible to approach from different angles. But there are no angles without a beginning — a definite beginning. The beginning is God — impossible to define, and still defining both Jesus (as Christ), as well as the angles from which we can approach him. In the following sections of this chapter, we will have a closer look at the conditions that the word "God" and the reality of God might provide for Christology.

God — the Word

Although we might now anticipate some of the issues to be dealt with more extensively later, there is a need in this initial part of the book to say something more about the framework within which the word "God" appears, and consequently, on what the following considerations are based. The use of the word "God" claims to represent a specific reality. To use the word "represent" means that God is not necessarily *present*. It still remains *relatively* open what kind of possibilities (and not necessarily realities) are

---

Siebeck, 2004): "Um ihn zu erkennen, kann man also niemals von Gott absehen. Um Jesus zu erkennen, ist es nötig nachzuvollziehen, was für ihn Gott ist — und wie er, Jesus, Gott versteht" (p. 12).

implied when using that word. Nevertheless, by the very use of the word, a possible reality *is* opened, a reality that would not be present to the listener without this representation by the word. Hence, this is a word opening possibilities that we would have no access to without that very word.

The word is a representation of a possible reality. But what kind of reality is this? What do we mean by using this word, by letting the word "God" be the beginning? Something has already been indicated by saying that "God" is a word that logically demands to be invoked at the beginning if it is to make sense at all. But we are still within the sphere of thinking when we deal with the concept in this way. To think about God cannot prove God, or secure God's existence. Thinking is not the beginning; thinking comes after. The German philosopher of religion Ingolf Dalferth rightly asserts that thinking alone does not have the competence to decide if God exists or not. The semantic necessity implied in the fact that one cannot think of God as non-existent when one really attempts to think God is neither an ontological necessity in terms of God's existence nor an epistemic necessity in terms of having to think of God. Rather, if one is to talk of a necessity concerning God, it has to do with the unavoidable *pragmatic* conditions for *thinking about God,* and not as a consequence of the semantic coherence of the thoughts about God. Accordingly, Dalferth claims that the alternatives, of either necessarily existing or non-existence, are false.[5] It bases the argument too much on the coherence of a notion (which cannot after all decide existence) instead of asking where and how God can be identified (p. 444). The reason for the alternative approach that Dalferth suggests is obvious:

> As with all questions of identification, this cannot be answered in an abstract and generic way; it can be answered only concretely and within the horizon of a concrete praxis of religious communication, and by the way in which we make clear who or what the expression "God" (or its equivalent) signifies or makes thematic. God is, however, not tied to a specific religious context of praxis, but who or what the sign "God" is pointing towards can only be determined by means of its concrete use in a specific context of praxis. In answering the question of identification, we can always only explain the way language is used,

---

5. Ingolf U. Dalferth, *Die Wirklichkeit des Möglichen: Hermeneutische Religionsphilosophie* (Tübingen: Mohr Siebeck, 2003), pp. 438f. References in parentheses in the text in the following are to this book until further notice.

and every explanation of "God" allows the question about the identification of God to emerge again. (p. 444, my translation)

To talk about God out of context, or without designating further what is meant, makes little or no sense. There is no general God, there is only a God implied in concrete historical events and occurrences, including language-games or practices. Dalferth claims that what Christians hold to be God, or identify as God, is linked to the eschatological events of the crucifixion and resurrection of Jesus Christ (p. 445). Without leaping ahead of ourselves, we can agree on this, but only on the condition that what happens in the crucifixion and resurrection must be seen as intimately linked to the life and praxis of Jesus before Easter. Given, however, that this condition is fulfilled, it is not hard to follow Dalferth further: He says that the cross itself cannot make apparent what the word about the cross can; only the word about the cross can identify God as present in what happens there. Hence, the word reveals more than the eyes can see. Both the content of the word (the event and its meaning) and the proclamation of the word are rooted in the salvific acts of God. So when Christians talk about God, they talk about one whom they assume to be present there, without being apparent.

At this stage in his considerations, Dalferth makes a valuable distinction between what Christians hold to be God, and what is the identification of God. For the one who believes in God must let this belief be more than a mere opinion; the reality implied has to become visible in the life of the believer. The identification of God is linked to how one fulfills one own life. Writes Dalferth:

> According to Christian insights, God is not to be identified except when one identifies oneself in the presence of God and understands God's presence as the Horizon of one's own life: the identification of God can only emerge in a self-committed engagement, and not in the mere language-based elaboration of the fundamental Christian experience. (p. 445, my translation)

It is possible to link what Dalferth says here to what I wrote above in relation to the prologue in John about how the word "God" is providing some kind of orientation for our own lives. God is to be identified in the lives of those believing in God. That is the starting point of Christology, and this insight does not only apply to those who are called Christians; it also applies to Christ himself. This is the very reason why Christology is linked closely to understanding Christ's life as God's self-revelation.

The task of defining the reality of God is impossible. What we can do, however, is to make some definitions of the word "God" (nominal definitions) that might explicate the semantics for certain uses of the word. These definitions do not allow us to understand the essence of God (that would make them *Realdefinitionen*), but they might help us to understand how to use the word in a meaningful manner (Dalferth, p. 446).

Dalferth understands the word "God" as an *index-word*. Such words do not have an ontological correlation, but serve as words by which we orient ourselves in the world. Examples of other such words are "I," "you," "here," "yesterday," etc. Such words cannot be conceptually defined or semantically explicated, but can be exchanged by names and dates. They function as signs for the pragmatic situation of use and speech in which they are employed. Hence, they function as establishing and identifying something in a concrete context of praxis (p. 463). They become meaningful by that very function, and they cannot be understood outside their context of use. When the word "God" serves as such an index-word, it is because it helps us shape our world and makes it possible for us to conceive of ourselves in a given situation in a specific manner. We understand ourselves in another way when using the word "God" than when we do without it. Such words structure the world we live in, and help us orient ourselves. "God" is consequently a marker that shapes the horizon and perspective from which everything else in the world is perceived, understood, and considered. And just as the place where you stand cannot be observed when you are looking at something else, God is only accessible in the mirror of that which is perceived through the horizon that the word establishes (cf. Dalferth, p. 467). But contrary to other index-words, we cannot substitute the word "God" with other indicators. Instead, the function of the index-word "God" makes us aware of the fundamental contingency of the context in which other indicators appear (p. 468).

Starting with God is thus the only appropriate start. That is what John has realized in the introduction to his Gospel. In order to understand the importance of this insight, we can look at the infamous text written by Nietzsche, in which he declared God dead. This declaration makes visible how the death of God deprives humans of all points of reference and orientation:

"Whither is God?" he cried; "I will tell you. We have killed him — you and I. All of us are his murderers. But how did we do this? How could we drink up the sea? Who gave us the sponge to wipe away the entire horizon? What were we doing when we unchained this earth from its sun? Whither is it moving now? Whither are we moving? Away from all suns? Are we not plunging continually? Backward, sideward, forward, in all directions? Is there still any up or down? Are we not straying, as through an infinite nothing? Do we not feel the breath of empty space? Has it not become colder? Is not night continually closing in on us?[6]

The perception of lack of orientation in this quote is startling. Nietzsche actually offers several parables that testify to the same experience: when God is dead, nothing is secure; there is no firm land on which to put your feet, no place or point of orientation.

Consider then what would happen if there were no word for what we call "God." There might not only be a lack of possibilities for orientation in the manner envisaged (although from different perspectives) by Dalferth and Nietzsche. In another sense, it would also mean that a specific mode of experiencing the world would remain closed and inaccessible to us.

In the present world, where there are so many different opinions on what or who God is, the task of providing a point of orientation (not to speak of a firm ground) when talking about God is a hard one. In order to locate such an orientation point, Christology might be a place to start. After all, it is possible, as we shall see, to read the whole story about Jesus as a theological struggle focusing on who God is. The important thing about Jesus is that it is in the combination of his practice and his teaching that the meaning of the word "God" becomes accessible as something more than a mere opinion. It is linked to realities that his ministry both presupposes and opens up to. These realities are the creative forces of God, allowing for a surplus in meaning and in resources for life.

6. Friedrich Nietzsche, *The Gay Science* (1882, 1887), para. 125, Walter Kaufmann, ed. (New York: Vintage, 1974), pp. 181-82.

Why Start Christology with God?

Discussions of Christology often look thoroughly into different methodological approaches. Which way is the best to take when talking about Christ? In what has been said so far, we have indicated that it is appropriate to start with the word "God." That should not, however, be taken as an indication that we start with an exclusively "from above" approach, which assumes from the start a position of the pre-existent Son who is then incarnated. Rather, our suggestions above imply that it might be more effective to start with the actual use and practice of the word "God" within the context of Jesus' history and ministry. In that sense, we are starting "from below."

Wolfhart Pannenberg has pointed out that to speak of God solely as a *presupposition* for Christology will not suffice.[7] Rather, he says, "the statements at which Christology arrives require conceiving of God as revealing himself in Jesus Christ" (p. 467). However, if we understand "God" in the sense just suggested, it is possible to work with "God" as a kind of non-metaphysical shaper of reality that does exactly this: reveals the divine within and through the life of Jesus. Furthermore, to understand the Jesus history in that way might already indicate that we need the kind of all-encompassing framework for talking about God that we indicated above when speaking of "God" as the beginning. Without contradicting his insights, our task will then be different from the one Pannenberg himself envisions, when he sees the need for developing Christology within the context of a full doctrine of God. He holds that the constitution of Christ's identity can only be conceived appropriately in a Trinitarian way (p. 469). Of course, he is right in this. Methodologically, however, I suggest that there might still be something achieved by a "modified approach from below" that not only looks into Jesus' theology, but also into his history and how it might be said to reveal God, without having to make any pre-given decisions on how this understanding fits within or conforms to a Trinitarian framework.

Furthermore, Pannenberg has pointed out that approaches to Christology from either above and below have shortcomings, about which we are not going into detail here. What he argues, though, is that the way out

---

7. Wolfhart Pannenberg, *Jesus — God and Man*, new ed., SCM Classics (London: SCM, 2002). References in parentheses in the text are to this work until further notice.

of this blind alley is to think of God and the historical Jesus as mutually conditioning each other (cf. what was said above about the oscillation between God and the human):

> Jesus' God is only accessible through the human Jesus, but the human Jesus is also only accessible through his God. To interpret the unity of God and humanity in the person of Jesus is only possible for the one who is able to enter into this circle where the human Jesus and the God who is present in and through him mutually condition each other, so that Jesus himself in person belongs to the divinity of God. Into this circle of divine life comes no one who is not already there. God can only be made known by God; this statement by Karl Barth remains correct with regard to this case. Without the Spirit of the community of Father and Son there is no knowledge of God and no knowledge of Christ.[8]

Pannenberg underscores that we need to think of the relationship between God and humans as an internal relation between God and creation, if God is at all. This position implies that everything that is, is included in the circle of life that God as the creator constitutes together with the creation. Given this internal relation, humans are already related internally to the life of God, and the link between them cannot be thought of as something contingent or arbitrary.

The consequences for Christology would then be that the basic relationship applies to Christ as to all other humans, and that this human (Christ) is no less possible to understand without the relation to God than any other human being. In this sense, what theology says about Jesus in his relationship to God is not totally different from what can be said about any human. The theology about the humanity of Christ cannot only explicate subjectively established decisions about who he is, but has to be based on argumentation that is intelligible to all, and in ways that relate to what is understandable to humans in general.[9]

The above position has two important consequences. First, as men-

---

8. Wolfhart Pannenberg, "Christologie und Theologie," in *Grundfragen Systematischer Theologie. Gesammelte Aufsätze* (Göttingen: Vandenhoeck & Ruprecht, 1980), p. 134. My translation.

9. Cf. Pannenberg, "Christologie und Theologie," in *Grundfragen Systematischer Theologie*, pp. 135f.

tioned, it affirms that Jesus in his relationship to God cannot be thought of as someone who is totally different from the rest of humankind. That implies that the *space of experience* the story of Jesus opens up is accessible and understandable without any prior faith in him as the Son of God, and so on. What confronts us in this history is not external to the rest of human history, but linked to this history. On the basis of these experiences, however, we are allowed to talk of God in new and different ways.

Second, this does not exclude a noetic perspective in which the relationship between Jesus, humanity, and God is disclosed through the very history of Jesus. The validity of the "approach from below" consists in the fact that the meaning, significance, and use of the word "God" and the understanding of what the phrase "the reality of God" means is given its context by and though this history. Through this history it becomes clear what "God" means. Although the reality of God has to be thought of as ontologically prior to our understanding, it is only by and through such a context of use for the word "God" that this reality is accessible to us.

Hence, there seems to be difficulties with a clear approach both "from below" and "from above." What is indicated here is that the choice between them might create a false dichotomy, not only in terms of contrasting a noetic and an ontological approach, but also in terms of determining the content of these approaches before actually looking at the context of use for the concepts used to define them. Accordingly, the best one could say about the position I have sketched out here is that it is a modified "from below" approach — seeking to understand how a word — "God" — is opening up and expressing a reality where we can talk about God's self-revelation in a specific history and with specific possibilities of experience — although not about a direct experience of God.

The angle I am struggling to develop is thus post-metaphysical in the sense that it does not start with something before and beyond history. Rather, it starts with a history which, when we speak about it in certain ways, points to something beyond what happens, but still is present in what happens. This "something" is only accessible by a specific use of God-language, which both represents and opens up to a reality implied in what is given. The language derived from the one specific word "God," and the contexts of experience and meaning it opens up to, address specific experiences of *surplus* in human life that might be related to the use of that word.

The above implies that "God" as a notion is a *generator of language*, and accordingly, this allows us to see the world differently or orient ourselves in another way than we do when such language is not generated. From this word flows a different language, other combinations of words, and other contexts of significance. For example, the word "grace" (that we will return to later) receives a different content when used in connection with "God", just as the word "creation" might not be fully understandable at all when used outside a context where the word "God" constitutes the framework for reference and significance.

To speak of Christ as *the incarnated word* might very well make sense in light of the above. Jesus is the human being within whose reality and history the word "God" is shaped in a definite manner.[10] The word "God" is here given context, shape, significance. It does not appear outside of history, but becomes part of a specific history. The main point in Christology is that it is in the history of Jesus that the word "God" has found its most appropriate context and use. Or, to put it otherwise: in Jesus Christ, Godself is revealed.[11] God cannot be revealed fully without the word "God" and its definite context of use. Of course, there has been and still are many contexts and many uses of the word "God" in the world. However, this story, this context, is the one most apt, most up to it, in terms of what this word means. Hence, another reason to link Christ, God, word.

These reflections have one important consequence. When we develop an understanding of Christ from other angles, we have to ask: How is "God" expressed, elaborated, and used in the stories about Jesus? This question cannot be answered only by looking at the Gospels and asking how Jesus speaks about God; we also have to see how he practices the word, and thereby try to get a better grasp on how the word functions.

10. I am of course fully aware that this is not the traditional way of thinking of Jesus as the incarnated word of God. However, what I am trying to do is to develop an angle that makes it possible to understand what this can mean also somewhat independent of the traditional philosophical framework of Christology, while still taking into account what this means for the understanding of God's self-revelation in Christ. Cf. John D. Caputo and Michael J. Scanlon, *God, the Gift, and Postmodernism,* Indiana Series in the Philosophy of Religion (Bloomington: Indiana University Press, 1999), p. 10: "The fundamental question of Christology is not the divinity of Jesus but what kind of God is disclosed in him. Jesus, of course, is not the only revelation of God for Christians [. . .], but for Christians he is the definitive Word of God."

11. The use of the male personal pronoun for God is increasingly problematic for me. However, no good and viable solution to this problem exists, and I use it sometimes, although I try to avoid it as much as possible. One of the reasons for using it is the necessity of keeping open a space in which God can be thought of as *personal.*

Desire

What has desire to do with Christology? This section is an attempt to suggest some consequences that might follow from using *desire* as an angle for reformulating some of the insights of Christology.[1]

Desire is what connects us to the world. Desire is shaping our orientations, giving us directions, suggesting aims to strive for. Our contemplation, consideration, and plans for action would mean nothing without desire. Sometimes desire is given content prior to such reflections; sometimes it is shaped and determined by them.

I deliberately use the word "desire" to indicate what I have in mind in this section. Desire occupies us, engages us in the world, relates us to something that we are not — and at the very same time, desire is part of us. Desire is not something you can decide to do without or ignore fully. A human who has no desire is without direction, and a person whose desires are not met is not thriving.

On the other hand, these insights provide no reason to claim that all desires should be fulfilled or all wants satisfied. The gratification of desire

---

1. As far as I am able to see, apart from the philosophy of religion building on Ricoeur and Derrida, there are not many extensive attempts to develop a full theology that integrates and develops an understanding of desire. One notable exception is the work of LeRon Shults, whose work on desire is integrated in an extensive matrix of theological inquiry. His conceptually oriented way of dealing with and differentiating desires exhibits an alternative to the more phenomenological approach that I am developing here. Hence, his work is directed along a trajectory that would be possible only *after* a project like the present has been carried out. Cf. F. LeRon Shults, *Reforming the Doctrine of God* (Grand Rapids: Eerdmans, 2005), passim.

is never a mere natural thing, but is interwoven with our conceptions of importance, with what we hold to be acceptable, how we relate with others, and with our perceptions of ourselves in general.

To illustrate what desire might mean within a Christological framework, we can start by reflecting on what faith is. Faith is a trusting relationship with something, usually something "outside" you. (Sometimes you also put trust in yourself — for good reason or not.) *In faith there is an implicit element of desire.* Not only in terms of engagement and commitment, but also in terms of wanting to be in relationship with that which you put your trust and faith in.

To be more concrete, when you believe in God, you desire to be in relationship with God, because you think that there is something in this relationship that is important — and good! — for you. However, I think that — for theological reasons as well as others — we cannot and should not talk about this desire as resulting from either *lack* or *need*. We do not believe in God because God is offering something that we need as we need water, sex, or oxygen. We believe in God because God is more than we need, because that relationship relates us to something that might be indicated as a surplus compared to what kind of reality we can constitute for and by ourselves and define by our needs. To define God's importance to us in terms of how God fulfills our needs is to make God a smaller god. That would be to define God on the basis of our world, and that is exactly what we should avoid if we are to hold open a conceptual space in which God can be God and hence not determined by us. We shall see later how this is an understanding of the relationship between God and desire that proves fruitful for an analysis of the theological struggles in which Jesus was involved.

Likewise, to define the belief in God based on a conception of lack would be to make another mistake: we do not believe in God because we lack something that God can give us. That does not mean that God does not give us something. He gives us what we need, and also something of what we lack, long before we believe in God. But God's function as gifting is never restricted to our lack — he transcends it in principle.

Hence, a desire based solely on our conception of needs and lack is a desire not fitting for understanding what kind of desire is involved in true faith. Note that this is a normative statement that we can develop also over against popular critiques of religion claiming that belief is due to people's needs for comfort, anxiety reduction, their will to power, or their need to escape from a boring everyday life. The valuable insights of such function-ally based critiques of religion are what we have to be aware of if we are to make a useful definition of the desire involved in true religious and Christian faith.

Desire transcending lack and need — but still deeply rooted in our own lives — is what we have to understand as implied in faith. Recently, several thinkers have contributed to such a more open — "metaphysical" — understanding of desire. However, to call this understanding metaphys-ical might be misleading: this is not due to some return to a metaphysic of pre-modernity. Rather, the use of "metaphysical" should here be taken to indicate a desire that is pointing beyond what is immediately present, be it in our understanding of ourselves, our needs, or what we want or strive for — and how we can concretely perceive of all this. Again, this might be seen in correlation with our understanding of the necessity of starting with God and not with something in the world when developing a theological conception: this desire is for more than what is in the present world; it is an openness to something new, something else, something that represents a surplus compared to what is presently given.

This surplus might also be called *the impossible,* i.e., that which does not seem possible when seen from the present conditions of life. This dream for the impossible is what constitutes Jacques Derrida's and John Caputo's approach to postmodern theological thought. They want to over-come or pass through the constraints and conditions imposed by moder-nity, and to think that which cannot be thought as possible within a mod-ern framework, and which for that very reason is what we desire most. The desire for something that is not *the same,* that is not a repetition, a contin-uation of what now maintains us in our given identities is what is ex-pressed in such desire: "The incoming of the same, on the other hand, would simply further confirm the present, already familiar horizon, would be more of the dreary, pedestrian, humdrum sameness of the possi-ble. . . ."[2] The alternative to this sameness is an eschatological reality that we relate to through *eschatological desire.*

Derrida's notion of the impossible is developed as a means to explore that which cannot be understood in metaphysical terms. To think other-ness, or to think infinity, is always "to be at risk of exposing it to the re-

---

2. John D. Caputo and Michael J. Scanlon, *God, the Gift, and Postmodernism,* Indiana Series in the Philosophy of Religion (Bloomington: Indiana University Press, 1999), p. 3.

incorporation by metaphysics, unless we proceed by the way of the aporias," of the *impossible*. "An aporia cannot be solved through recourse to reason but only re-solved through recourse to a kind of faith," says R. Horner about Derrida's position here. This aporia interrupts metaphysics, and suggests that there is something beyond or prior to it.[3] This interruption cannot be deduced by our systems of understanding, rationality, and interpretation. The Impossible means, says J. Caputo, "something whose possibility we did not and could not foresee, something that eye has not seen, nor ear heard, that has never entered into the mind of human beings (I Cor. 2:9). So I am plainly advising us to revisit the idea of the impossible and to see our way clear to thinking the possibility of the impossible, of the impossible, of the possible as the 'im-possible,' and to think of God as the 'becoming possible of the impossible,' as Derrida also says."[4]

What Jesus does is that he creates the eschatological desire for the impossible by his presence, and makes the impossible seem possible. Those healed, saved, recognized, find their desire more than fulfilled, since he destroys the circle of sameness, liberates from the bonds of the present conditions, changes the conditions of life. Who can have a dream about and a faith in the impossible? The one who knows that something is im-possible, who finds no possibilities in the present, which is captured, locked into the circle of sameness, economy, and merit. As Richard Kearney says:

> The desired of eschatological desire exists before memory and beyond anticipation. It is immemorial and unimaginable, exceeding the horizons of historical time. But if the desired good gives itself thus from "beyond" history, it is nonetheless inscribed, as vigilance and summons, in each instant of our existence. It is incoming at all times. It is, moreover, on embracing this eschatological paradox that Levinas goes beyond Plato.[5]

3. Robyn Horner, *Jean-Luc Marion: A Theo-Logical Introduction* (Burlington, VT: Ashgate, 2005), p. 45. More concretely, such interruption is manifested in the saturated phenomena of gift, forgiveness, hospitality, etc.

4. John D. Caputo, *On Religion: Thinking in Action* (London and New York: Routledge, 2001), p. 10.

5. Kearney, "Desire of God," in Caputo and Scanlon, *God, the Gift, and Postmodernism*, pp. 116-17. Cf. Richard Kearney, *The God Who May Be: A Hermeneutics of Religion*, Indiana Series in the Philosophy of Religion (Bloomington: Indiana University Press, 2001), p. 64.

Kearney here points to the same phenomena that I tried to indicate in the previous section: What we call God, the impossible, announces itself in and through our history, and cannot be grasped independently of that history. It thereby also shapes and alters the present. On the other hand, it still remains something else than what is present, and represents more than what is present. In this sense, the desire for God — and the belief in God — is a desire that is open for more, more than can be conceived or anticipated concretely by us. Moreover, there is also here a correspondence between the Christian understanding of the reality revealing itself in Jesus Christ and postmodern deconstruction: in the negative moment implied in the relation to the present and what it does not contain in itself, theology opens itself up to a God not yet defined, a God ineffable. Caputo says aptly: "Like negative theology, deconstruction turns on its desire for the *tout autre*."[6]

Faith is thus closely related to the impossible, as Derrida conceives it. He rethinks the impossible "in a way that is not simply negative or disabling. The impossible needs to be affirmed because [. . .] it is precisely impossibility which opens up possibility and makes it possible."[7] Faith thus implies a far more radical and encompassing desire than the desire for food, sex, or other things in the worldly realm. At the same time, this desire is rooted in this world, exists in this world, and is constitutive for a believing relation to the world. But as it is more all-encompassing than such desires, it might also be more critical towards what takes place or is desired in this world. The desire for justice or forgiveness might transform the immediate desire for being right or winning the game or gaining honor or money. Justice, as we shall see, indicates an attitude of openness to something more than what is controlled and regulated by limiting and clearly defined desires.

At this point it is necessary to elaborate the understanding of this eschatological desire by looking at what takes place within a positive relationship between two (or more) parties who recognize each other. In such a relationship between persons there is an element of openness, of something indefinite, that cannot be fully in one's own hand.[8] By entering into a

6. Caputo and Scanlon, *God, the Gift, and Postmodernism*, p. 3. Cf. Kearney, "Desire of God," p. 95.

7. Kearney, "Desire of God," pp. 96f.

8. This openness has been thoroughly described by Emmanuel Levinas, and the following considerations are indebted to his work. See esp. Emmanuel Levinas, *Totality and In-*

relationship with someone else — and not only by using him or her for our own purposes — we allow for ourselves and the fellowship to find its own way. There is arguably an element of similarity between the trust we invest in such relationships and the eschatological desire. By entering into relationship based on such desire, or by engaging with God's future, we allow ourselves to be open for what the other can give us and for what we do not yet already have. We desire the hitherto unknown world of the other, the world which we are promised by his or her presence, but which we still cannot grasp totally, and which will always elude us.

A constitutionally different desire is the one based on what we already are. That desire aims at control and is basically not open to anything new, different, or other. Rather, it strives to remain in control of the given world. In such a world, relationships with those different, those who are the real others, might prove disturbing to such control. In the controversies between Jesus and the Pharisees, as the New Testament records it, this desire is expressed in the need for marginalizing those who do not conform to the given rules of conduct or fit the religiously and socially accepted patterns. Jesus confronts such desire, and thereby he opens up for new community and other forms of desire. Instead of closing the world to those who are different or appear as unacceptable, he opens them up to a new world, by taking their desire for salvation (i.e., new life, freedom, community) as an opportunity to change their world. He lets the word "God" enter their world(s) in a new way that reorients their perception of themselves and of him (more on this later). There is a difference between the desire to control and master reality and the desire to enjoy, participate, and communicate. The first emerges out of concern, worries, and insecurity, the other out of trust and gratitude.

Another and perhaps even more serious element of "closing" desire is the desire for money. Money or wealth creates the illusion that one can gain control over one's own reality or make it more secure. It thereby shapes a focus that is not open to others, but only to securing the needs of the individual.

---

finity: An Essay on Exteriority (Pittsburgh: Duquesne University Press, 1969). The openness and lack of narrative closure can also be seen as manifest in the stories of the resurrection, as the empty tomb reveals both absence and presence, and thereby allows us to avoid any kind of triumphalistic appropriation that bases itself on the fact that the story is closed. Cf. David Hadley Jensen, *In the Company of Others: A Dialogical Christology* (Cleveland: Pilgrim Press, 2001), pp. 101-2.

Furthermore, one feature of desire that might prove theologically important is that it *individualizes*. Desire is never generic, but is always somebody's. To become aware of the fact that one's desire is one's own is thus to become aware of ourselves in a new way. To be asked "What is your desire?" and thereby invited to state it (or them) is to be taken seriously as a person. On the other hand, not to be asked for your desires is to be refused access to a world that could open you and others up to more than what is already present. In some of the brief analyses we will do of narratives in the Gospels, we shall see how this individualizing element plays an important role in the reshaping of people's lives.[9]

Exploring Christological Doctrine from the Angle of Desire?

Consider what might arise if we look at traditional Christology from the angle of desire just outlined: when God becomes human, God engages with the world, desires community and full relationship with the world in a manner not previously revealed. It is not due to lack, but to love. The incarnating God thus appears as a God desiring another mode of fellowship with creation than was hitherto the case. This desire is implicitly stated in the famous words in John 3:16-17 about how much God loved the world, and his desire for saving it by giving his son.[10] One could perhaps also say that by incarnating himself in the world, the Son opens up God to another type of *vulnerability:* he might be rejected; his desire for community might be refused. That is what ultimately takes place at the crucifixion, where God's vulnerability over against human sin comes to its foremost expression when Christ is delivered into the hands of those who take his life. The desire for being vulnerable in this sense can be seen as a willingness to not control the outcome of the process of incarnation. It is also, as we shall see, one of the risks of loving and giving a gift. Even God thus opens up to something that is not controlled beforehand. This might be taken as an indication of God's desire for a true relationship and a true community with

9. However, as should be apparent already, desire is socially conditioned and shaped, and despite its ability to individualize, it is not a phenomenon easily used for promoting an individualistic ideology.

10. This argument suggests that there is an internal relation between the mission of the Son, his incarnation, and a gifting God, but without suggesting that these are one and the same. But I will not develop this claim here.

humankind, where others are not instruments of God's will, but real participants in God's story.

There is a link here also to gift and giving, a topic we will deal with more extensively in the next chapter. S. H. Webb comments on God's excessive generosity in an analysis of E. L. Mascall's account of Thomas Aquinas:

> If God gives because God wants or needs something in return, then God would be dependent, limited, and vulnerable. God would become implicated in a process that could alter or even damage God's very being. This is unthinkable in classical theism because it assumes that God's being is infinite, perfect, and simple and thus incapable of change. However, God's vulnerability in giving is not based on our ability to respond or return the gift, but in how his gift is received. As God finally gives his Son, it would be impossible to think of both the giving and the rejection of this gift as something not affecting God.[11]

Webb himself develops this along Trinitarian and Hegelian lines that we will not be able to follow (yet), when he says: "God's giving puts God's being at risk in the destiny of the gift. If the Son loves the Father through the Spirit, then the gifting community is the way in which God comes to be God. We, in turn, enter the love of God not through an emotional state or cognitive decision but when we give to others what has been given to us."[12] The openness of God's desire for community with the world is also reflected in God's desire for the world's desire for God: ". . . that whoever believes. . . ." God desires our desire for God — our faith in him. The desire God desires from us goes under other names in Christian theology, usually faith, hope, love. This desire for our desire is part of what makes God vulnerable in the incarnation. I can reject another's desire for me. So also with God's desire for me.

We can also see that God's desire to become human is a desire to become material, in order to be loved, to be saving. God materializes in the incarnation. Moreover, the desire for the other's desire is constitutive for the recognition of the other as other, and part of how the other (Human) makes God incarnate (i.e., a new identity) in a way that both presents (makes present) and re-presents God. God's presence is still a surplus of

11. Stephen H. Webb, *The Gifting God: A Trinitarian Ethics of Excess* (New York: Oxford University Press, 1996), p. 156.

12. Webb, *The Gifting God,* p. 156.

his re-presentation in Christ. God is fully present there, but also more than what is present there.[13]

The human response to God's loving desire for the world is most clearly present in Jesus' desire for the reality of God, which he sets above anything else. In the teachings and practice of Jesus there is a desire for the reality of God, for his kingdom. No one can pray "Thy kingdom come!" (Matt. 6:10) without expressing a desire for that which transcends the given and opens up a hope for a world of surplus and grace. Jesus' desire for God is the true answer to God's desire for the world: it is by seeking the kingdom of God prior to anything else that something beyond the world can direct our desires and open us up to the impossible, to justice, to something more than the mere calculation and return of favors might make possible.

Hence desire provides us with an angle for some of the concerns of a traditional "two-nature" doctrine (which will receive my critical scrutiny later): Desire, as expressed in Jesus, is both God's desire for the world and a true human's desire for God. One desire is received by and reciprocated by the other. They are not identical, but complementary; and they are internal, i.e., they are desires desiring the desire of the other, and thus not only wanting the other for the sake of oneself (which would imply that the desire would be for an external, "tangential" or "closed" relation to the other who is desired).

Desire Within a Broader Framework of Human Life — and Its Possible Implications for Christology

The above understanding of desire is developed as an alternative to the more Freudian understanding of desire that has dominated much of psy-

---

13. Cf. Robyn Horner, *Rethinking God as Gift: Marion, Derrida, and the Limits of Phenomenology*, 1st ed., Perspectives in Continental Philosophy, No. 19 (New York: Fordham University Press, 2001), p. 244, saying that "God cannot be seen, not only because nothing finite can bear his glory without perishing, but above all because a God that could be conceptually comprehended would no longer bear the title 'God.'" Naming God does not result in a theology of presence, but one of absence, a phrase Marion immediately qualifies: "By theology of absence . . . we mean not the non-presence of God, but the fact that the name that God is given, the name which gives God, which is given as God . . . serves to shield God from presence . . . and offers him precisely as an exception to presence." Horner cites Marion from Caputo and Scanlon, *God, the Gift, and Postmodernism*, p. 37.

chology of religion for many years. One author who has argued for a revision of that framework is Sebastian Moore. In *Jesus — The Liberator of Desire* (1989),[14] he sees desire's meaning as linked to the mystery of human life. As he says, "The desire for a full life stretches out to the infinite source of life in which we must become lost as, desiring to know life's meaning, we are lost in an answer that is mystery" (p. 7).

Moore explicitly links desire to crisis and loss. When we want something new, this demands a breakdown in our own present perception of the world; this opens up to the liberation of desire. Moreover, he stresses, as I did in the previous section, that a self-affirming and trusting component is present in the desire that is able to change and produce a new reality in which to live in:

> Self-love trusting in the mystery that embraces me is that essential act of living that we call desire. Desire, whereby alone a person lives, is the trusting relationship. [. . .] This relational context of desire is vital to our understanding of desire. (p. 10)

Moore's approach to desire allows us to see how desire might have important consequences for the way we understand its gratification. In what we have so far called "open" or "metaphysical" desire, there is not final gratification. When this desire is satisfied, it *increases:* "This increase of desire with fulfillment, of course, is only intelligible once we understand desire as a trustful relationship. One can always be more trustful, more connected, which means more desirous" (p. 11).

Moore elaborates his understanding of desire further than we can follow here, but there is one more point to make, which is linked to the question of how one recognizes oneself and others in new ways when it comes to desire. This approach is linked to what we said above about the individualizing function of desire, but it also underscores more strongly the social dimension of the effects of desire in *recognition*, which is an issue I will deal with later. Moore uses an illustrative example about falling in love to make his point:

> One of the puzzles of falling in love is that desire is not only fastening on a new object (this I understand) but finding a new subject (but who

14. Sebastian Moore, *Jesus the Liberator of Desire* (New York: Crossroad, 1989). References in parentheses in the text are to this work until further notice.

am I?). Intrinsic to the excitement of "you" is a new "me." [. . .] "Who am I?" and "What do I want?" — these questions exist in a dialectic that is in the nature of growing selfhood. It can be most frustrating. Thus the growth of a person is the progressive liberation of desire. It is the process whereby desire finds ever more deeply its subject, whereby desire comes to be in one who can say, ever more deeply and wholly, "I want." (p. 17)

As Moore here points to how desire is both relational and individualizing, he also implicitly suggests that all desire presupposes an undetermined I, or ego. This ego becomes disclosed and grows, becomes individualized and differentiated, articulated for itself and others, by how it relates with, in, and by desire. The increasing liberation of desire is thus a liberation of the self by which the self becomes aware of itself — realizes or discovers the contents of its soul, so to say.

This process comes from the first cry of infant desire to the final liberation of desire in union with God. [. . .] Desire is fully liberated when a person comes to the deepest self, where identity is at one with the God in whom we "live and move and have our being." (p. 17)

In a certain sense this means that the trusting relationship with God that is expressed in desire is not aimed at becoming satisfied or by getting something for which I can feel pleased. As indicated earlier, that would imply an understanding of the relationship with God based on lack or need. It is more a question of finding one's own identity in the relationship with God: "The desire whereby I am drawn to another is partly constitutive of who I am. To be drawn to another is to become more myself" (p. 18).

One can see this liberation of desire as something people undergo when they are confronted with Jesus and his message about God. But also from a specific Christological point of view, Moore can see the life of Jesus himself as one that continually died to ego and into fuller life. But his is not a private spiritual quest: By dying to ego, Jesus becomes progressively more in solidarity with others and alive to the nerve of pain, desire, and hope that runs through us all:

His was the suffering inherent in living out the self's true being, which is being-in-oneness, in a way that questions all the defensive barriers between people, all the role-based relationships, that institutionalize

the normality and permanence of ego as a way of being. Hence the table friendship with disreputable people; the seeing of women as
equals, unheard of in his time; the relativising of the Law; the unmasking of all forms of self-righteousness; the unpredictable behaviour of
the leading characters in the parables; the wild exaggerations of the
Sermon on the Mount; the image of the grain of wheat dying applied
to himself. (pp. 37f.)

With this positive affirmation of how desire functions and guides life, action, and practice, Moore can also say that Jesus' suffering is a consequence
of the fact that he was following his own desires, and not that he put them
aside: "His desire, totally liberated toward union with God, totally reso-
nant with God's will, draws upon him the vengeance of an unliberated and
tearful world" (p. 90). Hence, Christ cannot — on this basis, at least — be
used as a model for humans, indicating that the neglect or repression of
one's own desires is necessary in order to do God's will. Rather, Jesus' desires were shaped by his relationship with God, and it is from that angle
that one has to understand also his union with the Father (to put it in classical Christological terms).

The strength of Moore's conception is how he relates desire to
growth, relatedness, and the overcoming of ego. Hence, desire does not re-
side in, or is not only situated in, the lustful and self-seeking ego, but expresses itself in the very ways the person relates to the world and thus is individualized. Moreover, this calls for an understanding of desire that
allows the individual to *enjoy* his or her own desire: the enjoyment of desire is not only present in its fulfillment, but in the striving relationship
with that which one desires. To enjoy my desire and to enjoy the other's desire for myself is to exist in a trusting relation where I can grow. That is
what happens when we can see ourselves as wanted by God, and relate to
God in our own desiring faith.

The methodological consequence of the above sketch of desire and its
possible function in Christology is that we have to ask for what and how
desires are expressed, and what identities are being disclosed by the way
desires articulate themselves in the narratives about Jesus and in the different relationships he enters into.

Gift and Grace

Grace has always been an important theological notion. Recently, however, there have risen new opportunities for understanding grace, given the intense discussion on *gift* in literature from fields other than theology. The interesting thing is that this discussion has not been conducted for specific theological purposes. Rather it seems as though philosophers and others have realized that there are important elements related to the phenomena of gift that might have bearings on the quality of human life in general. However, there is no reason why, from a theological angle, one should not try to appropriate the insights of this discussion in order to find a philosophical angle from which one can also develop a theological understanding of the issues that are central to human experience and human life in general.[1]

The present discussion of the phenomenon of *gift* has its point of origin in the work of the French anthropologist Michel Mauss.[2] This discus-

---

1. For other theological attempts to appropriate this discussion, see, for example, Risto Saarinen, *God and the Gift: An Ecumenical Theology of Giving, Unitas Books* (Collegeville, MN: Liturgical Press, 2005), and Stephen H. Webb, *The Gifting God: A Trinitarian Ethics of Excess* (New York: Oxford University Press, 1996). Also much of J. Milbank's work centers around the question of gift, but as critics have pointed out, his work emphasizes reciprocity more than does those I engage in the following. For a critical analysis of Milbank on gift, see J. Todd Billings, "John Milbank's Theology of the 'Gift' and Calvin's Theology of Grace: A Critical Comparison," *Modern Theology* 21, no. 1 (2005).

2. Marcel Mauss, *The Gift: The Form and Reason for Exchange in Archaic Societies* (London: Routledge, 1990). There can be found more extensive analyses of Mauss in both Webb and Saarinen.

sion has clarified a lot of the dynamics related to gifts and gift-giving. However, from a more postmodern and critical angle, some more recent contributions suggest that there might be problems with the understanding of gift as found in Mauss, if we are to take seriously what a gift really is. They try to develop an understanding that is not based on gift-giving as an act of reciprocity and as a specific mode of economics, but try to "purify" the concept of gift from all calculating intentions and motives. Among those critics from a philosophical angle is Jacques Derrida.[3] On the other hand, from a theological angle, we have had several contributions, among them American theologian Kathryn Tanner.[4] In the following, I will pay special attention to these two works, as they, in combination, might provide us with an angle that could serve Christological purposes.[5]

A gift is a common thing in human life. However, by looking at it, we can easily detect that a gift might serve different purposes: On the one hand, it might be part of an already existing economy of exchange and expectations, of anticipations and desires. On the other hand, it might disrupt this economy, by presenting something that is unconditional, surprising, something that represents a surplus or an excess compared to what is already present in and between agents and parties and in the economies that shape the relationship between them.

In many ways, these differences between different types of gifts and conditions for gift-giving or -receiving might be laid bare by looking at how *grace* is understood in theology: either as something you are making yourself deserve to receive (merit), or something that is given unconditionally. In the first instance, grace becomes part of some type of exchange economy (merited grace), while in the latter case, it is an expression of

3. See Jacques Derrida, *Given Time: 1. Counterfeit Money* (Chicago: University of Chicago Press, 1992), as well as John D. Caputo and Michael J. Scanlon, *God, the Gift, and Postmodernism,* Indiana Series in the Philosophy of Religion (Bloomington: Indiana University Press, 1999). For a critical analysis and comparison with the present work of Jean-Luc Marion on gift, see Ingolf U. Dalferth, "Umsonst. Vom Schenken, Geben und Bekommen," *Studia Theologica* 60, no. 2 (2005).

4. Kathryn Tanner, *Economy of Grace* (Minneapolis: Fortress Press, 2005).

5. The choice made here might also be seen as a confessional one: I hold that J. Milbank's approach to gift neither makes us able to understand the relation between gift and grace properly, nor is it well suited as an angle for developing a Christology like the one I am attempting here. This might of course be due to my position as a protestant (even Lutheran) theologian, who has problems in relating to a Roman Catholic framework in which merit is part of the totality for understanding gift and grace.

something out of the recipient's control, and even might be prior to one's expectations or conception of what one deserves. In the following, I will address these two types of framework for gift under the headings of "an economic gift" (suggesting that the gift is part of a value system or an exchange system) or as "an unconditional gift." As a conclusion to the analysis I make of Derrida and Tanner, I will then suggest some Christological implications of this differentiation.

Derrida on Gift (1992)

In his understanding of gift, Derrida[6] tries to separate it from an economy of exchange. He thereby not only distances himself from what Mauss found to be one of the most important characteristics of gifts, but he also discloses several aporias related to gift and gift-giving.[7] Derrida lays bare the possible unconditional character of a gift, by showing how we constantly turn it into something other than gift by understanding it from the point of view of an economic exchange. Hence, in speaking of gifts, we name a trace of something, but on closer examination we do not encounter the gift, but only an illusion of it, already deconstructed and shown to be aporetic.[8] Derrida thereby discloses a possible understanding of gift which, in my opinion, is close to a biblical understanding of *grace*. Grace is what cannot be determined by humans, and cannot be fully grasped, but we can see its traces.[9]

Interestingly enough, Derrida juxtaposes the economic and the law (which he also calls "the nomic"). Without suggesting that there is a theo-

6. The following is, if not otherwise indicated, based on Derrida, 1992. References in parentheses are to that work until further notice.

7. A remark typical for the way Derrida deals with Mauss is the following: "On the one hand, Mauss reminds us that there is no gift without bond, without bind, without obligation or ligature; but on the other hand, there is no gift that does not have to untie itself from obligation, from debt, contract, exchange, and thus from the bind" (Derrida 1992, p. 27).

8. Cf. Saarinen, *God and the Gift*, p. 25.

9. It is hard not to notice how Derrida here offers an approach that is developed further in Jean-Luc Marion's work on God and gift. Marion's work constantly points to how there is in God an excess of givenness that does not allow for any limited objectification. Hence, God also represents what he, from a phenomenological angle, calls "a saturated phenomenon." For a summary of Marion's position, see Saarinen, *God and the Gift*, pp. 27-29.

logical background to this understanding of the law, he nevertheless formulates it in a way that makes it tempting to use his reflections for theological purposes. The reason for this is that sin, law, and human action are linked in the human who centers around herself in the construction of her world.[10] Moreover, when Derrida suggests that it is a connection between law, economy, and partition, this might be read to indicate that in a system of economic gift, there will always be outsiders, marginalized ones, those who cannot participate.

Also, in the *economically* constituted exchange of gift, there is nothing new happening; there is no opening for surplus or for radical change. All remains within the sphere of what can be constituted by human action. Says Derrida: "This motif of economy is the — circular — return to the point of departure, to the origin, also to the home" (1992, p. 7). This return to the "home" can also be read from Levinas: it is *a return to the same;* there is nothing here that is breaking in as an announcement of the infinite or something radically transcending the world constituted by the ego.

This announcement of the infinite is exactly what Derrida suggests is present in the unconditional gift. Here he comes close to an understanding of gift that I find most fruitful in developing a theological understanding of both gift and grace:

> But is not the gift, if there is any, also that which interrupts economy? That which, in suspending economic calculation, no longer gives rise to exchange? That which opens the circle so as to defy reciprocity or symmetry, the common measure, and so as to turn aside the return in view of the no-return? If there is gift, the *given* of the gift (*that which* one gives, that which is given, the gift as given thing or as act of donation) must not come back to the giving (let us not already say to the subject, to the donor). It must not circulate, it must not be exchanged, it must not in any case be exhausted, as a gift, by the process of exchange, by the movement of circulation of the circle in the form of return to the point of departure. If the figure of the circle is essential to economics, the gift must remain *aneconomic.* (1992, p. 7)

To develop an understanding of the gift outside the circle of economy seems to indicate an attempt at the impossible. Derrida claims that such an

10. More on the relationship between these instances below.

understanding "announces itself, gives itself to be thought as the impossible" (1992, p. 7).[11] As Stephen H. Webb points out, for Derrida, the extravagance of the gift *(don)* thus "makes it a particularly suitable symbol for the 'other' and all the problems of understanding otherness in general."[12]

From a temporal point of view, the "impossible" gift will have no determinant and no predecessor in anything prior in a circle of economics. It must present itself at an "instant" — not as part of a sequence of events of exchange. Derrida formulates himself similar to Kierkegaard in his *Philosophical Fragments*[13] as he speaks of the gift as something that is based on an instant that means the interruption of all circulation (1992, p. 9). That a gift is given on the condition of this instant means, in practice, that it has no clearly defined place in history. Accordingly the gift emerges from no condition that we can identify or determine as part of a previous sequence of incidents:

> For there to be a gift, there must be no reciprocity, return, exchange, countergift, or debt. If the other gives me back or owes me or has to give me back what I give him or her, there will not have been a gift, whether this restitution is immediate or whether it is programmed by a complex calculation of a long-term deferral or difference. (p. 12)

Among the things that make it hard (or impossible) to give a non-economic gift is that in order for something to be a real gift, Derrida claims that it is necessary that the donee not give back, reimburse, or enter into a contract: "It is thus necessary, at the limit, that he not recognize the gift as gift. If he recognizes it as gift, if the gift appears to him as such, if the present is present to him as present, this simple recognition suffices to annul the gift" (p. 12).

Derrida here drives his own logic of the unconditional character of the gift outside of circulation to the edge, and ends up in a situation in which the gift is annulled once it is recognized as such (1992, pp. 13-14, 16).

---

11. This impossibility of the gift is what has caused Dalferth, in "Umsonst. Vom Schenken, Geben und Bekommen," to criticize Derrida for dissolving the phenomenon of gift. However, I still maintain that there are many fruitful insights in Derrida's approach.

12. Webb, *The Gifting God*, p. 67.

13. In the *Philosophical Fragments*, Kierkegaard defines the instant as the moment in time when eternity breaks into the temporal. See Søren Kierkegaard, *Philosophical Fragments: Johannes Climacus* (Princeton: Princeton University Press, 1985).

Any such recognition of the gift might suggest its possibility for becoming dragged into a conditional economics again. At this point, I think Derrida would be served by using the notion of *grace:* grace is not, as gift, part of an exchange, not something possible to deserve, but something one cannot merit without annulling it.

This recognition of the gift as gift does not annul the gift, but it makes it hard to pinpoint what it means for a gift to be a gift. Derrida suggests that something happens when there is a gift given that makes a change; something matters, something is not as it was previously. I want to suggest that this *interruption* of the same, this *event* of something new, is paralleled by the undetermined in what I previously called eschatological desire: it is something more than what can be determined from the present — in this case the presence of the economic circle. It breaks into, or rather, *out of* this circle of determination. It thereby also suggests that there is something more in the reality than what can be determined within a framework of previous conditions in space and time:

> For there to be gift event (we say event and not act), something must come about or happen, in an instant, in an instant that no doubt does not belong to the economy of time, in a time without time, in such a way that the forgetting forgets, that it forgets itself, but also in such a way that this forgetting, without being something present, presentable, determinable, sensible or meaningful, is not nothing. (p. 17)

Trying to see this from a Christological angle, how can we think of the gift in such a way that the giver is not destroying or dissolving the gift by merely presenting it? Is there, in other words, a way out of the impasse that Derrida's understanding of gift suggests? The way out, I suggest, is to think of this gift not only as gift, but rather as a manifestation of a *gracing relationship* where the parties involved are recognized by each other as existing outside any kind of circulating economy of gifting. The remaining parts of this Introduction will develop an understanding of how this might be possible, from different perspectives.

By a "gracing relationship" I mean a relationship where both parties are recognized by each other as someone not determined by the conditions of one's own horizon, but rather as an Other, a relationship that is not part of the world and the concrete expectations (or anticipations) of the other. Hence, in such a relationship one is invited into the world of the other by means of an open invitation, one that is not prescribing the conditions for participating in the community with the other.[14]

This suggestion tries to get around the problematic of gift in Derrida by seeing the element of gift as part of a wider phenomenon: that of *a true community of grace*. Within such a horizon, what Jesus does when he feeds the hungry, restores the health of lepers, or asks "What can I do for you?" is not to present a gift, but to allow an un-determined gracing relationship to appear. Moreover, this context of community sets free the concrete phenomenon that can be understood as a gift from the entanglements that threaten to dissolve the gift as a gift of grace. But such an understanding can only be developed if we allow grace to manifest itself as the constitutive element for what is taking place. As this notion of grace is what is lacking in Derrida's elaborations of the gift, he is unable to rectify the problems arising from his understanding of gift, and this makes the gift seem impossible to him. Once this is rectified, however, we can allow ourselves to conclude as he does when he describes the entanglements from which the gift must be liberated — but we can now see more clearly that this must happen in order to be a manifestation of grace:

> It is also on the part of the donor "subject" that the gift not only must not be repaid but must not be kept in memory, retained as symbol of a sacrifice, as symbolic in general. For the symbol immediately engages one in restitution. To tell the truth, the gift must not even appear or signify, consciously or unconsciously, as gift for the donors, whether individual or collective subjects. From the moment the gift would appear as gift, as such, as what it is, in its phenomenon, its sense and its essence, it would be engaged in a symbolic, sacrificial, or economic structure that would annul the gift in the ritual circle of the debt. (p. 23)

This quote also indicates that a *sacrifice* might easily appear within the same economic circle as a gift. Accordingly, to understand the gifts of grace manifesting themselves in the ministry of Jesus as *sacrifice* would be problematic from Derrida's point of view. If this sacrifice means that you have to give up something in order to achieve something else, it implies ex-

---

14. I note here in passing only that this mode of understanding the gracing relationship is partly informed by later discussions of both recognition and hospitality. But it is not necessary here to go into detail about this.

actly what he tries to avoid in order to safeguard the gift: a sacrifice means entering the logic and conditionality of economy. It would, however, be too hasty to let Derrida's reflections prevent us from trying to see Christ's death as a sacrifice. We just have to come to it in another fashion than the one immediately presenting itself here. As we shall see, sacrifice can be seen as the offering of a community-shaping gift.[15]

What I would suggest is that this critique of sacrifice as part of an economy could be made fruitful for Christology if we were to apply it with respect to what usually counts as Christ's sacrifice: his death. Without anticipating the results of our more extensive discussions later, let me just indicate that if we were to understand his death as a sacrifice, it would mean that he is entering into an order that he is not accepting, but trying to dissolve or overcome through the whole context of his ministry. When Christ dies, he relates to an economy of law and retribution, and not to a realm of grace. Hence, his death may be seen as a sacrifice from within the perspective of the "economic circle" — while this death might also mean that he is dissolving this circle "from the inside." Exactly by sacrificing what should not be sacrificed (his own life), or paying what cannot be paid or paid back, he is suggesting an element of surplus and excess in relation to such economies that makes it problematic to maintain an "economy of life and death." Rather, this is the final instance necessary for making visible that such economies are not able to maintain true human community in the long run. We will be going into more detail about these suggestions later.[16]

Desire and Gift

The persistent and hyperbolic elaborations of Derrida on gift seem to be dictated by two concerns: first, to make sure that there is something called gift. The insistence on the existence of the phenomenon of the gift is closely related to the second concern: that gifts are indications of the graceful and unconditional elements of human life, something elusive,

---

15. See below, pp. 287-88.

16. This is partly informed by, and partly supports, the approaches to the death of Christ as they are made possible by the work of René Girard. Girard's work will be dealt with later.

something finally beyond grasp and control, but something we still deeply desire — without knowing what it is. For this reason, one might agree with one of his interpreters, who says that "The gift, one might say, is how things 'come,' how the impossible happens."[17] The impossibility of the gift, the fact that we cannot spell out or determine the conditions for giving, makes it easily understandable as something of a gift of grace, theologically speaking. This im-possibility arises out of our lack of grasp on the conditions of possibility (die Möglichkeitsbedingungen) for a gift. The deconstruction of these conditions seems then to provide the condition for gift, to put it paradoxically. Hence the gift is also something that escapes the economies of desire based on lack and need. From the understanding of gift in Derrida follows that a gift that is truly a gift cannot arise from or be an answer to a specific desire — but when it appears it is nonetheless a gratification of our desires. It is this gratification that makes the gift welcome, that makes us want to receive it. Caputo, in his interpretation of Derrida, develops these elements further by pointing to how a gift is thus also related to the unexpected event:

> The gift is an event, e-*venir*, something that really happens, something we deeply desire, just because it escapes the closed circle of checks and balances, the calculus which accounts for everything, in which every equation is balanced. The circle [of economics] prevents the event, blocks the incoming of the new, tethers the *tout autre* to the horizon of the same. The tighter the circle is drawn, the less there is of gift.[18]

Derrida develops his understanding of the gift further by making clear that the impossibility of the gift keeps our desire for it open: we never encounter the gift, because the gift should, he says, never be confused with the presence of its phenomenon (1992, p. 29). This presence of the not present I find as a good expression of how the ungraspable reality of the divine might still be present in the concrete experiences of the world — and of gift. Our de-

---

17. John D. Caputo, *The Prayers and Tears of Jacques Derrida: Religion without Religion,* Indiana Series in the Philosophy of Religion (Bloomington: Indiana University Press, 1997), p. 160. The point made might be illustrated by how one, when receiving a gift, is far more surprised when one receives an unexpected gift than when one receives something already anticipated. In the latter case, the event of gift opens up to something new, a realm or a new dimension, something that might change the perception of both the giver and yourself, your own reality.

18. Caputo, *The Prayers and Tears of Jacques Derrida,* p. 160.

sire for God — as indicated already in the presentation of S. Moore's understanding above — is something that is deepened when our desire for God is met; it gives rise to more desire and is still something gratified, although not in a complete way. Our desire for God might in this case be compared to our desire to know: it is something satisfied by learning, but nevertheless still keeping the horizon open for further learning. A gift in Derrida's sense, i.e., what can be thought of theologically as grace, is similar: it is something received, and still stirring more desire. Writes Derrida:

> Perhaps there is nomination, language, thought, desire, or intention only there where there is this movement still for thinking, desiring, naming that which gives itself neither to be known, experienced, nor lived — in the sense in which presence, existence, determination regulate the economy of knowing, experiencing, and living. In this sense one can think, desire, and say only the impossible, according to the measureless measure [mesure sans mesure] of the impossible. If one wants to recapture the proper element of thinking, naming, desiring, it is perhaps according to the measureless measure of this limit that it is possible, possible as relation without relation to the impossible. One can desire, name, think in the proper sense of these words, if there is one, only to the *immeasuring* extent that one desires, names, thinks still or already, that one still lets announce itself what nevertheless cannot present itself as such to experience, to knowing: in short, here a gift that cannot make itself (a) present. (p. 29)

All this suggests that the gift of grace, that constantly deconstructs itself and eludes a definite grasp or control, might be understood as a *borderline phenomenon:* it is a phenomenon on the border between control, openness, and indeterminacy. What Jesus does when establishing gracing relationships with others is exactly to direct them to this border, and to give them a chance of experiencing something beyond their immediate desires, something that is a promise of a wider horizon for life, beyond their control, but nevertheless offers a new point of orientation. However, as we shall see in the light of Tanner's theology below, this also requires that we are able to understand what he offers as more than deeds of *charity,* as this is usually understood.

Finally, this also suggests that the gift of grace is something outside the realm of the law (theologically speaking). In light of what was just said about the gift as opening up to a realm beyond control, it is interesting to see that Derrida himself seems to have realized this when he claims that the gift does not belong to the realm of practical reason. It is — as both Levinas and Hegel will say about recognition — something pre-ethical. When Derrida addresses this issue, it is striking how much he takes a normative position:

> It [the gift] should remain a stranger to morality, to the will, perhaps to freedom, at least to that freedom that is associated with the will of a subject. It should remain a stranger to the law or to the "*il faut*" [you must, you have to] of this practical reason. It should surpass duty itself: duty beyond duty. If you give because you must give, then you no longer give. This does not necessarily mean that every law and every "you must" is thereby excluded from the gift (if there is any), but you must then think a law or a "you must" that are not determinable by some practical reason. A law or a "you must" without duty, in effect, if that is possible. (p. 156)

To conclude, so far, this means that we by way of Derrida can get a grasp on the traditional conceptions of law and grace from a philosophical angle. I have already hinted at how this might provide another angle for understanding what happens when Jesus confronts people with the message about the kingdom of God. We will, to say it again, have to develop this more in detail later. First, however, we shall see how these insights from Derrida's philosophy are echoed in the recent work of theologian Kathryn Tanner.

The Economy of Grace: Tanner

Tanner's project does not have a specific Christological focus, but is directed towards developing alternative and more theologically sound types of economy than those we face in today's world, which tend to reduce the language of altruism, sacrifice, and generosity to economic terms. However, she also makes important observations relevant for this project, and provides us with insights that are much in accordance with what came out of our analysis of Derrida, but less hyperbolic in character.[19]

19. Tanner, *Economy of Grace*. Tanner herself comments on Derrida's work as "the most famous hyperbolic effort to purify the category of gift" (p. 147, n. 39). References in pa-

Tanner points out one instance of giving that seems to be at the other end of the spectrum from Derrida's conception of gift: that of *charitable giving*. This way of giving differs from gift exchange. Charitable giving meets the needs of the recipient. It is not intended to keep gifts circulating, but to allow the gift to settle with the one who needs it. Unlike in an economy of exchange, the relationship between the parties is tangential and external; there are no other links between them than the giving of the gift. Thus the very giving cannot be taken to symbolize anything about the character of the relationship: giver and recipient are strangers to each other. Tanner writes about this type of gifting:

> The point of the giving is not to keep the relationship up. To the contrary, charitable giving often justifies the donor's not having anything further to do with the recipient. The giving of gifts now means that the recipient can be excluded in good conscience from all the usual social or exchange relations that make up the donor's life. The fact of charitable giving might help to legitimate, for example, the fact that one is not empowering the recipient for the sort of participation in capitalist exchange that might make him or her less needy. Unlike gift exchange, in which circulation seems almost to become an end in itself, the important thing about charitable giving is the gift and the benefits it brings to others, not the act of giving and receiving or the sort of relationship it sets up. (p. 55)

Although Tanner writes with reference to a capitalist society, this understanding might still have bearings on understanding the practices of Jesus as something other than deeds of charity. The fact that Jesus changes people's lives and invites them to fellowship with him suggests that there is another type of graceful giving at stake here than the one presently and commonly understood as charity. This also fits well with Tanner's conclusion, which is that neither gift-exchange nor charitable giving can provide us with good models for an economy of grace (p. 56). In light of what we have presented earlier, the latter form of giving fails to establish exactly that which we have indicated might be the most important horizon for providing a gift of grace, namely the *relationship*.

---

rentheses in the following are to her work until further notice. A study that thematizes Tanner's work on gift prior to her recent book is found in David Albertson, "On 'The Gift' in Tanner's Theology: A Patristic Parable," *Modern Theology* 21, no. 1 (2005): 107-18.

Tanner also offers a formulation for the "pure" gift that might be easier to make operational than the one we found in Derrida. She formulates the commonly held insight that "A real gift has to have the spontaneous expression of good will behind it, over and above the call of duty. Something is really a gift only when it is not being used to put pressure on you, when the gift is given simply for your benefit and is not serving any ulterior motive" (p. 58). By pointing to the gift as both transcending duty and by seeing it as an expression of the spontaneous will, she is actually formulating conditions "outside" of what might be an economic circle. When the only thing in focus is the *benefit* of the recipient, this is a good *in itself*, not something one attempts to achieve for the sake of something else. I deliberately phrase it like this because it allows us to say that *such a gift is a good in itself.*

Tanner describes, not surprisingly, God's giving as unconditional. She is thereby able to formulate the basic distinction on which we have operated so far, along the following lines: God's unconditional giving is "not obligated by the prior performance of the recipients and [. . .] not conditional upon a return being made by them. This principle marks all these relations off from *do ut des* giving, or 'I give so that you will give,' the alternative principle of conditional giving that covers barter, commodity exchange, and debtor-creditor relations of all sorts" (2005, p. 63).[20]

This is clear first and foremost in how God creates the world. Creation cannot be a response to anything creatures have done. Tanner calls this God's "total gift." Nothing obligates God in any way in creation or in God's setting up covenant relations with Israel. This is done out of "sheer free beneficence and not because of this particular people's special merits" (p. 63). However, when it comes to what God gives humans as salvation gifts in Christ, her description suggests that God is then — despite the free relation to the recipients — still working within one kind of economy, which is qualified as follows:

> They seem to be given to us simply because of our need, our sufferings and incapacities, not because of our righteousness and bountiful living in communities where justice and peace reign, not because of our good use of gifts already given. Christ is the way God comes, not to the righteous and the already blessed, who fully expect their privileges of

20. Cf. Kathryn Tanner, *Jesus, Humanity and the Trinity: A Brief Systematic Theology,* Scottish Journal of Theology. Current Issues in Theology (Edinburgh: T. & T. Clark, 2001), pp. 2f.

moral standing and good fortune to bring with them all the further goods of life, but to sinners in the midst of their sin, to the poor crushed by burdens of pain and injustice, to all who seem to be owed nothing. (pp. 63-64)

Reading this from an economic angle, it seems first of all obvious that those Jesus offers gifts to are often those who have no prior part in the ordinary economy of exchange, be it in terms of merit, honor, or social or religious recognition. Or, they are people who have realized that they are not able to fulfill their desires within such an economy. Thus, the gifts of salvation meet the lack and the needs, but there is more to it than that: salvation is not there in order to restore people's position within a community based on economic exchange or merit. Rather, it is the manifestation of another type of community that is different from, and hence critical towards, any kind of community based on such economies. The gracing fellowship we suggested above is *inclusive in the sense that everyone who sees himself or herself as a possible participant is allowed to enter.* The only thing that would keep them out of this would be if they thought there were certain merits or privileges that conditioned this participation.[21]

Does this mean that faith is an answer to lack, and that we are again falling into a logic of faith that is determined by need and desire? In order to avoid this pitfall, we have to understand that the gifts of salvation are offered not primarily as the satisfaction of present needs, but rather as a transformation of the situation out of which these needs occur. This situation is, in biblical context, determined by lack of community with other humans, and an assumed lack of community with God. The establishment of a gracing fellowship changes that.[22] From this it follows that the needs

21. An obvious example of this is the story about the prodigal son (Luke 15:11ff.), who finally finds himself excluded from fellowship and economic exchange but is welcomed back by the father, though not by the other son, who thinks he has specific privileges. J.-L. Marion has a reading of the same parable that underscores these points further. See Jean-Luc Marion, *God Without Being: Hors-Texte, Religion and Postmodernism* (Chicago: University of Chicago Press, 1991), pp. 97-98 (and below).

22. This should not be read as a way of "spiritualizing" the community of believers, so that this fellowship has nothing to do with the care for the hungry, ill, etc. Rather as the opposite: because the hungry, destitute, etc. are part of the created community, and are recognized by believers as images of God, it follows from this that their needs cannot be ignored without jeopardizing the very basis of the human community. This way of formulating the order is echoed in Jesus' words in Matthew 6:33.

might be met, but in the present context, it is important to underscore that this demands another order than the one of economic gifting. The order of grace is a community not determined by economic or other capacities. As long as we are living with the lack of grace, there are lacks and needs for which we know neither name nor remedy — because we might then be referred back to ourselves in order to overcome this situation. The human predicament is that we are not able to achieve this by ourselves: we are dependent on grace to really overcome the exclusion from community. This is what the kingdom of God is about.

Tanner suggests that what God does, no matter what the human response is, is to continue to give. The non-conditional character of God's giving expresses itself also in how he continues to give in spite or our misuse of his gifts. Had God then stopped giving, it would have placed God's giving within the economy of exchange again, where our failures prompted a response forfeiting these gifts. But this is not what happens. When we experience the loss of these gifts, says Tanner, it is not because of God's ceasing to give, but rather because of our sin:

> It may seem to us as if God takes away gifts in response to our sin. But it is our sin itself that interrupts the reception and distribution of God's gifts, bringing suffering and death in its train. The loss of what we might have enjoyed is not God's punishment of us, but the natural consequence of our turning away from and refusing what God is offering us for our good. God's gifts continue to stream forth to us in the way they always have; we are simply failing to avail ourselves of them, to our own destruction and harm. (2005, pp. 64-65).

As is obvious, Tanner's understanding of a gifting God might be seen as in accordance with the approach of Derrida above. However, her theological angle also allows for three insights that are valuable in the present context: *First,* she underscores how God's giving is not dependent on our reception, but on the other hand, there are some of God's gifts that humans cannot simply fail to receive as part of the created world (cf. p. 66). *Second,* "the unconditionality of God's giving is saved despite all our failures of reception and response because anything that might look like a condition for the reception and good use of God's gifts is really itself the gift of God. There is nothing good about us that is not also the gift of God, and this includes the acts by which we receive those gifts and put them to good use" (p. 67). *Third,* she affirms that we cannot make an adequate return to God's giving (p. 68). This final point underscores how it is impossible for humans to integrate the gifting of God within an economy that is under our control.[23]

We have now established a hermeneutical framework for understanding gift and grace and the place it has within the narratives about Christ. We have suggested that this understanding might shed light on the teachings of Jesus himself, as well as on the understanding of the reality opened through the life of Jesus. The contrast between two frameworks for understanding the relationship between God, the law, and gift may also have important bearings for understanding the theology of Jesus. Consequently, the present chapter suggests angles to Christology that might prove fruitful in relating the content of Christology to our present-day understanding of what gifts and gifting might involve. The reflections presented can provide an *optic* for reading the Gospels that might suggest how what is at stake in them is not something very different from what also can be part of present-day human experience.

23. In order to complete the picture somewhat more, it is necessary to add here that Tanner also has a lot of valuable insights into the responses we might have to God's giving without making it part of the closed economic circle. She also has more to say on Christ as a gift (pp. 66-67, 65, 147, n. 41) — and I will have to return to that at a later stage. Among the problems in John Milbank's work on gift is that he is not really clear on how the conditions for avoiding ending up within such a circle can be maintained.

Recognition

One of the important gains of postmodern theory has been its ability to develop an understanding of the constitution of human identity and self-hood that overcomes the idea that humans are what they are in themselves, and that they constitute the conditions for their own life. These insights echo concerns already expressed in early Christian theology, but are presently articulated without specific religious presuppositions. The overcoming of a *centered* understanding of the self and a focus on the pre-subjective conditions for subjectivity are among the lasting contributions of such theory. Focus on the pre-subjective elements that condition subjectivity has been developed from different angles, among them also the angle of desire. Desire is not something immediately under the subject's control, and one's desires might often shape the way the subject understands himself or herself. Moreover, how desire is itself constituted and given content by social and cultural relationships and symbolic exchange prior to the constitution of a (self-) conscious subject is another element in this picture.[1]

Another phenomenon that points to the pre-subjective conditions for establishing both subjectivity and identity is *recognition*. Although there are forms of recognition that simply involve our capacity for seeing and re-cognizing, the most important forms of recognition are interpersonal, in a way that separates it from simply *knowing*.[2] One important

---

1. To name but a few of the persons who have developed theories that might be relevant examples here: Ricoeur, Foucault, Kristeva, Lacan, Irigaray, Bordieu.

2. Cf. Paul Ricoeur, *The Course of Recognition* (Cambridge, MA: Harvard University

mark of what brings about recognition, according to Ricoeur, is *change:* varieties of temporalization accompany varieties of change, and these varieties of change and temporalization constitute the occasions for identification and recognition (p. 62). This observation indicates that recognition is closely bound to the very conditions of history and of understanding oneself or others in historical time. Time indicates that the identity is not given, but that it, due to its temporalization, can change and be recognized as something else. Hence, the flexibility of recognition is based on the possibility of change in time. This is important to notice in order to counter the criticism that recognition implies an oppressive form of maintaining difference.

Ricoeur develops the difference between recognizing people from things along lines that underscore a similar type of flexibility and openness. While to recognize things is mainly to identify them through their generic or specific features, people, on the other hand, recognize one another principally by their individual features (pp. 65f.).

A basic feature shaping and underlying my concerns in this book is that humans have a desire to be recognized — seen, respected, and accepted as responsible. Such recognition is not always present, and we then find ourselves in the *struggle for recognition,* which underlies the struggles for justice, for truth, and for responsibility.[3] Recognition involves inclusion, while lack of recognition implies the exclusion of the other, due to him/her not recognized as being on equal terms with me. Hegel, to whom we will return shortly, sees *the final expression of recognition in the interweaving of love and right.* Only thus can one be recognized in a way that is without the opposition of the will (p. 182). Ricoeur formulates it thus: "We can say that lovers recognize each other in models of identification that can be held in common" (p. 190). My reason for using recognition as one of the analytic angles for this book is exactly this insight: Jesus opens up to such positive forms of recognition, while he opposes forms of identifying the other that lead to suppression. Such forms neglect the fact that time and history always make the other's identity open to change and to be recognizable in an affirmative and positive manner.

Press, 2005), pp. 12ff., esp. p. 19. References in parentheses in the text in the following are to this book until further notice.

3. For this, see Axel Honneth, *The Struggle for Recognition: The Moral Grammar of Social Conflicts* (Cambridge: Polity Press, 1995), on which Ricoeur also builds.

This means that there is an alternative to struggles for recognition. Ricoeur sees these alternatives in what he calls peaceful experiences, which are based on symbolic mediations exempt from the juridical and commercial orders of exchange (p. 219).[4] As the primary example of this, he names *agape,* the love that "renders unnecessary the reference to equivalents because it knows nothing of comparison and calculation" (p. 220). Agape is something that transcends the ordinary conditions of action and behavior, and expects nothing in return (p. 224). As such, agape as gift is the excessive gift of recognition of the other.[5] By being recognized in this way, the individual who is recognized is not only given a new type of freely accepted identity, but he or she is also given a new place in his or her world, and can relate to his or her history in a way different from before.

Against this backdrop, we need not see recognition as resulting in or resulting from oppression.[6] Kelly Oliver, who has challenged present ways of understanding recognition, thus seems to overemphasize the objectifying relation to the other in her critique of contemporary theories of rec-

---

4. Note how this fits in with my understanding of gift, as developed above. Ricoeur also makes this connection explicit; see Ricoeur, *The Course of Recognition,* p. 219.

5. Ricoeur's development of love and gift here seems to address some of the criticism voiced against the notion of recognition in Kelly Oliver, *Witnessing: Beyond Recognition* (Minneapolis: University of Minnesota Press, 2001). Oliver focuses on the repressive elements that may come to the fore in specific types of recognition and lack of recognition. She nevertheless develops her own conception of love and witnessing in a way that to me seems to be much in accordance with Ricoeur. Her own considerations on love develop it as an alternative to objectification. Building on Irigaray, she sees a deep link between love and the recognition of *difference:* "Love does not exist without difference. And difference is not recognized beyond recognition without love. The love imagined by Irigaray, however, is itself beyond recognition. Irigaray's discourse of love would challenge many, if not most, of our contemporary cultural representations of love. The notion of love itself — the experience of love and its representations, which cannot be separated — must be open to social and political transformation. Love too must be reinterpreted and elaborated, especially in terms of its performative dimension. What is love beyond domination?" (p. 216). I also think that she supports Ricoeur's understanding of the relationship between love and justice when she says that "Love is an ethics of differences that thrives on the adventure of otherness. This means that love is an ethical and social responsibility to open personal and public space in which otherness and difference can be articulated. Love requires a commitment to the advent and nurturing of difference" (p. 20).

6. This is the main difference between the understanding outlined here, and the one found in Oliver (cf. *Witnessing: Beyond Recognition,* pp. 3-4). References in parentheses in the text are to this work until further notice.

ognition. Her own suggestion is to substitute recognition with the concept of *witnessing,* and I want to make use of that notion here, not in order to replace that of recognition, but to call attention to an important reason for deepening our understanding of how both humans and Christ can be recognized as witnesses to God. As has become clear already from our understanding of the conception of *imago Dei,* witness is internal to it. To be recognized as a witness is to be affirmed as a specific type of subject and a bearer of a specific type of subjectivity.

Oliver sees "address-ability" and "response-ability" implied in the process of witnessing. Hence, subjectivity is also the result of the process of witnessing, and she is here in full accordance with my description of the negative elements in the lack of recognition when she writes that oppression and subordination work to destroy the possibility of witnessing and thereby undermine subjectivity. For her, witnessing is not only the basis for othered subjectivity; witnessing is also the basis for all subjectivity (p. 7). The crucial question is then how she understands the concrete function of witnessing. On this she writes:

> Witnessing is [. . .] defined as to bear witness, to testify, to give evidence, to be a spectator or auditor of something, to be present as observer, to see with one's own eyes. It is important to note that witnessing has both the juridical connotations of seeing with one's own eyes and the religious connotations of testifying to that which cannot be seen, in other words, bearing witness. It is this double meaning that makes witnessing such a powerful alternative to recognition in reconceiving subjectivity and therefore ethical relations. (p. 16)

For Oliver then, recognition implies an openness to the incomprehensible that cannot be captured by the concept of recognition, as this is a concept building on memory or the ability to fit something from past experience into our present world. But as she defines witnessing and our relation to witness, recognition in this narrow sense is overcome. She holds that to recognize others requires acknowledging that their experiences are real even though they may be incomprehensible to us. Although she says this in a context devoid of theology, this implies one important thing for theology as well: we must recognize that not everything real is recognizable to us: "Acknowledging the realness of another's life is not judging its worth, or conferring respect, or understanding or recognizing it, but responding in a way that affirms response-ability. We are obligated to respond to what is beyond our comprehension, beyond recognition, because ethics is possible only beyond recognition" (p. 106).

The strength in Oliver's approach is linked to this opening up to recognition as a radical concept for receiving the witness of the other. It thereby also has important ethical elements, based in the presence of that which is witnessed. This other-based and other-related way of understanding recognition of the other's witness to what takes place is an opportunity to conceive the world differently, to become aware of new possibilities (cf. pp. 135f.). This, in turn, makes her insights theologically fruitful.

Recognition and Desire in Hegel

Despite the often-announced postmodern traits in such an understanding of the human, this decentered approach to human subjectivity has its predecessor in one of modernity's most distinguished philosophers: G. W. F. Hegel. Hegel articulated the famous dialectic between master and slave, and his description might serve as one of the most important renderings of the socially constituted identity of the individual. In the following, we shall provide a brief account of the implications of this model, while arguing that the model itself does not imply a necessarily repressive relationship between the parties. Rather, the dialectic taking place in the exchange of recognition between the parties is one in which every kind of identity is based, and the recognition might be either oppressive or expressing equality. In what follows I shall try to appropriate the philosopher R. R. Williams's account of Hegel's concept of recognition to attempt to make it theologically fruitful.[7]

The basic point in the dialectic of recognition is that we are what we are due to how we experience others' understanding of us, and it is by accepting their view of us that we establish an identity. Hence, a master is a master only if he has someone who recognizes him as such, and a slave is a slave only when she accepts that identity. If no such acceptance takes place, there is a struggle for another kind of recognition. Hence, the relationship to yourself comes through the relationship that others have with you, and you thereby relate to them as well as to yourself.

7. See Robert R. Williams, *Hegel's Ethics of Recognition* (Berkeley: University of California Press, 1997). References in parentheses in the text are to this work until further notice.

Williams's own reading of Hegel underscores how recognition is a general concept of intersubjectivity. He consequently takes issue with an understanding of recognition in Hegel that relates it solely to the master/slave dichotomy. Instead, Hegel's description of the master-slave relationship is only one, first phase of unequal recognition. In order to secure freedom, this phase must be transcended. Accordingly, it is not the final, but merely a transitional, inherently unstable, configuration of intersubjectivity (p. 10). The lack of stability is due to the lack of freedom: here one or both parties are forced into a relationship that is without the possibility of experiencing freedom. Alluding to our previous presentation of the phenomena of gift and desire, we might say that in an unfree and unstable relationship there is something deeply dissatisfying in terms of how the exchange is taking place or how desires are ordered and gratified. The parties (one or both) are not able to find the recognition in the other that might liberate them, including their desires (in the sense of S. Moore) for autonomy and satisfaction. We are talking, in fact, of the opposite of a gracing relationship.

A genuinely gracing relationship might be based on another type of recognition than the one that leads to oppression. Williams points to how genuine recognition in Hegel is fundamentally reciprocal and involves the mutual mediation of freedom (p. 10). There are two interrelated points to underscore here: First, this means that there can be no substantial freedom unless the subject is given (sic!) an identity that allows for this. Second, freedom is tied to recognition, and cannot be separated from the social realm. Moreover, freedom as a socially constituted phenomenon also implies that both parties have to be free: freedom can only be mediated between two persons where each allows the other to be free. If that is not the case, true freedom is not manifested.

I think this analysis is of tremendous importance to a reading of the gospel that focuses on human liberation from oppressive structures. It might also prove important for a critique of theological conceptions that have petrified structures of oppression in which people find themselves trapped. Of course, this is a claim not possible without implying that faith and freedom are two sides of the same coin. The theology of Jesus is accordingly structured around another type of recognition than the one practiced by his adversaries: His is not a recognition that needs to oppress others in order to develop a self-understanding implying certain privileges or a specific status. On the contrary, by offering (giving) an alternative way of recognition, he contributes to both liberation and a new and different identity for the one who accepts his recognition. In this sense, recognition is a presupposition for manifestations and instances of surplus, compared to what can be achieved outside the realm of recognition: There is more to the whole of the relationship than the mere presence of two (or more) individuals.

Williams points to how freedom achieved by recognition only can be established when both parties renounce coercion (p. 10). Coercion might not only be physical, it might be social or religious as well. Typical for coercion is that it keeps the subject in a state where he feels trapped and is unable to relate to himself in a manner determined by his desire for something outside of the given situation. Referring to Honneth's (and Habermas's) development of the more social-psychological elements in recognition, he offers a wide variety of patterns for understanding such coercion and its opposite. Honneth distinguishes what he calls three positive forms of recognition: (1) primary relations as love and friendship, (2) legal relations, and (3) a community of value and solidarity. "The three forms of recognition in turn make possible affirmative self-relations. Love makes possible self-confidence, right makes possible self-respect, and social esteem develops self-esteem." However, the full impact of these forms of recognition for theology is only accessible if we look at their opposite: The disrespect of the other that manifests a lack of recognition is (1) abuse and rape, (2) denial of rights and exclusion, and (3) denigration and insult (p. 15). Altogether, I think that we are justified in saying that we might find examples of most of these forms of recognition or disrespect in the narratives about Jesus, especially regarding his death. Thus, Hegel provides us with important interpretative tools for reading what takes place in the Gospels as examples of ordinary human phenomena — and how they might be overcome.

Another important gain from Hegel is that, by means of his understanding of recognition, he is able to link recognition to *desire*. Desire provides the ground for freedom. Writes Williams:

> Hegel conceives the self not as a simple, stable, quiescent self-identity but as a complex, restless, self-repulsive, negative identity that, as desire for the other, is driven beyond itself, including its natural existence. The doubled ground of freedom implies a mediated autonomy, where the other is no longer merely external but mediates the self's relation to itself. (p. 48)

The struggle for freedom is anchored in desire. Hegel suggests that freedom is not to be conceived as a theoretical aim or only related to the "higher" interests of man. The desire I bring with me, and with which I meet the other, implies that I am struggling to achieve more of my own freedom. If we allow ourselves to depart from Hegel momentarily, we might suggest that this is illuminating our previous analysis of desire in an interesting way: Desire is always struggling to be recognized and met, and by being met, it is allowed to be free. However, when desire is not met, the subject is confronted negatively with his own desire. He then might be challenged to recast his understanding of himself in light of the role desire played in the relationship. Let us illustrate this by means of two examples:

- When Jesus heals the blind man, Jesus meets his desire for sight. This not only changes the man's perception of himself, but also his status in society. It is a desire that allows him to become free. Without acting on his desire, he is not able to be free. What Jesus does when asking "What can I do for you?" (Mark 10:46-52; cf. Matt. 20:32) is to allow for the recognition of this individualizing and witnessing desire.[8]
- When I desire something that is not good for me — and I am hindered from achieving it — the Other's understanding of what my desire might mean confronts me and changes the way I look upon or understand it. The immediate understanding I had is now sublated by means of the intersubjective approach that has been established. Accordingly, I change my own self-understanding because my desire now appears in a new light.

Hegel sees the parochial self as hidden from itself. Hence, it depends on the other for its own critical self-consciousness. That is why self-knowledge for Hegel takes the form of self-recognition in the other. As Williams aptly put it,

The road to interiority passes through the other. The self is for itself only by being for an other, and the self is for an other only by being for

---

8. It is, of course, also possible to relate this to how Jesus' own self-understanding changes when confronted with others, for example, the exchange with the Canaanite woman (Matt. 15:21f.). Thus, the Gospels should also be read from the point of view that Jesus is coming to terms with who he is, becomes his identity in relating to others, and by doing to others what he does.

itself. The "for itself" formulates not the beginning but the result and *telos* of the process of recognition. (p. 49)

Although desire can be conceived as something that struggles for its immediate satisfaction, the above indicates that this is not always the case. But the understanding of desire as based on lack and struggling for satisfaction is the least original of the components of Hegel's analysis. What is more important is how he understands desire as a condition of individual consciousness (cf. what we already have suggested about the individualizing functions of desire in the analysis of Moore previously). Because desire is prior to this consciousness, Hegel understands it as both pre-ethical and pre-rational.

At this point, we can see the importance of Hegel's thinking for overcoming the understanding of the individual as a rational and self-establishing entity. For the individual to become aware of herself, recognition through and by the other is of utmost importance. However, for recognition to occur, the immediate desire must be overcome, or, to phrase it in Hegelian terms, sublated. Desire is thus part of the individual's process of becoming self-conscious:

> Desire begins as a kind of natural solipsism that is naively self-centered and narcissistic; its self-centeredness is manifest in the fact that it regards its objects as non-essential, that is, as consumables to be used and consumed at will. The natural "solipsism" of desire is a condition that must be transformed and sublimated if the self is to become capable of enduring relationships with others. Hegel's account of the process of recognition is at the same time an account of the sublimation of desire. In this process desire is not eliminated but deepened: "Self-consciousness attains its satisfaction only in another self-consciousness."[9]

To understand that what one desires is essential for oneself, and why it is so, is thus a basic condition for the transformation of desire. When I really understand that someone else is important for me, I want to engage in communication with her and maintain lasting relations with her. Desire is thus a desire for the other, but a desire that does not only center on my

9. Williams, *Hegel's Ethics of Recognition*, pp. 49-50, with reference to and quotation from Hegel's *Phenomenologie des Geistes*, p. 139.

own needs, but also around who or what the other is and how I am present in her life. This desire for the other thus shatters the narcissistic self, and liberates the individual from its "solipsism" (cf. Williams 1997, p. 50). This is perhaps most clearly illustrated in the way that sexual desire might appear in two forms: either in a narcissistic form that desires the other only as an object of gratification, or as a desire that desires the other's desire for oneself, and thereby also the implicit recognition in the other's desire for oneself. The mutuality and reciprocity in the latter also shape the initial desire in new ways, and one can say that this transformed desire is — by means of recognition — something that truly has its origin in the Other — but now, not the other as object, but as recognizing subject.[10]

Hegel thus helps us to deepen the understanding of desire by his understanding of recognition: it shall not be overcome, but it needs transformation. It has a lasting impact on human life and self-development. Readings of the New Testament, and of the Gospels, that suggest that desire is something that must be rejected or suppressed, will likely be unable to account for this situation. Verses that are read to suggest how Christians must deny themselves (Mark 8:34 par.) would accordingly have to be read in light of this insight. They would not be about repressing desire, but about overcoming and transforming the immediate and self-centered desire in order to develop a different and *relational* desire, where the importance of the relation to the other is what constitutes the self-understanding of the believer.

The Hegelian reading of the constitution of the subject also offers important insights into an understanding of sin as a relational phenomenon. As Hegel makes clear, it is by relating to others that we can understand ourselves as those we are to become. Or to put it even stronger: that we can become those we are called to be by living in a relation to others and to God. This goes for Jesus as well as for any other human being. Hence, it becomes important how one relates to others. Williams calls this the necessity for the sublation of the other as one opposed to me.[11]

The negation of the other, the denial of the other's importance in my life and for the constitution of my identity will then not do. Any attempt to isolate myself from the other will fall back on me. The other is in my life as

10. We shall see in later chapters how the relation to the other is opening up to different forms of desire, among others through the work of René Girard.

11. In the next section, we shall see how Levinas can help us overcome the problem that this sublation might present in terms of making the other a part of the totality of the subject, or, as he says, a part of the *same*.

long as it is understood as my life, and appears for me as thus. If the individual by way of her immediate desires appears as closed off and self-centered, the relation to the other then seems to provide her with no opportunity for living another life and becoming another self. To put it theologically: it is by relating in an affirmative way to God and God's presence that we can become our true selves, rather than being determined by our immediate desires. Williams describes the common phenomenon of the mediation between self and other in a manner that against this background also has a strong theological significance, as it points to how the relationship is transformed:

> In this case the self negates itself, that is, its exclusive parochial identity. Since this identity is expressed primarily at the level of immediate desire, which regards the other as nonessential, this self-negation is not really negative. Rather what is negated here are the negative limitations of parochial self-identity that exclude the other or lead to its coercion and domination. In other words, the parochial self is negated, enlarged, and opened up to what is other. This recognition means that it renounces domination and ceases to dominate the other.[12]

One could perhaps say that the function of the immediate desire is to exclude the other as other, and to see him or her only as an extension of the self that seeks gratification. The way this mode of subjectivity constitutes itself is consequently by excluding or marginalizing the other as one who can shatter or disturb the already conceived self-understanding given in desire. This approach is also a good explanation of sin as the destruction of relationships. In such a context, the desire in question is not for the other, but a desire for the continuation of the narcissistic self that seeks itself in the mirror of the other. Alternatively, this self seeks itself through the negation achieved by confronting the other. Or, to put it in terms that might be more familiar: This mechanism emerges when the pious needs to see his piety in the mirror of the assumed impure and impious. Hence, excluding mechanisms are needed to maintain one's own identity as pure, privileged, righteous in the eyes of God, etc.

---

12. Williams, *Hegel's Ethics of Recognition*, pp. 55-56. One could formulate the same with reference to Levinas, when he claims that "Transcendence is not negativity." See Emmanuel Levinas, *Totality and Infinity: An Essay on Exteriority* (Pittsburgh: Duquesne University Press, 1969), p. 40.

The positive and affirmative self-knowledge achieved through the recognition of and by the other Hegel calls "being at home in an other" ("bei sich im Anderen"). This basic form of relationship is prior to and constitutes the realms of ethics, rights, and Spirit Existence in a community of true recognition, which means that the individual no longer exists with a limitation or restriction of her freedom. Rather, the relationship with the other is the enhancement and concrete actualization of freedom. This underscores both the intersubjective conditions for freedom, and how desire and recognition should now be seen as prior to ethics (cf. Williams 1997, p. 59). Ethics is what comes after the transformation of desire into freedom has taken place. When ethics is "practiced" outside the context of recognition, it might easily be just another way for the self-enclosed subject to promote her own interests.

The true result of recognition is love: in his *Philosophy of Right*, Hegel describes love as the consciousness of my unity with another. Love means that I am not isolated by myself. I gain my self-consciousness only in the renunciation of my independence, by knowing myself in relation and union with another. That is what takes place in love. Hence, the recognition fueled by desire ends up in love for the other.

Recognition of the Other and Desire in Levinas

It is hard not to read Emmanuel Levinas's understanding of how the Other constitutes the ego without looking back at Hegel. In spite of their differences, Hegel and Levinas share a common point in understanding the individual from the point of view of the Other, and they are both critical toward understanding the self as a self-constituting entity based on a rationally conditioned self-creation.[13] On the other hand, whereas Hegel is concerned with mediation and sublation of differences, Levinas[14] strug-

---

13. Levinas is nevertheless critical of what he calls Hegel's totalitarianism. Williams takes issue with this critique and affirms that ethical life (which is the first philosophy of Levinas) in Hegel's sense "is not totalitarianism but a bulwark against it. Hegel's ethics of recognition not only remains relevant to contemporary concerns as a counterdiscourse to modernity; as a correction to both the ancients and the moderns it still has much to offer our disrupted and fragmented cultural situation at the end of the twentieth century," he claims. See Williams, *Hegel's Ethics of Recognition*, p. 412.

14. The following is based on the English version of Levinas, *Totality and Infinity*.

gles to maintain an understanding of the Other as different in such a way that the differences are not neglected or abolished, forcing the Other to be the same. This is most likely the reason why Levinas calls the relationship between the self and the Other metaphysical: something is at stake here that cannot be reduced to the immanence of the self. Typically, Levinas asks: "How can the same, produced as egoism, enter into relationship with an other without immediately divesting it of its alterity? What is the nature of this relationship?" Going deeper than we have been able to go so far, he also claims that to see the Other as a representation is indeed problematic, because the "other would therein dissolve into the same."[15] Hence, to understand the other from the point of view of the subject would be to fail to see what or who the Other is:

> The other with which the metaphysician is in relationship and which he recognizes as other is not simply in another locality [. . .]. The metaphysical other is other with an alterity that is not formal, is not the simple reverse of identity, and is not formed out of resistance to the same, but is prior to every initiative, to all imperialism of the same. It is other with an alterity constitutive of the very content of the other. Other with an alterity that does not limit the same, for in limiting the same the other would not be rigorously other: by virtue of the common frontier the other, within the system, would yet be the same. The absolutely other is the Other.[16]

To maintain the other as an absolutely Other, Levinas underscores that this Other cannot be integrated into the totality of the intentional subject. In a profound sense, the other has to remain inaccessible, or outside the system of totality. Once the Other is integrated into the totality of the same, it loses its changing and disrupting significance. The formulation of this as a "metaphysical" other is thus very apt, as it suggests someone or something outside the realm of nature, outside of the presence by which the mind of the subject constitutes her world.

The "metaphysical" here cannot be thought of in terms of Plato or any other classical metaphysics. As in Plato, that which is beyond the present conditions of the subject and her world, remain exactly as that — as beyond. "The Other" is a marker of the boundary between the world of

15. Levinas, *Totality and Infinity*, p. 38.
16. Levinas, *Totality and Infinity*, pp. 38-39.

sameness or the totality of the ego on the one hand, and that which remains inaccessible on the other. Against this backdrop, it is possible to call God "the Other" as well; i.e., God is among the instances that fit into this category. As this other cannot be made into the same, but remains a boundary concept, God cannot appear as part of the metaphysical system. In Levinas, the very word "metaphysical" implies just the opposite of system: it is what eludes a totality. When Levinas defines religion as "the bond that is established between the same and the other without constituting a totality" (1969, p. 40) it makes sense, accordingly, to say that God is understood in post-metaphysical terms.[17]

For the present project, Levinas's understanding of God and totality is fruitful because it suggests how a god that is integrated into a kind of totality constituted by the subject is not god anymore. When all of a human's life is oriented around his own actions, for example, this would imply that God is seen only in relation to those actions. This is a valid perspective for reconstructing the discussions that Jesus has with the Pharisees about who God is and how God is to be understood.

Finally, if we want to take an even more critical angle, we can also make use of Levinas's definition of *atheism*, as this suggests a mode of existing that by definition is based on the totality of the ego, and thereby seems to exclude any conditioning by the Other:

17. I contrast here the post-metaphysical with the metaphysical or, in Heideggerian terms, with the onto-theological. Joeri Schrijvers, in "Ontotheological Turnings? Marion, Lacoste and Levinas on the Decentring of Modern Subjectivity," *Modern Theology* 22 (2006): 222, defines this onto-theological endeavor as "an ultimate reason that can account for the totality of beings. Its point of departure — beings — forbids that onto-theology encounter anything other, at the end of the chain of beings, than a being. Onto-theology proclaims that a being is what it is only insofar as its contingent mode of being corresponds, and is thereby grounded by, the essence of this particular being. This essence of a being, however, stands itself in need of a foundation, since the essence of a being, in one way or another, is dependent upon the (material) existence of the being of which it is the essence (in the same way as one abstracts a unified essence from diverse empirical tables). For this, onto-theology has recourse to God as the one who, supposedly un-founded or founded in and through Godself, grounds the essence of beings, by simply thinking them or by creating these (imperfect) beings of which God is said to have the perfect idea eternally. 'God' can thus only appear here in the light of a correspondence theory, as that being, be it the highest, who assures a perfect fit between the essence or the 'being' of a being and the empirical being itself." By "placing" God in the category of "the Other" and suggesting that this other appears at the boundary of totality or is beyond the grasp of it, I want to make clear how Schrijvers's understanding of the onto-theological corresponds with my understanding of Levinas as post-metaphysical.

One can call *atheism* this separation so complete that the separated being maintains itself in existence all by itself, without participating in
the Being from which it is separated — eventually capable of it by belief. The break with participation is implied in this capability. One lives
outside of God, at home with oneself; one is an I, an egoism. The soul,
the dimension of the psychic, being an accomplishment of separation,
is naturally atheist. By atheism we thus understand a position prior to
both the negation and the affirmation of the divine, the breaking with
participation by which the I posits as the same and as I. (1969, p. 58)

Against this background, we not only get an understanding of the original
position of the ego as atheistic, but we also come to a description of what it
means to be an atheist, phenomenologically speaking. The fruitfulness of
this is apparent in how it can also make a believer — who believes in her
own actions as conditions for being righteous in the eyes of God — an
atheist. From a postmodern perspective, this suggests that the Gospels and
the provocative teachings of Jesus might not only be about what at surface
appears as different understandings of God, but rather, and more radically,
they deal with the question about theism or atheism disguised as piety.[18]

*   *   *

We have now presented the framework by which we will develop the following understanding of Christ from other angles. At the same time, we
hope that there have been sufficient hints in the previous presentation as
to how these angles might be relevant and what they could imply for
Christology. The next sections of the book will then be a test as to how well
this works, and to what extent the attempt to see Christ from these angles
might also be of relevance to more than the affirmation of traditional
Christology.

18. Cf. in relation to this the reference to Sobrino below in footnote 1, page 112, who
says that the question for Jesus is *who* and not *if* God is. It is possible to agree with Sobrino,
but nevertheless allow for Levinas's insight here as one that deepens the way we address the
problem of atheism: to relate to a god who is an idol is only a different form of atheism.

PART II

IDENTITY ISSUES

Who Is This Human?

It is striking how much of Christological debate and reflection center around questions of identity. There is hardly any surprise in that. Already the Gospels voice a lot of different stories about questions of Jesus' identity. In this chapter, we will look at some of the insights that can be gained from discussions on this topic. Our analysis will be framed by the different angles that we presented in the Introduction to the book.

Before proceeding to some of the identity issues that might be discussed with regard to Jesus, it is, however, appropriate to note that in much postmodern theory, the issue of identity is treated with a fair amount of suspicion. Attempts to define identity, or to clarify what establishes identity, often fail. Such failures could contribute to a lack of understanding rather than the opposite, especially if the failure is not recognized. Moreover, one might deal with such questions in order to gain control over, get a grasp of, or relate all previous elements of one's knowledge to the one whose identity is of concern.[1] In that case, the definition of identity might express a will to power, a certain interest in conceptualizing that does not fit into pre-established schemes of thought, and that therefore is exactly the reason why we question someone's or something's identity.

1. For this, see, e.g., Kelly Oliver, *Witnessing: Beyond Recognition* (Minneapolis: University of Minnesota Press, 2001). Oliver also questions to what extent an identity based on recognition is sufficient to liberate humans fully, and develops an attempt to move beyond a mere Hegelian model of recognition. However, I still think I am justified in using Hegel in the way I have so far suggested, given that I qualify the understanding of recognition as I did in the previous chapter.

Here we are going to discuss issues of identity related to Jesus, but this discussion is not made in an effort to "get it all" and establish an exhaustive understanding of his identity. Rather, what I will attempt is not only an effort to get more, or to get something other, than what is often all too easily presented and/or taken for granted as the identity of Jesus Christ. There is a kind of openness allowed by the witnesses of Jesus that should be considered in framing the questions of his identity. Hence, as I am not going to say all that I think there is to say about Jesus in this book, I approach questions concerning his identity with no aspirations of completeness. Furthermore, in this respect, Jesus also, as every other human, testifies to the validity of the old hermeneutic rule that the *individuum est ineffabile.*

This last point is a lesson learned already from the early days of Jesus scholarship: As every epoch in history inevitably will establish its understanding of the identity of Jesus against the background of its own context, we cannot reasonably claim to have immediate access to everything that makes him important. His identity is thus constantly in need of being reestablished for us. In a certain sense, Jesus is — as everyone else — no one in himself. He is what he is by and in his relation to others. Albert Schweitzer expresses it thus: "He comes to us unknown. . . ."[2] Someone who comes to us unknown, we have to get to know. The challenge in the process of getting to know is to let the Other come forward on his own terms, and let him be exactly that — Other.[3] Although he belongs in another time than ours, we nevertheless have to understand him from our own point of time in history. That makes dealing with the identity issues even harder, and should make us approach them with openness and a consciousness of the preliminary character of the task.[4] Or to put it in a differ-

---

2. A. Schweitzer, *The Quest for the Historical Jesus* (1906). Here quoted from Donald Capps, *Jesus: A Psychological Biography* (St. Louis: Chalice Press, 2000), p. 268.

3. Cf. the hermeneutical considerations for Christology in Werner Jeanrond, "På Väg Mot en Kristologi i Dag," in *Jesustolkningar i Dag. Tio Teologer om Kristologi* (Stockholm: Verbum, 1995), pp. 238-39.

4. Graham Ward underscores also the need for making "the word strange," and he writes aptly: "We cannot winnow the historical from the theological, in the belief that the historical is 'nearer the truth.' We move always within the circle of faith and the economy of redemptive response; within a hermeneutical activity that I wish to call 'discernment' to distinguish it from the philosophical goal of interpretation, 'understanding.' As such the Jesus we enquire into is always the Jesus who makes himself known to us today. The Jesus we figure forth and discern is always a contemporary Jesus. Since, then, all our figuring issues

ent manner: no matter where we are in history, we are always at another place than the one we are trying to grasp. That should make us allow for different approaches. I hold, consequently, that an approach that allows for a plurality of approaches to the questions of the identity of Jesus is the one most fitting the circumstances that shape our understanding of him.

Unstable Identities of Descent and Assent as Reflected in Matthew 1

There is something almost ironic about the way the evangelists present the initial phase of Jesus' life. When we get beneath the cultural layers of modern Christmas celebration and the idyllic function of the nativity stories, we get a glimpse of something different, although also quite disturbing: Here are involved elements of power, desire, sex, and shame. The assumption almost every reader has about the glorious king is effectively deconstructed. We see this most tellingly in the first verses of Matthew (who is, by the way, the one among the evangelists who is most concerned with legitimating Jesus' position in a Judaist context).

The aim of the genealogy of Jesus offered in Matthew seems to be to provide a link between Jesus and David. Jesus is first presented, accordingly, as a descendant of this most glorious king of Israel (cf. Matt. 1:1f.). However, contrary to what one should expect, this link is deconstructed and given a twist, and in two ways: First, the genealogy ends up with Joseph, the husband of Mary, and second, it is said that Jesus was conceived before Joseph had been living together with Mary. Hence, the very link that should be established by way of the genealogy is actually made problematic: The one who was — biologically — to secure Jesus' place in the glorious genealogy is the one who is recognized as not immediately providing the means for doing that: the biological fatherhood is, contrarily, disputed. To put it otherwise: the father is not the father, is not recognized as father; is his father and is not his father.[5]

---

from within the matrices of our own cultural embeddedness, Christology is always a cultural undertaking." Ward, *Christ and Culture: Challenges in Contemporary Theology* (Oxford: Blackwell Publishing, 2005), pp. 19-20.

5. This unstable position of Joseph, and thereby also of the relationship between Jesus and Joseph, is underscored in the story in Luke 2:48-49, where the use of the word "father" is

Similarly, this also jeopardizes Jesus' own identity: if he is to be recognized as the son of David, he is dependent on Joseph's recognition of him as his son. This identity is not something to be taken for granted, but it is an identity offered, given, by Joseph in his recognition of Jesus as his son. By recognizing Jesus thus, Joseph is himself given a recognized place in the history of Jesus.

The lack of stability in the constitution of Jesus' identity as the descendant of David is underscored by the apparent elements in the story: Joseph could have rejected Mary and her child, and Mary herself would not be recognized without the recognition of Joseph as having a legitimate stand in this genealogy. Moreover, Mary's situation is one not marked by honor, but by potential shame. The only thing that can save her from this shame is that she is — concretely, physically — welcomed into a community that recognizes her as bearing a child who has its origin in the life-giving powers of the Holy Spirit. That is what Joseph does. This we can see as the first modeling trait of the story. It models some features that are often repeated in later stories about Jesus and the community he shapes.

As Matthew puts it, Jesus' identity is thus an identity by assent, and not (solely) by descent. It is constituted by Joseph's active recognition. From a legal point of view, Joseph could have rejected Jesus as his son. At the same time, we can read the story as giving another account of the origin of Jesus: his life originates in the life-giving powers of the Holy Spirit. That is not unlike any other human; rather, it is, from a theological angle, identical with what is the origin of all other humans.

By reading the beginnings of Jesus in this way, what become underscored are not questions about some miracle birth, or the virginity of Mary, but the vulnerability of his identity as seen from the perspective of a family. In his story is involved what is common to many humans: the possibility of being rejected by a father or a family, the fact of being conceived out of wedlock, the fragility of your social status — especially if something "goes wrong" in terms of what is socially accepted.[6]

---

given two contradicting contexts. Jesus thereby even suggests that his house (the house of his Father) is a different one than the house of Joseph and Mary. This contributes to the general destabilization of family ties as a marker of Jesus' true identity in the Gospels.

6. Cristina Grenholm, *Moderskap och Kärlek: Schabloner och Tankeutrymme i Feministteologisk Livsåskådningsreflektion* (Stockholm: Nya Doxa, 2005), calls this the ambiguous open space where Mary becomes the site for the creative processes that constitute Christian faith, and, with reference to E. Schüssler Fiorenza, parallels this open space with

What can we make out of this? First, as suggested, we can see these experiences from the early life of Jesus, and related to the constitution of his identity, as later giving shape and content to his preaching and his ministry. The inclusion of those not socially accepted, and the recognition of others based on their origin in God, rather than based on what they have done or not in terms of social acceptability, is prefigured in the model of Joseph. Second, we can also see here how there is no stable identity without positive recognition: even a descendant of David might need some recognition based on assent. Interestingly enough, Jesus himself at later stages of his life puts equally little emphasis on the biological origin of humans when determining their relationship with him (cf. Matt. 12:46ff.).

King Among Kings?

From the outset, one can read the Synoptic Gospels as establishing the identity of Jesus in a way that challenges human power.[7] The importance and validity of the genealogy in Matthew for establishing the identity of Jesus are made also by the sequel to the narrative about Joseph and Mary: When King Herod learns of the child, he is said to be using his powers to kill every infant who threatens his position as king. This places the position of king in a problematic light: he is not so glorious after all. On the other hand, the Gospels are throughout recounting the good tidings of the kingdom of *God*. Hence, there is a tension between earthly powers and kings, and the kingdom of God, and this tension is portrayed as one between life and death.[8] The narrative in Matthew also suggests two different

---

that of the empty tomb after resurrection. These "places" where we do not know what took place open up for new visions about the possibilities of life — partly because they are told as stories about what we take to be impossible.

7. Marcus J. Borg, *Jesus: Uncovering the Life, Teachings, and Relevance of a Religious Revolutionary* (San Francisco: HarperSanFrancisco, 2006), pp. 66f., sees the stories about the birth of Christ as a direct challenge to central claims of Roman imperial theology. As indicated in the following, I think the frontier here is more plural and cannot be reduced to that aspect alone.

8. This contrast becomes even more gravely spelled out when we see the practice of Herod, as it is echoed in the narratives of the killing of infants, with the way Jesus himself as an adult preaches and practices the kingdom of God: "In its fullness, therefore, Jesus' message of God's lordship and his kingdom is: God's universal love for men as disclosed in and

approaches to the newborn child, which are modeled in Herod and the Magi respectively:

- Herod rejects the child and seeks to eliminate him. Jesus is — if king — someone who challenges Herod's position of power, wealth, and social position. Herod does not seek to give the child anything, but seeks to deprive him of *all conditions for receiving gifts and recognition* (as king) by taking his life. Herod's identity as king is at stake if he recognizes Jesus as king. Hence, there is here a struggle of mutual exclusion: one of them must yield. The struggle of recognition here is of the kind that Hegel described as unstable: it is one carried out by force, and as such, it cannot end up in a mutual recognition expressing freedom. Matthew's narrative thus expresses clearly the brutality and wickedness of the violent struggles for recognition.

- The Magi recognize Jesus as king — in spite of the not kinglike environment and the circumstances under which he is born. Their recognition is also mirrored in their *gifts,* which are gifts of surplus and worthy of a king. Without being able to develop it much here, we should nevertheless note that these gifts of affluence and excess are given to someone who is likely to be very poor, and who has no means himself for establishing any conditions for the gifting. The gifts thus appear as exactly that: as gifts outside the economic circle, in Derridaean terms. Neither reciprocity, nor any hope for return later on, is suggested here. The Magi disappear out of the story afterwards. The point of their appearance in the narrative is thus twofold: to offer gifts, and to make visible one way of recognizing the identity of this child: as a king — but on conditions other than those on which Herod lives.

In the tradition, the Magi are sometimes also themselves called kings. This description then makes the question of kingship acute in the present narrative: not only can the kings of this world relate in different ways to Jesus; but the way they exert their kingship also suggests that there are no

---

through his actual mode of conduct, consistent with and consequent upon it, and thus as an appeal to us to believe in and hope for this coming salvation and kingdom of peace, 'imparted by God,' and likewise faithfully to manifest its coming in a consistent way of living; the praxis of the kingdom of God." So Edward Schillebeeckx, *Jesus: An Experiment in Christology* (New York: Seabury Press, 1979), p. 154.

necessary links between being a king and recognizing Jesus positively. Whereas the Magi are said to prostrate themselves and give Jesus homage (Matt. 1:11), Herod operates from a distance and never confronts Jesus personally, and never in a similar way, which would then suggest that he recognized Jesus as *his* king.

When we then look back on the initial two sequences in the Gospel of Matthew, and ask what they can say to us about the identity of Jesus, we get a differentiated picture. The narrative expresses the tension between possibilities of rejection or positive recognition. However, the rejecting position also presupposes that Jesus is recognized in a specific way: as an illegitimate child who is a threat to Joseph's righteousness, or as one who challenges Herod's position as a wealthy king. In both cases, the mere appearance of the child, before he is himself able to do anything, is by way of his indirect relation to these two, posing them with different options as to how they will understand themselves — either as someone who welcomes or as someone who closes off to a personal relation with this child. My reason for pointing this out here is that we already in these initial narratives find that the question of identity remains open, and that different ways of understanding the identity of Jesus are modeled in these texts. I underscore here the modeling element, as this is clearly not a feature that offers mere historical information, but rather points to how one, as a reader, might still relate to and recognize Jesus. At the same time, these texts suggest already, from such a reading, patterns that can be disclosed in later parts of the Gospel narratives about Jesus.

When we then ask, "Who does Jesus appear as in this story?," the immediate answer is that he appears as one who can be (positively) recognized, but who need not be. He is identified in manners that hold a strong element of contingency. We become more than aware that this is not the way it needed to be. Thus, Jesus appears in the split between shame and glory. What could have become shameful in a family context is overcome. On the other hand the kingship of Herod that could have appeared as glorious in its recognition of Jesus is instead disclosed as mean, low, and ungenerous. What Jesus' own kingship means remains open and undefined.

Moreover, as the installation of Jesus in the tensions of this story also suggests that he can be recognized as king, we must then let go of any previously conceived idea we have about what a king is. Nothing in the story so far gives us a clear idea about how and why he can be recognized as king. Perhaps we can say that the narrative opens up a space where Jesus, by his mere existence, is a placeholder for a kingship yet to be determined, but clearly not to be determined by the usual means for identifying a king. In the narrative, Jesus' identity remains open as a placeholder for this identity.[9]

There are thus only two elements that are clear contributions to his identification so far: he is the son of Mary, and he is the origin of struggles about identities (not only his own, but everyone who has to ask: Who am I in the presence of this child?) from his early childhood on.

The Mother and Identity: Perspectives from Kristeva

Mary's position and relationship with Jesus is never disputed, although Jesus himself questions the *significance* of the family ties between them later on. At the beginning, Mary is the stable point, a point of orientation. In the Gospels, Jesus is unquestionably Mary's son. It is striking how she continues to remain identified as such throughout the Gospel narratives. We can say that she is accompanying the Jesus story, and thus she offers the story about him a point of reference. The identity of Jesus as a man born of a woman is maintained by the presence of his mother. Mary is thus the one who more than any other in the narrative contributes to underscore the identity of Jesus as a true human.

Mary's own identity is also, of course, dependent on her status as the mother of Jesus. However, postmodern theory has contributed to make problematic the immediate reduction of Mary's role to that of (the) mother (of Jesus). When looking at her function as a mother in light of how Julia Kristeva understands mother identity, we need not understand her solely in light of this function. By identifying the mother's relation to the infant as a function, Kristeva separates the function of meeting the child's needs from both love and desire. Both love and desire transcend the determinations of motherhood, a point that is possible to detect later in the Gospels where we can see Mary as a social and speaking being who both loves and desires (cf. Matt. 12:46f.). Moreover, this also allows for love

---

9. In Luke, there are stronger allusions to Jesus as king than those we find explicit in Matthew. On the other hand, the witness to his kingship is constructed in a quite different, if not opposite, manner: The angel in Luke addresses Mary, not Joseph, and the Magi are replaced with shepherds in Luke. The references to the kingship of David are also made far more explicit (cf. Luke 1:32).

to have a place outside of mere mother-like relations. Love is given, so to say, a more independent place, in Kristeva's reading.

One of the implicit but fruitful suggestions of Kristeva is that both men and women can fulfill the maternal function, because this is not necessarily a sexed function that only women can maintain. Given that this is the case, Mary should not be reduced to a model for motherhood that excludes men from defining themselves as possible practitioners of that function. Nor should her subjectivity be seen as only emerging from her function as a mother: she might love and desire apart from that function.

There is, however, one point in Kristeva's understanding of motherhood that might have a special bearing for our reflection on how the identities of both Mary and Jesus are constituted. Kristeva claims that the maternal body operates between nature and culture. This situation precludes the position that maternity can be reduced to nature. As Kristeva uses the maternal body with its two-in-one, or Other within, as a model for all subjective relations, she presents a model for the desire to know, to relate, and to develop as a subject that is of great interest: As the maternal body, each one of us is what she calls a *subject-in-process*. In this process, we are always negotiating with the Other who is there as part of what constitutes us, and the presence of the Other (in Jesus' case: Mary) makes us who we become. Our identities are consequently never given without a process in which we relate to important others. As subjects-in-process we are always negotiating the other within our own fragile totality, and thus, we can never fully be the subjects of our own experience. This approach not only points back to Hegel, it also contributes to the questioning of a traditional notion of an autonomous unified (masculine) subject.[10] There are also possible links here to the understanding of the Other in the constitution of the identity of the self in Levinas.

To put this last point in an actual context would mean to say that anyone who relates to a conception of Jesus exists in a "mother-like" relationship to this conception. He is the Other whom we are constantly called to learn more about, and thereby learn more about ourselves as well. This goes for men as well as women. To deepen this insight somewhat more,

---

10. See Julia Kristeva: *Desire in Language: A Semiotic Approach to Literature and Art* (New York: Columbia University Press, 1980), as well as Kelly Oliver, "Kristeva and Feminism," Feminist Theory Website, ed. Kristin Switala [http://www.utc.edu/~kswitala/Feminism/Kristeva.html] (1998).

this makes it impossible to establish the identity of Jesus as an object, as something that can be determined independent of our personal relation to him. This should be a kind of critical marker against any objectifying dogmatic statement about the identity of Jesus, as well as against a kind of misconstrued apologetics that makes it appear as an objective truth about who he is and how we, accordingly, should relate to him. The presence of Jesus in our perception of him and his otherness puts our own as well as his identity at stake. To suggest otherwise would be to neglect the very effects of identity-shaping that his presence — in the different representations of him — might contribute to. When mystical theology opens up to ideas about Jesus being born in the heart of the believer, this is one of the backgrounds against which this could be read.

Furthermore, Kristeva's theories might shed some light on the background for what constitutes the identity of Jesus in his relation to his mother. In her Introduction to *The Kristeva Reader,* Toril Moi points to how the free subject is able to construct imaginary fantasies and new languages, precisely because she is able to situate herself in relation to the law.[11] The law in Kristeva stands for the symbolic, that to which the subject is subjected and must relate. The law is also that which enables us to become speaking subjects in the first place.[12] Hence, the law is the influence of others upon us; that which allows for us, by their recognition, to become subjects. Given that the law is present in the life of Jesus through his mother, and that the law might be read against a more theological background as well, this would imply that it shapes and orders the created world in which they both believe. Then the following picture emerges:

Kristeva understands the cured subject, the one free to develop *a new language,* as a subject of love. Moi points to how the cured subject in Kristeva is marked by transference love, which consists in an imaginary process of identification with an archaic ideal ego (the "father of personal prehistory"). The subject is accordingly one who loves, who is able to create new languages and thereby get access to imaginary resources, as well as one who relates back to a father-figure in the prehistory of his own subjectivity. I would argue that the picture we get here is not hard to apply to Jesus.[13] His

11. Cf. Introduction, in Julia Kristeva and Toril Moi, *The Kristeva Reader* (New York: Columbia University Press, 1986), p. 18.

12. Introduction, in Kristeva and Moi, *The Kristeva Reader,* p. 14.

13. The relation to the imaginary father is a conception that is extensively treated in Capps, *Jesus: A Psychological Biography.*

personal development of a new language, new practices when relating to the law and the way it is understood, as well as his personal and intimate relation to the imaginary "father" God, who is not Joseph, might become more understandable in light of this reading.

Against this background, when we look at the relationship between Jesus and his mother it is first relevant to say that Mary is the one who constantly presents (in both meanings of the word) him with his origin. Simultaneously, she is the one who has contributed to his entering into the social world and his specific experiences, and given him opportunities for love. Her maternal function has thus provided Jesus with the features of his subjectivity. She is the origin from which he cannot distance himself. In this respect, Mary has a function parallel to God.[14] However, this is a function that, although parallel to God's function in all humans' lives, Mary only has in relation to her children. Whereas the ability to distance oneself from God accordingly is something that no human can fully possess (at least not from a theological angle), *we* can distance ourselves from Mary as our origin. Mary had a singular and unique function and relation to Jesus that no other humans have, and this uniqueness is not parallel to our relationship with God. Not even his brothers and sisters are likely to have had a similar relation, as we have to assume that their paternal origin was more transparent than it was in the case of Jesus.[15]

The above analysis should make clear that it is not only how one relates to Jesus (or not) that contributes to his identity. We cannot make of Je-

---

14. Cf. for this also how Ward, *Christ and Culture*, p. 213, uses Kristeva's work to argue "that she roots a theological examination of the doctrine of *kenosis* in an anthropology that relates the fundamental experience of human existence as one of dispossession (or in Schleiermacher's term, 'absolute dependence') to our nature as the creators of signs and symbols. We are makers of images because we are 'made in the image of.'" As indicated in the way the present book is constructed, I think we mostly can do without the language of *kenosis*, though.

15. Further on this, see Capps, *Jesus: A Psychological Biography.* Capps discusses a vast variety of psycho-historical material which I cannot go into here, but which basically also suggests that some of Jesus' approach to organized religion, as well as his attitude towards the God he calls "Abba," may be due to him growing up without a father, or without some of the privileges of the oldest son, due to his ambiguous position in the family and in relation to Joseph. Capps's book is very interesting, but the aim of the present work is to relate our understanding of Jesus to the indisputable traits common to him and other humans, not to develop his individual biographical traits as they might appear in a more or less speculative psychological pre-history of the man we know as Jesus from Nazareth.

sus whatever we like, and the determining factors for his identity do not only lie in the present. As with the rest of us, his is also a relation to a mother, and this relation cannot be disregarded. The mother-relation — for better or worse — contributes to the basic traits of every human's life. It is by and through the relation to his mother that Jesus himself is most likely to have had his desires shaped and given content. Accordingly, in his process towards individualization and the shaping of subjectivity, Mary is a central person. Hence, it is more than understandable how she appears again and again in the Gospels. Her presence throughout is a constant reminder of the personal and psychological background environment that made Jesus the one he is. By appearing on the scene now and then, Mary also continues to recognize Jesus as her son, and thereby to remind us of his true humanity.

Let me make just one methodological point in relation to Christology in general, when developed along these lines: any approach to the person of Jesus that applies psychological or other approaches that can also be applied to other humans, unavoidably lets him appear as a human. We should consider this observation a gain for constructive theological reflection, as this enables us to see how the history of Jesus is not remote from the sphere of that which shapes the experiences of any human. When we come to understand more about what shapes the fate and identity of Jesus, we will also come to understand more about what might shape our own lives — or not. This "from below" approach thus not only has gains in terms of providing a more concrete understanding of Jesus, but also in terms of the challenges and predicaments of humanity in general. When I suggested reading Matthew's narrative as one that models different approaches to the recognition of Jesus, I was also claiming that this approach is one that Matthew would *like* us to engage in.

In the Conclusion to his book on Jesus, Don Capps writes that "the single most important thing about him — as far as the identity issue is concerned — was that his identity was, as noted, other than his socially attributed identity." His identity is accordingly something that cannot be decided on ordinary social terms.[16] We have to look into other elements than solely those constituted by his social environment. Hence, to reconstruct elements of the pre-history of Jesus' subjectivity in a way that is not only relevant to him, but to all humans in some way or another, is a relevant enterprise in this regard.

16. Capps, *Jesus: A Psychological Biography,* p. 268.

Relativizing Family Ties as Basis for Identity — a Different Community

Most people seem to render family ties as important for their identity and for the way they commit themselves. The emphasis on family is not only so among our contemporaries, it also seems to be a rather general trait across the borders of time and culture. It shapes the preconceptions underlying the reports about how Jesus related to his biological family as well. One of the striking features in the Gospels is how Jesus seems to render family ties as of little importance in terms of belonging, loyalty, or preferences. This suggests that he did not primarily define his identity along such lines. Moreover, as we can see in Matthew 10:45ff., he also does not seem to allow for family relations to have importance for defining *any* ultimate value in terms of guidance for conduct. In the mentioned passage, family ties are rather modeled along the same lines of struggle as those suggested in the previous sections of this chapter: what it all comes down to is who one recognizes Jesus to be. By his own saying, he will divide households, and recognizing him is more important than recognizing and relating to your own family. Hence, family relations are, according to Jesus as portrayed in Matthew, of secondary importance to other things.[17] In a subsequent passage, Matthew 12:46ff., we can see this even more vividly described in the relation of Jesus to his own family: he there substitutes the recognition of his own followers with the recognition of those who are his biological family.

The reason for this exchange of emphasis on biological family with the community of those who recognize him lies exactly in this: the *recognition*. Not only is the question about recognizing Jesus positively as representing the most important relation at stake, however. Rather, what is at stake is the question about recognizing *God*. To put it bluntly, it is only the recognition of God, and the fact that God is the one we are to love more and above any other, that allows for relativizing the importance of family ties. When Jesus says, "Whoever receives you receives me, and whoever receives me receives the one who sent me" (v. 40), he indicates that there is a recognition taking place here that not only implies that they recognize *him*

17. I think Borg overstates the issue in anachronistic ways when he writes that Jesus "saw the patriarchal family as a constricting institution that demanded a loyalty inconsistent with loyalty to God. To give primary allegiance to it locked one into the world of convention." Borg, *Jesus: Uncovering the Life, Teachings, and Relevance of a Religious Revolutionary,* p. 207.

in a manner that makes him recognize *them* as more important than his own biological family. Something even more important is taking place: by recognizing Jesus, they recognize the God who sent him. This is the basic reason for Jesus' positive recognition of them. Moreover, this is the reason for eliminating any reference to biological family ties as those who constitute belonging and defining relationships.[18]

The bottom line is that in these stories, which are clustered around the questions of Jesus' identity in relation to his family, *God* emerges as more important. Not much more is said about God, but enough is said to see that in the passages just referred to, God takes a crucial role in Jesus' self-identity: Jesus sees God as the one who has sent him. This understanding of God shapes the practice that Jesus conducts vis-à-vis his family. His conception of God, the conception on which he is acting, accordingly has two consequences: First, it implies that his family relationship is not privileged over his relationship with any other people. This is not to be taken as a downgrading of family, but rather as an upgrading of the relationship of others. What I am aiming at here is to understand the practice that Jesus develops as emerging from his understanding of being sent by God. God does not make some people less worthy than others; rather, the overall project of Jesus seems to be to make visible that all have as much worth as everybody else. The response to the requests of his family must therefore *not* be seen as a *devaluation* of them, but rather as a higher evaluation of those with whom he is sharing a community based on trust in God and in God's positive recognition of them.

Second, from the angle of identity this opens up a space where everyone has a place, and where familial/biological relations are second to the relation based on having our origin in God. That is the positive side of these relativized family relations. It means that the identity of those belonging to this community is based on what they have in common: belief in God, and in the one whom God has sent. The other side of the conditions for this identity is that familial or other contingent features of identity have no bearing on who belongs to this community or not. In this sense, later Christianity's (final) opposition to oppression due to ethnic, cultural, or gender identities is prefigured here. No one is privileged in

18. For how this leads to an understanding in the first Christian communities of the church as a "new family," see Karl Olav Sandnes, *A New Family: Conversion and Ecclesiology in the Early Church with Cross-Cultural Comparisons* (Bern and New York: P. Lang, 1994).

terms of such characteristics. As we shall see later, this implies that such understanding of God makes it impossible to use God as an identity-marker that excludes anyone who believes in God, and accordingly, sets God first. If someone is excluded from a community, it is because something other than the relationship to God shapes his or her priorities.[19]

When one then asks, "What are the consequences of belief in God?," the answer is to be found in the identity of the community that Jesus shapes, and which is practiced in his own ministry: To believe in God means to recognize all others as being created by and loved by God, and as someone having the same standing as yourself over against God.[20] Hence, the belief has practical consequences also in terms of how one treats others and relates to (recognizes) them. In this respect, belief in God is linked to practice, community, and identity. The God that emerges out of this practice, or, the practicing of the word (of) God in the family context, includes rather than excludes others from community.

Matthew contributes to making problematic the importance of family ties for defining Jesus' identity from a different angle when he narrates the story of Jesus in the synagogue: When people respond to his teachings, they seem unable to understand from where he has gotten his wisdom and capabilities. Reflecting on how he got them, they are reported to say: "Is he not the carpenter's son? Is not his mother named Mary and his brothers James, Joseph, Simon, and Judas? Are not his sisters all with us? Where did this man get all this?" (v. 55f.). John 6:42 also suggests that people perceive a lack of correspondence between Jesus' family origin and his teachings: His message and appearance simply do not become understandable from the family angle. These approaches of

19. Parallel points have been made by other, more exegetically based approaches: Rowan Williams, in *Christ on Trial: How the Gospel Unsettles Our Judgement* (Grand Rapids: Zondervan, 2002), p. 29 says that "Due to the full presence of divine Sophia (Wisdom) in Jesus, 'membership within a patriarchal family is dramatically replaced by membership within the family of disciples gathered around Wisdom . . . and the metaphors used for this discipleship are inclusive — brother and sister and mother (12:46-50).' Refusal of Wisdom is a refusal of this inclusive vision; refusal of Wisdom is going to be, ultimately, an act of violence against what seems incongruous and discontinuous — even though it is in truth the hidden logic, the hidden unity, of the world." Williams refers to Elaine Wainwright, "The Gospel of Matthew," in *Searching the Scriptures: A Feminist Commentary,* ed. Elisabeth Schüssler Fiorenza (London: SCM Press, 1995), p. 654.

20. As we shall see in a section later in this part, this has specific implications for the understanding of every human being as created in the image of God.

the narratives underscore the problem of defining or understanding Jesus against the background of family. He cannot be understood for what he is on those terms.

Who Do They Say That I Am? The Outcome of Mark 8

The puzzles of Jesus' identity not only have to do with his family relations. We see also that he himself opens up to the question of identity in different parts of his ministry, as recorded by the evangelists. For example, in Mark 8, there is a report of an exchange that takes place just after a man is healed from blindness (and thus is able to see clearly).

> Along the way he asked his disciples, "Who do people say that I am?" They said in reply, "John the Baptist, others Elijah, still others one of the prophets." And he asked them, "But who do you say that I am?" Peter said to him in reply, "You are the Messiah." Then he warned them not to tell anyone about him. (Mark 8:27f.)

Several elements in this story are worth commenting on. First, it is Jesus himself who raises the issue about his identity. Mark, however, in no way indicates that this is done because Jesus is insecure about his own identity. Rather, the story becomes the function of showing that Jesus transcends the pre-given conceptions of identity ascribed to men such as Jesus, and which existed among his contemporaries. The story is thus construed as making it clear that Jesus *could* be recognized as the Messiah, but nevertheless that this identity is neither identical with any other category at hand, nor something that is fully in accordance with traditional conceptions of who and what the Messiah is.

Moreover, Jesus seems to have been very hesitant in attributing the title or role of the Messiah directly to himself. This is recorded in the warning he gives Peter after his testimony, but we can see something similar in the response to John the Baptist's disciples in Matthew 11:3, where he seems more eager to tell John what is happening than to apply any kind of title to himself. Surely, he is not denying that this title applies to him (this would also not be possible to imagine, given that the evangelists have the establishment of his identity as the Messiah more or less as a kind of overarching concern), but they nevertheless report a kind of reluctance in his approach to the title, as if to suggest that there is *no* title that might be appropriate for him.[21]

Given that Jesus himself was reluctant to accept, or even rejected, the use of the title of Messiah for himself, one has to ask what bearing this might have on the construction of a Christology. Given what has been suggested already, it seems to imply first of all that the title of Messiah is one that most likely emerges out of reflections about the totality of Jesus' ministry. When the evangelists report on Jesus' attitude towards the title, they indicate both its validity and its limitations. Or, to put it in more fashionable terms, they deconstruct the immediate and clear meaning the title can have as applied to Jesus, because he is in no way the king that was expected.

The preliminary conclusion here is that we do not have many more "stabilizers" when answering questions about the identity of Jesus in relation to God than we have to answering the question, "Who is this man?" Every time the question is asked, we get an answer, but a different one; and simultaneously, we realize that there is more to be said than what is explicitly said. This openness and lack of final definition suggest that a Christology developed around the central titles usually employed in Christological studies should be employed with care and with awareness of their limitations. When one title is given for identification, some other is simultaneously limited or deconstructed. There are no exhaustive terms, no means for establishing a final and definite identity for this person — just as there are none for anyone else. When the Gospels indicate this, they also indicate that the one we have to remain open to, in considering Jesus from Nazareth, is an Other — one who is more and different than our preconceptions, and who therefore cannot be subjected to or restricted by them. This is not said in order to undermine the actual content and importance of the different understandings we might get; rather, it is said in order to maintain the necessity for keeping them — but to keep them in a manner that allows for a plurality of such understandings, and not privilege any of them beforehand as more apt than others.

---

21. Some scholars take it that Jesus himself explicitly rejected the title of Messiah as apt for himself, and that the use of it originated in early Christianity due to the inscription on the Cross. For references to this opinion and its position in recent research, see Pannenberg, *Jesus — God and Man* (London: SCM, 2002), pp. 13, 138.

The Other Approach to Identity: John

We can read the prologue of John as an alternative approach to the identity issue that Matthew and Luke are offering. Although their Gospels — by way of different strategies — put great effort into building up or constituting a narrative that can open up to the identity issues related to Jesus, they both also, in a certain sense, fail to give a final account of his identity. As we have seen, this is related to how the narrative itself also deconstructs stable identity markers applied to Jesus.

John is the only one who begins with God. In the other Gospels, when the divine is introduced in the story, it is mediated by an angel, a messenger, or by reference to what God has said through the prophets (mostly in Matthew), or by the sayings of Jesus himself. Not so in John. He opens the overarching perspective by starting with God — and the Word, the logos.

We have already commented on how John goes back to the beginning of the beginning. By starting with God, and nevertheless stating that "he came to his own" (1:11), John is able to combine the origin in God with an immediate and intimate relation of the Son to the world. This construction allows for establishing different elements of identity: to come to one's own means to have a pre-established relationship of "property" or relation, but it also means a return, a revisit, and a recognition of those he is returning to as those to whom he belongs. The point of departure in John thus allows for spelling out the recognition of God for the world though his Son, before any subsequent report of their recognition of him (or lack of it: 1:11). Hence, not distance, but relation is what John is establishing by starting with God and claiming that Jesus came to his own.

John also rearranges the family issues that we dealt with in the previous sections, and establishes the theological angle fully by explicitly excluding human conditions as a basis for the community of freedom and faith. In John 1:12f., we read: "But to all who received him, who believed in his name, he gave power to become children of God, who were born, not of blood or of the will of the flesh or of the will of man, but of God." This can be read as John's version of the text we discussed in Matthew 12 above. But there is one important addition in John, underscored by how his angle is based on the perspective of God: when people receive Jesus, and thereby recognize that they are offered an identity as children of God, the establishment of this identity is *other-based*. Neither human flesh nor will can establish this. By affirming it thus, John confirms the radical character of gift and grace in the identity that Jesus and God bestow upon humans. As this identity is not originating from anything human, it not only stems from God's gifting and God's will to establish a gracing community, it is also something that one cannot hold on to without being in a relationship with God. The identity is given with and in this relationship. When John states how truth and grace came though Jesus Christ, he reflects these insights. In his prologue, John thereby strongly affirms and repeats the gifting and gracing element that is present in Jesus: "From his fullness we have all received, grace upon grace" (1:16). That is a different way to construe Jesus' identity.

John thereby makes visible how the God behind the identities of both Jesus and the believers is a gifting God. This God, external to any believer, is decentering the identity of humans, and thereby, paradoxically, making it more stable than it would be given that it was established on contingent, human-made or human-controlled elements.

In sum, John's prologue goes straight to the core of questions of identity, and is able to develop an understanding that underscores elements of both gift and grace, of recognition — how God is the origin of identity and the point of orientation for understanding what takes place in Christ. Simultaneously, like the other evangelists, he is clear on how not everyone recognizes (receives) Christ positively: the possibility of rejection is still an issue.

There is one more element in John's prologue that has a bearing on what we are trying to develop in this section: John identifies the Son with Logos, and thereby makes him pre-existent. The question immediately rises: How can this be meaningful in a post-metaphysical world? How can we understand the fact that John seems to identify Jesus with the logos that is there from the beginning of the world? In order to provide an answer to this question, we have to see how he construes the different elements of his presentation:

1. He identifies the logos with God — and claims that the word has its origin in God as Logos. Without going into the historical issues concerning how one is to understand the background of the logos-concept in John, we can nevertheless hold that this description links the world to an origin that we can experience through its structure, shape, and meaning. Or, to put it otherwise: the world is something that we, on the basis of John's description, might see as an expression of the divine logos that was there from the beginning of everything. John thus offers us a point of ori-

entation by which we can consider and estimate what takes place in the world, and that also makes it possible for us to detect that which is *not* logos-like, as something disrupting or destroying the creativity of the logos. I stress the *possibility* here, as this is not something that necessarily must be experienced in this way. But John's description makes it possible to be present in the world with this perspective, and to experience it from this point of orientation. Hence, the point he is making in 1:1 is not solely about heavenly affairs — it is also something that opens up to a specific understanding of the world. The other side of this is of course that when we understand the world from this perspective, we can also understand more of the reality that is present in Jesus Christ. John's description thus opens up to a twofold possibility of experience of both Christ and the world.

2. When John says that the Word (Logos) became flesh and lived among us, he is claiming that the reality that shapes and forms our world is present and detectable in Jesus. The theological way to put this is to say that Jesus is the self-revelation of God as the Logos. This description immediately calls for further qualification of what the word *present* means in this connection. Is the reality of God present in Jesus in a way similar to or different from what is the case in other humans? Pannenberg links this issue closely to the understanding of Jesus' unity with God, and from that angle, he states that

> When God's presence in Jesus is spoken of [. . .] as the extension of the question about Jesus' unity with God, it means that Jesus' relation to God cannot be ascertained by itself apart from the question of how God appears to other men through Jesus. Jesus' relation to other men is the sphere in which the relation to God arises, namely, insofar as he alone exercises God's authority towards the rest of humanity. Thus, from the very beginning the question of Jesus' unity with God involves the presence of God *for us* in Jesus. We must inquire about the way in which God is present to us, to the whole of humanity, in Jesus. Otherwise, the question of Jesus' unity with God cannot be posed at all if this unity is supposed to be found in God's revelation.[22]

Pannenberg here rightly points to how the question about presence cannot be thought of as separated from the question of unity. Moreover, it

---

22. Pannenberg, *Jesus — God and Man*, p. 116.

is likely to suppose that if the reality of God is revealed in and by Jesus, this implies that the presence by which our perception and understanding of what is important in reality might change. When something is revealed, it means taking a different perspective, another angle that opens up to something new and different from what was *present* previously. As this perspective is offering itself by and in Jesus, it lets humans perceive of *themselves* in modes different from beforehand, and allows for other forms of recognition that express freedom and dignity. To make the point from a more post-metaphysical position, this means that every human being can recognize who she is *to become* in Jesus. Here she can detect a new and different identity, which is not marked by social or other contingencies, but by the unity between God and humanity, as this is already present in Jesus from Nazareth. This is the logos we are to become, the logos that shall shape our lives in all dimensions.

Against this background, we seem justified in claiming that the reality revealed in Jesus Christ is not (yet) revealed in a similar way in any other human, and that, consequently, we cannot think of the unity of Jesus with God in a way parallel to how God is already present in other people's lives. It is exactly this difference that makes it possible to say that what appears to other humans through Jesus is something that so far cannot be found elsewhere.

At this point, I want to adopt Pannenberg's understanding of creation as something that happens from the future. Seen in this perspective, the logos of God as revealed in Christ anticipates the consummation of creation. In him is present what humanity is destined to become, and hence, one can say that here the destiny of humanity (and thereby implicitly: its identity) is present.[23] Hence, God is here united with Christ in the sense that the full realization of God's plans for humankind is present in him. In this sense, we can say that he is the one we are to become; it is on him (as logos) that our life is modeled.

This cannot mean that all are destined to become *men* like Christ, or to have the same individual physical or mental traits as him. Rather, when we speak of him as the one who reveals the logos and the model of humanity, the unity between God and humanity is in question, and not questions of sex or gender. This unity is not only revealed as something different from Christ, but it is with him, as him, that this unity is revealed. In the

23. Pannenberg develops this idea briefly in *Jesus — God and Man*, pp. 180f.

next section of this chapter, I will try to develop this further by seeing this unity in light of the understanding of humanity as created in the image of God. We are already now, however, in a position where we can say that in this man is concretely, socially, and historically present the reality from which humans are well advised to understand themselves, God, and the rest of reality. It is not necessary to develop any huge metaphysics in order to make this point.

3. In his prologue, John points to one more element that can allow us to develop a post-metaphysical angle to the question of Christ as God's pre-existent logos. John says that the law was given by Moses, but that truth and grace came through Christ. He thereby recognizes the law as well as its importance. The law is what orders social life and secures the life of the other, as well as ordaining what is needed to recognize God as God. In this way, we can say that the law makes present, or represents, God and the Other in human life. But this representation is one of order and demands, and rightly so. If such demands are not expressed, the Other as vulnerable cannot be secured, and if the Name of God is not safeguarded, God cannot be voiced. Hence, the law orients the individual into a reality where he or she is not alone, but has to consider the interests and concerns of others.

But there is no grace in the *demand* of the law as such. The law recognizes the Other through the demand, but not as a gracing presence. To realize that the basic order of reality is constituted by more than moral demands and socially mediated expectations, one has to experience love and grace. The truth about reality is that it is grounded in love and grace, a point to which all the Johannine writings testify. The former, the law, can be experienced and felt outside the reality of Christ, as can also love and grace. But their source cannot be identified. In the revelation of Christ we can see, perceive, understand, experience fully that the love and recognition that God has for all humans, is present and can shape another kind of reality and community than the one based on human agency, merit, and social or religious position. The presupposition here is that grace is differentiated from the law *qua* demand.

As we will develop later, this suggested reconstruction of the difference between the order of the law and the gifts of grace is not meant to obliterate the importance of the law. Rather, it is a question of what framework the law is supposed to exist within, or, to put it otherwise, it is a question whether the law as a condition of agency should constitute the framework for human community and action and for the relationship between humans and God. Is there something more important and basic beyond and above the law that cannot be subordinated to its order or defined from its perspective on human agency? As we shall see, the latter is the case. The law gets its proper standing only when it is not understood as the final basis for human agency. What makes humans what they are, and lets them be recognized in the eyes of God, is not how they fulfill the law, but God's free and graceful choice of entering into community with them.[24] There is accordingly a logos deeper and more profound than the one expressed in the law, and it is this Logos that is revealed in Jesus Christ as the one who is in full unity with the God who created the world. This logos is expressed in the community that Jesus creates and manifests, and it is through and by this shaping of a different kind of human reality and community that we are warranted in claiming that there is something new and more happening than what the law can establish. The question is to what extent we can develop an understanding of that unity of God's logos and Christ more extensively than has been done so far without engaging in metaphysical claims that are hard to support with human experience. One route to go in order to deal with this would be to look at Christ from the perspective of the true *Imago Dei*.

Christ as the True *Imago Dei*

The evidence for calling humans images of God is scarce in the biblical literature. Nevertheless, the places where this notion is used are sometimes very central. The most obvious example is Genesis 1:27f.: "So God created humankind in his image, in the image of God he created them; male and female he created them." Widely used and referred to, this designation of humanity nevertheless is not quite clear as to what it means. The approach

---

24. This comment is echoing the debate about the assumed "anti-Semitic" character of the Fourth Gospel. As I try to make clear here, there is no warrant for such accusations only on the basis of these comments on Moses and the law, and even less so, as the way of understanding God's grace as something prior to the law is given as a basic feature already in the Old Testament. Jesus also presupposes and confirms the undisputable demand of the law — on behalf of those in need, and thereby he gives it a different context of function than those against whom he directs his polemics. Cf. also how already the gift of the law (sic!) in Exodus is given after first having presented the gifting and salvific acts of God towards Israel. God's acts are thereby presented as primary.

that then recommends itself, and even more so in the context of the present work, is to provide a reconstruction of what might be taken to be its main systematic content, in light of the historical knowledge we have access to. Such reconstruction would then imply the following factors:

The "image of God" might historically point back to markers signifying who was ruling in a certain area or country. Kings erected such markers, and thereby it became visible — and present — who was the king, even when the king was not physically present. Applied to the understanding of humanity as the image of God, this would mean that humanity is visibly called to represent God and mark his presence on earth. Against this background it also becomes clear why humans are called to fill the earth: it is not to overpopulate it, but to make clear that all of the earth is God's creation and domain.

Furthermore, this designation of humankind must necessarily be understood in light of God's calling of humanity: it is not something the human has in itself, but is *given* because of the relationship that God has established with humanity. The one who is called to be the image of God is called to be God's representative. As humans are *created* in the image of God, this designation is given as an element that contributes to their very existence. It is not something optional, but the very basis on which humankind is to be understood, theologically. The relational character and content of the *imago Dei* is not added to the act of creation, but is integral to it. Hence, it serves as a designation of the basic character of what it means to be human.

Humanity can fulfill the calling to be the image of God or fail to live up to it. That is what Genesis 3 indicates in the story of the fall, which suggests that humans break out of their relationship with God. But no matter how much humanity fails this calling, it nevertheless remains valid — as a calling. This double option makes it necessary for biblical writers, and especially those of the New Testament, to differentiate between the image of God that we are called to realize and the *true* image of God which is already realized in Christ.

At this point it is important to make sure that the understanding of humanity's lack of fulfillment of its calling does not have mere moral content. It is not only due to the fact that humans do this or fail to do that which makes them fail their calling. Rather, in light of the relational character of the *imago Dei*, we must understand the failure as one that indicates a failure in the way the relationship is constituted from the human point of view. It would however, be wrong to see it as a total dissolution of the relationship, as God's calling is still valid, and God is still relating to humans due to God's designation of them and the calling implied in that designation. The failure is thus one in which the lack of full unity between God and humans is manifested. How can we, against this background, understand the conditions of this unity?

The unity between God and humanity is constituted by God's recognition of humanity as called to become his image, but also by humanity's recognition of this calling, and thereby, implicitly, by recognizing God. The fundamental structure in this process of recognition manifests itself in an awareness of the difference between humans and God. Humans cannot partake in their vocation without being aware of the fact that they are not themselves God.

To establish oneself in a position where one takes over the functions of God might, if this difference is forgotten, be an ultimate expression of sin. Such functions might then be expressed in terms of, for example, determining who is righteous, or attempting to secure the means for upholding one's position socially, religiously, or otherwise, or it might have to do with simply ignoring or rejecting God's call to have concern for the neighbor, as this call might indicate that you are not yourself the center of the world. To put it in Lutheran terms: It is when humans start trusting in themselves and their own work and merits that they make themselves into God. They thereby indicate that they do not trust in God's own designation and calling of them, but prefer to understand themselves outside of this relation.

The recognition of difference is thus a marker of humanity's identity as the image of God, and simultaneously, this recognition is the condition for its unity with God. It is by allowing God to be God that humans can become fully human, and it is by becoming fully human that humans can bear full witness to the glory, love, and grace of God. The goodness of human life is, accordingly, not only to be found in obedience to the law, but is present when humans allow for God's grace, mercy, and love to become manifest in the world — including in their own lives. That is something not secured only by human agency, but can become present even to, and in, humans who are beyond what we can call the capacity for agency. Hence, goodness and glory transcend the law, and comprise an excess and surplus compared to what can be established on "reasonable" and mutually conditioning grounds.

At this point there is a need for defining the difference between this way of understanding the basic conditions of human life, and those found in one of modernity's most famous attempts to define them otherwise: Friedrich Nietzsche's claim that the basic feature in human life is the will to power. The will to power may easily be defined as humanity's attempt to become like God, given, i.e., that God is to be defined as power in this way.

EXCURSUS

Nietzsche's Understanding of the Human as the Alternative to the Notion of *Imago Dei*

Nietzsche sees it as his task to enlighten us about the real conditions of reality, and included in this are his insights into what determines us as subjects. A religious subjectivity is, from his point of view, marked by lack of insight into its own will to power as the determining power. The amount of power that this subject actually possesses is not more than what one needs in order to create an understanding of the world by which most things can be referred back to the powerful God. This must be seen as a kind of compensation for not referring the understanding of the world back to the subject's own powers and will to power — something that would demand more strength than a religious subject possesses. Thus, the real condition of the subject is not only made obscure by religion, but the subject is also given the possibility to endure the suffering and the absurdities of reality by interpreting them in a way that gives the subject the chance to experience itself as affirmed, as recognized, as chosen.

Against this background, there are two similarities between the believing and pious subject on the one hand, and the ungodly, atheistic subject on the other. Both have a will, and both interpret the world according to this will. Nietzsche claims that the results of the different *interpretations* can be seen as manifest in the ways these subjects relate to and understand the world. Or, to put it otherwise, and in accordance with our established vocabulary: Nietzsche sees our point of orientation when living in the world as a result of our own agency, based on the will to power. The point of orientation is accordingly not something that is given or offered, but rather, it is something construed by the human. What he neglects is that in order to interpret the world, there has to be *something* to interpret. In this sense also, the subject in Nietzsche is dependent on something *given,* something from which one has to take one's point of departure.

A related comment in the same vein is that will is also something intentional, something directed, something with an aim. Admittedly, that at which one aims one's will may be different, but no will is given without an object of desire. Hence, also in this sense, the subject turns out to be related in its activity to something that exists before this activity.

I point this out in order to observe what seems to be the target of Nietzsche's position. His alternative to acknowledging that there is something prior to the subject that determines it and that also contributes to its shape and life seems to be that only the subject and the subject's will should be affirmed. This is the only way in which we can avoid the inauthenticity he seems to think is internal in any type of subjection to otherness. Much of his anger and scorn is directed against forms of life that are determined by them. I think we can see this very clearly in the way he deals with compassion and charity.

Nietzsche's suspicion about compassion and charity we see in *Zarathustra,* but it is echoed in, for example, *Ecce Homo,* where the point is that these traits of human life must be overcome. The real proof of power is to be able to offer resistance to the impulses of compassion.[25] Charity and compassion are thus to be seen as ways in which the morality of the weak attempts to support the life of the weak — those who are dependent. In this manner, charity is nothing else than the will to possess more, in order to extend one's rule further.[26] A commandment to love one's neighbor is nothing else than a hidden will to power — for the weak.[27] By the means of charity, the situation of the weak can be improved, as the weak, through it, can find affirmation of their life. Again, this is a life in which there is no transparency and no authenticity, as the subject has not been able to see that his ideals and deeds of charity are motivated by his nihilistic will to power, which affirms mediocrity. Here, one is kept in a relationship that links one to the one in need, or keeps the one in need in a relationship to the helper. We thus see vividly illustrated how Nietzsche's understanding of the subject is one who tries to free himself from any kind of determination by others, and from having to recognize others as having valid claims over against oneself. Nietzsche's struggle is for a human with no

25. Cf. Friedrich Nietzsche, Giorgio Colli, and Mazzino Montinari, *Sämtliche Werke: Kritische Studienausgabe* (Berlin and New York: De Gruyter, 1988), vol. 6, p. 270.

26. Cf. Nietzsche, *Sämtliche Werke: Kritische Studienausgabe,* vol. 3, p. 386 [*The Gay Science,* aphorism 14].

27. Nietzsche, *Sämtliche Werke: Kritische Studienausgabe,* vol. 5, p. 383 [*Genealogy of Morals,* book 3, aphorism 18].

relations that are not determined by the subject itself. It is in a profound sense a centered subject, that cannot allow for the disturbance in the call from the Other.

Nietzsche accordingly develops an understanding of the world that is opposite to one in which we can experience any kind of feeling of dependence, vulnerability, or exposure to the face of others. In the bulk of Nietzsche's work that portrays what a human life should be like there is no such element present. The reason for this might be found in the very human experience that Nietzsche is unable to recognize: dependence. Any occurrence of dependence has to be overcome, neglected, and annihilated as a threat against the life-fulfillment of the strong individual. Nietzsche seems to conflate relationship and a determining relationship, and is not able to make a distinction between the two. There is consequently no recognition in Nietzsche of the original dependence of humans upon one another. Nietzsche's ideal is *distance* towards others. We can read in *The Twilight of the Idols:*

> For what is freedom? That one has the will to assume responsibility for oneself. That one maintains the distance which separates us. That one becomes more indifferent to difficulties, hardships, privation, even to life itself. That one is prepared to sacrifice human beings for one's cause, not excluding oneself. [. . .] How is freedom measured in individuals and peoples? According to the resistance which must be overcome, according to the exertion required, to remain on top.[28]

Freedom is thus not to be fulfilled in the recognition of and by the other, and the community that emerges from such relationships, but is to be acquired in the *overcoming* of dependence. The individual has to make freedom her own task. To speak of free will is, according to Nietzsche, something that theologians do only in order to make people responsible, and responsibility in this connection only means "sie von sich abhängig zu machen."[29] Accordingly, his task is to spell out how the human being has to establish herself as independent of everything, and must struggle to remain so, even if this implies an emotional numbing, where natural impulses to be charitable or compassionate are silenced.

The question of *freedom,* accordingly, is closely related to the question of the will in Nietzsche. In that context, he distinguishes between strong and weak wills.[30] Feeling, thinking, and affect are all parts of the will as the central and de-

---

28. Nietzsche, *Sämtliche Werke: Kritische Studienausgabe,* vol. 6, pp. 139-40.

29. Nietzsche, *Sämtliche Werke: Kritische Studienausgabe,* vol. 6, p. 95.

30. Nietzsche, *Sämtliche Werke: Kritische Studienausgabe,* p. 95. Cf. *Beyond Good and Evil,* vol. 5, p. 36.

termining element behind subjectivity, but all these are also related to the *other* of the will. The freedom of the will is mainly the emotion of being superior to the one who has to obey; everything else is subjected to my will and my decisions.[31]

Hence to be free in Nietzsche is to be strong enough to determine your own reality independent of others. The sketch offered here should now be sufficient not only to shed some light on his critique of Christianity, but also to illustrate how he develops a modern form of individualism in the extreme. From a critical angle, we have to ask if Nietzsche is not working under the illusion that we can find ourselves, our identity, without having to stand in an affirming relation to others that includes mutual recognition.[32] He thereby also neglects or tries to overcome the fact that constitutive elements in human life, such as dependence, vulnerability, and weakness, are part of what makes us human.[33]

For Nietzsche, the subject we should struggle to become is a subject of control, of mastering, of struggle and self-rule. The world is to be made useful for the one who has the strongest will to power, the one who is able to recognize and bear that everything that happens in the organic world is about mastering and subjecting others. Hence, what counts is to interpret and reinterpret what so far has been considered as the meaning and purpose of all things, until former forms of understanding are eradicated.[34]

The human being who exercises her will to power determines the world fully according to her own internal and independent standards.[35] She is thereby a human being that understands herself not from who she is in relation to others,

---

31. Nietzsche, *Sämtliche Werke: Kritische Studienausgabe*, p. 95. Cf. *Beyond Good and Evil*, vol. 1, p. 19 [vol. 5, p. 32].

32. In this, we can see in Nietzsche what is theologically addressed as *sin:* how the human being does not acknowledge her relationship to God as the constituting power of her own existence. An additional comment related to the history of ideas: it is not by accident that the relational element in human life is in focus within the horizon of the Christian cultural tradition.

33. Cf. for this point also Nietzsche, *Sämtliche Werke: Kritische Studienausgabe*, vol. 6, p. 125. That this insight is also related to determining elements in Nietzsche's biography is argued in Jørgen Kjær: "Nietzsches psykologi," in Jan-Olav Henriksen, ed., *Friedrich Nietzsche. Filosofi og samfunn* (Kristiansand: Høyskoleforlaget, 1999), esp. pp. 103-4.

34. Nietzsche, *Sämtliche Werke: Kritische Studienausgabe*, vol. 5, pp. 313f. [*The Genealogy of Morals*, vol. 2, p. 12].

35. This interpretation is supported by the analysis offered by Hans Ebeling, "Grundsätze der Selbstbestimmung und Grenzen der Selbsterhaltung" in Hans Ebeling, ed., *Subjektivität und Selbsterhaltung. Beiträge zur Diagnose der Moderne* (Frankfurt: Suhrkamp 1976), esp. p. 388, cf. pp. 384-85.

from the recognition of others, or from the calling of others, but only from herself. Critically, we have to ask if this radical alternative to the conception implied in the idea of the human as *imago Dei* is possible, from both a theoretical and a practical point of view. When there is no recognition of the Other, or of dependence, how are we to understand this mode of understanding subjectivity?

The basic question turns out to be: Is a subject constituted by powers of her own, by drives and desires and a will to power "within" herself, *or* is she basically and primarily living in a relationship with the world, so that her drives, desire, will, etc. are shaped by the ways this relation is maintained and exists? Recent psychology suggests the latter, and thereby lends significant weight to the theological position we are trying to develop as an alternative to Nietzsche in this book. We can see mirrored in Nietzsche an approach to the understanding of the human that contradicts not only the theological position indicated in the present work, but also insights of recent psychology, as articulated by the American philosopher and psychologist James W. Jones. Jones claims, contrary to Nietzsche, that

> The capacity for personal relationships makes us human. Our uniqueness as a species lies not in our existence as individual subjects of consciousness. Rather, we exist as persons because of our relationships with each other and the world surrounding us. This mutuality of interaction is the defining characteristic of the personal. Selfhood would be unthinkable apart from relationship.[36]

Nietzsche thinks of the subject as basically body-based and generally naturalistic. Culture is secondary to how the subject expresses itself, and the relationships that are configured by and within culture are never for him seen as constitutive for the self in a positive way. This is part of why dependence for him is to be overcome or outgrown.[37] Jones, however, points to how the human needs for dependency, connection, and affirmation are never left behind, just transformed into more mature forms. Object relations such as God are the result not of the biological instincts seeking release but, rather, of the inherent human condition of relatedness and the drive for those emphatic resonances that sustain us as human beings.[38]

Nietzsche is not in a position where he can acknowledge how the originally

---

36. James William Jones, *Religion and Psychology in Transition: Psychoanalysis, Feminism, and Theology* (New Haven: Yale University Press, 1996), p. 26.

37. A critique similar to the one I offer here is found in Alasdair MacIntyre, *Dependent Rational Animals: Why Human Beings Need the Virtues* (Chicago: Open Court, 1999), esp. p. 162.

38. Jones, *Religion and Psychology in Transition*, p. 37.

given relationship to the Other can be understood in a positive manner — as a source of creativity and positive interdependence. Anything other than the subject, understood as a will to power, is something he thinks must be overcome or controlled. This creates a kind of dichotomy between self and world that is really only making the world an object that the subject should attempt to subject to its own will. However, according to Winnicott, for example, we understand something as an object first when we have realized that it cannot be fully subjected to our control. Hence, there is an in-built contradiction here: on the one hand establishing the world as an object for the subject (i.e., an object whose influence is to be overcome and replaced by our control of it). On the other hand we have the fact that the world can appear as an object only as a consequence of our realization of it as something that cannot be fully subjected to our control. This contradiction is only possible to maintain as long as we think of the self as an independent entity, whose identity and basic traits are established prior to its relation to the world. This is an idea that has played a large role in the modern idea of what it is to be a human being, but it is nevertheless deeply mistaken, viewed from a psychological point of view. It is no surprise that God and morality in this framework suggest a threat to the subject, notions that delimit and repress it. However, there is an alternative, suggested in Jones, which is carefully enough spelled out to take into consideration some of the relevant and valid criticisms of religion that have been advocated in modernity. Jones sums up his position in this way:

> A model of human nature that sees the self as embedded in a network of relationships, which sees positive as well as negative aspects to connection and interdependence, which orients us more toward the importance of subjective experience, which champions the deepening of interpersonal encounters, contains the possibility of a more open approach to, if not rapprochement with, religion. The connections in which we are embedded may include a connection to a larger, sacred reality without doing violence to human selfhood, because selfhood and interconnection are not antithetical but potentially mutually strengthening. Likewise, dependency on a higher power may not contradict individuation, as the need for interdependence stays with us all our lives.[39]

Nietzsche would probably reject this description. However, what is more important here is that by the discussion in this excursus, we have been able to de-

---

39. Jones, *Religion and Psychology in Transition,* p. 68.

velop a psychologically related understanding of human relationships, recognition, desire, and creativity, which might indicate that Nietzsche's alternative to understanding the human being as the *imago Dei* is not so viable after all. Subjective experience, creativity, a positive relationship to others, and an affirmation of individuality were something he strived for all his life, but these are not ruled out in the approach we have argued for, but affirmed. Such affirmation needs, however, to be based on a different conception of the other than seeing the other as a danger and a threat to personal life-fulfillment. It has to recognize the Other, be it God or the other human, as one who offers us chances for living more fully, more creatively, more relaxed and laid back, and not to struggle for control in every part of life. Hence, it also allows for a life lived in trust — or faith.

Contrary to Nietzsche's dictum, "If there were Gods, how could I then cope with not being a God?," the human being who lives according to her vocation to become *imago Dei* understands and recognizes herself from the necessary difference between God and humans. The calling to become God's image thus presupposes the *boundary* between God and humans, and that humans can never be God. The attempt to become like God destroys humanity's calling (cf. Gen. 3:3-5). Humanity exists *according* to its calling only when we are aware that we are not, and cannot be, like God. To be living in the image of God is to live in such a manner that the glory and grace of God are revealed, and not try to establish such a glory on our own.[40] This is why the New Testament can call Jesus the true image of God (Col. 1:15), and even as the firstborn of all creation: Christ was the first to fulfill this calling towards which all of humanity is directed.

Goodness in human life is accordingly manifesting itself in what happens when humans live and receive life according to this calling, and thereby let God be God. The gifting of this goodness suggests that it is not constituted by human agency, nor is it exhausted in human action, although it is emerging through others: Goodness is just as much in the receiving of a gift as it is in being creative, thriving, comforting, and in sustaining relationships of love and recognition. The *inexhaustive* character of goodness or desire for goodness in human life also points to how hu-

---

40. This is a main point in Christof Gestrich, *The Return of Splendor in the World: The Christian Doctrine of Sin and Forgiveness* (Grand Rapids: Eerdmans, 1997).

manity's existence as *imago Dei* is rooted in a reality that is beyond what can be grasped, fully articulated, or calculated. This is a point that can be elaborated by looking at J. Kosky's analysis of Levinas. Kosky discusses the relation between goodness and desire in Levinas:

> The infinite is good, above all, in that it does not accept what desire offers but directs this desire to an other, *Autrui*. The Good thus compelled disorients desire, turning it away from the infinite which aroused it and which it wants, in order that the infinite might escape a present shared with desire. The infinite is "Good in this very precise, eminent sense: He does not fill me with good but compels me to goodness, which is better than to receive goods."[41]

The combination of presence and transcendence of goodness in human life is one of the main reasons why Christianity could find an ally in Platonic thought. This character of goodness might also shed some light on our attempts to develop a framework for a more positive approach to the notion of desire in Christian theology: as desire is always directed towards the *assumed* good, the question becomes to what extent we can see desire as something to be fulfilled, or as something that lets us exist in a position of enjoyment without full consummation. The enjoyment implied in not being able to reach fully the desired "object" might thus stem from the recognition of the character of *difference* in the object: by recognizing that this object (goodness, or even God) is different from what is present but nevertheless also expresses itself in the present desire, it is given a different character that no longer relates to the desired as an extension of itself, but sees the desired as the announcement of otherness.

In spite of its transcending character, this makes goodness something *internal* to human life, as goodness announces itself in our desire for it. This desire can then also be said to be an expression of the calling humans are given by their very existence. Jesus responded to this calling towards goodness in the way he acted with others, and it is as a true fulfiller of the calling to be an *imago Dei* that we are consequently able to interpret what he did as expressing the goodness of God. Thereby — and by still marking the difference between himself and God, as is witnessed in Mark 10:18: "Why do you call me good? No one is good but God alone," Jesus ful-

41. Cf. Jeffrey L. Kosky, *Levinas and the Philosophy of Religion,* Indiana Series in the Philosophy of Religion (Bloomington: Indiana University Press, 2001), p. 181.

fills his calling by bearing witness to the goodness of God: When goodness expresses itself in his own life, it still witnesses to the goodness of God.

To understand the designation *imago Dei* as a calling, it is necessary also to state that it is a gift that has to be realized and recognized as gift. When the character of gift is not given priority, the *imago Dei* easily ends up being understood as the capacities of humankind to do this or that. Only as *an unconditional and determining gift* prior to all that humans can be and do can this designation be a marker of human dignity: only then does it express itself as God's unconditional recognition and gift to every human being.

As a gift given with our existence, the unconditional character of the *imago Dei* might be expressed from our point of view in the pure, trusting reception of it. Humans live as images of God by receiving in trust and openness. The way the gift is received is, however, not a condition for it to be a gift. But, as Kathryn Tanner points out, some gifts call for an appropriate response. In the following quote, she also underscores the element of joy, gratitude, and freedom as what might be seen as enrichment to the gift itself, and not as something that should be understood as a kind of obligatory return:

> It would be odd to say, for example, that the gift of a delicious meal for twelve obligates your eating it and sharing it with eleven friends; that is just an appropriate response to what it is. There is no external constraint being placed on the recipient; this response emerges from the recipient's own reaction to the gift, from what the gift means to the recipient. If a return to the giver seems the right thing to do, that is not because of a condition placed on the transaction, because this was the deal going into an exchange that began with the gift's being handed over to you, but because of what the gift is, how good it is. The gift's goodness is what inclines one to affirm that fact, to thank the one who brought it, to praise and honor the giver for her kindness and generosity. One doesn't make a return like that to the giver because one has to, but out of a free and joyful testimony to what one has received from another's hands. The more unconditional that giving was — the giver had no prior relationship with you, the giver could have avoided having anything to do with you, you hadn't done anything for them, and so on — the more wondrous the sense of gratitude and joy.[42]

42. Tanner, *Economy of Grace*, p. 69.

To receive a gift is to recognize the giver. To receive in faith the gift of being the image of God is accordingly to recognize God as the source of my own designation, calling, and destiny, which allows for the joyful response. It is possible to say then, that due to his recognition of this giver, Jesus appears to be the true human being; in him something is realized that has never previously been realized in the same manner. His unity with God is related to how he recognizes God and God's calling of him.

This preconception of *imago Dei* serves as the hermeneutical tool for understanding Jesus as a true human. We can thereby combine the scriptural resources on the *imago Dei* with our systematic reconstruction as well as with the concrete actualization of this calling in the life of Jesus. What it means to be truly human is then not seen as something realized solely out of the example of Jesus. Rather, we have been arguing that Jesus can be understood as a true human because he makes visible what it means for all humans to be true humans and live as images of God.

We are now in a position to see more clearly what it can mean to say that Jesus is a true human, as this understanding emerges from the understanding of him as the true image of God. By fulfilling his calling and by bearing witness to God's giving and recognition, Jesus does what any representative of God is called to do but what all other humans except him fail to do. The true humanity of Christ is thereby something that does differentiate him from God — who sends him; but this differentiation does not jeopardize his *unity with God* — rather it expresses, confirms, and realizes it. The unity Christ manifests with God is from this point of view not exceptional in the sense that it discloses a total discontinuity with the rest of humanity; rather it is in continuation with the designation and calling for *all* of humanity.

The approach we have developed here might suggest that the unity of Jesus with God can — along these lines — be taken as something related to the life-conditions of every human being. Moreover, this approach is apparently in opposition to the claim Pannenberg makes in his Christology, namely that the unity of Jesus with God "was not yet established by the claim implied in his pre-Easter appearance, but only by his resurrection from the dead."[43] Am I here then attempting to downplay the importance of the resurrection for establishing the identity of Jesus? In no way is

---

43. Pannenberg, *Jesus — God and Man*, p. 39. In the German edition the word used is "begründet."

that the case. My point is that from the position of a post-Easter recon-struction of Christology, although the resurrection may be seen as the final event that warrants Jesus' position, we must also be able to understand this unity from other angles manifest in the pre-Easter life of Jesus. This is es-pecially important in light of the reconstruction of what it means to be an image of God. As we shall see in the following parts of this book, how Christ concretely fulfills his calling to become the image of God is what leads to his crucifixion at Easter, and it is against this background that we can also understand why he was vindicated by God in the resurrection. In this perspective, the resurrection might be seen as a confirmation of the unity that manifests itself already in the ministry of Jesus. The suggested approach thus also indicates that we might have a warranted claim for Je-sus' unity with God apart from how we understand the historicity of his resurrection.[44]

Looking finally back at Nietzsche, the following reflection offers itself: If there is any will to power expressed in the ministry of Jesus as he realizes his designation of *imago Dei*, it is the will for a *different* power, one that is not aimed at control and subjection, but at empowering others to become more fully images of God — by letting them receive community, relation-ship, and grace. The attempt to contrast our systematically developed un-derstanding of *imago Dei* with that of Nietzsche's will to power suggests that the underlying issue in the contrast is linked closely to one of our main angles: that of the true recognition of the other. The power of God lies in a positive ability to be recognized as God and as the source of goodness and grace, not in the ability to subvert human freedom and community.

The understanding of God that is implicitly witnessed in the minis-try of God thus becomes an ambiguous character: on the one hand God is the gifting, who reigns by shaping community and offering people chances to live another life, not marked by exclusion and marginalizing, by sin and suffering. On the other hand, allowing for the consequences of our recon-struction here, God is also vulnerable. To be able to realize God's kingdom in the world, God is in need of representatives who are witnessing to God's gifts. If that does not happen, God is not voiced, but remains silenced.

---

44. This last remark should not be taken as an indication of my rejection of the his-torical basis of the claims for Jesus' resurrection. It is rather meant as suggesting that there is something about the reality of God to be experienced and understood in Jesus regardless of how one understands the issue of resurrection.

God's presence is not expressed or manifested. God's presence and the manifestations of God's power are thus not something given and secured, they are always partly, at least, dependent on someone who responds to God's calling. God is manifesting Godself not as a necessary power, but as an impossible possibility. This understanding of God is linked closely to how humans are fulfilling their destiny: *God's destiny in the world is dependent on how humans respond to God's designation of them as images of God. The specific and unique character of Jesus' life was that he was able to manifest this possibility in a manner unforeseen, and in a manner that we, today, can say changed the world.* This change is not due to coercive power, but to the power of love that manifests itself in the ministry of Jesus.

This analysis then provides us with an angle from which we can understand Jesus as the self-revelation of God: It is because Jesus voices and manifests the power of God as he does that we can say that Jesus is God's self-revelation. Jesus does not reveal *himself;* he never points to himself, but always to the one who has sent him. This he does in accordance with God's calling, and hence, it is as ordained by God that Jesus reveals God in the way he does.

Unity Between Human and God — Identity Again

Our deliberations in this chapter started with the question, "Who is this human?" We are now able to claim that we have developed some features in an answer to that question, which mainly are along the line of understanding Jesus according to conditions to which every human can relate. Moreover, we have also indicated that, as an *Other,* Jesus is a person who transcends the religious or political categories ascribed to him. In that sense, the evangelists themselves contribute to the deconstruction of the very titles and designations they use for him — and they still nevertheless continue to use them.

Regardless of the latter point, we can set forth the following thesis, in which light the following chapters can be read: *In Jesus, we are able to recognize that this is what God is when and if God is a human.*[45] Or, as Kathryn

---

45. This is my alternative to the formulation by W. Pannenberg: "Jesus' unity with God is not to be conceived as a unification of two substances, but as this man Jesus is God." Cf. Pannenberg, *Jesus — God and Man,* p. 319. In order to avoid any modalistic misinterpre-

Tanner puts it, "In Jesus, unity with God takes a perfect form; here humanity has become God's own."[46] The first of these formulations is the one I will stick to in the following, as it tries to safeguard the experiential dimension in Jesus' ministry: if, and when, God should be human, the reality of God could be expressed in the manner Jesus expresses it. Hence, the self-revelation of God as Logos — as the revealer and the revealed through the word about the logos of reality — is here *incarnated* in a human. An alternative formulation aiming at similar concerns is the following: *In Christ we can recognize God,* or, *we can recognize Jesus Christ as God since it is about him that it is possible to say the impossible, namely that it is in him revealed what God is when and if God is a human being.* Jesus Christ not only then reveals wisdom's or logos' embodiment in ordinary life, but he is this wisdom or this logos embodied by the very way he lives.

The statement given by one of the soldiers standing at the foot of Jesus' cross is an expression that echoes the confession of the early church about Jesus. It says something important about the conceived unity between Jesus and God: When the soldier says "Truly this man was God's Son!" (Mark 15:39 par.), what is voiced here is the concluding answer to the question that we started out with in this chapter: more than being the son of David or Joseph and Mary, Jesus is recognized as the Son of God. By ending their construction of the narrative about Jesus in this manner, the evangelists suggest that this is the most important conclusion to the question about Jesus' identity. Moreover, the attribution of sonship to him suggests that — at the very end of his life in the total abolition of power — Jesus is manifested as the Son of God, which means that it is in God he has his origin; it is from God that he has his heritage and his resources. This underscores other elements in the unity between Jesus and God. To die in a manner that reveals him as the son of God calls forth the question: How could this happen? Not: How could the Son of God die, but rather, how could this death make it possible to recognize Jesus as the Son of God? That question will continue to occupy us.

We cannot develop more extensively the possible meaning of the unity between God and Jesus before we have considered in more detail

---

tation, it is important to maintain that my formula is made on the presupposition that as this man, Jesus is still dependent on God as something to be differentiated from his concrete humanity, as humanity is always only possible on the grounds of God acting.

46. Tanner, *Jesus, Humanity and the Trinity: A Brief Systematic Theology,* Scottish Journal of Theology. Current Issues in Theology (Edinburgh: T. & T. Clark, 2001), p. 9.

what Jesus says about God. It is only by looking more closely at how Jesus voices God, or lets the reality of God be heard and seen, that we can assess his unity with God.

Attempts such as the above to formulate the link between Jesus and God suggest that it is very hard to make any rich elaboration of the content of their relationship without taking into account the question of the identity of God. However, as already indicated, we cannot say much about who God is without addressing the identity of the one who bears a true witness about him. Now is the time to turn more explicitly to that witness and ask: Who is this God, about whom Christ bears witness?

Who Is God?

Jesus' *theology* sent him to Golgotha. That is one of the main theses of this book, and one that might seem surprising and calls for some hermeneutical considerations, from at least two angles:

First, his understanding of God, and his God-practice, so to say, has through the course of history become apparent and understood as inclusive, benevolent, and hence, to be appreciated and welcomed. This response is not so different from the one the Gospels report from people during his own lifetime. Nonetheless, this welcome message also created new antagonisms. In order to understand these, we need to frame his understanding of God in a way that makes it understandable *why* the proclamation of a God who has mercy for sinners and desire for community leads to tensions and finally, to a successful attempt to get rid of Jesus. It is only when we see Jesus' struggle as part of a struggle about who God is that this outcome becomes possible to understand.[1]

Second, some present readers might not like the idea that we talk of Jesus' *theology*:[2] Is not Jesus more an object of theology than a subject of

---

1. As J. Sobrino points out, this makes the crucial question in Jesus' life a different one than that of modern atheism: the question is not *if* God is, but *who* God is. Jesus defends a vision of God that is not only opposed by his adversaries, but can also be seen as a struggle against idols. See Sturla J. Stålsett, *The Crucified and the Crucified: A Study in the Liberation Christology of Jon Sobrino* (Bern and New York: Peter Lang, 2003), pp. 289f., 338f. Cf. nevertheless also the comment above on atheism on p. 69, n. 18.

2. This assumption is not taken out of the air — I experienced it myself when, more than twelve years ago, I published an introductory textbook in dogmatics, making a similar claim.

such, and even more so, by those who conceive of him as himself being God? This latter response is understandable from the point of view of later Christian theology, but it misses the point we are aiming at here: When we do Christology we must understand Jesus as a subject in both meanings of the term. It was due to the way Jesus preached and practiced a specific understanding of what "God" meant, that people might today even call him God. He did this as a historically situated subject. It is as such a subject, and due to his acting as such when witnessing about God, that we make him the subject of Christology. To put it more bluntly: we cannot even start thinking about Jesus as God or the son of God today without considering the theology he preached and practiced.

The last point above we need to stress from the very beginning of this chapter: By introducing Jesus as a theologian who has a specific response to the question "Who is God?," we introduce him exactly as an active subject of theology. This subject-status makes it impossible to approach his message and ministry as something enclosed in itself and as being accounted for by purely objective means of reporting. Rather, it allows for understanding Jesus in a web of relations from which it becomes understandable how he understands God, including what is expressed in the creative language enabled by love and by Mary, as well as by his Jewish theological context. We are ourselves, in a wider sense, part of this web — as is the present reality in which we live. This relational dimension suggests that when we are dealing with his theology, we are, by relating to Jesus ourselves, involved in coming to grips with the question "Who is God?" Hence, the question cannot be answered out of context, but demands a hermeneutically reflected approach, from which we are enabled to see how Jesus' understanding of God challenges and changes our preconceptions. It is against this background that it also becomes fruitful to look at Jesus' proclamation of God, and his God-practice, from the angles of postmodern philosophy.

This phenomenon of challenging people's preconceptions of God, as these are involved in the specific forms of life, of self-understanding and practice, is the most likely reason why Jesus' theology made him enemies in all camps. Enemies appeared among ordinary people, among the priests and the religious establishment, and among the politicians, who feared that his proclamation of God might cause a new uproar. He met a lot of expectations, emerging from different contexts and from a variety of desires, and not surprisingly, he also had to let some of these expectations remain unfulfilled. But many people do not meet the expectations of others, and they still live well and prosper. What is it with Jesus' understanding of God that finally leads to his execution? This is one of the underlying questions here, which will be taken up again more extensively in the next part of the book.

Difficulties Concerning God-Talk in the Markian Narrative

The picture of God emerging from Mark's narrative about Jesus is not very broad: God is present mostly in an indirect way, as a point of reference, or an index-word. When Jesus speaks about God, it is about how *God's kingdom* is to be, i.e., how it is where God rules. Thus the content of his message is not God as such.

God functions as an index-word at the initiation of Jesus' ministry, when in Mark 1:14f., it reads: "Now after John was arrested, Jesus came to Galilee, proclaiming the good news of God, and saying, 'The time is fulfilled, and the kingdom of God has come near; repent, and believe in the good news.'" In this passage also, it is the *reign* of God more than God who is the subject of teaching. "The good news about God" is actually never specified or addressed in words other than those describing the kingdom of God. This observation can be taken as an indication that *what the word "God" means can never be understood apart from our understanding of this kingdom!* Moreover, here as in the other Gospels, the kingdom is basically presented in parables.

Given that the word "God" is more a point of reference or orientation than one that is developed substantially in a way that contributes to the content of the narrative itself, it serves as the kind of index-word I suggested in the Introduction. It relates the word "God" to the familiar, but nevertheless serves to open up the familiar to something more, to an *unrecognized surplus* that is both part of the present and also transcending what can be grasped in the concrete present. In Dalferth's words:

> The one who uses the word "God" as an indicator of what takes place in the life-world where he realizes his life in faith, thereby does not only designate the world in which we orient ourselves with our systems of indexing as contingent, but identifies these contingencies of our life as the place where God is present: God is to be found in all this, and not beyond or behind it. [. . .] The indicator "God" signifies that

which is the condition given with everything concrete, that without which the concrete is neither real nor possible.[3]

If we read Dalferth here as an insight into how God is related to ordinary life, we get a post-metaphysical picture of how God is at work: God is given with (mitgesetzt) the concrete elements of reality, the point from which we relate to all its elements, and not something to be found beyond the concrete experienced world. In this way, then, the kingdom remains inaccessible with respect to our possibility of fully grasping it; it is not in human control, based on human conditions. It nevertheless is present in the world we live in, but as a contingent reality. It could be otherwise; it is an expression of one among several other possibilities in the world, and it is certainly not a necessity. Thus, the kingdom of God is not only a gift — a gift of God's gracing presence — it is also something that constantly has to be expressed in new and different ways, because its content cannot be exhaustively presented or given a final expression in the world as it is now. The kingdom struggles constantly to express itself.

The basic contents of the gift of God can be expressed very simply as *the initial and basic recognition of every human as the image of God, and as the calling of the law in order to protect and serve the neighbor.* What is important in Jesus' theology is to see that these two elements are related to each other in a manner that makes the proper function of the law dependent on the recognition of oneself and the other as the image of God. Outside the framework of this basic designation, the practices of the law might become corrupted. Hence, Jesus' attack on theological elements in his own context was not an attack on the Jewish belief in God, but in a specific form of practice that neglected the basic character of gift and grace by which every human lives. God is the source of graceful recognition as well as the source of the law.[4]

As indicated, the kingdom thereby marks a *surplus* compared to what people's present resources can offer or establish, for understanding, practices, health, or otherwise. The surplus, or even excess, that the kingdom manifests is best expressed in parables because this character of surplus

---

3. Ingolf U. Dalferth, *Die Wirklichkeit des Möglichen: Hermeneutische Religionsphilosophie* (Tübingen: Mohr Siebeck, 1994), pp. 469-70.

4. Lutherans will see this as a variation of the distinction between God's gifts and God's demands. The structural direction is all that matters here: the gifts have ontological and epistemic priority, unless we are to make God's works conditioned by human agency.

transcends the horizon of our intentionally ordered worlds. What Jesus does, even when he is *not speaking directly about God,* is to bear witness to this reality, which rightly can be called a manifestation of *otherness* compared to the content of these worlds. This otherness is nevertheless something announcing itself in the present world, trying to break in.

The above point about the necessity of speaking in parables regarding the kingdom of God, due to its incomprehensible content, is, however, in need of a supplementary comment: It is clear that the listener, in order to understand the parables, needs to *invest* some of his of her competence, fantasy, ability to transcend the immediately given understanding of the world in order to grasp what is at stake. This demand points to what we can see as one of the basic requirements for understanding (but not living in) the realm that Jesus calls the kingdom of God, namely the ability to be grasped by and determined by something other than what we are by ourselves, or by what is present in our intentions and immediate desires. The parables, basically, confront listeners with an *otherness* that shapes a different point of view on life, practice, orientation, and self-understanding. Without the personal investment, which is an investment of openness more than of a substantial contribution, the understanding of the kingdom might become inaccessible.

Jesus, as said, says little about God apart from what he says about God's kingdom. What the good news is about God is more or less presupposed when Mark addresses his readers. And when God is spoken of in Mark, it is by others more than by Jesus himself directly. There are, of course, important and notable exceptions to this, to which we will return later. But it is notable that when God is spoken of, it is in *response* to what Jesus does. These responses then serve to underline *the recognition by others that God is at work in the practice of Jesus.*

Moreover, God is portrayed as the one who recognizes Jesus as his Son — twice (Mark 1:11 and 9:7). In both instances, it is God's direct word that does this. From the "recognition" angle that we have established, this testifies to the legitimation of Jesus by God, but it also says something about God: God is the one who can and will recognize Jesus as his son, and who encourages people to listen to him. Hence, these stories indicate that God accepts, authorizes, and can identify with the practices and the message of Jesus. They serve as markers of direction: Jesus is one to whom one should listen. This recognition by God is echoed in the way Jesus functions as God, and thereby witnesses to God as one recognizing him.

Against this background, it is interesting to see how "God" appears in the text. Often others speak more about God, or about Jesus as the son of God, than Jesus does himself. The Markian feature of the messianic secret also points to the withdrawn character of God-talk in the Gospel. In one of the stories about healing, Jesus tells the Gerasene Demoniac to go home and tell his friends how much "the Lord has done for you, and how much mercy he has shown you" (5:19). The reference here is clearly to God, and other stories as well suggest that Jesus is conscious of acting on behalf of God, or as sent by God (9:37; 12:1). Hence, the construction of the narrative indicates indirectly the close relationship between Jesus and God, but also makes clear that Jesus differentiates himself from God in a manner that allows God to receive the glory when he is healing people.

The element of recognition here is closely linked to the one about mission: When speaking of his *mission* the narrative suggests that Jesus not only sees himself as recognized and sent by God, but also that God is Jesus' presupposed point of orientation and reference. Contrary to the consciousness of present-day atheism, Jesus seems unable to understand himself apart from God. Even when he quotes Psalm 22 on the cross (Mark 15:14), accusing God of having forsaken him, this can only be done when presupposing that God is, or should be, present. The cry on the cross underscores Jesus' emphatic trust in God's presence. To live and act with God as his constant and continuous point of reference thus seems to be the foundation for the ministry of Jesus. It is based on this presupposition that we can understand the lack of much explicit God-talk in Mark. This lack is not due to the fact that God is not important, but more to the fact that God is assumed as such an important point of reference that one can hardly get a sufficient access to this presupposition only by articulating it conceptually. That has to be expressed in parables and practices that manifest what God means.

God's Care — Sufficient?

Jesus portrays God as one who cares for creation, and one in whom one can trust, because God is the one who can give people what they need for daily life. The warnings against worrying that Jesus issues in Luke 12:22 and Matthew 6:25ff. point to the importance of trusting first in God. The most likely interpretation of this prioritizing is that the only way humans can live under the reign of God — in God's kingdom — is when they put God first. If one starts worrying, one not only centers on oneself and one's personal needs, priority is also given to something other than the reality of God. Such concerns or worries close off humans from both God and the neighbor in need. The sayings reported about the useless task of worrying are also saying that God is generous, that there is no lack of what one needs where God reigns and is present. To strive for or direct one's desire towards God's kingdom will give access to all things needed.

How can this be the case? How are we to understand these words, which are clearly not to be "spiritualized"? There need not be any sophisticated solution to this. The point is simply that where God is recognized as the generous giver, and the wealth in the world accordingly is seen as God's gifts, people will share because they are not directed by their own worrying about whether there is sufficient or enough goods for them. It is worrying that leads to egotistic accumulation of wealth and keeps the neighbor away from her share. Moreover, where God reigns, the neighbor is recognized as created in the image of God, and with the same privileges and rights to the goods of creation as anyone else. To keep someone away from these goods is to keep them away from God's gifts.

Looking at this from the point of view of the present world, it is not difficult to draw the conclusion that this is a world in which God does not reign and where the trust in God is replaced by trust in the accumulation of wealth. Hence, when we look from this angle, there is important light shed on the kingdom of God, understood in the contrast between an economic framework for gift and a gracing one. Where God's kingdom is not practiced there is a lack of grace, whereas a gift-economy based on grace might not only help those most in need but may also contribute to a more just world.[5] By practicing such an economy, the disciples of Jesus not only bear witness to the gracious and gifting God; they are the salt of the earth (cf. Luke 14:33-34).

S. Webb underscores that sin, seen in this context, should not simply be equated with the existence of private property. Given the fact that a gift is something given, there also has to be someone to possess it. The real question is for what and whom ownership exists: Is it for the owner, or as a means for further giving? Webb thus suggests that we understand sin in

---

5. I see this as one of the underlying motifs of Kathryn Tanner's book *Economy of Grace* (Minneapolis: Fortress Press, 2005).

this context as "the denial of the essential mobility of goods."[6] Instead of equating sin with the striving for pleasure, theology should, suggests Webb, contrast the pleasure of giving with the greed of keeping.[7] He refers in this context to an insight articulated by Tillich, which might well serve to illustrate how greed narrows our reality and closes us off to the other instead of opening up and widening our reality and our possibilities. Tillich defines concupiscence as "the unlimited desire to draw the whole of reality into one's self," or the temptation of "reaching unlimited abundance" in which the self denies all limits.[8] To sum up with the words of Webb:

> The sinner tries to find abundance within the self, not in the relation between self and others. This is a false and illusory excess that actually creates borders and restrictions on the flow of goods and the enlargement of the self. We resist God most when we anxiously want our share of things, patrolling the excess that gives and taxing the mutuality of the return.[9]

Against this background, one has to see Jesus' warnings about wealth as something that might hinder people from entering the kingdom of God. When concerns for your own wealth and property are prioritized instead of the need of the neighbor, what is actually happening is that one says: "I do not belong in the same kingdom as the one in need. He is not of my concern." As we shall see in a later interpretation of the last judgment, *this exclusion of the other from my world is what leads to my exclusion of myself from the kingdom.* The exclusion from the kingdom that people may experience is not due to their lack of merits, but to their lack of granting others the same privileges as they hold for themselves. In effect, it means that the other is not recognized as the image of God with the same vocation and rights as myself, and that she is, accordingly, not considered as related to God and God's gifts in the same way as I am.

The parable where Jesus illustrates the difficulties made by wealth is

---

6. Stephen H. Webb, *The Gifting God: A Trinitarian Ethics of Excess* (New York: Oxford University Press, 1996), p. 145.

7. Webb, *The Gifting God: A Trinitarian Ethics of Excess,* p. 145.

8. Paul Tillich, *Systematic Theology,* vol. 2, p. 52, quoted from Webb, *The Gifting God: A Trinitarian Ethics of Excess.*

9. Webb, *The Gifting God: A Trinitarian Ethics of Excess,* p. 145.

telling: As a camel carrying a burden is excluded from entering a narrow gate, so is a wealthy person who tries to enter the gate to the kingdom. However, if the wealthy person is able to consider his own chances for getting into the kingdom as similar to the person lacking wealth, he has to leave his possessions behind and assume the same position for entering as the poorer one. By leaving it behind, he not only recognizes the other as one in the same position as himself, but he also recognizes himself as one dependent on God's generosity.

That *generosity* is the main point here suggests that there is more than an ethical dimension implied, i.e., to serve and take care of the needs of the neighbor. This might also be the case, of course, but the element of generous gifting that is the point of departure in the parables of Jesus testifies to something else and beyond ethics. In his analysis of the parables of Jesus, Webb points to how Jesus' rhetoric "does justice to the illogic of abundance [. . .] in which love is offered over and above the moderate and reasonable concerns of self-interest and self-preservation" (p. 145). Webb also holds that the parables do more than merely illustrate moral principles: I would say that they express the *weak* ontological foundation for a different and faith-shaped relationship with reality. I call this a *weak foundation,* as it is only, once the world is given as a gift, an ontological possibility that we continue to relate to it in a way that can make it appear as such a gracious gift. Webb formulates this in a profound way when he concludes his analysis of the gifting parables as follows:

> In the Gospel parables, a poetics of praise — an encomium celebrating the apparently impossible but the miraculously necessary — unfolds as an ethical discourse in which the other is situated above (in terms of priority) and in front of (in terms of accessibility) the self, demanding and deserving recognition. This ethical discourse, however, is not a prosaic reflection on the need for justice, the careful demands of fairness and equivalency. Instead, this hyperethics is disclosed through the poetics — the poetry establishes an appealing imperative — by a compact and tense account of an action that makes sense because it is narratable, but demands existential verification because it is extravagant. The parables themselves, the excessive stories of Jesus, become, then, an avenue of grace: they open a way toward a giving in which, no matter how much we resist, we can find the empowerment that permits us to give in — the end to which is our own beginning. (p. 146)

The extensive quote is important also because it tells us something about how the giver recognizes the recipient, and how he then places the recipient as an Other who is not part of the economy of the giver, at the center of attention. This can only be done in a gift constituted by the interest in a gracing community, and not in a situation determined by reciprocity and the circle of exchange. Moreover, Webb suggests that it is in giving that we can experience or come close to that which is our own beginning — a remark that makes sense once we orient ourselves from the perspective of life as something given by God.

The postmodern understanding of gift sketched in the previous part of this book thus seems to find striking resonance in the way Jesus preaches and practices the kingdom. Jesus even bids that one deliberately invite those who can pay no return: "When you give a banquet, invite the poor, the crippled, the lame, and the blind. And you will be blessed, because they cannot repay you" (Luke 14:14). It is hard not to think that it is verses like these that are echoed in Derrida's description of the gift and its impossibility. By giving to those who cannot repay, the disciples thus testify to a kingdom outside of economy; they are blessed, he says, because the guest cannot repay, i.e., *there is blessing in being liberated from an economy of exchange, merit, and retribution.* Moreover, however, Luke indicates that there is still a reward waiting, a future reward, but one that is outside the sphere of time and economy, and is linked to the resurrection of the righteous.

The Kingdom as Gift — the Impossibility of an "Economic" God

We will return to the understanding of the kingdom of God more extensively later, but note already here that the character of surplus, a dimension pointing beyond exchange and economy, is underlined in Mark and Luke. In the story about Jesus and the children (Mark 10:13f.), the gift-dimension is underscored from the point of view of reception: only as a little child receives is it possible to receive the kingdom. A child is by its mere trust in the gift and the giver a model for expressing the unconditional giving of the gift. This parable is important, not only because it underscores the character of gift in itself, but even more because God is here — through the praxis of Jesus receiving the children — made visible and practiced concretely as the one who receives. God's welcoming hospitality is revealed through this practice in a manner that underscores the relationship between gift, recognition, and the fulfilling of desire for community and fellowship expressed by the parents. Jesus thereby witnesses to the reality of God and fulfills himself the vocation to be the *imago Dei*.[10]

Moreover, Jesus is fulfilling the kingdom of God and his own vocation as *imago Dei* respectively when he preaches and practices the kingdom in this way. The close internal links between the motives we work with nevertheless do not eliminate that he is clearly differentiating himself from God: When he asks the rich young man "Why do you call me good? — no one is good but God alone" (10:17), he affirms the difference, and points the young man back to God — as the very basic point of direction and orientation.

Whereas the children are received and community occurs instantly, Mark's narrative construction shows that to enter into the community Jesus practices is not always easy. One might even ask if there are not some *conditions* formulated here for entering the kingdom of God, as Jesus tells the young man in the story subsequent to that about the children, to let go of all his possessions in order to enter the kingdom. Moreover, he stresses the difficulties of entering in a manner that makes his disciples ask how it can be possible to enter the kingdom at all. How can we understand this as a story about grace, when it clearly also points to the conclusion that something is required as a necessary condition in order to enter?

The story clearly suggests that one of its central motives is that of setting the priorities right. As we shall see below, this question of prioritizing is closely connected to understanding God as the highest good and the most important object of our desire. But the story takes another twist that is also worth looking at. At the very point when Jesus expresses the difficulties of wealth the story deviates in an unforeseen way. Jesus here not only points to the impossibility of humans entering the kingdom of God, i.e., how it is impossible on human terms to establish what is necessary in order to participate. He also expresses what it is possible for *God* to do in order to make humans enter. His is thus a rejection of the question about how to make it possible for humans to *merit* entering. There is no unilateral connection between humans and God here: humans cannot make this access possible in the same way as God — they cannot make it happen at all.

---

10. That Jesus is aware of this vocation is a point strongly argued in N. T. Wright, *Jesus and the Victory of God: Christian Origins and the Question of God*, vol. 2 (London: SPCK, 1996), passim, and Conclusion, p. 651.

Jesus virtually says that it is impossible for humans to enter the kingdom of God. At the same time, he says, as a response to the terror and the desire of those wanting to enter, that it is possible for God: *For God all things are possible* (Mark 10:27). This is not necessarily to be read as a metaphysical statement about the general potentials or capabilities of God, but can also be seen as closely tied to the question of entering the kingdom. Whereas the impossibility is on the side of humans, God's possibilities still remain open.

Humans orient themselves from what they can do, and from their past, which is the only reality they know. From that angle, entry into the kingdom of God is refused. We see this in the story about the rich man: his riches were accumulated in the past, and what he can now do with them amounts to nothing in terms of enabling him to enter the kingdom. Jesus' words mark as nil what he has. He has to be confronted with this in order to be able to receive the kingdom, because it can only be received when it is not a merit or part of an exchange economy. The time of humans is the past, and that is what locks us up in a closed perception of our possibilities, and in the game of exchange and merit.[11]

On the other hand, the future is God's time and the time of possibilities. Humans do not control the future, and it would be futile to think that we could. Moreover, the future is not time, but is time to come, thereby signifying the possibilities beyond our grasp. The future is what God holds. The future is possibility, once we let go of the determining factors of the past and trust God. Against this background, it makes sense to say that trusting in God opens us to a wider and richer reality.

Hence, the statement about God's ability to open the kingdom of God is not a statement about God being able to do the impossible, but that for God all is possible;[12] some of the things that are impossible for humans

---

11. Derrida stresses that what dissolves or even destroys the gift is its integration in our timeline: "For there to be gift event (we say event and not act), something must come about or happen, in an instant, in an instant that no doubt does not belong to the economy of time, in a time without time, in such a way that the forgetting forgets, that it forgets itself, but also in such a way that this forgetting, without being something present, presentable, determinable, sensible or meaningful, is not nothing." Derrida, *Given Time: 1. Counterfeit Money* (Chicago: University of Chicago Press, 1992), p. 17.

12. This goes also for the saying in Luke 1:37 that nothing is impossible for God. By this formulation, what is clearly circumscribed is not God's ability to do the impossible, but that nothing is impossible for God, and hence, he can do all that is possible. That statement

are possible for God.[13] Among the things impossible for humans is to establish the reality of God: the reality of God is beyond the scope of possibilities humans can control. Hence, it has to be *given;* it is necessary that, if a reality at all, it is a reality of gift.

In present postmodern philosophy there is a discussion about *the impossibility of God*.[14] The claim for this impossibility of God is not to be understood as atheistic; rather, it is based on the insight that "Deconstruction is a way of thinking that seeks to protect the truth against restricted description."[15] The truth of God lies in the impossibility, which here has to be understood on similar terms as the impossibility of entering the kingdom. In human terms, God is the impossible; God is that which cannot be circumscribed by limited description, or brought about by human action or calculation.

Jesus radicalizes the insight into God's impossibility when he states that it is only for God that God is possible, i.e., it is only on the terms and conditions set by God that God can be God. Every human attempt to grasp, control, or circumscribe God is doomed to fail, because it is a result of the ignorance about the impossibility of God. The desire to establish, control, or define God will be a failure as long as it is expressed on the basis of human interests and needs, and in accordance with our conditions for agency.

I am trying here to express a link between what Jesus says about what is impossible for humans and what is possible for God, on the one hand, and the present discussion about the impossibility of God on the other hand. The link is more than mere linguistic or conceptual. It emerges from the insight into what is impossible for humans. The negative dialectic of this insight is expressed in the fact that whereas humans cannot control the future as the horizon of possibilities, God can still be thought of as one who does that. But these possibilities nevertheless still remain *possibilities* for God, and hence, the future can still be seen as open. Only when the fu-

---

as well should not be read as a general metaphysical statement about God, but from its context: that God will make it possible for Mary to have a son, in spite of her lack of a husband.

13. A more extensive discussion about God and the impossible can be found in Marion.

14. See for this, e.g., Hugh Rayment-Pickard, *Impossible God: Derrida's Theology, Transcending Boundaries in Philosophy and Theology* (Aldershot, UK, and Burlington, VT: Ashgate, 2003).

15. Rayment-Pickard, *Impossible God: Derrida's Theology,* p. 149.

ture is seen from the limited perspective of the concrete conditions of human lives does it appear as limited, narrow, and sometimes even closed. The very stating of the possibilities of the future thus holds our perception for its openness open to us.

It is noteworthy that Jesus never says anything about *how* things are possible for God. The function of his statement is nevertheless apparent: humans have to trust God when it comes to the entering of the kingdom, and not what they can do in themselves. In this respect, there is a correspondence also between what Jesus says about the reception of the kingdom by the children and what he says about the possibilities of the rich man to enter the same kingdom.

God as the Object of Love and Desire

In his response to the question about what is the first commandment, Jesus responds: "'You shall love the Lord your God with all your heart, and with all your soul, and with all your mind, and with all your strength.' The second is this, 'You shall love your neighbor as yourself.' There is no other commandment greater than these" (Mark 12:30-21). This response opens up an understanding of the relationship between God and our love and desire. The absorbing or occupying character of the love for God makes it even more likely to understand his response from the angle of desire: Jesus suggests that God is the object to which our love and desire should first and foremost be directed. Anyone looking for explanations to how this might be provocative should consider to what extent humans tend to put things other than God first — including their own piety and their own conceptions about what God is like. His answer points to a dimension beyond that which can be controlled by human agency. This answer would be perceived as provocative for anyone trying to understand God from within the horizon of one's own agency.

Moreover, the response we deal with here is to a question about the first commandment *in the law*. Jesus answers by using the law here to point to what is behind and beyond the law, and towards the very condition for the law. Hence, he confirms the importance of this commandment in the law, but the object of love that it describes is singled out as more important than the law in itself. This is not to say that the law is not important, but to say that what the law is directed toward is primary. *The law is used to point* beyond the law. That which regulates human agency (the law) is exceeded by the love for the God that is the giver of life and the basic condition for human agency.

This being the case, we need to qualify what it can mean to say that the first and foremost object of our love is God. Even more so, as God cannot be the mere object of human love: God is the condition for our love. No one can love God unless God has already been active in her life. God is the subject of our love for God, before God is the object of our love. Hence, the love for God cannot itself be seen as rooted in human agency. It emerges from the fact that God's reality breaks into human reality and manifests itself as the center where humans are grounded in a reality beyond themselves.

Jesus' response thus displays the same structure that we have already disclosed in our considerations concerning the structure of *gifts:* they cannot be conditioned by the recipient, and they transcend the circumscribable conditions of human agency. The law points beyond the law, and cannot be absolutized as the basis for human agency or humans' development of self-understanding without ending up as atheist, in the Levinasian sense of the word: The atheist is one who closes himself off from the participation with that which is larger than himself and beyond himself.[16]

Applying a contrast from Jean-Luc Marion, we can say that Jesus deconstructs the law as the idol, and makes it an icon for the reality of God.[17] An icon is what makes you see into a different world; it offers the new and transcending perspective, while an idol absolutizes the present and creates the illusion of control and closure. Moreover, what he does is to point to God as an object for love that is not similar to any other objects of love: God is invisible and someone we cannot control or grasp. For Marion, Christ is the ultimate icon of God, or even more: he is the face of the invisible itself: "He is the visible image of the invisible as invisible," as R. Horner says in her exposition of Marion.[18]

Hence, the love and desire for God is different from the love and desire we have for property, for ourselves, or for other humans. At least to

16. Cf. Introduction, pp. 68f.

17. Cf. Jean-Luc Marion, *God Without Being: Hors-Texte, Religion and Postmodernism* (Chicago: University of Chicago Press, 1991), pp. 8-9.

18. Robyn Horner, *Rethinking God as Gift: Marion, Derrida, and the Limits of Phenomenology,* 1st ed., Perspectives in Continental Philosophy, No. 19 (New York: Fordham University Press, 2001), p. 168.

some extent, these can all be parts of (however, not necessarily fully parts of) our world. To love God is to love that point of orientation from which we can see that our love and our life are not based in us, but in the gifts of the loving and gracing God. Hence, to love God and desire God is to desire the one who *can* shape our whole world, given that we let this point of view be expressed and witnessed as gracing, giving, loving. The desire for God is what can make our desire and love for the world something more than an expression of our own love, desire, and need: By loving God in this way, more than any other, we are enabled to love those whom God loves, as God loves them. By loving others as God loves them, we are images of God, and we are conformed to the true image of God, who is Christ.

At this point, we can address more critically Derrida's understanding of love and desire for God. Referring back to the points in the previous section, the experience of the divine impossibility is for Derrida bound up with feelings of desire and love. The reality of God's impossibility is not a freestanding "fact" that we merely take note of as passive observers. Rayment-Pickard says that for Derrida, an awareness of God's impossibility is caught up with concern *for* God.[19] Given that this impossibility is manifested in the immanence of agency and intention, it becomes easier to understand what he can mean. Negatively, Derrida's longing for transcendence — a transcendence he cannot find secured anywhere, because it *of course* always is dissolved into immanence, leaves him in "an unresolved state of longing, an eternal Advent with no possibility of Christmas. This religion of God's impossibility, moreover, takes the form of a bleak fideism, where faith has become entirely performative, an act of abstract hope whose object remains 'undecided.'"[20]

While we can recognize Derrida's concern for God, we have to find a way out of his understanding for religion without religion, or as being based only on the impossibility of God. My suggestion, as indicated above, is that it is possible to overcome the bleakness and the abstraction of his approach by seeing how love and desire, from the point of view of love for God, can manifest itself concretely in the world as love for others. Thereby, as love, it contributes to a positive understanding of what "God" means, or about how God functions. *God can function only by and through images (icons) of God.* This need not be a permanent advent without Christmas, as

19. Rayment-Pickard, *Impossible God: Derrida's Theology,* p. 146.
20. Rayment-Pickard, *Impossible God: Derrida's Theology,* p. 147.

in Derrida. Rather, it can be God permanently revealed by Godself in the world. Derrida's deconstruction of the possibility for "Christmas" removes him from the very object of love that can make his (non-)religion more concrete: a God who is revealed in, and still transcends, human love and desire for the good and for justice.

The reason for the impasse of Derrida is that the approach of deconstruction leaves him as stuck in immanence as every other who lacks access to a revelation of the concrete gift in Christ. Without looking at the content of revelation, he has no access to this transcendence, although this transcendence is already inscribed in the very language he uses. He is unable to develop this transcendence as long as there is no concrete manifestation of its practice, meaning, and context of signification. Such a context is what Jesus offers and signifies when he connects the love for the unknown and ineffable God with the love for the concrete neighbor.

The ineffability of God suggests not only that God is not an object. Postmodern philosophy, most notably in the wake of Martin Heidegger, has pointed to how God — as the object of our love — cannot be thought of as a being like other beings: consequently, the constitutive "element" or source of our desire for God is not being, and this not-being underscores the no-object-status of the object of our desire. Most recently, Marion has pointed to how God has to be understood more from the angle of gift and giving than from the angle of being. The importance of this approach is even more understandable when we see it from the point of view of Heidegger's confrontation with onto-theology.

In the famous reply in his Zürich seminar in 1951, Martin Heidegger was answering the question of how he understood the relationship between God and being. His answer has much relevance for how we think about God and desire:

> Being and God are not identical, and I would never attempt to think the essence of God through being. [. . .] Faith has no need of the thinking of being. If faith has recourse to it, it is already not faith. Luther understood this. Even in his own church this appears to be forgotten. I think very modestly about being with regard to its use to think the essence of God. Of being, there is nothing here of impact. I believe that being can never be thought as the ground and essence of God, but that nevertheless the experience and manifestness of God, insofar as they meet with humanity, eventuate in the dimension of being, which in no

way signifies that being might be regarded as a possible predicate for God. On this point one would have to establish wholly new distinctions and delimitations.[21]

The quotation is important for several reasons: first, it makes it clear that Heidegger — and I think rightly so — holds that both science (as an objectifying approach to the world) and philosophy are attempts to understand, control, and explicate the immanent. They thereby deal with something other than theology. God is not being. God is the condition of being, and something that manifests itself in being, without making being an immediate manifestation of God's self. As desire is directed towards or anticipates the presence of being, in this way of thinking, God consequently remains *absent*.

Second, it is interesting that Heidegger here alludes to Luther. He is (in his understanding of theology) referring to Luther's explication of what it means to have a God in the explanation of the first commandment in the *Large Catechism*. To have a God is not to put one's trust in anything in the world, i.e., not in any kind of *being*. God is beyond the ontological difference between the different entities and that which distinguishes them, namely that they are grounded in being or are expressions of being. Hence, to think of God in a way that relates him to a philosophy of being is to fall short of what the notion of God is all about.

The final reason for referring to Heidegger here is that Heidegger in his philosophy always insisted that there is a kind of more original or genuine approach to reality than the one offered by the objective approach found in, for example, modern science. The immediate meaningful relation to the world as ready-at-hand (Zu-handen),[22] by which our relation to the world is constituted as *our* world, is primordial to a scientific, detached approach to, and investigation of, the world (present-at-hand, Vorhanden). This more primordial world is the world that we described as the concrete world of presence by way of Dalferth earlier.[23] Hence, the experience of the life-world as something meaningful, and of the word "God" as something meaningful in the context of the life-world, refers the

21. Martin Heidegger, *Seminare* (GA 15), pp. 436f., here quoted after Laurence Paul Hemming, *Heidegger's Atheism: The Refusal of a Theological Voice* (Notre Dame: University of Notre Dame Press, 2002), pp. 291f.

22. Cf. Heidegger, *Sein und Zeit*, esp. pp. 70-71.

23. Cf. above, p. 20.

human being to something not only embedded in the life-world, but also beyond what can be, and what can be expressed in philosophical and objectifying scientific language about the world.

I think this last point is of importance in the present context of our discussion for a specific reason: Any attempt to understand the world from a context-less or objective point of view, in Heidegger's understanding, is based on abstractions from a more immediate and primordial experience. It is due to such abstraction that the investigating subject loses sight of the meaning of the world. This way of approaching the world also makes it impossible to engage it with love and open desire. As the subject thus addresses the world as an object of control, she loses sight of the fact *that the meaning of the world that means something for us* is usually immediately given in our experience of it. In this sense, theology reflects on and refers more back to our experience of what is given in the life-world, than to what is articulated and explicated in objectifying inquiry.

Heidegger uses the notion *onto-theology* to describe how everything that is, is a unity or a totality, something we can oversee and consequently control. In order to establish such a totalizing concept of reality, it is required that there is a kind of theological point of reference, called God or logos, which itself is to be seen as standing over against or beyond all being and is its final and first cause. However, when humans articulate this first principle and name it God, God is simultaneously reduced to an instrument for human power and grasping. God becomes a God of thought, a component in a philosophical system.[24] This God, conceived as the *causa sui*, is a God that is fully enmeshed in the ontology of being — and conse-

---

24. "Der Gott kommt in die Philosophie durch den Austrag, den wir zunächst als den Vorort des Wesens der Differenz von Sein und Seiendem denken. Die Differenz macht den Grundriss im Bau des Wesens der Metaphysik aus. Der Austrag ergibt und vergibt das Sein als her-vor-bringenden Grund, welcher Grund selbst aus dem von ihm Begründeten her der ihm gemassen Begründung, d. h. der Verursachung durch die ursprünglichste Sache bedarf. Dies ist die Ursache als die Causa sui. So lautet der sachgerechte Name für den Gott in der Philosophie. Zu diesem Gott kann der Mensch weder beten, noch kann er ihm opfern. Vor der Causa sui kann der Mensch weder aus Scheu ins Knie fallen, noch kann er vor diesem Gott musizieren und tanzen. Demgemass ist das gott-lose Denken, das den Gott der Philosophie, den Gott als Causa sui preisgeben muss, dem göttlichen Gott vielleicht naher. Dies sagt hier nur: Es ist freier für ihn, als es die Onto-Theo-Logik wahrhaben möchte." "Die onto-theo-logische Verfassung der Metaphysik," in *Identität und Differenz* (Stuttgart: Neske, 1957), pp. 64-65. Cf. for this also Jayne Svenungsson, *Guds Återkomst: En Studie av Gudsbegreppet inom Postmodern Filosofi, Logos Pathos,* Nr. 3 (Göteborg: Glänta Produktion, 2004).

quently, is determined and conditioned by man's relation to being and his/her way of thinking. This way of thinking about God is exactly what postmodern conceptions of God criticize. When we think that we have grasped God in this way, we can be sure that this is exactly what we have not done.[25] Again, *here* God remains absent in the presence of the fulfillment of desire. To relate God to scientific results is not a way we can gratify our desire for control and oversight — any discourse in which God appears as a name has to open up to the fact that God is exactly *not* a fact.[26]

This postmodern way of understanding God immediately presents theology and philosophy of religion with a problem: here God's alterity seems to be so strongly emphasized that it seems hard to speak about God at all. In one sense, God seems to be absolutely transcendent, but this transcendence is itself determined by an onto-theological paradigm marked by the distinction between transcendence and immanence. Hence, to say that God is transcendent immediately calls for the negation and the deconstruction of the transcendence-immanence scheme. This is done for the sake of maintaining that it is necessary to articulate that there "is" "something" like God, but at the same time, this articulation negates itself for the sake of God.[27]

It is important to maintain that although God constantly eludes our

25. This is nicely done by J.-L. Marion in a small and telling contribution in *Modern Theology* 18, no. 2 (2002), called "They Recognized Him; and He Became Invisible to Them." For Marion's critique of Heidegger, based on Levinas, see also Svenungsson, *Guds Återkomst*.

26. Cf. Slavoj Zizek, *On Belief: Thinking in Action* (London and New York: Routledge, 2001), p. 89: "Christianity, however, renounces this God of Beyond [i.e., in Judaism, J.-O.H.], this Real behind the curtain of the phenomena; it acknowledges that there is NOTHING behind the appearance — nothing BUT the imperceptible X that changes Christ, this ordinary man, into god. In the ABSOLUTE identity of man and God, the Divine is the pure *Schein* of another dimension that shines through Christ, this miserable creature. It is only here that the iconoclasm is truly brought to its conclusion: what is effectively 'beyond the image' is that X that makes the man Christ God."

27. This is an ancient understanding of the conditions and limitations of theological language, expressed already in the saying *Deus semper maior*. Cf. Francis Schüssler Fiorenza, "Being, Subjectivity, Otherness: The Idols of God," in John D. Caputo, Mark Dooley, and Michael J. Scanlon, eds., *Questioning God*, Indiana Series in the Philosophy of Religion (Bloomington: Indiana University Press), p. 341: "Theology should talk about God. Yet, whenever it does, it confesses the inadequacy of its very language about God. Theology lives off this tension between the need to speak of God and the inadequacy of its language about God. This tension is the motor driving theology to search for adequate language and at the same time to reflect critically on the inadequacy of its language about God."

concepts and conceptions, as well as our desire, but also to claim that God — in, with, under, and beyond language — means something positively, something that is in a relation to everything else. This point has to be repeatedly stated over against postmodern and deconstructive approaches that leave God as silent or totally undetermined, and presenting itself mainly as a new version of negative theology. At this stage, it is not only the advent of the gift of transcendence that suggests itself as a way out of the impasse of deconstruction "theology," but also several of the other angles we developed in the Introduction.

- First, that "God" is the object of our love and desire suggests that there is a given point of orientation *that makes a difference.* This point of orientation is not necessary. However, its contingent character is sublated once we affirm it as our point of orientation: When we love and desire community with a God defined as impossible (from the point of view of immanence), we allow for understanding ourselves as *necessarily* linked to a horizon of transcendence that is not determined by us. This horizon we can only live within by trust and faith, unless we want to gain control and narrow the world down to immanence again. Against this background, we understand love differently, and this horizon makes it possible to love the neighbor not only because she is a neighbor, but also because she is loved by God. The point of view of God here is not just "an additional" motivation, but also implies a different recognition of the neighbor. She can now be *unconditionally* loved, and not due to her part in and function in our lives of immanence, constituted by merit, reciprocity, function, economy, egotistic desire, etc. Hence, the close connection of the point of orientation given in the love for God and the recognition of the neighbor.
- Second, the desire for God, implied in the love for God, is a desire for the impossible, and thus an eschatological desire, determined by the future and not by my past and present conditions. When Jesus says that no one who looks back is fit for the kingdom of God (Luke 9:60-62), this can be read as an indication of how an orientation determined by the past closes off from or excludes God's future. In this respect also, a god that is fully determined by my desire is not God. Hence, love for God has to be fulfilled being conscious of this, and so my desire must not and cannot be to control or determine God, but

is instead expressed in the desire to be determined by God. This desire for determination by God only makes sense when God is understood as love and as good: only the desire for being determined by love and the good is a desire to which we can give ourselves over freely and without restrictions. Against this background, we have a different basis for loving the neighbor as well: our love for the neighbor is the result of being determined by God's love for us.

So far, these elaborations make sense in a way that is consonant with traditional Christian theology and piety. We now run the risk of changing this when we claim that all this can be assumed without having to affirm God's existence elsewhere than in language. We do not know if something called God exists outside of the perspective of the world made by the God-language provided by Jesus. The point of view of transcendence described above is exactly that: a transcendent point of view, developed from the point of view of immanence, in a suggestive language.

I am not trying to make the point here that God does not exist in any ordinarily assumed way of speaking. Rather, I want to stress the point that the reality of God as it is opened in Jesus is not something that can be demonstrated. It must be *witnessed,* in Oliver's sense, as response-ability and address-ability. It is as such we can understand the practice of Jesus in the Gospels: God is something pointed towards by Jesus. To what extent it is meaningful to say that God exists is closely related to the way we can make sense of the practices of love and freedom that stem from belief in God, and the types of experience that are opened by a language about God based on Jesus' witness.

What I am trying to say here is that it is "God's" function for us, the way this symbol or word opens up to an understanding of something that transcends our regular ordinary life, that makes it meaningful to talk about God. The meaning of the word is primarily linked to the assumption of a separate existence of a specific reality. Its meaning lies in its ability to help interpret experiences that transcend what can be grasped by the other tools we have for understanding ordinary life events. It is in this way that "God" is related to and present in our lives, and not in any other ways. Given that this is the case, it becomes understandable why Jesus links the love for God and the love for the neighbor in the way he does.

The desire for God that occupies and shapes the believer, and which makes her trust fully in God, can be developed more fully also when we analyze it more specifically from the angle of representation and (self-)recognition. Rowan Williams has provided a fruitful approach here. When I by faith relate to my identity as a human being and as *imago Dei,* I hold this identity to be something still in need of being fully realized, still in the future. This is not to be considered negatively as a flaw, but as something that makes it possible for me to be liberated from my own instantly self-seeking self — and also, for example, to seek justice for others. Thus, it makes me future-oriented. How can that be? In order to develop a possible answer to that question, we have to look at the connection between Christ as God's representative and *imago Dei,* and the way his presence can contribute to the shaping of human love and desire in a way that becomes liberating.

Paradoxically, it seems that when the human being seeks himself or herself in a not-yet-fulfilled destiny, while realizing that this cannot be wholly appropriated or fulfilled at the present, this safeguards the possibility of living here and now in a way that recognizes the vulnerability of both others and oneself. We are not perfect, and to realize this is to be confronted with the vulnerability that is given with the fact that we are dependent on others, and live exposed to the power of others. I think this insight lies behind the inclusive practices of Jesus as he preaches the kingdom of God. Writes Williams:

> The self becomes adult and truthful in being faced with the incurable character of its desire: the world is such that no thing will bestow on the self a rounded and finished identity. Thus there is in reality no self — and no possibility of recognizing what one is as a self — without the presence of the other. *But* that other must precisely *be* other — not the fulfillment of what I think I want, the answer to my lack.[28]

The human being acquires a fuller identity by realizing or being confronted by what it is — and what it cannot yet be. A truthful engagement and confrontation with some Other can provide this. In the description above, Williams offers a possibility for spelling out the positive function that God as the Other can have in the development of human identity: God is the stability that no human can have in him/herself. The relation to God at the same time offers the human being a possibility of grasping her

28. Rowan Williams, *Lost Icons: Reflections on Cultural Bereavement* (Edinburgh: T. & T. Clark, 2000), p. 153.

self as an unfinished and problematic project, and to live with the impact of that insight. To see God here as the Other underlines how every attempt to try to make God a function of one's own gratification of desires implies the attempt to overcome God's otherness, and thus, to make God less than God. It also implies that by doing so, the human being loses its self, its soul.[29] God is excluded; the possibility of God is made impossible.

From this, we can show how the *true* self-relation configured in the presence of the other excludes idolatry: idolatry is here to be taken as the worship of oneself or of someone or something in the world (generally: the created). The self-relation in the presence of the other is the form of life that secures in the most profound way the basis for an authentic and sustainable life. How can we say that? We can point here to the experience of how therapies function in which there is a *distinct and realized representation (but not full or total presence!) of otherness.* Williams points to how different forms of therapy (and thus, self-relations) can be developed on the basis of either an embodying or reification of otherness, *or* on the basis of otherness as *represented.* I suggest that this idea of representation, offered by Williams, is fruitfully to be understood as a means for signifying the presence-absence of God, as God, when being represented by the word "God," remains in and with and working through consciousness without becoming identified with it.

At this point, the distinction between representation and embodiment is crucial. From this angle, we can realize how Jesus, in his affirmation of the commandment to love God, has to be understood as both the revealer and the representative of God. Such a distinction helps us to see how the presence of what is desired can be understood in two distinct ways, and thus contribute to two quite different functions for the self. Embodying or reification of otherness can be perceived as presence, and thus open for a kind of idolatry, as the actual presence of the other is assumed to offer some kind of (provisional or illusory) gratification for the self.[30] Such reification captures the human in a position of lack of identity instead of liberating its self to further development and quest. But as we can clearly see in the Gospel stories, when Jesus is recognized as God's representative, it is *God* who is given honor and glory, and Jesus himself is not

29. This is a point that, as indicated on p. 28 above, I think is important to argue against recent and former forms of critique of religion.

30. This would then be a relevant perspective on transference in psychoanalysis.

worshiped. Here, it would be appropriate to speak of Jesus as God's embodied representative and representation, as this definition still makes it possible for God to be more and other than what is present. Williams writes in the continuation of the quotation given above something that might point to how the very function of representing God might then serve as liberating:

> The therapy that releases or constructs the viable, truthful sense of self that is needed for a life without crippling misperception is a therapy that represents such otherness. And (here is a further twist of paradox) it must represent and not claim to *embody* it; if it slips into the latter, it becomes a new slavery and illusion. The claim to embody the Other says, in effect, that the Other is *here,* an answer, a gratification, a terminus of desire, so that the other is reduced to the dimension of my lack and ceases to be Other.[31]

We can understand "the Other" in the quotation to be both God and our future destiny as *imago Dei.* To be aware of the fact that neither God nor my own self is something that I can acquire and make present myself is also to realize that these are not controllable or reducible to something I know or can handle. This awareness is liberating to the extent that it lets me give up the search for constituting my own self, and live in trust and faith in God. It is to realize that life cannot be now what it shall be. But this also means that every attempt to embody or reify God by deifying something manageable, be it by putting my trust in other humans, money, sex, power, or ecstatic experiences, implies a human failure, theologically speaking: I only acquire myself when I am able to live with the awareness of an otherness that cannot be embodied in any kind of object, an otherness that is — exactly — represented, but not fully embodied in my reality. To put it in a more postmodern wording: This idea of and ability to live with representations instead of embodied substitutes for gratification rules out idolatry as well as closure. I think this can be seen as a parallel to what Kearney means when he speaks of eschatological desire as desire for that which is impossible, for that which cannot be seen as a fulfillment of my longing or desire (see p. 30 above).

God is thus only able to make us into those we are to become as long as God is not finitely embodied in the world, but represented there. God's

31. Williams, *Lost Icons: Reflections on Cultural Bereavement,* p. 153.

full representation we find in Jesus, as the one who fully manifests what it is to be God when God is a human. The above analysis thus not only presents itself as a possible psychological wisdom behind the incarnation, but also suggests ways of manifesting transcendence in a manner that implies that God can work and promote God's reality through and by our relationships with other people and the rest of creation.

Moreover, this is also the *motivation* for any type of critique of religion directed against the reification and finite embodying of the divine. Simultaneously, this is also the reason behind the rejection of every form of critique of religion that claims that religion is nothing other than symbolic constructions and extrapolations of the wishes and desires of humanity. Religion functions according to its aim exactly when it does *not* contribute to such fulfillment. When otherness is safeguarded by religion in a way that lets both God and human identity remain something still to come, something not to be fully acquired by human controlling powers, it realizes its aim.

If human desire is directed along these lines, and the love and desire for God occupies us in this way, something more than a meeting between two parties is taking place in an encounter between them shaped by one's love for the other. There is a third party involved, one who is present but not fully embodied, and who still contributes to the development of their selves as recognized and recognizing images of God. Although Williams in the following uses non-theological terms (he speaks about the non-ideological Other), the quotation shows how God in his paradoxical absent presence is constitutive for the content in the realization of the human destiny as the *imago Dei*:

> [This] is not just a skilled invitation to the life-giving contradiction or frustration of desire; it works as such by doing something significantly more, by invoking the necessarily absent, non-particular ("non-existent") Other. It is a three-cornered relation, not only a dialogue, in which the presence of the absent third makes possible some kind of liberation from the net of ideas and projections that binds us in the fantasy that some specific other can supplement our lack, once and for all, and end our desire.[32]

In this way, the presence of the Other (be it God or another human, the neighbor) opens up a new access to our lives and a new way of relating to

32. Williams, *Lost Icons: Reflections on Cultural Bereavement*, p. 154.

oneself, determined neither by the past and its actions, nor by the desire or the longing that is deeply situated in our own person and its experiences. Thus, the presence of the Other gives rise to new possibilities of experience, but these are only realizable when the individual is able to transcend his or her present self — and appropriate the resources made available by the Other.

We should also note in this connection the importance of the other human person, whom Jesus calls the neighbor. She is, in her own way, as an image of God, *God's representative,* and can help me realize and come to grips with my present situation. This is well illustrated in how people are recognized or not in the last judgment parable, where Jesus links the outcome of the judgment to how one treated the neighbor, indicating that this was also the way one treated him.[33]

God, as the present-absent third party — and thus as the not finally and finitely embodied object of love and desire, can become represented by an Other. Consequently, what God wants to give — as a gift of life, community, and identity — to a human being can be carried out in our meeting with another person, if we are able to realize her/his otherness, and not only see him/her as something we can turn into a controllable sameness on the basis of who and what we already are. This is an approach that can be developed in a Christological direction, but it also might have implications for our understanding of what it means to function as an image of God. Anyhow, the Other (Jesus, the neighbor) in this respect contributes to the clarification and transparency of who I am and what I am to become, and thus to my understanding of the given relationships in which I am challenged to live my life.

> And the absent "non-existent" third is manifest as the condition for the truthful recognition of my own limits, of the persistence of my incompleteness, because it is not itself *a* point of view, mirroring or competing with mine; it is not another system of desiring, any more than it is something being fitted into the system of *my* desiring. Its otherness is radical enough to allow me to be other — to be distinctive, to be this-and-not-that of temporal particularity. And the finite other who "holds" this perspective does so only out of the same aware-

---

33. Matthew 25:31ff. See for a more extensive analysis of this parable below, pp. 188-95.

ness of the permission given by the "third" to be a finite self; if this is not so, I remain trapped.[34]

By contributing to the clarification of these issues, Williams gives a profound account of what it means to be guided with the desire for God, and to maintain that God can be at work also when he is absent in the presence of desire. He thereby also suggests a way out of the impasse where Derrida found himself. Through his analysis, we are provided with an interesting example of a *theologia negativa*, although this theology is not totally negative, but informed by how desire works in the attempts to fulfill our lives.

By insisting on how God is present in desire, desire is thus not to be understood as a blunt negation of God. It is a chance for conceiving of God's distinct otherness, and at the same time, through this, to see that such a God is a larger God than the one who gratifies human desire, or is interwoven with some kind of onto-theological conception of reality. Thereby, paradoxically, the presence of God manifests God as the *infinite* Other — in the presence of desire.[35]

As a conclusion then, God as the object of desire, the one who is worthy of the full engagement of human love, God who is a gifting non-being shaping being, is the only one who can present Godself as worthy of our trust and love. This is so because God is the only one who can lead us towards our destiny, without us having to know or secure beforehand what this means or what it fully implies. The suggestion by Jesus that our love for God must occupy us totally, with all heart, mind, soul, and strength, suggests that a life occupied by God by means of our desire for him is not only a fuller life. It is a *different* life, in terms of orientation and priorities, and accordingly, in terms of recognition of what is important when living in this world. The God at work in this desire is worthy of love and trust. This God is not one that humans can use in order to control others or to marginalize them from their lives. Hence, this God might still be perceived

---

34. Williams, *Lost Icons: Reflections on Cultural Bereavement,* p. 154.

35. In this context, the infinite also points to the eschatological not-yet of the other, that which is not possible to acquire or appropriate. For God as the infinite other, and the theological connotations of this notion, cf. Jan-Olav Henriksen, *Grobunn for Moral: Om Å Være Moralsk Subjekt i en Postmoderne Kultur* (Kristiansand: Høyskoleforlaget, 1997). [Soil for morality. On being a moral subject in a postmodern culture], pp. 215ff., where I analyze this in relation to the work of Levinas.

as a dangerous threat against conceptions that serve as religiously moti-vated bases for control or power.

The Kingdom of God — as Witness About God

As mentioned, two elements are striking if we ask about the theo-logy in the Gospels: first, that so little is said directly about God, and second, that when Jesus talks about the kingdom of God — the place where we can ac-tually detect, experience, or realize what the reality of God means — this reality is described in parables. Hence, there is no direct access either to God or to an understanding of what the presence of God — manifested in God's reign — means. This elusiveness suggests in itself the *transcending* (but not: merely transcendent) character of this reality, and the parables accordingly give us clues, traces, or indications based on our own experi-ences about the larger horizon or reality that this reign implies for human life.

The purpose of the present section is twofold: first, to look into some of the elements where the parables about the kingdom of God offer details for understanding God, and second, to relate this result to our angles of in-terpretation. This task is even more important due to the fact that the con-tent of Jesus' theology would seem meager without looking into these par-ables. On the other hand, as the parables tell us something about the character of a reality in which God reigns, there is a lot of content to gain from them regarding Jesus' theology.

Jesus himself underscores that it is difficult to understand the para-bles about the kingdom (cf. Mark 4:11-13). The problem of understanding might well be seen as one of the effects of trying to understand the world from the angles of economy, reciprocity, and merit. For example, what the parable of the Sower says about God is that God distributes the word and offers possibilities of response for everyone, regardless of their position and response. It is not only about response, but also about generosity.

The kingdom of God breaks through beyond human control, as a seed grows without our awareness (cf. Mark 4:26-29). This is not surpris-ing, but it underscores, nevertheless, that God can only be God, and God's kingdom can only be his own, when God is not controlled or enrolled into a reign dominated by human purposes. That would render nil *God's* king-dom or reign. When Jesus points to God's lack of dependence in bringing forth the kingdom, the breakthrough itself suggests that there is more to life than what can be brought forward by human agency. In this respect, also, the kingdom appears as *gift*. On the other hand, we need to recall that this breakthrough needs to be kept together with what we previously said about God's vulnerability: God makes Godself dependent on humans in order to become apparent *as God* in the world.[36] The tension between these two motives can be expressed in the witness to *God as the vulnerable (and exposed?) sovereign,* who offers his reality to everyone as a gift that no one needs to receive, and for which someone must be there representing God in order for it to be given.

Moreover, the parable of the mustard seed (Mark 4:30f.) suggests that God's presence might go undetected: what brings God's kingdom forth is not glamorous or spectacular events, but the small events, which later on will be seen as the start of what can be experienced as overwhelming. The parable prompts us to consider what is small as no less important than the spectacular, but it does *not* say what this small thing *is,* in the kingdom of God. If it says something about God, it might be that God — in the course of history — might go unnoticed (cf. what was just said about vulnerability), and that for us to recognize God might demand that we look elsewhere than in the obvious places. Hence, the parable challenges the presupposition that God is to be detected only in the major events of history. It challenges humans to recognize that God is present in what happens in the smaller events and moments in life. By describing the kingdom in this way, Jesus makes people realize that God is at work in the lives of those not necessarily considered to be of great religious or moral importance. Events or people that appear unimportant might have important consequences on a long-term basis.

This way of describing the world implies that one should be alert to what is happening in a way that opens up understanding the normal as only one of several possibilities. God is surprising; God's advent might go undetected unless you are alert. There is an almost existential motif in Jesus' warnings about being ready that suggests one be *watchful.*

36. Cf. above, p. 33.

Summing Up Jesus' Teaching About God: God as Burglar?

In one of his parables, Jesus also uses the notion of watchfulness in order to say that the Son of Man will come at an unexpected hour (Luke 12:40). This should not be taken to indicate that the kingdom of God will come unexpectedly: it can be read from the signs when it is present. However, the parable in question suggests that the advent of the Son of Man[37] can be likened to the advent of a thief, a burglar. This raises the interesting question: What can we get out of understanding the advent of God or God's representative, conceived of as a burglar? Apart from the obvious motif of watchfulness towards the unexpected, what causes us to take up the subject in the present context are several other possibilities as well. Hence, we can turn to the exhortation to be watchful and see if there is something hidden in this parable that may help us understand *God*.

- To say that God breaks in implies that we do not consider — in our consciousness of ourselves and the world — God as present. Alternatively, God is so domesticated that God lacks the ability to disturb, change, or upset us. Such a god is no god, because this god is part of *the human world,* instead of a God who makes humans see themselves as part of God's world and *confronted and challenged* by God's presence. The importance — theologically, Christologically, and soteriologically — of a God who is perceived as *breaking in* is that such a God does not allow us to become too comfortable in our own world and defies our attempts to maintain a sense of false security. God's advent suggests there is still something to come, still justice to be done, still a kingdom becoming. The advent of the coming God opens our eyes to what is happening in the world, and lets us see the world not from our comfortable perspective, but from the uncomfortable perspective expressed in the question: Is God reigning here, is God witnessed here, is the neighbor recognized here as the image of God? This disturbing perspective is opened by perceiving God as a burglar.
- Second, as God *breaks in,* it means that what is closed is opened, and that something that is excluding is no longer effective. The in-

---

37. There is no indication in Mark or Luke that the advent of the Son of Man is identical with the breakthrough of the kingdom, which they both seem to think is a present but not-yet-fulfilled reality.

breaking of God is the breaking down of the world that I can possess and where I am the only lord. It effectively confronts me with *the Other,* the one who is not me, but who rearranges and reorders my vision of the world. Not only is the burglar contributing to this, but the very event of the *encounter* itself witnesses to a world beyond my own. An encounter is an event signifying something new in addition to what was the situation beforehand, adding or changing this situation into something different. Hence, the burglary implies a testifying to the difference from what was presently the case.

- Third, God surprises, both in time and in form: Echoing Derrida's understanding of the gift as beyond time, we can now see that God, as the burglar from outside of time, enters or breaks in at an instant. The surprise marks in *form* the unexpected, as God is not and cannot be anticipated: God is in the small things, that which is unremarkable (like the mustard seed). God might go unnoticed, until one realizes what his presence in the world really means. That is what Jesus indicates as well, when he points to God's generosity and God's care for creation, from the sparrows to the humans. The workings of God in these things are also a reason for trust and confidence in God, and not in your own possessions (cf. above, and Luke 12:22ff.).
- Fourth, a burglar changes our perceptions of the world also in the sense that he makes me ask what is most valuable to me, and what is it that I can afford to lose or not. When a burglar takes away what I assume to be my riches and lets me see what means most to me, he is enacting concretely the very same function as Jesus, when he says that whoever wants to enter the kingdom of God must get rid of his possessions.
- Fifth (and more speculative than the previous explorations), there is an element of suspense when a burglar comes to visit. The effect of too much familiarity in the presentation of God might end up in boredom. That might even be the case when God is presented as the solution to all your needs or as the gratification of all desires. Even as such, the perception of God might become too familiar, too domesticated.

The above cannot and should not be considered as exhaustive, and for a very specific reason: it might be taken to indicate that the people to whom Jesus preached about God had a completely different notion of God that made him present a new theology. That is hardly likely to be the case. One of the reasons why there is so little extensive development of the understanding of God in the Gospels is rather that the people Jesus addresses, as well as the people the Gospels are written to, share a common view of God, which makes even the God Jesus speaks of rather familiar to them. And it is exactly this familiarity that makes it so important to stress the element of excess, surprise, and difference that is present in the reality of God, when we see God in relation to the given. This is not because God is completely different from what they (or we) might expect, but because there might be something missing in recognizing God as God if we were not constantly alert to the possibility that there might be something more and other at stake than that with which we are familiar. More abstractly put: If "God" as a word partly represents an open and undetermined horizon for human life, that very horizon gets closed once you forget to look for the new, unexpected, or unfamiliar.

Hence, to understand God as a burglar is to see God as surprise and interruption, as one behind the experiences of the unexpected, new, and unconceivable. Such experiences are of excess and surplus, as they offer chances for ordering life in new and different ways. Faith can be seen as letting oneself be determined by that which God creates of goodness in human life. These goods are not the overcoming of deficits, but rather uncontrollable interruptions and surprising events — the unanticipated possibilities of life.[38]

A Major Image of God and Tensions: The Prodigal Son

The parable in Luke 15 about the prodigal son and his brother can be read from many angles.[39] Here we are first concerned with what it says about Jesus' conception of God. Assuming familiarity with the parable, we can sum this up in the following elements:

First, as said aptly by S. Webb, the story recognizes how "giving is a force that breaks boundaries, supersedes limitations, and thwarts expectations."[40] Hence, this story points to something beyond what can be expected.

---

38. Cf. Ingolf U. Dalferth, "Umsonst. Vom Schenken, Geben Und Bekommen," *Studia Theologica* 60, no. 2 (2005): 95.

39. I have developed an understanding of the anthropological implications of this parable in Jan-Olav Henriksen, *Imago Dei: Den Teologiske Konstruksjonen av Menneskets Identitet* (Oslo: Gyldendal, 2003).

40. Webb, *The Gifting God: A Trinitarian Ethics of Excess*, p. 144.

The background for this is exactly in the giving, or rather, in the radical affirmation of the character of generosity that characterizes the father's attitude; on two separate occasions his gifting seems to supersede the two sons' conceptions, which are shaped by an understanding of exchange economy and possession. The generosity is expressed in both the giving over of the son's inheritance and in the father's welcoming him back. There are no conditions stated in either case. The father is a generous giver, pure and simple.[41] The generosity not only implies the giving over of possessions; it also allows the prodigal to depart from the father's house, although the consequences might be fatal both for the son and for the values in question.

Second, the father recognizes both his sons as having the same rights, and fully as his sons. They can do nothing to change that recognition. This point is important, as it is not only expressed in this parable, but also several other places in the Gospels where Jesus considers the righteous of Israel to be in the presence of the father. Hence, from the father's side there is a basic positive recognition of both.

Not only are both sons fully recognized, but the father also accepts that both sons go the ways they choose. The generosity of the father is sufficient to allow the son who desires to go on his own to do so. However, as the story vividly suggests, the departure of the son — and his way of ordering and orienting his own life — leads to a breakdown in relationships: the prodigal loses the relationship to father and brother, and those he then lives with only stay with him as long as there is money left. All this suggests, of course, that there is a fatal flaw in human life, and a great amount of fragility in human relationships, when structured around (the struggle for) possessions. Moreover, as Jean-Luc Marion suggests, the son's request for his share of the inheritance converts the dynamic of gift, which he has hitherto lived by and from, into a logic of property.

> He asks that one grant that he no longer have to receive any gift: he asks to possess it and dispose of it, enjoy it without passing through the gift and the reception of the gift. The son wants to owe nothing to his father, and above all not to owe him a gift; he asks to have a father no longer — the *ousia* [possession] without the father or the gift.[42]

41. The generosity of God is present several places in Luke, cf. e.g., 11:5-13.
42. Marion, *God Without Being: Hors-Texte,* pp. 97-98, here quoted from Webb, *The Gifting God: A Trinitarian Ethics of Excess,* p. 145.

Stephen Webb says that this also implies that the son wants to turn the ground that the family shares into "liquid money, which, by definition, seeps and trickles between the fingers. The cost of the gift for the father in receiving the son back is forgiveness; the expense of property for the son is the loss of his humanity."[43] Webb quotes Marion with affirmation at this point.

However, Marion's reading, echoed in Webb, also calls for one criticism: he says that the cost for the father is forgiveness. But the story says nothing about that. Moreover, if we look at the other texts surrounding this one, they are all about the joy when someone repents, and not about the cost of forgiveness. Hence, the main point in these parables is the surplus of joy that repentance creates over against the lacks that are conditioned by the past (cf. Luke 15:8-10).

As we can see, the element of joy makes it even more possible to see Jesus' understanding of God from the angle of a postmodern understanding of gift. God's joy is over the return of the *recipient*, and not the gift. This underscores how God's gifting is always directed toward community and fellowship, and not toward getting something back in terms of what God deserves. Joy, furthermore, is among those goods that only get multiplied by being shared — as are all God's goods.

The parable is, however, also about changes or transformations of *desires*. The youngest son has a desire for property and wealth that directs and orients his initial actions in the story. The change in desire takes place when he is able to recognize that there is a world beyond the one present for him, represented in the conception of his father's house. Without the presence of the father's house, the son would not realize the chances still possible for community and recognition. Hence, the story suggests that the very *awareness* of the possibility of a receiving God who seeks community might open up to a new and different future for humans who are lost in the world.

Moreover, it is notable that the father welcomes both sons to the celebration of the return. Just as in the similar parables in the previous chapter in Luke, this one also suggests a willingness to share joy: As mentioned, joy multiplies by being shared. Hence, it makes sense to say that when God welcomes and includes anyone who will take part, God offers a participation in the gifts that cannot be possessed, but only shared.

---

43. Cf. Webb, *The Gifting God: A Trinitarian Ethics of Excess*, p. 145, with reference to Marion, *God Without Being: Hors-Texte*, pp. 97-98.

The portrait of the father suggests the close internal connection between the traits that we have seen repeatedly in this study: The father is marked by love for both his sons, and hence is merciful. This love is possible to see as the conditioning background for his welcoming and hospitality. The experience of such an unconditional welcome, which is physically manifested in the welcoming to a meal, also serves as the witness to an unconditioned community where all previously experienced *shame* is effectively blocked out.[44]

That Jesus is countering structures producing shame is underscored by A. Nolan. He points to the close relationship between being poor and hungry or thirsty, and shame. "The principal suffering of the poor, then as now, was shame and disgrace."[45] The social order makes sure that they never can be accepted into the company of "respectable" people. Hence, a logic of exclusion is at work here that denies them what they need most: the recognition in prestige and public esteem. Writes Nolan: "They did not even have the consolation of feeling that they were in God's good books. The educated people told them that they were displeasing to God and 'they ought to know.' The result was a neurotic or near-neurotic guilt complex which led inevitably to fear and anxiety about the many kinds of divine punishment that might befall them."[46]

The challenge of the parable, however, remains: Who will take part, who will recognize the prodigal as one with whom we can share joy and relate in a community on equal basis? This question might basically be phrased in the following manner: Is the kingdom of God and the community of those who believe an inclusive and potentially universal community, where no one is excluded unless we distance ourselves from those who partake there? This question will be dealt with more extensively in the next chapter, when we ask: Who is righteous?

44. The presupposition of this argument is the understanding referred to above of how shame can be overcome only by concrete and physical acts of integration and recognition. For the function of meals as places for manifestation of social order and hierarchy, cf. Marcus J. Borg, *Jesus: Uncovering the Life, Teachings, and Relevance of a Religious Revolutionary*, 1st ed. (San Francisco: HarperSanFrancisco, 2006), pp. 158f.

45. Albert Nolan, *Jesus Before Christianity* (Cape Town: David Philip, 1986), p. 22.

46. Nolan, *Jesus Before Christianity*, p. 24.

God as Abba

Although it is often referred to as a feature specific to Jesus, the evidence for his intimate relationship with God as expressed in the name "Abba" is not very large. This, of course, need not have any importance or bearing on the historical correctness of his use of this term. However, it does suggest a likely conclusion to the presentation of his understanding of God in the previous section.

When God is addressed as Abba, it suggests that there is a close relationship expressed in the usage by the addresser, marked by confidence and immediacy. This is usually developed in different ways in order to establish the image of God as confidant, and there is no reason to oppose such images of God. Nevertheless, there might be more to say about this picture than that.

One who addresses God as Abba is most likely to see God as his closest relative. A relative is one with whom we have a relationship that cannot be dissolved. When Jesus teaches his disciples to address God in this way, he is suggesting that this is how they should recognize God: as one with whom you are in a close and unending relationship, one you can trust as a good father. Moreover, this father is present in a manner that is unconditional, a manner that allows for relating to God as someone involved in ordinary, daily life. God is not remote, or too holy to be encountered on a daily basis. This image of God is reinforced by stories such as the one about the prodigal son, whom the father unconditionally welcomes back. In the presence of such a father, there is no place for shame.

In light of the issue of recognition, to address God as Abba is likely not only to imply a close relationship but also one's own origin in God. To understand oneself as originating from a loving and merciful God might have important bearings on how one orients oneself in the world: to be merciful, loving, or generous is from this point of view a natural consequence of the gifts recognized as received from this father. We can thereby also see the close relationship between witnessing to God as Abba and the practice of mercy, healing, and community.[47]

---

47. The close ties between these features are supported by D. Capps's interpretation of the healings of Jesus as based on his change of the psychological conditions for suffering. Capps offers a reading of the healings that makes it possible to see the illnesses as both manifestations of problems in the social order of the society, and as overcome by Jesus' different

Jesus Functioning as God

Jesus forgave sins, much to the annoyance of those who had conceptions of God as the only one who should do that. The offense in this forgiving was possibly also due to the opinion that the given did not deserve this, or that they were not appropriately situated to receive forgiveness. By doing it, Jesus not only implies that he is one who has a mandate to forgive, he also suggests that *God* has given him this mandate. At least three things regarding Jesus' practice of forgiveness shed light on the manner in which he reveals God:

1. First, this practice testifies to a forgiving God who is ready to forgive those who turn to God for forgiveness. In this respect, Jesus is in accordance with the picture of God present in Israel, as the one who is willing to forgive those who repent. This understanding is, for example, echoed in the story about the Pharisee and the tax collector in Luke 18:9ff.

2. Second, Jesus treats those turning to him as if they had turned to God. Hence, he acts as if he is God's representative, as if his is the presence of God. He thereby recognizes their recognition of him as someone sent from God, and God appears in this situation to be the non-present third party who is manifested through and in the acts of Jesus, including the act of forgiveness.[48] That God is actually present here as the non-present third party is obvious when we see how people praise God as a response to what Jesus does (cf. Luke 5:26).

3. Moreover, the way Jesus acts implies that God gives such a mandate to this specific person. This is one of God's possibilities. By granting Jesus this mandate, God allows Jesus to act on God's behalf. This is the theo-logical implication of Jesus as one who forgives sins. Hence, the forgiving practice of Jesus implies that God is a forgiving God, acting out of mercy. The ability to forgive is not restricted to God — it is something a human can do.

Accordingly, not because of this, but nevertheless connected, Jesus teaches his disciples to pray "forgive us our debts, as we forgive our debt-

---

vision of what the community is like. See Donald Capps, *Jesus: A Psychological Biography* (St. Louis: Chalice Press, 2000), pp. 211-16.

48. Cf. above, pp. 137-39.

ors." Thus, he draws implications from the above-indicated understanding of himself as one who widens the possibility of forgiveness to something also being distributed among humans. By confronting a perception of God that says that only God can forgive sins, Jesus contributes to a wider and more concrete proliferation of forgiveness that also may create changes in human relationships. By functioning in this way, Jesus — by giving forgiven-ness — opens up a surplus in reality, something excessive or abundant compared to the restriction of resources that is the case when forgiveness for sins is not occurring among humans.

There is one more feature in Jesus' functioning as God that needs to be addressed here: Jesus addresses everyone, but those he calls to *repent* are those who think they are secure. His call for repentance is accordingly marked by generosity and openness. He challenges first and foremost not moral failures, but people who exclude others from community due to what are perceived as such failures. In this way, he confronts the negative side of being obedient to God's law, as this might make people become more concerned with their own righteousness than with their neighbor. Moreover, when Jesus warns against judging others, it is interesting to see how this exhortation can be understood as excessively generous and closely related to giving and forgiveness. We thereby get an indication of what God is like:

> Be merciful, just as your Father is merciful. Do not judge, and you will not be judged; do not condemn, and you will not be condemned. Forgive, and you will be forgiven; give, and it will be given to you. A good measure, pressed down, shaken together, running over, will be put into your lap; for the measure you give will be the measure you get back. (Luke 6:37-38)

As God is merciful and generous, it is reasonable to expect the same of those believing in such a God. Moreover, the commandment not to judge and condemn is important not only from the point of view of establishing and maintaining community. It is also important because when someone is condemned, she remains tied to, even chained to, her past, and this past then remains definitive of our relationship with her. By not judging or condemning, the future of otherness, of new possibilities, is still kept open for her.

The positive reception of the call for repentance then implies an overcoming of divisions and exclusions based on moral agency.[49] We will develop that issue more concretely in the next chapter, where we look into how Jesus practices his understanding of God. Thereby, he also overturns conceptions about who is righteous and who can be granted community with God.

Hospitality and Forgiveness in Derrida: Opening Up to God

The above development of forgiveness as a radicalization of human community can be developed further if we look at how Derrida has related forgiveness and hospitality.[50] Hospitality means welcoming the other into your own world — even when he or she is unannounced. In this way Derrida stresses how forgiveness and hospitality (which he deliberately misspells as "hospitiality") represents the same type of impossible phenomena as forgiveness, gift, or justice. He echoes the words of Jesus in Matthew by challenging us to serve also those from whom we are not expecting any return:

> If, in hospitality, one must say yes, welcome the coming, say the "welcome"; one must say yes, there where one does not wait, yes, there where one does not expect, nor await oneself to, the other, to let oneself be swept by the coming of the wholly other, the absolutely unforeseeable stranger, the uninvited visitor, the unexpected visitation beyond welcoming apparatuses. If I welcome only what I welcome, what I am ready to welcome, and what I recognize in advance because I expect the coming of the hôte as invited, there is no hospitality. (pp. 361-62)

Hospitality consists in welcoming the other that does not warn me of his coming. Seen against the background of what we have already devel-

---

49. Cf. Nolan, *Jesus Before Christianity*, p. 64: "If Jesus had refused to argue, discuss and mix socially with the Pharisees, then, and then only, could one accuse him of excluding them or treating them as outsiders. The gospels abound in examples of his conversations and meals with them and of his persistent attempts to persuade them. In the end it was they who excluded him; at no stage did he exclude them."

50. See "Hospitiality," in Jacques Derrida and Gil Anidjar, *Acts of Religion* (New York: Routledge, 2002). References in parentheses are to this work until further notice. For a critical, but not fully convincing treatment of Derrida's work on forgiveness, cf. Chris Kaposy, "'Analytic' Reading, 'Continental' Text: The Case of Derrida's 'On Forgiveness,'" *International Journal of Philosophical Studies* 13, no. 2 (2005).

oped above in writing about God as a burglar, hospitality now *reveals* itself as something far more than a means for community. *Hospitality is the preparedness for the unprepared, the openness for that which one constantly forgets:* "In regard of this messianic surprise, in regard of what must thus tear any horizon of expectation, I am always, if I can say so, always and structurally, lacking, at fault, and therefore condemned to be forgiven or rather to have to ask for forgiveness for my lack of preparation, for an irreducible and constitutive unpreparedness" (p. 381). Because of the unexpected advent of the Messiah, Messiah is always the one who is not welcomed, the one who is not recognized as the coming guest, and thus he reveals that even when we might have a *disposition* for hospitality, this disposition is nevertheless insufficient to recognize or welcome him when he arrives. Thus, Messiah represents all those who are unwelcome, and when he reveals the impossibility of hospitality — as welcoming the unwelcome — he also reveals our need for forgiveness.

Hence, the positive phenomenon of hospitality reveals that there is built into the human condition something that calls for *forgiveness*. Forgiveness is also the most extreme form of allowing the other into my world, in spite of what he or she has done to me or not. Both forgiveness and hospitality cannot then be understood as phenomena that result from calculations or simply from obeying a rule. Derrida can say that "forgiveness granted to the other is the supreme gift and therefore hospitality par excellence" (p. 380). This gift-character of hospitality places it, like all other phenomena of a similar kind, outside of economy and calculation. Hospitality presupposes forgiveness, but is outside of control, as a gift: "Whoever asks for hospitality, asks, in a way, for forgiveness and whoever offers hospitality, grants forgiveness — and forgiveness must be infinite or it is nothing: it is excuse or exchange" (p. 380).

Derrida ends his discussion of hospitality and forgiveness by pointing to the problems inherent in offering others forgiveness. The reason is not because the perpetration is too large to be forgiven, or the impossibility of forgiving on behalf of others. Both these might sometimes be the case. What he addresses is the kind of position in which I place myself when I forgive someone — or, to play a little on the Hegelian dialectics of recognition, in what position the other places me when she asks *me* for forgiveness. What Derrida does, however, is profoundly theological: he points to how this dialectic between two parties refers them to a third, who is then — as the God of justice — the only possible giver of forgiveness, and the only one to which one can give oneself over. *I cannot give myself the right to forgive,* stresses Derrida:

> "I beg your pardon" is a decent statement — "I forgive you" is an indecent statement because of the haughty and complacent height it denotes or connotes. Who am I, who do I pretend to be to thus grant myself the right to forgive? If forgiveness can be asked for by me but granted only by the other, then God, the God of mercy, is the name of he who alone can forgive, in the name of whom alone forgiveness can be granted, and who can always abandon me, but also — and this is the equivocal beauty of this word abandonment — the only one to whom I can abandon myself, to the forgiveness of whom I can abandon myself. Thus, I have to ask the hôte for forgiveness because, unable to ever receive and give him enough, I always abandon him too much, but inversely, in asking the other for forgiveness and in receiving from him the forgiveness of him, I abandon myself to him. (p. 389)

The beauty and importance of this quote lies exactly in the connection it makes between hospitality and forgiveness: God is the host who invites to the banquet where everyone is welcome, and God is the source of and sharer of — giver of — forgiveness, as well. We shall see that this triadic relation between God, other, and self is even more emphasized in the way Jesus practices the hospitality of God when calling humans into a new community. Rowan Williams describes this in an apt manner:

> Jesus' characteristic hospitality extended to the rejected and marginal, and his acceptance of their hospitality extended to him (see, e.g., Mark 2:15ff., and parallels) is a paradigm instance of "embodied" grace. In word and act, Jesus rejects the world's rejections, and causes the rejected to become accepted. In his sharing of food with the tax-collectors and sinners, he creates for them a new relation with each other and by bringing them into relation with himself. The means by which God is met is a transaction which perceptibly changes the prevailing human state of affairs so that the victims become guests, receivers of gifts. Thus the shared table is the natural and indispensable extension of the "embodiment" of grace in Jesus' person: embodiment takes effect in the acts of the person.[51]

51. Rowan Williams, *Resurrection: Interpreting the Easter Gospel*, rev. ed. (Cleveland: Pilgrim Press, 2002), p. 99.

By practicing hospitality and forgiveness in this matter, Jesus is also revealing a new dimension in the answer to the question: Who is righteous? To this question we now turn.

Who Is Righteous?
The Kingdom and the Disruption
of Economies of Merit and Money

How does Jesus practice his understanding of God? The answer to that question is given in the way he preaches the kingdom of God and calls for a new and different community, a community that he, accordingly, both verbalizes and practices. Here, humans are not only invited into a new community, but ascribed a righteousness that is deeply connected to their recognition of Jesus as God's representative.

In the Beatitudes (Matt. 5), Jesus praises those who direct their longings and desires towards the future of God. Inherent in the situation of everyone who is described as blessed here is a *desire* for something else: for peace, for righteousness, for a better situation for those who need mercy, for a situation different from the one that creates mourning. This desire is for *the impossible,* i.e., for something that they cannot achieve or bring about themselves. Hence, they have to trust that this will come from the future — God's future. In this respect, they are blessed because they believe in God as the one for whom all things are possible. The desire for the impossible is therefore coupled to a belief in the one for whom all things are possible. From this angle, thus, the Beatitudes seem to express elements that are in accordance with the angles suggested in the Introduction.

However, there is more to be said here, as one also has to ask what is the content of these impossible desires? Apart from the last (Matt. 5:10-11, on persecution), all the desires recognized by Jesus as important (but not constitutive, see below) for being blessed, express the longing for a different world: where no one mourns, where righteousness and peace rule, where mercy is shown, etc. These features express a social world in which people are positively related to each other, and where conditions for a common life — in recognition and witnessing — are sustained far better than in a world where these features are missing.

When Jesus speaks about the future like this, he describes what is to come in the future as the constitutive reason for the blessedness of the people in question: They are blessed because they orient themselves from the point of view of hope for God's future. To be open for *that which is not yet,* for that which one cannot make happen, but which the future may make happen, is to be open for the reality of God. Jesus links the future to the experiences, desires, and longings of people by bringing witness to what they can expect and continue to hope for in the future. He confirms the validity of their desires, and recognizes them as not in vain. He thereby makes it possible for those who are peacemakers, etc., *to identify themselves as part of God's future.* From the described future determined by God, they can recognize themselves as directed towards a common future.

Again, we can consider what might be the case if the word "God" was not linked to the desired future of such people. They would then have no chance of recognizing what they strived for as part of God's world. Hence, they would also have no chance of understanding the goodness of their desired world as something related to the one who created this world for the good. By expressing how their longings and desires will lead them to a full realization of community with God, Jesus not only testifies to the relations between them and God. He also suggests that the relation and the community in question have this quality because they are directed towards the good of others: those who are in need of mercy, peace, righteousness, etc. Hence, a relation between three parties is involved here: this is not only a way of expressing how God and the listeners are related; it is a way of expressing how God and the listeners are related *when the listeners relate to others.* The three parties taken together thereby express the commonality and sociality of the future of God, where no one is excluded or marginalized by injustice, war, suffering, etc. The Beatitudes thus express the social and inclusive character of the kingdom of God, and the impossibility of assessing the blessedness of a person as separated from how he or she relates to the Other, and thereby — implicitly or explicitly — to the future of God. Those described as blessed by Jesus are already practicing and anticipating a community in which justice and peace are present.

The blessed are not so because of their merit, though. They are blessed because of their expectation of the future of God, and the fact that their good works make people "glorify their Father in Heaven" (Matt. 5:16).

They witness to God; they are images or representatives of the kingdom and goodness of God.

It is against this background and in the context of the triangle God–Other–Self that Jesus' call for wholeheartedness and his radicalization of the law make sense. Those who can be righteous are those who are open to the future of God, and practice the law according to an openness for the Other that is behind and beyond the concrete commandments of it. Moreover, this context of interpretation also makes sense of *who* it is that Jesus calls to repent: not those who seek him and his company, but those who are offended by the fact that he mingles with "sinners." When Jesus addresses some of his contemporaries as hypocrites, it is because they live within a horizon where the other — as the third party of the described triangle — has no place. Hence, there are no real fruits from their piety, and accordingly, no righteousness either. The only way to overcome the temptations in a piety based on the law is to focus on the Other as the recipient of such fruits.

The practice Jesus calls for is one beyond calculation and reasonableness; it is one of excess, to go two miles instead of one, to lend to anyone who asks, etc. — all this points toward practices that break down any pattern of mutuality, reciprocity, and calculation.[1] On the other hand, it is still possible to claim that such practices open up to *the good*. They signify that the other is recognized and considered as one who has a share in your life, and suggest a social world where goodness is beyond what can be secured by conceptions of merit and mutual accountability. To radicalize the demands of the law to the extent Jesus does also serves to expose whom one is most concerned with in one's practices: with either oneself or the other. Hence, this radicalization contributes to the revelation of hypocrisy. Consequently, hypocrites are disclosed as needing salvation just as much as those standing outside the circles of social and religious establishment.

I think we can see the social dimension in Jesus' ministry clearer against this background as well. What Jesus does when he dines with sinners is to establish a community that is not based on merit and that manifests grace and gift. Of course, the inclusiveness of his practices offended

---

1. These practices can also contribute to opposing the practices of repression and exploitation, as is pointed out by Marcus J. Borg, *Jesus: Uncovering the Life, Teachings, and Relevance of a Religious Revolutionary,* 1st ed. (San Francisco: HarperSanFrancisco, 2006), pp. 247ff.

those who had established their position on their assumed difference over against that kind of company. However, Jesus calls both parties, those who are marginalized by others and those marginalizing, into the same community. He thereby indicates that they have something in common, both in terms of the gifts they receive from God and in terms of their calling to be God's image. The recognition of this God-constituted community is part of his call to reconciliation: he is calling people to reconcile and to overcome diversities and splits that are due to human-based conceptions about who does and does not belong to such a community. In this way, Jesus reveals that the righteous are those who long for community, for participating in a world where the Other has a place. Righteousness is not primarily a question of agency, but of relating and relationship. Implicit in the community Jesus opens up is the recognition of the Other as one with whom I share a common destiny as being called to the future of God. I need to repent if I exclude the other from my conception of that future, and see it as something I merit by my own work, instead of seeing it as a gift of God.

To say that Jesus is calling the marginalized into community is not original. It is nevertheless important to realize what it means. As we become persons by being in relationship with others, and are shaped through social interaction, this call to community can have dramatic effects — salvific effects, even — on human life:[2]

> The individuality recreated by Jesus' call re-orientates the called person in his or her future relations, and it is this which is its essential feature. That it means being at Christ's disposal rather than at that of "the things of this world," however, must not be individualistically misunderstood. This transformed individuality is not an ascetic retreat from the world, still less from every reality except the disciples' own. The transformation propels them either back into the social context from whence they emerged or else into some other.[3]

Alastair McFadyen holds that this is saying something about both Jesus and the people he is calling. As for Jesus' personal identity, it was marked

---

2. Cf. Alastair I. McFadyen, *The Call to Personhood: A Christian Theory of the Individual in Social Relationships* (Cambridge and New York: Cambridge University Press, 1990), passim, esp. pp. 47ff.

3. McFadyen, *The Call to Personhood*, p. 56.

by what he calls a liberatory aspect. In Jesus' invitation to others, he established relations on a different basis from those in which they were currently situated. In this way, the *recognition* he offered also had a strong impact on their self-understanding:

> In his communication he intended people in a radically different form from others' intention of them and their own self-intention; different that is, from the prevailing patterns of co-intention from which their personal identities had been sedimented. He could therefore decisively reject the expectations others had of them and which had been ossified into self-identities appropriate to such a network of expectations. Jesus found broken, closed and communicatively distorted people in distorted and closed relational networks. The Gospel set people free by placing them firmly in an alternative communication context from which a new identity could be sedimented, even though their social situation might remain materially unchanged. [. . .] He pulled the possibilities of future emancipation into the present and thereby established new possibilities of identity with and for them.[4]

Against this background the overcoming of marginalization is not only to be understood as "being included in a community" but also as a new chance for developing future possibilities, including that of identity. This practice, in which Jesus confirms that he is not complacent with present religious or social conditions, could not be manifested unless Jesus had a radically different understanding of himself and the people he met than the one offered by his contemporaries and present in the dominant religious and social context of understanding.

A Community of Excess

Sharing in community with Jesus leads to surplus and excess. This feature is most vividly expressed in the reported feeding of large crowds. All the evangelists report such incidents. In these reports the point seems to be not only to report how many people were actually fed, but also how much food was left as a surplus after the meal.

However, such reports are not only signals of the surplus present

---

4. McFadyen, *The Call to Personhood*, pp. 117-18.

where the kingdom of God manifests itself. When such excess is at hand, no one is left outside the circle of sharing; everyone can have a part. Thus, these stories testify to the same kind of community as the one indicated above, one in which the focus on the other is mirrored in the lack of consideration for oneself. When one is not keeping the goods for oneself, there is a different kind of social world possible. It is when the other is closed off from my world that a future like the one God promises through Jesus becomes impossible.

The presence of Jesus, or the presence of the kingdom that Jesus manifests in the way he relates to and shapes a community with others, also leads to a revaluation of all values, to speak in Nietzschean terms. This revaluation implies that what is valuable is considered differently than it would be in a context in which the price of commodities is in focus. It is exactly the inclusive and accepting presence of Jesus that leads to such a revaluation. Mark also suggests that there is a close link between this revaluation and the final rejection of Jesus: In Mark 10, the question of what is an appropriate use of the costly nard is framed by narrative elements that lead to the betrayal of Jesus. The woman who pours the ointment on Jesus manifests her will for relationship, while those disputing this use of it, calling it waste, point to its monetary value. This also discloses what cannot be manifest when this gift is exchanged for money and given to the poor: money cannot testify in a similar way to Jesus as king, as the story implicitly suggests. It is clear that Judas takes offense at this use of resources, and that he is unable to see how apt it is to anoint Jesus as king.[5]

The revaluation of values in the practice of the community of the kingdom seems to disrupt an order or an economy where everything is estimated according to its monetary value. By positively recognizing the excessive use of the ointment by the woman, Jesus directs attention to the fact that there is a different reality than the one shaped by the value of money — and that this is manifested in the recognition of him as the king. Of course, this does not exclude considerations for the poor, but as indicated above, the inclusion of Jesus in the relation between the poor and the giver manifests a triangle relationship in which all three parties need to be recognized in order for the community not to be instrumentalized for egotistic purposes.

5. Cf. B. Chilton, "Friends and Enemies," in Markus N. A. Bockmuehl, *The Cambridge Companion to Jesus*, Cambridge Companions to Religion (Cambridge and New York: Cambridge University Press, 2001), p. 85.

Furthermore, stories like these — and we can include here also John's story about the wine in the wedding at Cana — may be read as *signs:* they signify a reality of surplus and excess where the affluence in question is not derived from the wealth of the people possessing it, but from the gifts of God. As signs, they point to a reality determined by God, and a reality in which scarcity and poverty are not determining the content of people's lives. Thus, these stories can create hope and articulate a vision of a different world that is nevertheless rooted in the needs, desires, and experiences of people, then as well as today. There is no need to spiritualize these stories as being about spiritual gifts. Such spiritualization allows them to have no connection to the experience people presently have of an unjust world where no such gifts are accessible. The signs of excess and surplus are, as indicated, signs of a reality where there are sufficient goods to care for the needs of everyone, and where competition for possessions, accordingly, is rendered unnecessary. In this way, the way Jesus describes the kingdom may also have an impact on how we critically assess the way the present world is ordered, and the principles according to which it is governed.

Excursus: The Community of the Church as a Sign of the Kingdom

The above interpretations suggest that the kingdom of God is the eschatological reality that becomes present in and through Jesus from Nazareth. The kingdom manifests God as creator, sustainer, and savior of the world, and expresses itself in the community of people recognizing this call. As the kingdom creates and sustains a new community between God and humanity and is linked to the presence of God in Jesus, *the church* is based on the acceptance of the proclamation of this kingdom by Jesus.

Against this background, the church is linked to and can be a sign of the kingdom, although it cannot be fully identified with it. This signifying character indicates that in some way or another there is a relation between the salvation given in the community of the kingdom and human morality. To find out what this relation is, we have first to ask in what way the church can be a sign of this eschatological reality that already manifests itself in the existence of the church. In the present excursus I will discuss this from the perspective of the church as a sign of the kingdom. While weight is given to the *moral sense* here, against the background developed in the book so far the moral dimension is a consequence of, and consecutive to, the *gift-character* of the kingdom, which manifests itself in the calling to God's inclusive community.

God's will and gifts in his creation appear as closely linked in this understanding of the kingdom of God. The underlying assumption here is that moral agency is informed by and carried out most adequately if it is based on what God has done already, and that this also helps us to understand the possible moral content of the proclamation of the kingdom of God. The gift is prior to any demand. It is important to stress this in order to reach the conclusion I am aiming at with the present discussion. Moreover, by suggesting a distinction between sign and symbol (see below) I try to spell out how we can also see signs of the kingdom outside the church. That there are signs and symbols of the kingdom *in* this world — also in the moral sense — tells us that there is a connection between what God does as creator and as savior of the world.

Since St. Augustine, theology has been familiar with the distinction between *signum* and *res* — sign and reality.[6] This distinction still proves a valid point of departure for discussing an understanding of the church as a sign of God's kingdom. By stating this, we are not saying that the church is the reality that it signifies, but are claiming that there is a specific relationship between the church and the kingdom of God. The differentiation of the two can be seen as an expression of the eschatological reality of the church: It is the place where the future is anticipated in faith and practice through the distribution and reception of the Word and the sacraments, where every human is placed in the same relation to God as recipient and part of God's community.[7] It is also a place where the reality of God's impossible future can already manifest itself in the works of love.

However, that the future can manifest itself in the present points beyond what the simple distinction between *signum* and *res* can capture. I therefore turn to Paul Tillich's understanding of the *symbol* to better understand what is going on. According to Tillich, a symbol is something that itself also takes part in what it symbolizes. Therefore, a symbol has an internal relation to that which it symbolizes. It also grows and dies according to the correlation between that which is sym-

6. See Augustine and R. P. H. Green, *Augustine: De Doctrina Christiana*, Oxford Early Christian Texts (Oxford and New York: Clarendon Press, 1995), vol. 2, pp. 1-3.

7. Cf. Wolfhart Pannenberg, *Systematische Theologie* (Göttingen: Vandenhoeck & Ruprecht, 1988), vol. 3, p. 50: "Die Kirche ist also nicht identisch mit dem Reiche Gottes, aber sie ist Zeichen seiner Heilszukunft, und zwar Zeichen in der Weise, daß die Heilszukunft Gottes darin selber schon gegenwärtig und den Menschen durch die Kirche, durch ihre Verkündigung und ihr gottesdienstliches Leben, zugänglich wird."

bolized and the persons who receive it as a symbol. Tillich holds that something can be a true symbol "only if it participates in the power of the divine to which it points."[8]

To understand the church as a sign or symbol of the kingdom of God lets us understand it as a place where this kingdom manifests itself *through* and *in* symbols as well. Such symbols, be it in acts or signs, point behind and beyond the present, and link the present to that which is not yet present, that which is not yet realized. The church must not be mistaken for being the kingdom of God itself, but there are good reasons for saying that it is constituted by the kingdom that it signifies.[9] The direction here is important: The kingdom of God is not something that is constituted by the faith or the acts of the members of the community. Members of the church believe and act as they do because they have already met and received the community of the kingdom of God.

This excludes understanding the kingdom as something being brought forth by human action. Instead, it seems more appropriate to say that faith and action are being brought to presence by the (promise of) the kingdom. This way of understanding the relationship between the church and the kingdom of God reflects a central insight in Lutheran theology, developed on the basis of reflections on how to understand the good works of a Christian.

In his treatise *On Good Works (Von den Guten Werken)* Luther emphasizes that the point of departure for the moral conduct of a Christian is his/her reception of the new life through the gospel. An important tacit assumption is that the gospel gives the human being her true basis for agency in the world. This is not an argument that only the Christian is able to do good works, but more an argument for what good works are in their *proper* function: They are to be understood as means by which God's will becomes visible in the world. Hence, we can see Luther's understanding as fully in accordance with what has been developed so far in this book. For Luther this is important, since it reframes the good works from one functional context to another: They are taken out of a context where the human being uses good works to glorify himself and establish his own righteousness by merit, and instead they are integrated in a context where the law is not used for expressing human *hubris,* but for serving God through the neighbor.

The discussion in *On Good Works* is relevant in our context, since it points exactly to the role ethical works play in the life of believers. If one underscores faith exclusively, and ignores works, one easily ends up in *antinomism.* For Luther

---

8. Paul Tillich, *Systematic Theology,* vol. 1 (London: SCM, 1978), p. 239.
9. Cf. Pannenberg, *Systematische Theologie,* vol. 3, p. 42.

(as for the more recent writers of the *Joint Declaration on the Doctrine on Justification*), it is important to avoid such misunderstandings.[10] Taking his point of departure in tradition and in the Ten Commandments, he interprets those commandments from his understanding of the gospel.[11]

Luther interprets the commandment "You shall have no other gods before me" in a way that makes visible how the human being ought to trust no one but God in his agency. Anyone who is self-confident in a way that ignores her basic dependence upon God has already acted against this commandment. Hence, there is no neutral status for the moral agent: We are already qualified *either* by our faith and trust in God *or* by the lack of faith and trust when we act.[12] Accordingly, no works can make the human being appear before God as righteous if these acts are not based on faith in God.[13] Anyone trying to appear *coram Deo* as righteous due to her own merit, is *de facto* making visible how she has broken the first commandment. Thus, the basic element in relation to God is faith and not works. We could perhaps say that faith encloses the good works and thus gives them their truly right position in relationship to God.

The major theological point behind this is, accordingly, that it is God, and what God has revealed in Christ, that human beings should put their trust in as a basis for their good works. The human being does not constitute the goodness of the world through her acts. Therefore, we are to take our point of departure in what God has already done, and make visible — witness to — how our works are accomplished because of God's gifts to us. This is the only way our works can serve the glory of God. Any attempt to base agency on our own capacities or abilities Luther interprets as idolatry.[14] Faith turns out to be the fundamental relation to God,

---

10. See *Joint Declaration*, § 16: "Together we confess: By grace alone, in faith in Christ's saving work and not because of any merit on our part, we are accepted by God and receive the Holy Spirit, who renews our hearts *while equipping and calling us to good works*" (my emphasis). Cf. § 35, which states that "God's commandments retain their validity for the justified."

11. In doing so, Luther continues a long tradition of natural law in theology, building on the assumption that those commandments are sufficient in order to shape our moral conduct (cf. WA 6, 204). See for this more generally Gunther Wenz, "Die Zehn Gebote als Grundlage Christlicher Ethik: Zur Auslegung der ersten Hauptstücks in Luthers Katechismen," *Zeitschrift für Theologie und Kirche* 89 (1992): 409.

12. This is perhaps most vividly expressed in Luther's *De Servo Arbitrio*.

13. WA 6, 211.

14. Cf. WA 6, 210. R. Schäfer interprets the righteousness that the non-believing human seeks to base on works as practical atheism: "Wenn der Mensch meint, daß er Gott nur durch die Werke gefalle, dann vertraut er nicht auf Gott, sondern auf sich selbst. Er ehrt

and therefore also the basic condition for living as God intends. This is why Luther also can say that faith may be enclosed in a commandment.[15]

As indicated, what Luther does is then nothing else than reformulate the functional context in which ethics appears in the teachings of Jesus. He makes apparent how the lack of confidence in the gifts of God, and in the righteousness God offers, is the object towards which Jesus directs his harsh critique of the piety of the Pharisees, etc. When this confidence is wanting, the human is forced to put his trust in himself — and to neglect that only God is God. But this critique in no way means that humans who believe are again "under the law" (cf. Rom. 7:6). Faith and freedom are tied closely together. Faith does not act due to force, but gladly and with good conscience. Faith shapes a trusting attitude towards the challenges of this world and openness toward the neighbor. That is why everything is dependent on faith — and the first commandment — in terms of our moral agency. The human being who is obedient to the first commandment, and lets God be God, is thus a theonomous being. Human theonomy is not opposed to human freedom, but a condition for freedom, as the human being through the relationship with God gains the freedom from sin (circling around oneself) and from the destroying power of the law (which tempts us to act for self-righteousness). When the law operates on the basis of the sinful human being, it is destructive. Hence, we are liberated by faith in Christ from the necessity of making our own merits constitute our righteousness.[16]

Luther thus reminds us of how we can regard our own works as signs of the kingdom: not as constituent elements of the kingdom, but as signs that manifest its presence already here and now. To the same extent as the good works of the church serve as a means for glorifying God, it can also be said that churches are signs of the kingdom.[17] They are so in an ethical sense as well, because any division between them also has an ethical dimension to it: Lack of unity is due to a lack of mutual recognition of equality. Such recognition, and consequently, such unity, is

---

äußerlich Gott, setzt sich aber inwendig selbst zum Abgott ein." See Rolf Schäfer, "Glaube und Werke nach Luther," *Luther* 58 (1987): 76.

15. See G. Wenz, "Die Zehn Gebote als Grundlage Christlicher Ethik," p. 420, where he points out that this indicates how the commandment to believe in God expresses how the relationship towards God in no way can be taken to be neutral, or to indicate that human freedom is grounded in the human being itself.

16. WA 6, 211.

17. We could here add that an alternative and obvious approach to the one here presented would be to develop the Lutheran and other understandings of the *notae ecclesiae*, and show how they also have a tacit ethical dimension.

necessary in order that churches can fulfill their calling to be signs or symbols of the kingdom. However, this calls for further clarification of the relationship between the kingdom on the one hand, and ethics on the other.

There are many reasons for regarding the ethicizing of the notion of the kingdom, which at least partly has taken place in theology since Kant, as a limitation of its full content.[18] There are also similar reasons for more postmodern attempts to interpret religion within a basically ethical framework, where it finally remains little more than a sophisticated call from the anonymous Other. There are two dimensions in the understanding of the kingdom of God that need to be seen as differentiated from each other, but are also in need of being held together if we are to provide a theological foundation for a fruitful discussion of the relationship between ethics and ecclesiology. In the following, I will develop these dimensions in somewhat more detail, with reference to recent discussions.[19]

The Norwegian New Testament scholar Hans Kvalbein argued some years ago that there are two basic approaches to understanding of kingdom of God in New Testament scholarship: On the one hand we find those following the line of, for example, H. Merklein, B. Chilton, and Jon Sobrino, stressing the kingdom of God as God's reign. To be in the kingdom of God is, according to this position, primarily to be under God's reign and to do his will. Kvalbein himself argues along a different line, where the kingdom of God — at least in the Synoptic Gospels — is "a concrete expression of the gift of salvation, the place of salvation and the time of salvation. It is not an abstract phrase for God's position or rule as king."[20]

Now, the first understanding of the kingdom as God's reign immediately opens the ethical dimension implied in the notion of the kingdom. However, it is also a line of thought that, if it is not interpreted carefully, can easily lead to a legalistic or moralistic ecclesiology. The basic challenge for this approach is to make clear that the kingdom of God is not constituted by our works, but that our works follow from the fact that God reigns and is offering his gifts. This seems to open up space for

---

18. I am thinking here especially of the theological tradition following Kant and partly also Hegel, e.g., R. Rothe, W. Herrmann, and A. Ritschl.

19. The following is partly based on and partly further elaborating elements from Jan-Olav Henriksen, "Guds Rike og Etikken — Uten Sammenheng? Linjer til en Systematisk-Teologisk Rekonstruksjon," *Tidsskrift for Teologi og Kirke?*, no. 1 (1998) ("The Kingdom of God and Ethics — No Connection? Lines for a Systematic-Theological Reconstruction"), in which I critically discuss the contribution of Hans Kvalbein in *Studia Theologica* 51 (1997).

20. H. Kvalbein, "The Kingdom of God in the Ethics of Jesus," *Studia Theologica* 51 (1997). He follows studies done by S. Aalen.

the intentions of the other line of interpretation: Here, the kingdom of God is exclusively understood as the place where God offers God's gifts to human beings.

I think, however, that it is mistaken to see these two lines as mutually exclusive.[21] I also think that the ethical claims put forward in the teachings of Jesus make sense only on the presupposition that there is a place and a time where God is acknowledged as the one who rules and offers gifts of salvation. In other words, the two lines should be seen as mutually dependent, and as something that *together* constitute the relationship between ecclesiology and ethics.[22]

Thus, the kingdom of God is a place where God is recognized as Lord, and where those who recognize his Lordship also — correspondingly — live by his gifts of salvation. Before the final coming of the kingdom this place is present in the Christian community, gathered around the gifts of Word and sacrament, and in visualizing the unity of humankind striven for. This community and its worship are also constituted by the tension between what is already present in the gifts and what is yet to come. As said already, the community and its worship cannot be identified with the kingdom of God. Yet it signifies the kingdom of God to the same extent that it anticipates this kingdom in its faith and practice.[23]

The crucial question, then, is how and to what extent the church can be said to be sign of the kingdom in its actual practice. How does the church signify the kingdom? First of all, I think there are good reasons to claim that any moral conduct connected to the kingdom of God is not set apart from the ethos possible for every human being to identify and understand. In other words, there can hardly be any ethics for the church that is not also aspiring to be an ethics for "the world" — for all God's creatures. Accordingly, the kingdom is not setting standards or norms that are relevant only for Christians. The demand for wholehearted love is a demand that God directs towards every human being. Hence, the rationale of the

---

21. Hence, I do not agree with Kvalbein, who tends to see the kingdom of God as an absolutely eschatological entity with no connection to the present in terms of ethics.

22. In this I agree with Wolfhart Pannenberg, *Grundlagen der Ethik: Philosophisch-Theologische Perspektiven* (Göttingen: Vandenhoeck & Ruprecht, 1996), who defines the kingdom of God as "Ort der Vollendung der Gemeinschaft der Menschen durch wahrhafte Gerechtigkeit und durch den darauf begründeten Friedenszustand" (p. 72). In other words, he too brings together the idea of the kingdom of God as a place, with an understanding of his reign. This also opens up the ethical relationship between the kingdom and the present situation: "Eine Begründung der Ethik vom Gedanken des Gottesreiches als der Zukunft des Guten her schließt darum auch die Bedingungen menschlicher Gemeinschaft in sich, wie sie in der Naturrechtstradition und in den zweiten Tafel des Dekaloges formuliert worden sind" (p. 72).

23. Cf. Pannenberg, *Systematische Theologie*, vol. 3, p. 44. Pannenberg does not, however, in his context stress the link between faith and practice the same way as I do.

commandments is rooted in the experienced goodness of their fruits, as I argue elsewhere in this text.

However, from what was said above about Luther's theology, the specific *point of departure* for moral conduct is different in the church than elsewhere: This point of departure is to be found in the sacramental community. From this flows the service of the church for the world, and in the liturgy the unity of humankind promised to be realized in the kingdom of God is already emergent. In the following, I present the outcome of some contributions that can help deepen the understanding of the church as a sign in a way specifying the ethical task of the churches:

To affirm the sacramental community as the point of departure is closely linked to one of today's challenges for the church: that of privatization and individualism. It is only by affirming that moral formation[24] takes place in a community where you are offered something, and where you are not asked to contribute everything yourself to the development of your continuing formation, that such formation can endure. On such a basis we can achieve a development of personal responsibility that is able to withstand, for example, the manipulative attempts of modern and postmodern consumer marketing. Without such community as its basis, Christian faith also lacks the resources for the full expression of its life.[25]

In this respect, a lesson can be learned from the understanding of ethics to be found in recent communitarian philosophy. Although I am critical of some of its expressions and its effectiveness as an overall framework for ethics, I think communitarianism is basically right in describing a local community of people sharing some of the same values and interests as an important and unavoidable factor in the constitution and development of moral character.[26] As communitarians consistently remind us, morality does not start with ourselves, but with the community to which we belong. Further, our moral agency also has its meaning only in relation to the shared worldview or beliefs of the community. Over against

24. I here adopt the vocabulary of the WCC report on Costly Obedience (1996), printed in Thomas F. Best, Martin Robra, and World Council of Churches, *Ecclesiology and Ethics: Ecumenical Engagement, Moral Formation and the Nature of the Church* (Geneva: WCC Publications, 1997).

25. "Der Christliche Glaube bedarf des Lebenszusammenhanges einer Gemeinschaft und kann nur im Zusammenhang einer Gemeinschaft sein Leben voll entfalten." Wolfhart Pannenberg, *Ethik und Ekklesiologie: Gesammelte Aufsätze*, 1. Aufl. ed. (Göttingen: Vandenhoeck & Ruprecht, 1977), p. 192.

26. See, e.g., Stanley Hauerwas, *A Community of Character: Toward a Constructive Christian Social Ethic* (Notre Dame: University of Notre Dame Press, 1981). I emphasize that this should not be taken as an advocacy for a general communitarian approach to Christian ethics (see next note).

any kind of "thin" description of morality based on human choice that is to be found in recent liberalism, the "thicker" description of the moral self offered by communitarianism seems to me more adequate if we want to reconstruct the moral contribution of the sacramental community in more philosophical terms.[27]

This can be further elaborated if we look to Wolfhart Pannenberg's work. He says that the sacramental community that links the individual Christian and Jesus together is also the basis for solidarity among Christians. Moreover, this bond to Jesus also implies a demand for solidarity with *all* human beings.[28] This has to be a central issue for the church, as the God of Jesus is the God of all humankind. Because of this, the communal life among Christians is to be understood as vicarious for all. Pannenberg writes:

> The Christian church has from its origins understood itself as a community that already on behalf of everyone who carries with her a promise of the consummation of all human community, lives a communal life in the spirit of love, freedom, and justice. To put it otherwise: The Christian community fulfills already in its present form of living together the reign of God, which is the future of the world and the whole of humanity.[29]

Although this is a rather ideal picture of what the church *de facto* does, I still think it is correct in terms of a theological description. Simultaneously it becomes visible how the church can be a sign of the kingdom in terms of its ethical life. It serves as such a sign to the same extent that it brings to vision how the reign of God is the true condition for peace and justice. It goes almost without saying that most churches still have some way left to go in terms of fulfilling this function. But Pannenberg's description also seems to suggest how the present life of the church still can be seen as a symbolic manifestation (in Tillich's sense) of what the king-

27. Hence, it is the communitarian understanding of the development of moral self-hood that I find most fruitful. Although I cannot develop it further here, I think that in today's pluralistic world it would be ignorant and perhaps even irresponsible to make communitarianism the sole basis of the ethics of the Christian church.

28. Pannenberg's point here can be taken as a minor correction of the WCC Uppsala 1968 report, which spoke of the church as a sign of the future unity of humankind (Uppsala 1968, German ed., p. 15), without making clear that this unity is based on the unity with God — a perspective that is found in Vatican II. According to Pannenberg, this leads to an overemphasis on the ethical, and a corresponding ignorance of the church's mission to proclaim a faith that is more than ethically relevant. Cf. Pannenberg, *Systematische Theologie*, vol. 3, p. 60.

29. Pannenberg, *Ethik und Ekklesiologie*, p. 193.

dom of God constitutes as the ethical basis for our priorities. As we are one in Christ, the unity we express in the celebration of the Eucharist, or the lack of such unity, also brings witness to the world of how we relate to each other, and how we deal with the challenge to recognize this unity in word and deed. It should not be underestimated how churches are a sign to the world in the negative sense also: They also witness that the unity and mutual recognition that will take place in the kingdom of God (see further on this below) is not yet present.

In many ways, there is an overlap between the ethical conduct of the church and that of other communities in respect to actual ethical content. The churches are not alone in the struggle for peace, justice, and love. Theologically speaking, this is due to the fact that all human beings have an insight into the law of God, and can act according to it, even outside the community of believers. However, such moral agency is only a *full* symbol of the kingdom when it is rooted in the recognition of and sharing of God's gifts of salvation, offered through the manifest presence of the means of grace. Without such a founding, any moral attempt is cut off from the new functional context of the law, as I develop it in the next section.

Based on the distinction between sign and symbol presented previously, I would like to suggest that non-church communities through their practices can offer signs of the moral content of the kingdom of God in terms of peace and justice. Such practice is also a manifestation of God's continuing work as creator. However, such practice is not a *symbol* of the kingdom, as it is not constituted by the kingdom. Symbols of the kingdom are only such practices that spring from the hope shared by the Christian community and shared in the anticipation of the kingdom through the Eucharist. Hence, the Eucharist is the point of departure of any symbol of the kingdom of God. Such symbols are not rooted in human action, but in the reign and will of God, and in the reception of God's gifts.[30]

From this it follows — and I want to emphasize this — that *there is no new normative moral content implied in the notion of the kingdom of God.* Sometimes the radicality of the moral teachings of Jesus is taken as an indication that it cannot be applied universally. Against such an understanding, I would say that it is radical — and it is for all. But it is given its rationale only by the notion of the fullness of gifts offered by God: This is clearly illustrated in the parable of the king and his servant debtor in Matthew 18:23ff., where the radical demand for forgiveness is

---

30. Cf. Pannenberg, *Ethik und Ekklesiologie*, p. 196, where he states how the church functions as sign and instrument not due to achievements of human power, but due to the community that is constituted by, and only can be constituted by, God.

only legitimate and appropriate on the basis that the king has already forgiven. The ungrateful servant is confronted with a demand that is clearly and rightly perceived as just, but only because of what he has already received himself.

We have already argued that the ethical demands put forward by Jesus are rooted in the gifts of God. It is these gifts that offer the good works a new functional context — by which our deeds and works can serve as symbols of the kingdom. There is one implication following from this that must be spelled out clearly. This understanding of what the kingdom of God consists in has material influence upon ethics. This is true in at least two directions: First, this understanding of the kingdom confines the function that the ethical realm has in the life of the Christian. It is not a presupposition for salvation. Hence, it is not morality that frames the totality of the life of a Christian but what she has received. Because of what she has received, ethics becomes a meaningful enterprise and not an unbearable burden.

Second, this relativizes the function of ethics in the life of the church. Although it is not to be taken as a statement that "ethics does not matter," it still implies that ethics is not the only thing that matters. There is something more fundamental to church life than ethics. And it is by making this visible that churches can serve as true signs of the kingdom *in* their diaconal work. If this is not made clear, churches are easily understood as tools for or institutions of moralism. Moralism expresses an approach to life that sees morality and law as the determining and most important frames of life. Hence, it ignores the claim that life is basically something good — and something received.

As said above, the kingdom of God does not give us any radically new ethical insights. But it must be stressed again that it gives us insight into a reality that provides us with another *framework* for our moral task. This is intimately linked to the understanding of the church as a symbol of the coming but already present kingdom, manifested in Word, sacrament, and works of love (in that order). As far as I can see, this is of importance for the relationship between ethics and ecclesiology in at least one important way: The churches have an obligation to realize coherence between their present practice and the stories and parables told by Jesus about the kingdom. This does not mean that the church shall understand itself as an example of the kingdom of God; but there has to be some kind of coherence if the church really can be said to participate in the reality to which it points and from which it derives its life. Without such coherence its life in witness to and service for the world will not be apparent.

The key *ethical* challenge emerging from the reality of the kingdom is to realize equality among human beings in a way that makes visible how God is the God of *every* human being, black and white, rich and poor, gifted and deprived, healthy and sick. The kingdom of God is an offer for everyone: We are offered to participate in the unity of all humankind in a way that recognizes that the other belongs to the same community as ourselves, a community with no recognized differences in status, privileges, or rights. The basis of this community is the realization that we are all equal before the God[31] who offers gifts to everyone. Speaking of this "kingdom of equality" in ethical terms implies the following:

- All human beings, morally speaking, are considered to be on the same level *coram Deo:* No one is righteous, and everyone is dependent on God in order to live and do good.[32]
- All human beings are equally dependent on God's grace.
- All human beings are equally dependent on God's rule and God's gifts and works in creation, whether they recognize God as Lord or not.
- God, who sends rain upon the just as well as the unjust (Matt. 5:45), can rightly demand that we recognize everyone else as recipients of God's love and care, and that we in our relationship to our neighbor take seriously our calling to realize and symbolize this love and care in the world, even if we can only do this in an imperfect and provisional way.[33]
- We can no longer judge people only by ethical standards. Any such judgment would rule out that our relationship to God is not only determined by the life we live, but by how we relate to and recognize God and God's presence in our lives. To judge a human being only on the basis of ethical standards is to ignore that it is something more and other than ethics that can and must tell us ultimately who this human being is.

Even though the equality of all human beings is given with creation, this equality is something that is renewed and recalled, recognized and deepened, through the salvific work of Christ and his proclamation of a kingdom for every

31. This position is also reflected in the following quote: "The Church becomes a Sign of the Kingdom of God when relationships within the Christian community are characterized by the recognition of the personal value and worth of each human being." World Council of Churches, Commission on Faith and Order, *Church and World: The Unity of the Church and the Renewal of Human Community: A Faith and Order Study Document,* Faith and Order Paper, No. 151 (Geneva: WCC Publications, 1990), p. 19.

32. Cf. *Joint Declaration,* § 25.

33. Cf. more concretely on this Charles S. Layman, *The Shape of the Good: Christian Reflections on the Foundations of Ethics,* Library of Religious Philosophy, vol. 7 (Notre Dame: University of Notre Dame Press, 1991), p. 126, where he discusses Galatians 3:28 and Ephesians 2:13f. as spelling out the consequences of this understanding.

human. This opens up an understanding of peace and justice as central values in human life as well as in the kingdom: Justice implies the recognition of the other's right to the same goods as I have myself, and a willingness to struggle for his/her participation or share in these goods. In a society where equality and justice are recognized, there will also be peace *(shalom)*. Such peace is more than the mere lack of conflict, more than is contained in the Roman *pacem.* It expresses the qualities necessary for a good life, and it constitutes this good life. Lack of peace is, *inter alia,* due to restriction of rights and abuse of power to protect privileges, and henceforth, due to lack of recognition of the other's equality with me. I think that the churches, as global communities, are today more than anything called to recognize that human-made borders and our established privileges in the western part of the world are not something the churches can promote and still be signs of the equality of the kingdom.

To serve as a sign of the kingdom is first to make clear that the church is not the kingdom, and that the final consummation of the kingdom is God's work and not the task of the church. But to be a sign is to *bear witness to the coming kingdom in word and deed.* If the church does not make clear the distinction between itself as symbol and the coming kingdom itself, the consequence will be that its proclamation of the kingdom loses its credibility. The all-too-human perception of the church's presence will provide for that.[34]

If the church is to serve as a sign, or better, as a symbol for the kingdom of God, it must through its witness in practice and proclamation make clear that human life in its fullness is something different from moral life. To make people see this is a way of making the kingdom be seen. The liberating force of this kingdom sets people free to serve God, without making them ultimately trust in their own works but on the gift of the promised kingdom. To help people to realize that human life is more than — but still also — moral life is a way of making human life better; it is a way of framing things in the right perspective. It is also a condition for avoiding any moralistic understanding of our moral agency. In this sense, the proclamation of the kingdom as something not dependent on our works is something that also fulfills a moral purpose, because it makes human life better, and moral life more modest in terms of what it can constitute and symbolize. Our moral life does not symbolize perfection — but it should point towards God who is the giver of all good gifts, the One who will eventually bring everyone and everything to perfection also as a gift.

---

34. Cf. Pannenberg, *Systematische Theologie,* vol. 3, p. 45.

Jesus' Reinterpretation of the Law: The Law in the Triadic Relation

Jesus deconstructs the function of the law as a means for being favorable in the eyes of God. Still, he emphasizes the importance of the law. It is as if he says: "You shall be righteous, but you cannot." This almost absurd paradox expresses the predicament of human existence. In order to make sense of it (yes, to make sense of the absurd) we have to understand the demand from another angle, which is the purpose of this section.

The law is not about achieving merit, or about getting a fair reward from God for good works. The law is the presence in the social world of the seen or unseen neighbor who is calling us to justice and to a manifestation of the structural order that allows for the presence of goodness in her life. God stands ultimately behind the call of the law. Thus there is a triadic relationship within which questions of the law belong. It is against this background that we can understand Jesus' attitude towards the law and the way he deals with its demands. According to Matthew, Jesus did not come to abolish the law — but to fulfill it (Matt. 5:17). There are two connected elements in his emphasis on the validity of the law that are important to note when we enter a discussion of this issue:

- The law still is valid — for the neighbor's sake.
- The law is not fulfilled by Jesus' opponents.

As said, the law is present as a calling to every human. The demands are high. They are so high that Jesus repudiates the Pharisees for not living up to the standards. The question then immediately arises, whether this does not mean that the standards are *too* high, such that no one is able to live up to them. And if this is the case, that no one is able to fulfill the law in a manner that can justify the claim for one's own righteousness, why continue to emphasize its demands? Is there any reason for perpetuating the claims of the law when no one can live up to them? The answer is yes. As long as the neighbor is in need, the presence of the calling of the law is valid. To understand the depth and warrant of its calling, we have to see God as the creator of the community to which all belong, and the one concerned with the welfare of the neighbor. The law exists as a means for recognizing the neighbor in need and my relation to her — and the function of the law is thus not to serve as a means for establishing own my righteousness. The high demands are thus for the neighbor's sake, not for mine. This comes to the fore most explicitly in the demand for neighborly love, which can never be for one's own sake, but always has to be for the sake of the other.

The reason why Jesus attacks the way the Pharisees practice the law is, against this background, most likely to be his opposition to the function *they* apply to the law, and for which purpose or in which context they understand its *rationale*. They seem to use the law as a means for establishing their own righteousness, but this righteousness is not conceived of as relationally conditioned in a way that allows for the presence of a relevant third party (in this case: the neighbor). By understanding the law as a means for gaining a status of righteousness, religiously understood, they in fact exclude the neighbor as a relevant party. Even admitting that Matthew exaggerates his critique of Pharisee piety (which no doubt was a sincere and deeply religious one), he still points to how the law in this context again functions to close off others, or to use others as mere negative or positive indicators of what you yourself wish to be.

A *recognition* of this negative use of the law underscores how the Pharisees used it to secure their own elaborated status, and not for serving the needs of the other. Thus, the relation of the other to the law becomes *instrumental:* the other is there only as a confirmation of my own ability to fulfill the law. I can understand my own position with regard to the law without taking the situation or the need of the other into account — she should take care of herself by means of her own relation to the law. When Jesus criticizes this way of understanding the righteousness gained from keeping the commandments, he is thereby not only questioning the ability of humans to obey the law, but also questioning the relationship to the other and *the functional context of the law.* Against this background it also becomes more understandable how he can confirm the validity of the radical demands of the law. But who can then be righteous? In what does righteousness then consist, given that all humans seem to be centered on themselves and their own agency, gain, and possibilities?

The only way to solve this seemingly unsolvable problem is to realize that, in spite of the confirmation of the validity of the law, Jesus also points to something *beyond* the law in his affirmation of its validity. Every human being — good or bad — is referred to the gifts of God, including the gifts of care and forgiveness. There is a realistic trait in Jesus' proclamation of the law, which we have already seen in his affirmation of the double commandment of the love for God and neighbor. Jesus knows that no one lives up to the demand of these commandments. But the consequence he draws from this is not — as one is tempted to immediately think — that one thereby is rejected. Instead, one is made dependent on forgiveness, and on the basis of this forgiveness, which implies recognition of a giving (and for-giving) God, one is included in the community of those who trust that the forgiveness and the gifts of God are the basis for participation in community with God.

Contrary to a scheme determined by human action and agency, the context for Jesus' proclamation of the law is thus the gifting God. The justice and righteousness that the law seeks to provide, and the community it shapes, have to be thought of as determined by God's gifts as they are recognized and testified to by humans, and not determined by what can be acquired by human agency alone. Hence, the righteousness that fulfills the law consists not so much in the concrete fulfillment of specific descriptions of demands as in the full desire for God and the love of the neighbor.

In one sense the one who responds to the demand of the law by saying, "This demand is too much," is justified in doing so. However, by realizing this, one is called to a new form of self-recognition: As incapable of fulfilling the law, one has to see righteousness as something conferred on us by God, and not established by our own agency. The new understanding of oneself in face of the law refers us back to a realization of how we — like every other human — are dependent on a forgiving and generous God and a forgiving neighbor. This is in itself a basis for a new community with other humans, and a reason for including others in our world instead of keeping them out or marginalizing them. Moreover, in this context the function of forgiveness appears: It is important in order to receive a new chance for reestablishing a positive relation to the other. This reestablishment is then and thus not determined by the failures of the past, but by what we can perceive as a common future in which we all belong.

There is a humanizing effect in forgiveness, not only in terms of softening and reestablishing relationships that might have been injured in the past, but also by making it possible to maintain the high standards of the law while realizing that it might not always be possible for us to fulfill it. The demands of the law would be inhuman and depressing without the possibility for love, mercy, and forgiveness. But to be referred back to the possibility of forgiveness allows for a space where humanity can flourish, and where the demand in the commandment of love is still recognized as valid and as something under which I stand. The importance of this configuration appears more clearly if we consider how it would be if the demand for neighbor love was relative. A relative demand would give us a chance to calculate, negotiate, or withdraw from it, given the "right" circumstances. This again would let the situation be determined by *us*, and not by the one who needs our attention, mercy, and care. It is exactly this radical demand determined by the other that secures a humanity where a self-sufficient subject is not the originating source of goodness. Rather, the source of goodness is a call from the other through the law. To obey this call is to bear "good fruits."

We can now spell out a connection between the commandment of love and forgiveness: Forgiveness is the radical reverse side of the commandment, and is not meant to abolish the commandment, but *make it possible.* Moreover, in a situation where people are not willing to forgive each other, it might be an expression of how they recognize themselves to be in a better moral position than the one being denied forgiveness. Although this might sometimes be justified,[35] such a denial could also mean that they are more concerned with their individual desires than with the other and her needs. When Jesus radicalizes the law, he points to how we nevertheless are dependent on the same gifts and conditions for life-fulfillment. This can be a motivation for meeting the other as we would prefer to be met ourselves (cf. Matt. 7:12), and it can prevent a form of self-righteousness that might place us outside some moral demands or consider them as something we have already fulfilled. A parable that illustrates this is the one about the unforgiving servant (Matt. 18:23ff.). It is the lack of love he himself shows to other debtors, and not his debt to his Lord, that in the end leads to his fall, in spite of the fact that the latter debt was much larger. Hence, what constitutes and justifies the accusation against him is a lack of love. This love could have been motivated by how much he himself had been forgiven. The parable also makes it apparent that God does not want our debts towards God to put at risk the relationship with God. What complicate the relationship are our own attempts to appear justified in our claims apart from or isolated from recognition of what we have received from God.

---

35. Hence, this should not be read as legitimating unconditional forgiveness against every perpetrator: Jesus' call for self-criticism here is directed toward those who consider themselves as morally superior in a manner that precludes them from seeing their own moral failure, cf. Matthew 7:4f.

By taking his point of departure in the double commandment of love, and focusing on the wholeheartedness toward the Other as the object of the law, Jesus opens up a different understanding of the law than the evangelists report as typical among his contemporaries. Keeping the law is not a question of keeping up appearances or of maintaining cultic purity, but has to do with understanding oneself as part of a triadic relation with God and the neighbor.

The Theo-logy of Generosity: Let God Be God!

It is easy to develop Jesus' criticism of how the law is practiced as simply directed toward a specific form of piety. However, if we do that, we miss the underlying *theological* concern of this criticism, a concern that is vital if we are to understand what made his theology one of conflict. The theological concern I am thinking of can be formulated as this: *God cannot be integrated into a framework in which human action is the main, constitutive component, as this would make what God does and does not do dependent on what humans do.*[36]

From this angle, we get an interesting framework for understanding the parable about the workers in the vineyard (Matt. 20:1ff.). They all get paid the same, no matter how long they have been working. One of the usual interpretations of this is that this shows how God is willing to give everyone according to their needs, and that providing the workers with one day's wage is an appropriate response to that need. This interpretation can be supplied by one that underscores how God is generous toward every human, no matter how much or little they are able to serve God. While there may also be relevant points along such lines of interpretation, I would suggest that there are two, far more striking features in the parable that are also more in accordance with the angles we have suggested previously:

First, the parable suggests that God refuses any attempt to be drawn into a humanly conceived economy. God is not paying according to labor done, but according to what God sees fitting. Hence, the work done is not the main condition for how the workers are paid. If they try to understand

---

36. I need to make a distinction between the senses in which God is dependent on humans and not: on being witnessed to, but not *fully* in order to give gifts and allow for generosity to flourish in creation.

the wage from that perspective, it appears unjust. However, if we understand the payment from the perspective of the landowner, what he does when paying according to his own richness and generosity, is that he maintains his sovereignty; he is not subjected to any other's rule, nor determined by them. Given that this point is valid, what Jesus does in the parable is to say that any attempt to determine what God should reward or not, according to a human understanding of an economic world, is totally in vain. As a result, God can be God only by being outside such determination.

Second, the order expressed in the wages paid is an order not only of goodness and generosity, but of excess. Some of the workers are paid far more than they expected. Nevertheless, no one can claim to be unjustly treated in terms of having been paid too little, or of not having been paid according to the agreement. The conclusion to the parable, where the landowner asks "Are you envious because I am generous?," suggests not only that generosity is an issue here, but also that the responses of the workers who had labored all day are inadequate in terms of considering the neighbor's needs. Had they evaluated the wage from the other's perspective instead of from their own, they would have appreciated the payment of others as much as they appreciated their own.

From this angle the challenge is directed against those who try to restrict the generosity and the excess of God's gifts by introducing their own conditions for whether or not generosity applies. This is just another way of attempting to make oneself (a controlling) god (as the one who determines reality) instead of letting God be witnessed as a generous God. There is also a critique implied in this parable that is directed against any kind of human-made modes of inequality and human conceptions of what is just. The very rejection of using merit (and of versions of the law that can be used for achieving merit) as a condition of a privileged relationship with God, and a relationship where the other is excluded, might be provoking for anyone who thinks there are reasons for such conceptions. The overcoming of such conceptions seems, however, to be a prerequisite for establishing a form of social justice in which the needs of everyone are cared for. Moreover, the rejection of a merit economy is also consonant with the primary commandment to love the neighbor as yourself: when the commandment is fulfilled, one does not primarily have a concern for getting what one merits oneself, but cares for the other as the object of love.

Against this background it becomes even clearer why Jesus sees *wealth* as a challenge for achieving true righteousness. As indicated, wealth allows us to draw a circle around ourselves, and distracts us from living wholeheartedly for God and the neighbor in the triangle where the law can fulfill its function in human life (cf. Matt. 6:19ff.; 19:16ff.; Luke 12:13ff.). However, not only wealth does this, but also human traditions may contribute to empty practices that are of no help to the other or the one in need. Jesus addresses such practices, for example, in Matthew 15:3ff., where he uses his own understanding of the rationale of the law (as expressed in the above-formulated triangle) as a basis for criticizing a tradition in which the law no longer serves those in need. The case in question is one in which the elderly father and mother are neglected for the sake of appearing concerned about religious issues instead.

Rationale of the Law and Justice Behind the Law

Given that the law is there for the neighbor, and can serve its proper function only within the triangle of God, other, and self, Jesus' opposition to the contemporary traditions of law-abiding practices becomes understandable. When he rejects these practices, it is not because he is against the law as such, but because he is against uses of the law that leave the neighbor out of the picture. Moreover, we can apply the resources that this interpretative framework offers us not only for understanding the critique of Jesus against practices of the law in his contemporary situation, but also to back the claim that the concrete interpretations offered by this framework are of relevance in the present as well. We might also, with the help of this framework, be able to understand what postmodernists aim at when they talk about *the Law behind the law:* that there is something beyond the ethical demand that cannot be fully and exhaustively expressed in human action and agency, but which nevertheless demands that we direct our concrete actions towards the well-being of the neighbor.

Against this background, there are two issues that call for discussion: the first is whether the elusive and non-articulate character dimension in the law makes it completely irrational, and consequently, if it makes the one who obeys it, and his or her practice, opaque or irrational. The second is what sense we can make of this understanding of the law from postmodern angles, in addition to what has already been suggested about its non-disputable demand mediated by the presence of the Other.

There are good reasons to reject an understanding of the law as grounded in some kind of opaque or irrational mystery. Two examples might indicate why this is so. First, there is Jesus' opposition against the way the Sabbath commandment is practiced (Matt. 12:1ff.; Mark 3:2ff.). Although his critique creates disturbance, he is nevertheless able to argue that the insights of the hearers themselves testify to the rationale of doing good on the Sabbath. By appealing to such insights (as in Luke 6:9 and 13:15), Jesus makes apparent the connection between *experienced goodness* and *the law:* it is because of the consequences of goodness (the fruit produced) that we evaluate some deed appropriate and not. Any attempt to make empty or vain actions more proper in religious terms immediately establishes a practice outside the triangle of God–Self–Other.

We need here only to make a short remark about the present relevance of this point. It basically implies that there are criteria in experience for claiming that an action is according to the law of God or not, and that these criteria are derived from the fruits of the actions in question. Hence to claim that something is good only because it is expressed in a specific and contextually conditioned version of how one understands this law will not do the trick of convincing those who are not able to see the good in the action in question, and rightly so. When there is no possibility of establishing corroborating experience that can warrant an action as good, there are — given this understanding of the rationality of the law — no reasons whatsoever for holding this as a valid position for Christian ethics.[37]

There might be one objection raised to this way of arguing for the rationality of Christian ethics from a contemporary point of view: some of the ethos of Christianity is not directed directly toward the neighbor, it is said. Instead, it has to do with holiness and with the purity that the people of God are called to exhibit. With regard to this strategy, there are two things to be said: First, the argument then seems to root the understanding of what is right and good in more than 2000-year-old convictions of pu-

---

37. This position also implies that I reject an approach that tries to understand the law within the framework of the *Divine Command Theory,* saying that whatever God has commanded is good, just because God commanded it. What characterizes Jesus' approach to the law is that he not only displays its *rationale* in the concern for the other, but that he also argues for the experienced goodness, and from the force of this goodness for understanding what is the good to do. See also below on the discussion of Derrida on the force of the law.

rity and defilement, related to a totally different culture and different concerns. As this argument is presently made to secure a special way of understanding proper sexual relations, one then immediately has to ask why this way of arguing is not applied in the same manner to other issues, for example, those of eating.

Second, the above argument immediately falls short of understanding Jesus' own opposition against a blind practice of purity and defilement, most vividly expressed in his and the disciples' plucking of grains, but also in his reassessment of what is to be considered clean and not (Mark 2:23-27; 7:19ff.). Thomas Kazen, who has investigated thoroughly Jesus' relations to purity, concludes his study by pointing out that Jesus' behavior may be understood as indifferent towards such practices, and there are clear signs that it was interpreted as such by his adversaries. He concludes by addressing how we are today challenged to interpret and understand the attitudes of Jesus:

> In this process of reflection and interpretation, participants may find something revealed in Jesus' behavior and attitude to impurity, which may be wrought within the bonds of a given social context and cultural paradigm, although not without conflict and tension — something which gives priority to human needs, preference to social fellowship, and power to overcome segregation, and thus has relevance not only in an historical past, but in our contemporary world.[38]

Given that Kazen is right, and I think he argues the case convincingly, Jesus puts the ethos related to purity behind the concern for the well-being of the neighbor. Hence, he not only evaluates them as different in terms of how much they should inform our actions, he also stresses that there are some concerns that basically override others. This means that an ethos based on purity will have little or no impact in itself — it will probably most of all serve the function of establishing a specific *identity*. However, we can read the totality of Jesus' practice as directed *against* such an identity politics, where some people are distinguished from others in terms of what they do and how they practice. Such identities are only superficial: it is the fruits in the life of the neighbor that count, and hence, your identity cannot be separated from how you relate to her and what conditions for

---

38. Thomas Kazen, *Jesus and Purity Halakhah: Was Jesus Indifferent to Impurity?*, Coniectanea Biblica. New Testament Series, 38 (Stockholm: Almquist & Wiksell, 2002).

life you contribute or offer her.[39] Moreover, by always calling attention to *the other* as the third party in the relation between self and God, Jesus can be seen to *destabilize* any religious identity *based* on a specific ethics.

There still remains, however, the question of how we can make this understanding of Jesus' attitude toward the law, and of its rationality, something that also speaks to present postmodern understandings of law. In an essay called "Force of Law: Mystical Foundation of Authority,"[40] Derrida distinguishes between the force of the law, the law itself, and justice, in a way that I suggest sheds important light on Jesus' approach to the law.

First, Derrida holds that the way the law is practiced is internal to the law itself: "Applicability, 'enforceability,' is not an exterior or secondary possibility that may or may not be added as a supplement to law. It is the force essentially implied in the very concept of justice as law, of justice as it becomes law, of the law as law" (p. 233).

Derrida points to how law is thus not only rooted in practice, but also that this practice or enforceability can manifest itself in different ways: from being enforced, on the one hand, to being practiced based on understanding and insight, on the other. When law is practiced, it consequently implies more than law. It implies force, be it in terms of the power of understanding, or be it in terms of coerciveness. The law is as a result something that, in one way or another, *forces itself upon us,* but it is not something purely external; often the force is internal. However, my point in using Derrida here is to underscore how the law that functions and forces itself upon us might be very different in different situations, and is strongly tied to the kind of social situations and contexts within which it is practiced:

> There are, to be sure, laws [lois] that are not enforced, but there is no law [loi] without enforceability and no applicability or enforceability of the law [loi] without force, whether this force be direct or indirect,

---

39. At this point I am critical of understanding Christian ethics as solely communitarian. If such an ethics is presented as the ethics expressing Christian identity, it again expresses a binary direction where the other as the third is left out of the picture, giving priority to the relation between self and God in the way ethics and good works is understood. Such binary constitutions of ethics easily marginalize the other as the third, and render him/her as secondary, and not as primary, in the fulfilling of the ethical task.

40. Jacques Derrida and Gil Anidjar, *Acts of Religion* (New York: Routledge, 2002). References in parentheses in the following are to this volume until further notice.

physical or symbolic, exterior or interior, brutal or subtly discursive —
even hermeneutic — coercive or regulative, and so forth. (p. 233)

Derrida holds the law as something that is essentially possible to *deconstruct*. By being such the law is per se not to be taken as the final expression of the moral demand. He gives himself two reasons for this
deconstructive possibility of law. It may be constructed upon interpretable
and transformable textual strata. Given that this is the case, any kind of
historicizing of the law will have deconstructive impact on it. But the law
may also be deconstructed "because its ultimate foundation is by definition unfounded" (p. 243). Such a lack of foundation opens up to all possible transformations and interpretations. Nevertheless, as he says, "The fact
that law is deconstructible is not bad news." The possibility of deconstruction (note: not abolition, not rejection) of the law may be part of what
constitutes political progress. However, it also opens a paradox:

> [I]t is this deconstructible structure of law or, if you prefer, of justice as
> law, that also ensures the possibility of deconstruction. Justice in itself,
> if such a thing exists, outside or beyond law, is not deconstructible. No
> more than deconstruction itself, if such a thing exists. Deconstruction
> is justice. It is perhaps because law (which I will therefore consistently
> try to distinguish from justice) is constructible, in a sense that goes be-
> yond the opposition between convention and nature, it is perhaps in-
> sofar as it goes beyond this opposition that it is constructible — and so
> deconstructible and, better yet, that it makes deconstruction possible,
> or at least the exercise of a deconstruction that, fundamentally, always
> proceeds to questions of law and to the subject of law. (p. 243)

What Derrida says here is basically clarifying the structure in Jesus'
attitude toward the law as well: The law can be deconstructed because
there is something behind or beyond law that expresses itself through and
by it: Justice. When justice no longer is secured by the law, the law has to be
deconstructed — but justice is in itself not possible to deconstruct. By
identifying deconstruction with justice, Derrida makes it possible for us to
identify Jesus' criticism of law as deconstruction, but this is then exactly a
deconstruction that is identical with the attempt to secure justice.

The most important claim in the quote from Derrida above, however, is that he says that *the law makes deconstruction possible*. The corollary
to this is, of course, that justice and deconstruction in one sense can be

identified. By claiming that the law makes deconstruction *possible,* Derrida in fact says that the law makes justice possible. On the other hand, they cannot be identified, and the model of thought he applies suggests that justice also expresses itself in the law. That, on the other hand, would mean that the law also implies what makes it possible to deconstruct it: By always pointing to justice, it allows for justice to break in and deconstruct the concrete shape of the law for the sake of Justice, and this justice can never be thought of apart from the Other. What Jesus does when he radicalizes the law and makes it impossible to keep, is that he appeals to the law for the sake of justice — and he thereby deconstructs the absoluteness of law by making its claims absolute *in the name of the Justice for the Other.* This radicalization points to the impossibility of justice, which nevertheless has to be proclaimed for the sake of Justice, but justice is never exhaustively captured in the enforcement of law:

> Justice is an experience of the impossible: a will, a desire, a demand for justice the structure of which would not be an experience of aporia, would have no chance to be what it is — namely, a just call for justice. Every time that something comes to pass or turns out well, every time that we placidly apply a good rule to a particular case, to a correctly subsumed example, according to a determinant judgment, law perhaps and sometimes finds itself accounted for, but one can be sure that justice does not. (p. 244)[41]

The shortcoming of law lies in its inability to express the *surplus* of every situation, the surplus that might express itself *positively* as justice. Hence, Derrida and Jesus both seem to realize that there is a finitude, even a kind of confinement, implied when the law is absolutized or envisaged as saying it all. Moreover, Derrida pinpoints another feature of the law that links it to what we have already developed critically: law is not justice, because

---

41. Kevin J. Vanhoozer, "Theology and the Condition of Postmodernity," in *The Cambridge Companion to Postmodern Theology,* ed. Kevin J. Vanhoozer (Cambridge: Cambridge University Press, 2003), p. 18, elaborates on this in a way that links the impossible to faith, and allows for the struggle for justice to emerge from the same source as faith: "Derrida's affirmation of the impossibility of justice, and the gift, is a gesture not of nihilistic despair but rather of faith: the desire for something *other* than what obtains in the present world order. Some such expectation of 'the other to come' is inscribed in the very structure of deconstruction and what gives it its 'messianic turn.' Postmodernity abolishes conceptual idolatry, one might say, in order to make room for faith."

"Law is the element of calculation" (p. 244). By contrasting calculable law with incalculable justice, Derrida not only opens up a richer understanding of what justice means than the one possible when one identifies justice with living in accordance with the law, he also suggests that *justice relates the impossible and the incalculable:*

> [I]t is just that there be law, but justice is incalculable, it demands that one calculate with the incalculable; and aporetic experiences are the experiences, as improbable as they are necessary, of justice, that is to say of moments in which the decision between just and unjust is never insured by a rule. (p. 244)

When we then relate this to Jesus' criticism of blind obedience to the letter of the law, as in his criticism of the practices surrounding the Sabbath, Derrida as well suggests that the decision about what is just cannot be secured by a norm alone. Derrida calls experiences of justice aporetic exactly because they cannot be derived from calculation or directly instigated from a certain practice: they contain a surplus in terms of what can be anticipated or calculated that make them belong to the realm of the impossible. Nevertheless, as both Derrida and Jesus suggest, the impossible happens — justice *reveals* itself again and again.

Regina M. Schwartz, in her article "The Revelation of Justice,"[42] contributes further to the parallelizing of Derrida with the teachings of Jesus as we have developed them here, when she contrasts justice understood as revelation with injustice as idolatry. As she indicates, the reason for this is to be found in the fact that idolatry does not only imply that there is a false object of worship, but that there is a false manner of worshiping as well. Schwartz identifies one of the main features of this wrong way of worshiping as *possessing,* and claims that there are violent costs to such a form of idolatry: "When we imagine that we possess God, we can use him as a legitimating instrument for our violence. Such a God can authorize the slaughter of our enemies" (p. 340).

This violence might come from a religiously masked form of piety that claims that God *possesses us* as well. The picture (idol) we then get of God is completely opposite to that of a gifting and giving God, and *we* be-

---

42. In Yvonne Sherwood and Kevin Hart, *Derrida and Religion: Other Testaments* (New York: Routledge, 2005), pp. 337-50. References in parentheses in the following are to this work until further notice.

come instead an idol god who creates even more of our self-centered concern for our possessions and ourselves:

> When we imagine that God possesses us, we can explain the terrors of history as his righteous wrath at our infidelity. The violence of possession proliferates: as God possesses us, so we possess land and men possess women, and all of this ownership leads to anxiety over the borders of possession and inevitable violence. (pp. 340-41)

Schwartz thus problematizes the possibility of possessing the law as well as to be possessed by God.[43] She nevertheless suggests that a theologically valid alternative to these pitfalls is given in Exodus, where justice shows itself as prior to the law but also inheres in the law and constitutes it (p. 340). The justice of the law is, according to her interpretation, conditioned by the first commandment: "Without this condition — obeying only one God — there can be no justice, and no law. And the law is: only one God, only his law, only his law is just." At this point, however, she radicalizes the interpretation we developed by way of Derrida above, when she suggests that the biblical case defies the usual logic that would separate justice from law, in order to secure as justice that which exceeds the law. Instead, she formulates an alternative way of looking at the relationship between law and justice. Exodus is, according to her interpretation, radical in the sense that it says *justice is the law*. This is a different way of expressing the unavoidable call of the other, and the revelation of God as the one who is there for the third. Such an interpretation of justice/law makes the charges of pharisaic legalism ludicrous, she claims.

Given this close connection between justice and law, law cannot be identified with specific norms (as Derrida seems to do, at least in the last quote above), but enforces itself as the unavoidable call to justice that must reveal itself in any given situation. As justice is prior to law, in Exodus it is depicted as something radical and unavoidable. Writes Schwartz:

> The force of the law is executed, in this narrative, on those who are in the very process of receiving it. They are accountable to the law, must answer

---

43. In this way, she makes a point that is in accordance with Marion's when he sees idolatry's problem not so much in an image that has reference to a god, as in the fact that it makes a god of the idolater. Cf. Horner, *Jean-Luc Marion: A Theo-Logical Introduction*, pp. 61f.

to the law, but are not yet under the law. This radical understanding of the Institution of law — that authority and justice are both outside and inside the law — makes it utterly impossible to reject. This law can and is broken; but it cannot be refused. The option of living within this law or not is not offered. It comes into being in a condition of complete inevitability. While political theory may call this totalitarianism, Judaism has called it revelation. Once it is given, there is no way to be outside of this (divine) justice. Anything else is false, a fake. (p. 340)

That God reveals God in justice, and that this justice is not to be identified with obeying a rule, suggests that not only law, but justice as well, points to a surplus. Behind and beyond justice is the God who reveals God in justice, while still remaining ineffable. This, nevertheless, does not render justice irrational or moral insights something to be based on specific revelations as opposed to use of reason. It is with and in reason, shaped by the welcoming of the Other as the third, that justice manifests itself.

Looking back then at Jesus' critique of the law, we now have a more nuanced background for claiming that more than anything, Jesus addresses the idolatry that consists in believing you can *possess yourself*, and be a full subject by yourself, by means of the law. The law is not a means for becoming a full subject, but for being subjected to the call to justice from the other. Jesus' rejection of the delusion of self-sufficient subjectivity by means of the law is nevertheless not solely grounded in a Levinasian-like appreciation of how the Other makes me a subject. It is based on the recognition of God as gifting, and consequently in a rejection of the practice of those who try to make God's gifts (including the law) a means for possessing oneself as a subject or the other as an object.

The Last Judgment: Christ as Judge and Witness to Justice

The question "Who is righteous?" is answered in several of Matthew's parables, of which one of the most important involves the judgment of the nations (25:31ff.). The parable presents us with a crux, especially when dealing with it from the position of protestant theology: Is Jesus here claiming that humans shall be judged according to what they *do*, after all, and do we then have to conclude that everything said about the grace of God is to be rendered invalid in the end?

In the following, I will present an interpretation of the parable that suggests that there are two interrelated issues at stake in it: one is related to the issue of *recognition,* and the other to *differentiation.* As for differentiation, Matthew strongly puts forward that what humans do and do not do have implications for the outcome of their lives. To suggest otherwise would be to say that in the end there is no justice for those who are suffering. Hence, differentiation between good and bad deeds (or lack of such) is a main concern here — not in itself, but for the sake of justice for those who suffer.

Consequently, one has to ask if the existential meaning of this parable is primarily to underscore that God takes seriously the suffering of those who are not met by their neighbors in ways that show mercy and compassion. Given that we identify the judge, named by Matthew as "the son of Man" (which points to an eschatological dimension that Matthew attributes to Jesus) who is Christ, God's representative, the point of the judgment is that Christ performs a justice that gives the suffering their right and recognizes their suffering. Without judgment, there is no real recognition of the one who suffers, or of suffering and injustice. The judgment makes us see and recognize, and verbalizes the injustice and justice alike.

That this is the main point of the parable is suggested by the detailed description of the different forms of injustice that "the Son of Man" addresses, and which more or less is repeated four times in the parable. It is against this background of securing justice that we then have to consider how the judgment is carried out. This is so, because those judged are judged according to how they identified and recognized needs and injustice.

At this point the discussion of gift again appears relevant: Those who are positively recognized by the judge are recognized because of actions that they did not themselves perceive as being done for a specific, economic purpose. They lack an understanding of what they have done in terms of *what their actions are giving in return.* They have not acted in order to achieve some goal for themselves. They have acted solely for the sake of the other. That is also why their surprise is so large when they learn that their actions have the implications pointed to by the judge.

The lack of *personal motives* for doing good to others need not exclude an internal relationship between the one doing good and the recipient of that deed. Moreover, it is possible to see how the good deed is marked by, or constituted by, a perceived relationship on the side of the agent, which then also reveals itself as a relationship to the judge: The judge says that "what you did to the least of these that are members of my family, you did to me." This suggests, again, the triadic structure of God's justice. There *is* a return here, but it is not linked to an economic circle by the one who invests his or her actions or deeds. Rather, the return is freely given, a point not only marked by the words of the giver, but also by the recipients' wondering and surprise when confronted with the gift of the kingdom. This is something unexpected and hence, something outside their perception of the context for action. This non-necessary connection between reward and action suggests not only that the inheritance of the kingdom must be understood as a gift of grace, but also that the actions rewarded have some kind of quality or content that is not realized by those who performed it. The lack of calculation or deliberation of personal concerns makes the beneficence a real gift as well.

The surprise expressed when the positive judgment is given turns then into a question of recognition: "When was it that we saw you?" This question of recognition is not only about being able to recognize Christ, but it is also a question about who belongs to the community of Christ. The response of the judge makes this clear: When the suffering are visited, fed, given clothes, etc., Christ himself is visited, fed, and given clothes. This suggests that there is an internal link between three parties, and that Christ is the non-present third party in the relationship between the one who gives and the one who receives. He is nevertheless not openly recognized. How can we come to terms with this puzzle? I suggest that the answer to the puzzle consists of three parts.

The first part is that when you address someone who is suffering in the manner described above (unconditional, without personal interest, even without an interest in relieving your own uncomfortable status when confronted with someone in an unjust situation), you are addressing them as someone who belongs to your world, and who rightly breaks into your world with a call for justice. You thereby recognize them as being justified in their call for calling you to justice. What you do to them is not only determined by *you*, it is determined by them and their calling of you. You recognize yourself as the other's neighbor, and the other as yours. That is the first step of recognition. Hence, you belong together, and your self-perception means that you are in no way justified in excluding the other from your world. The bottom line of this recognition then, is that you see the other as the image of God (be this explicit or not): he or she is reminding you of God's justice, and is calling you to be an image like him or her by being a response-able witness in action.

Second, the parable then continues to indicate exactly that they are related to, or belong to Christ, and are among *his* family. Revealed is not only Christ, but God as concerned with injustice and in solidarity with those who are suffering under it. Moreover, by suggesting that one recognizes the other as *imago Dei* when one shows mercy to those who suffer, the consequence of this recognition is that they have a common vocation with Christ's: to be the image of God. Hence, there is a close relationship between the three parties involved, most expressively manifested in the notion of *imago Dei*. The notion of *imago Dei* thus helps us to reconstruct the extensive theological dimension in the designation of the suffering as "the least members of my family."

The third part of the answer is the implication of the above, namely that you confront Christ in your neighbor. Because Christ is the true image of God, all of humanity is related to him, and is in some sense represented in him. As the true image of God, Christ is what all other humans are called to become. We are accordingly in a position where we can see Christ in the face of every other human — as the one who calls us to mercy, compassion, and love.[44]

We can now allow the question from the introduction to this section, which was motivated by a protestant context, to resurface: Does all this mean that good works are what is required, in the end? What the parable seems to suggest is that good works are important, not for the final judgment as such, but for the neighbor. However, their importance for salvation seems to be undermined by the fact that what ends up as most important is the ability to *recognize* the other as part of my world, as a person with a valid and justified call to justice. The good works are not only part of my world as such, but part of my world as gifts from God that I am called to share with others.

The recognition of the other, and of his valid claim to break into my world and call me to justice, thus implies that I *believe* that my world is

---

44. Allen Verhey, in a recent article, makes an observation on the parable's contemporary meaning: "The parable is eloquent testimony that watchfulness takes the shape of care. And it is an elegant reminder to care givers that the presence of God is mediated to them through their patients, that patients — in their very weakness and vulnerability, in their hurt and loneliness — (re)present Christ to the care giver." See Allen Verhey, "Science at the End of Life: Contributions and Limitations," *Princeton Seminary Bulletin* 28, no. 1 (2007): 18.

God's gift, and that the Other is the *imago Dei* who calls. In other words: The basic and underlying presupposition for the whole outcome of the judgment is the ability to recognize oneself, the other, and the world as all rooted in the creative act of a giving God. The theological expression for this recognition is usually faith. By living from the faith in these gifts, one is set free from concern for oneself and is able to care for the other. This opens up to salvation in the broad sense of the word.

However, the *faith* expressed in this recognition is not necessarily articulated or expressed as an extensive faith in Christ: Christ might still be unknown, but one might nevertheless be able to respond to the calling of justice and to offer the gifts to others. One can thereby act as the image of God also outside of faith, by giving others the chance to experience God's world as gift. However, this unthematized witness is in need of a revelation in order to be acknowledged and recognized as God's gift. The parable suggests that this revelation takes place in the final judgment.

The parable thus suggests that faith is important for developing a full recognition of the other and of the world, but faith in a Christian sense of the word — as belief in Jesus Christ as the savior of the world — is not required in order for humans to be able to function as images of God in relation to others in need. But faith serves as the personal commitment where what is at stake is fully recognized and can be interpreted adequately. It is in faith that the link between the three parties involved is revealed and manifested — outside the context of reciprocity or an exchange economy.

The element of *surprise* is, as suggested, closely related to the fact that there can be no determination of the outcome due to any kind of calculative economic concerns. One can say that the only way to express the kingdom as gift is through a surprising judgment — one in which the other is there first and foremost by herself and for herself — so that we are not tempted to treat the other as a means for pleasing God. Or, to put it the other way: we are not first and foremost asking if the other is someone representing God — because that would easily and accordingly lead us back to a situation where we met the other by asking if he or she might be representing God or belong to God or not. The point is that the beneficial works are to be done solely for the neighbor. They express a desire for the neighbor's good, well-being, and welfare. The judgment is the place where it shall be revealed that there is more at stake than this desire and the recognition of the other — but this cannot be revealed beforehand, or the non-economic logic of gift runs the risk of being compromised. Hence, the judgment reveals a new dimension in recognition of what has to be hidden for the sake of the gift to be a gift — seen from the perspective of the giver.

In a certain sense, one can say that the basis for the judgment is not human agency as such, but rather the *other in the way she is recognized by me,* and thereby directs and guides this agency. This approach lends even more weight to an understanding that does not see the good works in themselves as what qualify for a positive judgment, but rather *the relationship to the other as it is expressed in recognition and community.* It is also from this angle that it becomes understandable what those people lack who are confronted with a *negative* judgment.

Primarily, the parable seems to imply that those who face a negative judgment lack the ability to recognize the other as related to them. Secondly, and accordingly, they thereby also become unable see that Christ is present as the third party in these (lacking) relationships. There is, accordingly, a double problem implied in the answer they give to the judge when he confronts them with what they did not do for him. First, they ask when they have met him in situations of suffering, hunger, etc., and thereby they indicate that if they had done so, they would have given him what he needed. This response reveals the ignorance of relationships between the needy, Christ, and themselves. Second, the same answer thereby also reveals self-righteousness. They try to justify their lack of good works by saying that they have not been able to recognize Christ in any of the people they have met, but what this discloses is their own lack of faith in Christ, and in God as the one present in the presence of the Other's face, calling them to satisfy her justified needs.

Put bluntly, the rejected try to justify themselves by saying that they had no chance to do good works toward Christ. But this justification does not work, because it implies that they can establish their righteousness regardless of their relation to their neighbor in need. That is what they cannot do. The one who is unable to meet the other's needs by recognizing her as one at the same level immediately faces the challenge of being self-righteous in a way that excludes the other. It is this type of self-righteousness that Matthew addresses throughout his Gospel, and which is related to his call for good fruits. A piety that is oriented towards doing the good for the sake of the agent easily ends up as a self-centered form of self-seeking, where the other is only an indirect object or tool serving a desire to secure one's own position. Such an attitude cannot produce good fruits, as it is *constitutively* not concerned for the other.

The conclusion to this way of life, in which one basically is oriented only towards oneself, is that community is ruled out, or, that one excludes oneself from community and fellowship by not recognizing the other as part of one's own world. The one who is judged as not righteous is thus the one who by excluding the other excludes herself. It is the one who lets her own totality determine the world, instead of letting the other be a witness to the richness of infinite justice, to use the Levinasian pair of concepts that is most apt for describing this situation.

The present analysis implies that it is not God who excludes humans from relationships in the last judgment, but that it is humans who, by excluding others from community, exclude themselves. God — as Christ witnesses in Matthew — remains the welcoming host for both good and bad (cf. 22:10). Hence, the hospitality and generosity of God goes unquestioned, as does God's concern for justice.

The interpretation presented here then also implies that it is in no way a lack of justice that leads to a situation where some humans stand outside the kingdom: it is the result of *human* injustice, and the lack of recognition of both the other and of God's generosity towards all humans. Human injustice keeps humans shut out from the kingdom, opposed to how God's grace and hospitality welcome them to join. From a modern angle, this should not be difficult to understand: a God who cares for those suffering and who cannot tolerate their neglect, as well as a God who welcomes everyone that does good to them, is a God who is righteous. By revealing how he is himself subjected to what humans do to other humans, Christ also indicates that he (or God) is affected by what humans do and do not do. This points back to our previous point about the vulnerability of God: God is able to suffer (in terms of being subjected to) the consequences of human agency.

Against the background of this parable, we are now finally also able to construct a possible framework for understanding more of the Beatitudes in Matthew 5: Those who are poor in spirit, who mourn, etc., will be rewarded. The reason for their blessedness and their hope for a future different from what is now is not determined by the present conditions, but by the promise of a different future in the kingdom of God. The future is the reason for their blessedness, and when people are open to and relate to this future, their very relation to it integrates them in a new and different reality, where they are not closed into themselves.

When we ask what kind of people Jesus is addressing in the Beatitudes, it is the same as those who are judged righteous in Matthew 25: those whose practice is such that it creates community and fellowship: those who seek peace and righteousness and who show mercy contribute to the emergence of a better future without divisions between people. They might do so for different reasons, but *what* they seek is nevertheless in accordance with the vision for a better future.

I want to strengthen this argument from another angle: What happens if the hope for the future is not articulated in this manner? What takes place if one is to conclude that justice will not rule in the end, that there will be no peace on earth, and so on? As indicated earlier, the very articulation of goodness is a condition for goodness to be recognized and take place. A vision of a different world is a condition for a different world that is not determined by present conditions. That is what the Beatitudes point to, and what the parable about the last judgment suggests when it reveals how righteousness for those who suffer will be part of the future.

Summing up, then, we can say that Christ, also in his parable about the judgment, testifies to God's inclusive community. This is a community where everyone is perceived as mutually related to each other, and where justice is manifest in and through the recognition of this relatedness. Moreover, by revealing God as the one who has prepared the kingdom "before the foundation of the world," and implicating himself as the judge who welcomes to this kingdom, Jesus points to how justice and righteousness are internal and integral to the world as God created it — and as he, as the Logos, welcomes us to perceive and express it. Without the hope for justice and community expressed by him, hope would be less. But Christ calls humans to this community, in the same way as he also himself practices it, and thereby gives witness to what it means that God reigns.

You Are Saved by Your Faith!

In the previous analyses, we have emphasized how the identity of Jesus, God, and humans are all revealed by the way Jesus preaches the kingdom. Jesus is revealed as witness to God and as God's representative, God is revealed as the generous host behind the call to justice and righteousness, and humans as either open to or rejecting the community that Jesus proclaims and practices. While maintaining the validity of the commandments of the law, it has also become apparent that more fundamental than obedience to the law is trust in God, which opens up to (concern for) others instead of caring for oneself. Jesus' practice can be seen as a long history of calling people to such faith, and thereby, to participate in a more open world. As *faith* here seems to be of crucial importance, the following section will look somewhat more into it. The reason for this is that a close reading of the Gospels seems to disturb or make problematic the common understanding that salvation by faith is dependent on a belief in Jesus as the one who died on the cross for our sins.[1] How can salvation take place before the salvific work of Christ is accomplished? The answer we give to this problem might indicate the close link between his call to the kingdom and the final consequence this call leads to in terms of being crucified. To put it in a straightforward way: We might see Jesus' crucifixion not as an independent sacrifice, but as an expression of the sacrifices his proclamation of the kingdom of God might lead to, and as the final expression of

---

1. Of course, there is much lack of clarity in this expression, but I leave it for now, as my main point here is to discuss how Jesus is able to say that people are saved before he has died on the cross.

196

what happens when the reality he reveals is confronted with the destroying powers of this world. However, for now we are still concerned with the positive reception of Jesus as God's representative, and how faith is involved in the recognition of him as such.

Three Encounters

Let us look into how faith is present in three stories of close encounters that can serve as models (although not exhaustive) for the relation between faith and the interpretative angles we have used throughout the book.

1. In the healing of the blind Bartimaeus, Bartimaeus is perceived as one *breaking into* the world ordered by the intentions of others. This breaking into is conditioned by him as *recognizing* Jesus as the son of David, and thereby as God's representative (*Imago Dei*). Jesus' response, "What do you want me to do for you?," contains several important elements: First, it recognizes Bartimaeus as a *subject,* not only as an object of healing. Moreover, his calling into another, active subjectivity (as he is no more subjected to the eyes of others as a passive object, a beggar) allows Bartimaeus to express his desire: his desire is to see, but also to be seen and recognized as a subject, or as a witness, to use Kelly Oliver's term. He redirects his desire towards that which is the most fundamental for him, instead of desiring to receive money. He thereby asks for another world; he asks for or desires the *impossible.* This redirection of desire is dependent upon what he recognizes in the presence of Jesus, and it liberates him from his narrow and passive acceptance of the world in which he finds himself and directs him towards something radically different. Moreover, this fundamental change in desire calls him into a new and different identity, symbolized in the fact that he throws off his cloak. When he does that, it is *prior* to the conversation with Jesus, and it points to the strong conviction he holds that Jesus will change his life. When Jesus says, "Go; your faith has made you well" (Mark 10:52), he manifests the change in the man's identity; Bartimaeus regains sight and follows Jesus on the way, which then basically implies that he takes part in the community that Jesus generates. Hence, the kingdom's community is not only preached but also manifested as an ontological reality.

Kelly Oliver's comments on what happens in political and social oppression give us an important background for interpreting the present story. She says that such oppression makes people into faceless objects or lesser subjects (e.g., a blind beggar, not primarily addressed by his first name). The social exclusion is expressed by the lack of visage that renders him invisible in any ethical or political sense. This in turn allows for subjectivity to become the domain of domination: "Subjectivity is conferred by those in power and on those they deem powerless and disempowered. The desire to be seen, to be recognized is the paradoxical desire created by oppression. It is the desire to become objectified in order to be recognized by the sovereign subject to whom the oppressed is beholden for his or her own self-worth."[2] When Jesus acts, he is allowing the blind man to escape from this type of subjectivity, and to see, not only be seen (positively).

That faith saves seems against this background to mean that faith is what manifests openness towards, and a trust in, the reality that Jesus reveals and represents. By faith one is directed towards and integrated into this reality as one's primary concern or desire. There are things that Bartimaeus then simply ignores, like social customs that imply that one should shut up instead of calling for Jesus' attention. Without this trust and the desire or engagement expressed here, a different reality cannot appear in a manner that implies salvation, but remains closed.

There is one element in this story that needs to be highlighted, namely that the one breaking in, making disturbance, the one who is unwelcome (cf. the above discussion about forgiveness and hospitality) is entering into the community of those following Jesus and believing in the kingdom of God. This intrusion of the initially and apparently unwelcome is even more strongly affirmed in the next encounter we examine.

2. Luke 7:36ff. reports that Jesus receives hospitality from the Pharisee Simon. While eating with him, a woman — unwelcome — enters the company.[3] Although it is not clear what makes the woman unwelcome

2. Kelly Oliver, *Witnessing: Beyond Recognition* (Minneapolis: University of Minnesota Press, 2001), p. 149.

3. In Luke, the woman is unnamed. In other places (e.g., John 11:2), reports of this incident identify her as Mary Magdalene, who later appears as an important subject in the Jesus story, especially when witnessing about the resurrection of Christ. The narrative connection between her as an unclean sinner and as a witness to and a follower of Christ is important as an underlying element that sheds light on the encounter reported here. Jesus' meal practice, including the way he acts here, is both constructive for community and subversive, as the open community in the meals embodied an alternative social vision. "To eat

and/or unclean, it is clear that her touch means defilement and impurity. The reserved attitude of Simon is, accordingly, expressed toward both Jesus and the woman: He sees her as a means for revealing whether Jesus is a prophet or not; thereby showing that his hospitality toward Jesus emerges out of hidden interests. Hence, he is not interested in the woman as such, or her well-being, but only in what it means for him and his social status. To put it otherwise: she is not regarded or recognized as part of the liberating triadic relation that Jesus reveals as foundational for true community. She is the other who is not recognized positively as the third.

Hence, the woman crashes the party. She believes in a hospitality that is not present, and which seems impossible from the position of Simon's lack of welcome. By breaking in, she makes manifest that she believes; she believes in a different community than Simon's. Her faith therefore also opens her up to the community into which *Jesus* welcomes her. He recognizes and receives her gifts, and his hospitality manifests itself in forgiveness as well. Moreover, it is clear that Jesus, as Luke describes him, considers this faith, reception, and forgiveness sufficient for salvation: her faith in Jesus as the one who welcomes into community is the faith that saves her from what she is in the eyes of the others. Her status is redefined: she is no longer tied to her past as a sinner, but to her present fellowship with Jesus. This fellowship is a surplus compared to what that past can offer or consist in. Thus, salvation as it is revealed in her life is the surplus of the future kingdom, manifesting itself in the present community into which she is welcomed as forgiven, and recognized as believing in.

3. A final story giving evidence to the fruitfulness of faith in Luke is the one about Zacchaeus (19:1ff.). He expresses an eager desire to see Jesus, a desire that Jesus recognizes and reverses into a request for his hospitality. This request allows for, recognizes, that Zacchaeus is *capable of generosity* (thereby being himself an image of God's generosity), and not only of the extortive practices for which he was known. By welcoming Jesus, he thus not only manifests hospitality, but a redirection of his previous desires, desires that most likely had excluded him from much of the community. His desire for collecting wealth, and for possession, is turned into a desire for

---

with others without regard for social boundaries . . . subverted the deepest boundaries society draws: between honor and shame, patron and client, female and male, slave and free, rich and poor, pure and impure." Marcus J. Borg, here quoted from Donald Capps, *Jesus: A Psychological Biography* (St. Louis: Chalice Press, 2000), p. 25, cf. pp. 28-29.

giving and generosity. Again, the presence of Jesus brings about the change. When Jesus learns from Zacchaeus how his is now a desire to give, emerging out of his newly found community, he says that "Today salvation has come to this house" (19:9). Again, we see how salvation manifests itself in a relationship to Jesus that indicates a new orientation toward others.

Recognition and Rejection

The above short reading of the stories shows that salvation must be seen as emerging from a specific recognition of Jesus (in faith) as the one who brings about possibilities of a new life. This new life is not to be understood as something spiritualized or specifically religious, but manifests itself in the way human community is shaped and opened up to sharing, giving, hope, and mutual recognition. The same elements are present in many of the healing stories in the Gospels, where a similar connection between faith, community, and healing is manifest.[4]

Faith implies an openness to and positive recognition of the other, and the presence of this other (as the third) is often important when people address Jesus. It is striking how often Jesus says "your faith has saved you" when people are making intercessions to him on behalf of others (cf. Matt. 8:10, 13; 9:2; 15:28 par.). To bring forth a desire for the well-being of the other implies a faith that is not self-seeking. These intercessions nevertheless have positive consequences for both the one praying for help, and for the one prayed for: they both become, by the act of faith in Jesus as the one who can help, linked together in a community with the third (God's representative), who can respond to what they both desire.

Against this background, the easiest way to spell out the relationship between faith and salvation would be to say that faith is the personal openness to the community with Jesus as God's representative. To believe in him is to believe that he is God's representative for us. In the next section of the book, we shall develop how he might also be seen as humanity's representative before God. Faith is the way to recognize both these functions

---

4. The connection between healing and social inclusion is one that is underscored strongly in Capps's work, cf. the previous footnote. Capps not only describes one possible psycho-historic background for Jesus' ministry, he also analyzes some of the healing stories and makes them understandable against the background of the historical context in which Jesus worked.

of, or better, relations of, representation. Thus, faith is linked to community and salvation. While faith as trusting that God is present (represented) in Christ opens up to salvation, the rejection of Jesus as God's representative not only implies lack of trust in him. The rejection also implies that one does not trust in the God Jesus proclaims, and consequently, that one closes oneself off from the community that is made possible by the way Jesus reveals God.

The question we have to ask ourselves at the end of this section is then the following: What is it in Jesus' message that provokes such rejection? Why are his hospitality and forgiveness not received by all? Why is his welcome not welcomed by everyone? The Gospels suggest the answer: Jesus provokes by breaking into established patterns of belief that make salvation a binary relation between God and the individual. In this binary relation, the individual is seduced to trust in what *she* can do to please God. Hence, attention and direction of desire is always towards that which is possible for the individual to achieve. Within this framework, both the other and the impossible remain out of sight, and the new and disturbing patterns of the impossible are not perceived as liberating, but as disturbing, unsettling, and unwelcome. Jesus challenges to give up possession of oneself and live life within a community of gifting, where everyone is welcome. That is a radical calling, and one most humans are likely to reject. To be honest, it is also one that many today calling themselves Christians *in practice* reject, although they still recognize its validity. Jesus' call is to what is unheard of, uncalled for; he thus calls forward rejection, implicitly as well as explicitly.

The provocation by preaching an inclusive and generous God lies in the fact that this God of the impossible, in order to change the world, is a God outside of our control. When Jesus preaches this God, he reveals how much humans are locked up in their own worlds, how small their openness is toward the other. The exclusivity of the kingdom of God as a different community is therefore first and foremost expressed in its lack of exclusivity. Once this lack of exclusivity is given up, the kingdom deteriorates into institutions of negotiation and reasonableness. But where one has to negotiate for the place of the other as the third, a generous God is already out of the picture. By implication then, Jesus' provocation might not only call for outright rejection, it might also provoke the more subtle rejections that are expressed in attempts to negotiate and make reasonable.

God disturbs the picture we want to hold on to about the world and ourselves. What Jesus does, is not only to reveal that these pictures isolate us and finally lead to death (in more than one sense of the word). He reveals a different world. When that world is rejected for the sake of the present and unjust world, the consequence is that he must die. He testifies to a world that humans — implicitly or explicitly — might like to see eradicated.

Conclusion

Jesus as Revealing Answers to Questions of Identity

In many ways one can say that the ancient attempts to define someone's nature were predecessors to more modern questions of identity. What the ancient church struggled with in terms of defining the nature of Jesus from Nazareth is today most often phrased as questions of identity. The concept of "nature" itself, with all its problematic connotations, has contributed to this. We have in this part dealt with questions of identity — noting, however, that such questions might also appear as problematic. We noted initially that the narratives about Jesus establish his identity in a form that underscores the problematic of using pre-established categories. Hence, his identity remains partly elusive, but still charged by powerful notions of this tradition. Jesus himself is also described as reluctant to be clearly and openly identified as Messiah. Against the background of postmodern philosophy, we can see this reluctance as an expression of an awareness of the danger of being reduced to the same, i.e., understood only from a pre-established world of intentions and preconceptions that are not open to the special identity he exhibits as a witness to God. Jesus himself offers no closure to the identity-question, and hence, with what authority he speaks is up to the listener or reader to decide (cf. Luke 20:1ff.). The openness of or lack of closure to that question demands involvement and commitment. There is no objective answer to the question. To put it in a form that, against the present background, is hopefully more than a mere tautology: The identity of Jesus is dependent on whom he is recognized as; his identity is not only a question of *his* identity, but who the other who recognizes him also recognizes himself or herself as. Jesus calls for recognition, of himself, of God, and of the other. If he is recognized as one who does that, this then also implies that the one who recognizes him says something about how he or she understand themselves.[1]

We have seen that elements of recognition, gift, forgiveness, hospitality, and desire are all present in the ministry of Jesus, and that they are reshaped there when he opens people to the kingdom of God. God's kingdom is what matters most, and what is given priority, in his ministry. This priority is not at the expense of the other, the neighbor, but on her behalf. The kingdom as we have described it is based on a triadic relationship where the community of God, self, and neighbor is fully realized only in their mutual recognition of each other. God is fully realized as God only when God is perceived as gifting, while the Other is only perceived as a neighbor when she is understood as a gift to my world who witnesses about the giving God, and I am only realizing my own destiny as the image of God when I welcome the Other into my world and share God's gifts with her. Hence, the triadic relationship exhibits a specific form of recognition, where Jesus — as the witness to God and God's kingdom — represents both the other and God when he approaches humans with the message about the kingdom of God.

It is against this background that we can say that the questions of identity we have worked under as guiding headlines for the previous analyses, have a definite answer: When we ask "Who is fully human?," "Who is God?," and "Who is righteous?," the answers to these questions in all instances have to take their point of departure in Jesus: Jesus is the one who reveals what it is to be fully human. By living uncompromisingly according to his calling to be the image of God, he reveals (not only informs, but exhibits, makes manifest, practices, establishes ontologically as a reality not previously realized in the same manner) what it is to be a true human being — who witnesses to God and is open toward the other.

We also are thereby able to realize that to be a human is to live in a specific relationship to God: To live as a witness to God is to recognize God

1. The dialectic of recognition described here might have some bearings on the traditional distinction between law and gospel: To recognize oneself as called and given all in Christ is receiving his message as a gospel, but to reject his call to recognize God, himself, and the other (neighbor) immediately places the one who rejects him (and then God and the other, as well as one's own calling to be the image of God) under the judgment of the law.

as the one towards whom desire and love are rightly addressed; because God is not a name for an entity, God cannot be worshiped as an idol, as is possible with entities. By directing our desire towards God, we realize that our desires cannot be fulfilled in a final way by directing them toward other entities in the world, and, moreover, that the desire for God opens us up to a mode of desiring that helps us grow while recognizing its incompleteness. The desire for God might also — as a true desire for God, for the impossible, for the surplus of reality — make us open to the neighbor. God thus becomes the source of community. The God whom Jesus witnesses to is hence a God of community. Access to this understanding of the identity of God is given through the message and practice of Jesus, and accordingly, Jesus reveals God's identity. This identity is, as that of all other parts in the triadic relationship, something not accessible without conceiving of it in relational terms: God is revealed as the God of community due to the way God is revealed for humans through Jesus.

By constantly witnessing to God, and thus being open to the Other, Jesus also appears as the one who is righteous, i.e., as the one who lives according to God's law. He lives in love, and is directed by love, and this makes him criticize the way the pious of his time use the law; but his critical stance is always for the sake of justice. We have seen how his destabilization of the letter of the law is intended to secure justice, and how his non-negotiable call for justice is made human by exhibiting how forgiveness is the other side of a community striving for justice — because the fulfillment of the law is not an aim in itself, but only an instrument for the fulfillment of justice in community. The demand of the law is paralleled by the call for forgiveness. Taken together, the two are a basis for a new and inclusive community of righteousness and love. When Jesus preaches and practices this vision, he is himself revealing the answer to the question: Who is righteous? He is. He also reveals all others as not living up to the standards of righteousness. This, however, is not a realization that serves as a reason to exclude anyone, but rather to include all those who realize their own shortcomings, and who are thereby able to recognize others as being on the same level and hence potentially belonging to the same community.

We have suggested that Jesus, in his proclamation of the kingdom, and in his development of an alternative framework for the law, represents not only God — he also represents the other human, the other as the third. It is this living in openness toward and for the one who is not present in the binary relation to the immediate other that makes Jesus represent both God and man. As such, he is *imago Dei*. It is because of this implicit or explicit claim to represent both that he is rejected. Then not only are his claims rejected, but God and the other as they are recognized and witnessed to in his life are then also rejected. We are here entering that place where it becomes understandable — also from our way of reconstructing the identity of Jesus — why he faced death in the way he did.

The warnings from present postmodern theory against delineating too static or restrictive understandings of identity are met by the relational approach we have built here. They are also relevant for the understanding of Jesus' identity. His identity is still relatively open, given that a true recognition of the other, as we have tried to delineate it here, implies the willingness to meet the other on his/her terms. To be in a dynamic and evolving relationship where even the question of your identity might be answered differently as history continues is part of this open process. Hence, in spite of all that is said so far, the full identity of Christ cannot be determined before we have dealt with his death and resurrection.

At this point, Paul Ricoeur's distinction between two ways of describing identity might actually prove helpful. In *Oneself as Another*, he distinguishes between idem and ipse-identities (expressing sameness and selfhood respectively). While idem-identities are those that denote what is constant, the ipse-identities may develop and vary throughout the course of life.[2] Ricoeur underscores how the understanding of a person's identity is constituted by both components, and that identity accordingly can be disclosed only through a consistent narrative that integrates them both.

Given that this is the case, it is deeply problematic to try to answer the question about the identity of Jesus Christ apart from the narrative of his life. While his idem-identity describes the permanence and continuity throughout his life, this identity is operating at a level of abstraction that is only able to say what he has *in common* with others. This commonality is usually described by means of conceptions of nature, species, etc., as expressed in the form *What* am I? On the other hand, the ipse-identity is grasped by means of elaborating the unique and idiosyncratic, that which makes one different from others, and hence it is an answer to the question *Who* am I? In Christ's case, this means that the answer to his identity in

2. Paul Ricoeur, *Oneself as Another* (Chicago: University of Chicago Press, 1992). See pp. 2f., 18f., 116ff.

terms of *What is he?* is too narrowly answered by saying "He is a Human" or "He is God." These answers only refer us back to questions about what it means to be human and what it means to be God. Given that Christ in his life reveals what it means to be human and what "God" means, we have access to answers of these idem-questions only through answering the ipse-question about *who* Christ is.

Ricoeur's differentiation not only helps us to get a new and fruitful perspective on the question about Christ's identity; it also helps us see that we need to talk about the identity of both God and humans as something developed by means of the Christ-history, even when we are talking about their idem-identity. Accordingly, the perspective offered has great importance for how we talk about humanity in theological terms. Hence, there is no abstract or context-independent way of defining what is God or what is human — apart from the specific history of Jesus Christ. It is in this story that we can identify God — but only when we recognize Jesus as the representative of the reality of God.[3] It is by reflecting on the ipse-identity of Christ that we achieve access to something that can be taken to define the major content of the idem-identity of both humans and God. But as indicated, this does not mean that the definition of the idem-identity helps us very much. If we keep to the insight that Jesus manifests or reveals God, and at the same time maintain that he is definitely a human being as we are, then this will most likely mean that we have to alter our conceptions of both what it is to be a human and of what it means to be God.

Continuing from this then, we might say that the idem-identity of God and humans is related to the non-necessary ipse-identity of Christ as this is expressing itself in the history of Jesus from Nazareth. And it is against this background that we can see how diversified the question of identity is: not only is the idem-identity of God and humanity dependent on the revelation of Christ, also the ipse-identity of Christ is linked to the way he reveals the true destiny of humanity and the generosity of God.

So far then, the ipse-identity of Jesus might be circumscribed by trying to develop an answer to the questions delineated in this part of the book. There is, however, one question that cannot be avoided, but is closely

3. At this point we can see an interesting background for addressing the logos of reality as something revealed in Christ: when both God and humanity become revealed in Christ, it means that what we can *say* about God, and the language we need in order to speak about humanity on theologically distinct terms, are both dependent on the logos which Christ articulates.

related to the others: Emerging from the question "Who is God?" is the question "Is Jesus God?" We have tentatively suggested already that a possible answer to that question is given by saying that *in Jesus, we realize who God is when and if God is a human*. However, I gladly admit that this is a statement that calls for further clarification in light of the history of Christology. One thing is, namely, to say that this is who God is, when and if God is a human, but that is not the same as to say that this human is God. This was the issue dealt with in the early centuries of Christology, and one still pressing in the present situation, where postmodernism has made problematic all suggestions of things having or sharing a "nature" — suggestions that might provoke charges of "essentialism" and hence concur with the criticism against identity ascriptions we have already met. The identity in question here is the question about the idem-identity of Christ. That this question is pressing is even clearer from the fact argued above that the idem-identities of both God and humans are dependent on the revelation in Christ. When we then say that Christ reveals what it means to be human or God, are we then not ending up in a kind of self-reference? That is a question related to what has been discussed in the history of Christology.

Did Jesus Have a Nature? Or Two?

The Council of Chalcedon decided that Christ is true human and true God. The main aim of this decision was to safeguard this identification without confusing the "natures" or making Christ something unique in terms of his nature. He could not be a mixture of divine and human nature, because that would mean that he was not really sharing in both natures, but of a "third" nature of hitherto unknown status.[4] The council thereby safeguarded both cosmological and soteriological intentions — the difference between Creator and creature, as well as the true humanity of Christ, which was important in order to ensure his ability to save humanity.[5]

However, the Chalcedon creed mainly defined what Christ is in neg-

---

4. "We teach . . . one and the same Christ, Son, Lord, Only-begotten, known in two natures, without confusion, without change, without division, without separation."

5. In my terms, the latter point would be spelled out like this: Christ's true humanity was important in order for him to be a true representative of humanity before God.

ative terms — saying how his natures etc. should *not* be understood. Hence, the creed could not stop further reflection on these questions. The main problem with Chalcedon and the doctrine of Christ's double nature in the present day is found in the concept of *nature*. This notion is taken from Latin, and means something like substance, that which characterizes something, that which defines what something is apart from or in difference to other things. It is also, at least to some extent, a notion that addresses something static, immutable, and not alterable (idem, as above). However, in modern thought this concept is often, and for good reasons, not easily accepted, since we have come to realize that nothing has a static essence, but all things develop and change through the course of history. Moreover, to say that something has an independent nature also suggests that it is not internally related to something else. From a theological angle, human nature is not independent, but dependent: human nature is by definition God-related.[6] But it is also highly problematic to state empirically that there is something like a static human nature.[7]

Another problem, which is addressed by Paul Tillich and others, is whether it is even apt to say that God has a "nature." What could that mean? It cannot possibly mean something that is common to all gods. Tillich also asks — rhetorically — if a "nature" is a term that should be used as a concept for the Creator in the same way we use it for the creature? This critique also echoes Schleiermacher, to whom we will return below.

Moreover, another problem is whether we should use ontological concepts about Christ, when the intention of Christology is to address and articulate his *personal* unity and relationship to us and to God. F. Gogarten hence makes the objection that Jesus has a personal unity with God that cannot be expressed in ontological terms. Behind this critique we hear not

---

6. It follows from the argument so far that a relational approach makes every kind of talking about nature as something opposed to the more accidental characteristics achieved throughout history problematic. Not only does it rest on an abstraction from what history means to humans, but it also ignores the basically relational character of all that is in creation. Hence there are good reasons for avoiding speaking of a human nature in Christ — as something underlying his concrete historical appearance — without taking into account his history and his relationship with God.

7. For an extensive argument on this, which nevertheless also opens up for understanding humanity in the light of religion, see J. Wentzel van Huyssteen, *Alone in the World? Human Uniqueness in Science and Theology*, The Gifford Lectures, 2004 (Grand Rapids: Eerdmans, 2006).

only modern personalist theology from the 1920s; we also hear the emerging post-metaphysical theology of the later twentieth century. As Jesus is the one in whom God is revealed, one that stands in an obedient unitary relationship with God, ontological language falls short of expressing what is at stake. This, of course, provokes us to ask if there is any gain in using ontological language at all.

The tendency to avoid ontological terms in modern theology has potential costs. For many critics it means returning to an actualist or functionalist Christology, where Jesus is related to God only on the personal and ethical level, and not in a deeper way. The relational approach I have developed above tries to deepen the approach of non-ontological language, but without giving up on the concern for expressing a deep and continuous relationship between Jesus, God, and humanity, respectively, that cannot be easily dissolved. If desire is something that totally occupies us and also implies a certain determination by the desired object, as well as something that makes you the one you are, then these demonstrate how a deep and two-sided relationship is shaped. Moreover, as Christ is also receiving the gifts of God and passing them on, he is ontologically making manifest God's presence in his own life and in the world. This, simultaneously, also links him closely to other humans, who recognize him as a true human, a witness to humanity in both senses of the word.

Hence, the solution to the problems with the two-nature formula might be overcome by developing a framework within which the old formula *vere deus vere homo* becomes understandable. This formula makes no use of the concept of nature, while it still opens up to an understanding based on what takes place in the history of Christ. What is not explicitly addressed in the formula is the concern that actually motivated the Council of Chalcedon: That Christ is a person not divided, but one, united, coherent. However, this unity cannot be explicated by means of concepts or conceptions, but only by relating to the historical person of Jesus from Nazareth, who might then be understood from both the angle of his divinity and his humanity. The mystery of Christ is his total unity with both God and humanity, and that unity is only accessible historically, if and when God reveals God as a human, as he does in Christ. Hence, Christology might be said to exhibit the need for perspectivism: What we get to know from Christ, or what is revealed in him, is not one, objective truth; it is several truths, depending on what we are asking for. Christ reveals something about true humanity and true divinity. However, divinity and humanity still need to be understood as non-identical, though still related and connected, and even more so in Christ.

The point here is substantial as well as methodological: Substantially speaking, the two-nature doctrine was meant to safeguard the understanding that Jesus Christ is both a full human being and God (as the second person in the Trinity). Moreover, the doctrine expresses the *unity* of the two in the one historical person. However, what has caused so much confusion and difficulty in the history of Christology is the attempt to interpret the life of Jesus in light of these concepts, asking in what sense he is expressing his humanity and in what sense his divinity. This approach is doomed to fail, because it does not take its point of departure in the phenomenon it is aiming to understand, but instead starts with concepts that are based on an understanding of that very phenomenon. This approach then gives privileged status to the interpretative concepts instead of the phenomenon they seek to interpret. We have to see the history as explicated by and brought to the fore by the concepts, which then serve the interpretation of that history, instead of asking how preconceived concepts can be exemplified, illuminated, and clarified by the history.[8]

Nevertheless, the *veritas* — truth — of Christ's deity and humanity is safeguarded only when we are able to keep creature and Creator, God and human distinct.[9] We can realize the importance of this concern by studying the historical context of Chalcedon. It is only against the background of these concerns that the formula can still serve any clarifying purpose. It cannot be taken out of this history and repeated outside of that context of

8. This point is made strongly in Wolfhart Pannenberg, *Jesus — God and Man*, SCM Classics (London: SCM, 2002).

9. In this sense, James K. A. Smith is right when he sees, in the light of postmodern material as well, Chalcedon's formulation of the logic of incarnation as one helping us to understand *difference*: Chalcedon "provides an alternative way for understanding difference, or better, the relation between differences. In the Chalcedonian model we see a certain mutuality — a play of differences that permits relation without either reducing the terms to the Same or asserting a radical incommensurability that precludes connection. In his phenomenology of the icon, one finds Marion taking this Chalcedonian model seriously and we see hints of it spilling over into his anthropology — enough traces of an alternative to mark a difference between the philosophical anthropologies of Levinas and Marion." James K. A. Smith, "The Call as Gift: The Subject's Donation in Marion and Levinas," in *The Hermeneutics of Charity: Interpretation, Selfhood, and Postmodern Faith*, ed. James K. A. Smith and Henry Isaac Venema (Grand Rapids: Brazos Press, 2004), p. 225.

discussion without creating severe problems. The contrast with today's ways of understanding and making problematic the concept of nature and its function then becomes clearer as well.

Critique of the Two-Nature Doctrine and New Attempts

In his *Der Christliche Glaube,* § 96, 1, Schleiermacher deals with the question of how the human and the divine can be subsumed under the same notion (i.e., nature) and be used as examples of some common notion. Is it at all possible that they can be determined and defined from the same "universal"? When we talk about human spirit and God's spirit, we have to make clear that they are something quite different, and would that not be the case for the concept of nature as well? I take Schleiermacher's reasoning here to suggest even deeper problems with the concept of nature as used in Christology than hitherto indicated: even when we think we have clarified the content of the divine and human natures, we still have the prior problem of the appropriateness of talking of them as two different *natures* at all. Does this not subsume that which is totally different to a notion of the same, to put it in fashionable postmodern terms?[10]

One can understand Schleiermacher's criticism as an expression of his intention to safeguard the divinity of God from being mixed with the human, and as an attempt to clarify the conceptions of both nature and person (of which he claims that the latter notion is also used in two different ways in Christology). His treatment is nevertheless more oriented towards pointing to the confusing consequences of the doctrine than with providing a constructive solution to it.

Schleiermacher points to how the concept of nature is made out of limitations — but God is not limited, claims Schleiermacher. Although the last point here is a modern critique that does not address the old use of the ancient concept of nature *(substantia),* he is nevertheless right in that we cannot use "nature" of God and humans in the same way, as this creates confusion and misunderstanding. What Schleiermacher thus makes clear is that when we express how Jesus is related to God and to humanity, we

---

10. Cf. Friedrich Schleiermacher, Hugh Ross Mackintosh, and James Stuart Stewart, *The Christian Faith* (New York: Harper & Row, 1963), vol. 2, p. 392. The present discussion is based on § 96, 1.

cannot use the notion "nature" in any clear way in order to state what they might have in common.

Moreover, his analysis of classical Christology also clearly spells out another weakness: Usually we talk about nature as something that is common, so that a person is one who belongs to those who participate in a common nature. But in Christ one person has two very different natures: "For in utter contradiction to the use elsewhere, according to which the same nature belongs to many individuals or persons, here one person has share in two quite different natures" (§ 96, 1, 393).

Schleiermacher also claims that as nature is a universal, one nature can characterize an indefinite number of individuals. But one individual cannot simultaneously manifest two natures, especially two that are poles apart, such as the human and the divine. His arguments suggest that this would lead to a situation in which one of the natures would have to give way to the other. Hence, he reopens the struggle between Antioch and Alexandria and focuses on the dilemmas over the understanding of Jesus: either we risk confusing both natures into a third, or we risk separating the two natures and make just one of them the basic point of orientation in the description of the concrete person of Jesus from Nazareth.

As indicated above already, Wolfhart Pannenberg criticizes Chalcedon for not starting from the concrete historical Jesus, but from abstract notions. Also, like Schleiermacher, he holds that "nature" cannot be understood in the same way for both the human and the divine nature. Pannenberg also underscores how difference and not unity is the focal point in the discussion of the relations between the two natures. Pannenberg also sees the expression of *vere deus vere homo* as indispensable, but underscores that this formula should be seen as explicating different aspects of this very same historical person. Hence, he will safeguard both the true humanity and the true divinity of Christ, but tries to avoid the problems connected to the old formula. He also quotes Edmund Schlink, to which we can subscribe as well: "The Chalcedonian declaration is not concerned with the two natures as such, but with the completeness of Jesus' divine and human nature without which his substitution would be illusory."[11]

---

11. Pannenberg, *Jesus — God and Man*, p. 321. The quotation is from E. Schlink, "Die Christologie von Chalkedon im ökumenischen Gespräch," in *Der kommende Christus und die kirchlichen Traditionen*, p. 84.

Pannenberg also contributes to a more constructive approach to these problems. Affirming how Logos must be thought of as that which is behind the created world, he opens up to a relational approach that integrates some of the concerns previously expressed in ontological language. This relational approach makes it possible to see the world and humans as already related to the logos. In Jesus this logos then is incarnated in a way that makes a new unity between humans and God possible — a unity to which all humans are destined already by the fact that they are created through the logos. Pannenberg hence makes possible a conception of unity that safeguards distinction and difference, and that does not presuppose two totally different and unrelated aspects of reality.

We find two more attempts to explore new ways of expressing unity and difference in the Scottish theologian John Macquarrie and in German-Danish theologian Peter Widmann. Macquarrie shares Schleiermacher's critique of the two-nature doctrine, but he also offers a reinterpretation where the main points seem to be the following: There is in this world of process no finished human nature. Human nature must be seen as yet something unfinished, something still coming into being:

> If we move away from the static understanding of "nature" (*physis*) as a fixed essence to the dynamic and progressive understanding of *physis* as "emergence" or "coming into being," then the notion of the two natures "concurring" in the person of Christ becomes intelligible. On the one hand, humanity is seeking its authentic being in its spiritual quest for communion with God, while on the other hand, God is entering his creation and communicating himself through a human being which can both receive and express the presence of God.[12]

Like our attempt to interpret Pannenberg in a more relational fashion above, Macquarrie also seems open for interpretation along such lines: his emphasis on emergence and quest can hardly be conceived without paying attention to the aim of this quest, or alternatively, how God, when communicating and participating in God's own creation in the process of incarnation, is relating to it in a manner that makes a distinct contribution to how we think of both God and human beings.

Peter Widmann follows up similar intentions as those of Macquarrie

---

12. John Macquarrie, *Jesus Christ in Modern Thought* (London and Philadelphia: SCM Press and Trinity Press International, 1990), p. 385.

insofar as he underscores the unity of the divine and the human in Christ. Widmann uses the notion "symbiotic unity" in order to express what is taking place. Such unity implies that we have to see two distinct "lines" in Christ's life, each one intact in itself, but entering into a symbiosis in the concrete life of Jesus from Nazareth, where they live from each other, participate in one another, and thus make a unique entity. Widmann compares this to how Bach's works are composed: often there are two works merged into one, where the two have their distinct quality and specificity, but nevertheless become something more, a surplus, when joined with the other element.[13]

We can develop Widmann's insights further by this notion of *surplus:* It will not do to say that there are two individual modes of being united in Christ, as this might easily lead into either Nestorianism or some form of Monophysitism. When the two parts in the merger are thought of as intact, but still making up something more when they are together than what they are individually (against Nestorianism), the surplus expressed in this *more* is not dependent on them making something *third,* but more like the surplus emerging from unity in difference and community (not identity). Hence, the surplus is linked to the very fact that belonging to or participating in a community allows for a different kind of expression, which does not sublate individuality or repress the identity manifested in the mutual recognition that shapes the community.

This latter approach to the concerns of the two-nature doctrine has one more advantage: it allows us to connect the understanding of the reality that Jesus opens up when he proclaims and practices the kingdom of God to the unity of God and human in Christ. In both cases, something is taking place that is not given with the past or to be understood from the immediately present elements. The reality that manifests itself in Christ as well as in the realization of the kingdom is a surplus compared to what is present in the world when God is not present in it as the incarnated logos. Hence, the revelation of God in Christ is the manifestation of the surplus which is a promise to the future of humanity. This also allows us to see the unity as both relational and functional. The question still withstanding is

13. Widmann, in Niels Henrik Gregersen and Jens Holger Schjørring, *Fragmenter af et Spejl: Bidrag til Dogmatikken* (Frederiksberg, Denmark: Forlaget Anis, 1992), pp. 193f. Widmann continues a long tradition in theology when he develops metaphors like this one. One that comes to mind is Luther's picture of the glowing iron, which is both heat and iron, and still something that cannot be what it is in its actual presence without the other.

to what extent we can also express what traditionally was taken to be the *substantial* unity in a way that overcomes the problems with the concept of nature as it appears in Christology? German theologian Hermann Deuser might help us further with that.

Christ as God's Representation: The Semiotic Angle

German systematic theologian Hermann Deuser has developed an understanding of Christ using C. S. Pierce's philosophy as a tool for understanding Christ and incarnation in a way that might further clarify or define our already used conception of *representation*.[14] Like me, Deuser sees this notion as a possible basis for rearticulating the doctrine of incarnation. Moreover, he interprets this notion on the basis of categorical semiotics, which allows for the notion to be understood from a relational angle. This then allows him to see the issue of how God is represented in Christ as a problem of description (Darstellungsproblem), which calls for reconstruction, as this makes the central issue not one of substance but of relation. Hence, relation functions as the basic philosophical concept when dealing with this problem.[15]

Deuser understands representation as that which immediately shapes our relation to and understanding of the world. Representations are something original (in the meaning of being prior to interpretation, analysis etc.), and our relation to the world is mediated through them. Without primary representations there are no such things as impressions, and hence also no possibilities for understanding and action. Deuser claims that this is also valid for religious representations.[16]

Against this background he then differentiates between three different uses of the word "representation." Representation expresses itself (a) in the relation of the image in the mind to that which is the origin of that image. Different theories of cognition work with this; (b) in juridical representation (Stellvertretung), but also in the way the unity of the church is present in the bishop, or Christ in the sacrament (as either image [Abbild]

---

14. Hermann Deuser, "Inkarnation und Repräsentation," *Theologische Literaturzeitung* 124, no. 4 (1999).

15. Deuser, "Inkarnation und Repräsentation," p. 360.

16. Deuser, "Inkarnation und Repräsentation," p. 362.

or real presence); (c) in the semiotic approach, which Deuser himself uses in order to reformulate the doctrine of incarnation. The understanding of representation found in this last approach is what concerns us in the following, and it is important not to confuse this with more generic theories of representation in the human sciences. On this semiotic understanding of representation, he claims that it presents us with an alternative to mere understandings of mirroring the world on the one hand, or nominalist forms of constructivism on the other. The semiotic approach opens up a realistic sign-structure that has universal significance, and is rooted in reality itself. According to Deuser, the world itself cannot appear to us outside operations of representation, in which one relates to that which is other in acts of interpretation.[17]

Deuser distinguishes between three different elements in the process of representation: (1) The original creativity, which then finds its (2) definitive expression in an object of representation. The relation between (1) and (2) is then something that needs to be (3) acknowledged or recognized in an act of understanding. Every process of thinking, understanding, and interpretation is here given within a representation-structure, where the representation is what makes the undefined something to be appropriated concretely in a specific context of understanding. This means, ontologically speaking, that when one relates to a representation one has to assume that behind or beyond this concrete representation is a qualitatively prior creative foundation that comes to its expression in the very process of signifying. Although this foundation is not always made thematic, it *could* always be made so.[18]

Deuser holds that what is characteristic for religious representations is that they make explicit and thematic the otherwise often not explicated question about the basis of reality. Although this may happen in many different forms, it always happens in a way that strives to express the best possible answer to these questions.[19] It is against such a background that it also becomes clear how the two-nature doctrine can be understood as a way to answer what expresses itself in the history of Jesus from Nazareth. This doctrine is an attempt to articulate what it is that expresses itself as the creative ground of that which we perceive as a representation in him.

17. Deuser, "Inkarnation und Repräsentation," pp. 362-63.
18. Deuser, "Inkarnation und Repräsentation," p. 363.
19. Deuser, "Inkarnation und Repräsentation," p. 365.

In saying that God is here represented, Deuser makes five remarks in order to clarify what this might imply, and these remarks must be read in light of his differentiation between the three stages of the process above:

1. Representation does not mean identification.
2. Representation allows for immediacy and historical mediation to be thought together. The creative quality of God the creator is not determined or defined in itself, but only in specific definite acts of agency. The creative power of God is then expressing itself definitively in the representative mediation as this comes to the fore in Jesus. In him, the creative powers of God are present and manifest (gegenständlich). This has the important implication that Christology is always contextual. The fundamental creative quality cannot be represented in other ways than in specific historical contexts. The specific case of religious or Christological representation at stake in these contexts is God.[20]
3. Representation mediates also between revelation and interpretation. When explicated in a Christological context, this means that the character of creative indefiniteness is overcome and made into something that can be received and understood concretely by means of the representation of God in Jesus Christ.[21]
4. Representation always implies a specific determination of the relation between parties (Verhältnisbestimmung). In Christology, this is explicated in a way that makes the church understand Jesus as the one who is in the place of God, and hence, his presence is manifest in a way that surpasses death. It is against this background that the church can say that as Jesus Christ is, so is God.[22]

20. Deuser, "Inkarnation und Repräsentation," p. 366.

21. Deuser, "Inkarnation und Repräsentation," p. 367. Deuser illustrates this further: "Die sog. Hoheitstitel oder Prädikationen Jesu als 'Sohn Gottes,' 'Messias,' 'Menschensohn,' etc. bringen in ihren jeweiligen religiösen Kontexten diesen Zusammenhang repräsentativ zum Ausdruck. Dann wird es auch überflüssig, das Verhältnis menschlichen Erkennens zur göttlichen Wirklichkeit in der Figur einer Analogie beschreiben zu müssen. Göttliches und Menschliches sind nicht analog, sondern vermittelt in der Produktivität und Prozessualität eines realen Zeichenereignisses — genau so, wie es in der Zusammengehörigkeit von Gott und Mensch in Jesus Christus repräsentiert ist. So ist die christologische Grundaussage in der Passionsgeschichte bei Markus zu verstehen: 'Wahrhaftig, dieser Mensch war Gottes Sohn' (Mark 15,39b)."

22. Deuser, "Inkarnation und Repräsentation," p. 367.

5. Representation thus must be seen as pointing beyond the alternatives of either image or real presence (Jenseits der Alternative von bloßem Abbild oder Realpräsenz).

Deuser's contribution is now possible to sum up like this: His understanding provides us with reasons for saying that we cannot possibly think God as present and effective in other forms than by representations. The semiotic approach tells us that the presence of God in the world is like the presence of anything else in the world: it is present by means of representations. The specificity of Christianity is that God's presence is linked to Jesus as his representation: "The semiotic connection of divine creativity and the presence of love in the parables of Jesus and in the realizing appropriation of the parable that Jesus himself is; this structural as well as substantial trinity is a complete representation."[23]

Deuser underscores how the actions of representation consist of three irreducible building elements: the qualitative (creative) basic reference, the objective representation, and the spiritual appropriation or interpretation. This allows him to see the Trinity as a necessary basis of Christology. God's Creation represents itself in Christ like this: either as parables that express the presence of the kingdom of God, or his presence in the spiritual community. Christological representation understood as the teaching and personal appropriation of God's revelation is the essence of the creative productivity and the continuous dynamic process of the sign-as-event whereby God is experienced and thought about in the Christian tradition.[24] This means that the doctrine of the two natures is not the final word about the identity of God or Christ. It also means that Deuser offers us a way to formulate conceptually what is doctrinally formulated by speaking of the substantial continuity of God and Christ, in a manner that makes them both refer to each other in order to become what they are. Thus, we can see Deuser's contribution also as a philosophical underpinning of what Widmann above described as symbiosis.

*   *   *

23. Deuser, "Inkarnation und Repräsentation," pp. 368f.: "Der semiotische Zusammenhang von göttlicher Kreativität, Nähe der Liebe Gottes in den Gleichnissen Jesu und in der verstehenden Aneignung des Gleichnisses, das Jesus selbst ist; diese strukturelle wie inhaltliche Trinität ist eine vollständige Repräsentation."

24. Cf. Deuser, "Inkarnation und Repräsentation," p. 370.

When the church says: Jesus Christ is *vere deus* et *vere homo,* we have to ask: What does that mean — what is the concern behind saying this? How are these words to be understood? Truth in the biblical sense means primarily: reliability. If you want to know truly what a human is determined to be, you should look at Jesus. If you really want to know what God is, you should look at Jesus. The possibilities of establishing an understanding of human or divine identity both lie with Jesus. Taken together, however, this combination also makes Jesus unique, in the sense that it is only in him that God and the human can be *fully* identified. He is more like us than we ourselves are like our own destiny (Bestimmung); but he is also like God. Consider how the combination works: if we "only" say: he is a true human, we say of him only that he is something like us — the ideal human, the human of higher actuality or so on. But by also saying he is the true God, we say something more, something that cannot be said of other humans. On the other hand, by saying he is true God, we say something about other conceptions of God: no other God can be truly God in the same manner, as the God we are speaking of manifests/reveals God's divinity in being a human. The *differentia specifica* of Jesus Christ lies thus in the combination of *vere deus* and *vere homo* — not in only one of them. The specific character of the God we are speaking about is a God who appears/exists in this world as the true human that we are all called to become. The concern of the Christological formulae is to express this uniqueness. It does this in such a manner that the rest of humanity is included into the horizon within which we talk of Christ's humanity. Meanwhile, it also speaks of God in such a manner that God is defined by God's presence in the life and work of this human.

This revelation of the identity of God in Christ is disputed, and it was rejected. Its most apparent rejection takes place in the crucifixion of Jesus as God's representative. To this issue in Christology we now turn.

PART III

DEATH AND CIRCUMSTANCES OF DEATH: THE CLOSING OF THE OPEN WORLD

The Drama of Easter and Its Victims

The rejection of Jesus is openly acknowledged in the New Testament (cf. Acts 3:14; 4:11; 1 Pet. 2:4, 7). Contrary to what might appear as a convenient picture, this rejection was not made only by those who were negatively challenged by his preaching. The most prominent among those who rejected Jesus is Peter. There are good reasons for calling attention to this: the New Testament pictures a situation where ordinary people, usually likely to join with Jesus, suddenly reject him. Hence it is not only the "bad guys" or the ones addressed in the Gospels as "hypocrites" who are depicted as contributing to his death. The picture the New Testament suggests is one in which we can find people like ourselves on the side of the perpetrators — or as passive bystanders.

Against this background two lines for reading the passion stories suggest themselves. One reading would see the world that Jesus opened and promised as being rejected. One can perhaps say that putting Jesus to death is an attempt to close down the kingdom he envisioned and the community he founded. This attempt is — from a theological as well as a philosophical angle — one that makes his death a natural consequence: the life manifesting itself in him and his practice is the opposite of the lonely and despicable death he suffers.

This first line of interpretation makes us see the death of Jesus as a mark of the antagonisms that are present since the very beginning of his life. We started the previous part of this book by pointing to the tension between Herod and the Magi over Jesus, or between the notion of a kingdom in glory versus one that realizes itself in poverty and among ordinary people. The same tension between forces of life and forces of death are at hand when the law is not used for the well-being of the neighbor, or when Jesus heals the sick, casts out demons, or raises the dead. Against this background, his own death is only one more instance of this struggle between powers of life and death, but in this struggle, he apparently loses.

A second line of interpretation, and admittedly a more existential one, sees these tensions not only as expressions between powers in the world: it is also possible to see the drama at Easter as one that reveals what is humanity's true identity and calling: The personal ambiguity of each and every human is here revealed, with Peter and Judas as two models of the same human predicament. Against this background of interpretation, what happens to Jesus at Easter not only reveals him as the only human with integrity; it also reveals every other human as those who due to this lack of integrity are faced with the powers of death in their lives.

There are, of course, several other angles of interpretation and ways of discussing the death of Jesus. Some of these will be presented along our course of discussion. The underlying question, though, is this: How is God expressed in what happens at Golgotha? What has God to do with this? Is the death of Jesus God's failure to reveal the kingdom, or is it an example of the tragedy that befalls those living in uncompromising love? Is this the end for those responding positively to the vocation of becoming images of God?

The interpretation of what happens to Jesus may take as a point of departure the observation that how one understands his death is a result of how one is related to him. This claim is of pivotal importance if we hold that his death has some significance for us. His death has no meaning *per se,* but only if we see it as a part of the relationships into which he is woven. How can this be a justified claim? In the following, I will suggest that the main approach for developing an understanding of his death emerges from understanding *Jesus as the victim of evil.* This is a moral as well as a theological claim.[1] His victimization is not unique in the sense that he is the only one to be a victim of evil, but it is specific in the way that he, more than any other, bore witness to a God of goodness, justice, and community, and that he thereby challenged the dominating cultural pattern of his times in a way that finally made him a victim. C. F. Alford has claimed that our culture

---

1. To say it with S. Mark Heim, *Saved from Sacrifice: A Theology of the Cross* (Grand Rapids: Eerdmans, 2006): "The event of Jesus' death, his condemnation, suffering and execution, is a bad thing" (p. xi). The theological outcome of this judgment is aptly formulated by Heim when he gives one of his chapters the subtitle "Saved by What Shouldn't Happen" (p. 107).

. . . has lost the narrative resources to make sense of the experience of victimhood, above all the dread of what it is to be truly human. It has, in other words, lost the sense of tragedy. We are all victims, victims of life and death. It is against the victimhood of being merely human that evil is dedicated.[2]

Alford's quote suggests that evil as well as victimhood is deeply connected to the basic features of human life, and that we need to make sense of this in order to get access to and open up our lives in a better and more adequate way. This is not exclusively relevant to Jesus, but goes for every human. That the story of Jesus' death provides such resources is what I am going to attempt to show in the following.

2. Here quoted from Arne Johan Vetlesen, *Evil and Human Agency: Understanding Collective Evildoing*, Cambridge Cultural Social Studies (Cambridge and New York: Cambridge University Press, 2005), p. 138.

Judas and Peter as Models

Judas' Betrayal

Judas' betrayal of Jesus is prepared in the narrative by a story we have already dealt with: Judas' approach to the anointment of Jesus suggests that he might be reluctant to see him as a king in the sense that the woman does. The underlying motive here, as in other places where he is described, suggests that he has an issue with money, arguably confirmed by the fact that he offers to betray Jesus to the chief priests for a specific amount of it.

Already these small strands are enough to imply that there are two interrelated elements behind Judas' betrayal of Jesus. It is not unimportant which comes first: his lack of a positive recognition of Jesus as the Messiah, God's elected witness. Because of this lack of recognition, he is also able to understand himself as one doing a religiously laudable act when he gives Jesus over to the guards. He thereby models every person who, in the name of religion, is willing to do some harm to another for the sake of some higher aim. The question is then what this aim might be. I will suggest that Judas gives expression to the experience of *a threat against a desired object*. This threat may be perceived as directed against the identity and stability of the society in which he had his place.[1] This threat against this religious

---

1. In the following deliberations I make use of the presentation of the theory of securitization made by Arne-Johan Vetlesen. I use Vetlesen's study for quite different purposes here than he has in his book, but I nevertheless think that the bulk of theory he provides for understanding what we can call acts of evil might also prove fruitful in the present context. See Arne Johan Vetlesen, *Evil and Human Agency: Understanding Collective Evildoing*, Cambridge Cultural Social Studies (Cambridge and New York: Cambridge University Press, 2005), pp. 167ff.

society and the established worship is something he can experience as having in common with the religious establishment. His perception of Jesus seems to have changed from one he thought would contribute to the securitization of that object, to one who is himself a threat against it. This might explain both why Judas follows Jesus up to a point, and why he eventually is willing to give Jesus over. The two basic events that may have triggered the change in his opinion abut Jesus are the anointment of Jesus (which Jesus did not reject, thereby implicitly accepting recognition as the Messiah) and Jesus' "cleansing" of the temple. Both these events could be interpreted as attacks against the two traditional foundations of Judaism: the kingdom of David and the cult in the temple in Jerusalem.

In present scholarship the issue of "securitization" is one identified in different strategies and measurements done to secure a specific political or social form. The need for "securitization" emerges when a significant object is threatened. The measurements are usually made dependent on an assertion about a threatened object (state, nation, religion). The Norwegian philosopher Arne Johan Vetlesen describes these dynamics:

> The assertion that the object is threatened takes the form of an appeal; this appeal in turn triggers different dynamics and paths of action depending on the properties of the referent object. The issue of destiny of a selected and particularly significant (meaning both symbol-laden and indispensable) object is made into an existential issue whose resolution will be decisive for the destiny of all those in the group (the national community, the religious community, etc.) who are associated with the object. Since the alleged threat is existential, it will be necessary to implement extraordinary measures in order to protect it.[2]

Against this theoretical background, we can understand Judas' betrayal not merely as a banal action in which he exchanged Jesus for his desire for money. Rather, the construction of this higher aim might allow Judas to relativize or play down the importance of that which he instigates as a secondary object of desire, namely money. The money is only an expression, admittedly a desirable and useful one, of his ability to put first the things that are over and beyond his mere personal interest. Money serves as a secondary object of desire and a confirmation of his dedication to the primary task and the desire to which he is committed: to make safe and se-

---

2. Vetlesen, *Evil and Human Agency,* pp. 167-68.

cure a religious worship and the society in which he lives. His basic desire is thus not the desire for money, but for a stable and secure society where there are no threats to the worship in the temple. As indicated, we might even see Jesus' "cleansing" of the temple and his criticism of what took place there as the final event that triggered Judas to hand him over. Hence, Judas appears as strongly religiously motivated, as well as acting on behalf of the society to which he belonged.

Judas' actions thus become a model for how religious means can be used for maintaining stability and conserving given political and social systems, in a manner that sheds critical light over the way religion might function even today: When the desire to secure religious values and a specific form of society becomes a "security issue" in this sense, it might entail that

> a specific issue is lifted above the ordinary political discourse; it is elevated to a higher plane, reflecting its importance and urgency, in keeping with the action-compelling logic according to which "if not dealt with in time, it will be too late." Hence all other concerns must be put aside; those charged with dealing with the issue must be granted unlimited powers, and their measures will appear as legitimate in light of the utmost seriousness of their task.[3]

What Judas then does is to exchange one framework for understanding and regulation of society with another: He represents a fall back into the ordinary way of understanding society, and prioritizes security and stability over openness, lack of control, and equal relations that manifest themselves in the kingdom of God. The way value-bearers (as money or ointments) function in this context is also differently conceived: the money Judas receives is his to keep (it actually becomes a problem when he hands it back), while the ointment that Jesus was given only functions as gift in a relation caused by his being deeply recognized by another human. This re-prioritizing makes it possible to justify what he does in light of higher aims, and it also makes his own act something more than an individual consideration. The deliberation expressed in John 11:45ff. reflects that the concern of the nation is a concern shared by the council:

> So the chief priests and the Pharisees called a meeting of the council, and said, "What are we to do? This man is performing many signs. If we let

3. Vetlesen, *Evil and Human Agency*, p. 168.

him go on like this, everyone will believe in him, and the Romans will come and *destroy both our holy place and our nation.*" But one of them, Caiaphas, who was high priest that year, said to them, "You know nothing at all! You do not understand that it is better for you to have one man die for the people than to have the whole nation destroyed." [. . .] So from that day on they planned to put him to death. [italics mine]

Although there might also be a tacit expression of rivalry-desire in this text,[4] the main message is that Judas' betrayal is clearly linked to the concern for the nation and the temple among the people's leaders. To sacrifice Jesus is, in light of this interpretation, to make him dispensable for the sake of a higher good.

At this point we have to see a deep connection between desire and lack of recognition. The prioritized desire here is possible *as* prioritized only against the background in which there is no realization or recognition of Jesus as a true witness to God and God's kingdom. Hence, not only Jesus and God (as expressed and witnessed by him) are rejected, so are the ways the social and religious community is perceived by Jesus. The impossibility of the kingdom is thus reaffirmed, but this reaffirmation is now made at the cost of death. Thus, the antagonisms expressed in the presence of the kingdom are now revealed in a new light: it becomes clear that when the kingdom is perceived as *the impossible in terms of the absolutely not desirable,* this implies a justification of measures like putting to death, if necessary.

One more thing is worth noting when we consider a possible context for action in Judas: neither Judas nor any of the chief priests express in the above quote any concern for *God* or for the kingdom of God in their deliberations. To put it simply: the word "God" is totally absent from their deliberations. That is interesting from two points of view: (1) It means that the word "God" is not shaping the world in which they make their deliberations to any significant degree. God is not the overall concern, the ultimate object of love and desire in what they do, and why they do it. (2) This means that something else is seen as the ultimate horizon for their actions and concerns, explicated in the care for the nation and the holy place. To phrase it with Paul Tillich: their ultimate concern is with things of this world, and not directly with God. Hence, the nation and the holy place are made into idols, and for these idols they are ready to make a human sacrifice. It is of

---

4. This is a subject I return to in a later chapter.

course impossible to write these sentences without thinking of the actual situation in the world today, when humans are still sacrificed for what is advertised as religious values, and their lives are subjected to or subsumed under the desire for security and a controllable market that must function regardless of the effect it has on local communities and individual lives.

The unconditional community that Jesus offers to all is offered to Judas even after he agrees to betray Jesus. This we can see in how Jesus calls him *friend*, and in his participation in the Last Supper. Although Judas was about to do what he did, Jesus nevertheless seems undisturbed by this in his practice of hospitality toward him. This suggests that the practice of Jesus, and his calling, remains regardless of how human sin is expressing itself — even within his community.

The above interpretation of the fate of Judas was taken in order to shed light on two factors that still have relevance and might be worth considering from a contemporary perspective. First, to reject Judas because he was rejecting Jesus is too simplistic an approach to the way he functions in the narrative about Jesus. *Judas could be anyone.* He is one of those who are willing to sacrifice innocent blood due to his own conception of what is best. But he is also one who, eventually, realizes that this is wrong (cf. Matt. 27:3-4). Second, as this "anyone" he is one who is committed to what he perceives as the good of the community, and it is due to this commitment that he is willing to make sacrifices in order to secure these goods. This might even imply making sacrifices that *seem* personal: he has to give up his friendship with Jesus and the community with him (he parts from the Last Supper). Such sacrifices might even be interpreted as his serving a just cause without considering only his personal interests but those of the community. Nevertheless, one has to ask: Is Judas then not also modeling a possibility for humans today? Is not even the Christian community at risk, when it wants to "protect" values they consider important, in spite of the fact that the securitization of these values makes others pay more?[5] To es-

---

5. This is not to say that everyone who fights, e.g., for family values, for marriage, or against divorce or gay marriage (or whatever else is considered the present "Christian values") is a Judas. But I am implying that the model of Judas might call for a critical scrutiny of practices where one promotes values mainly at the expense of others, and in a way that does not create possibilities for community with those against whom one is fighting. That some Christians also perceive critical responses they face themselves when, for example, arguing against the ethical validity of homosexual partnerships as the "costs" *they* have to pay is hard to understand as anything but a mere self-centered conception of martyrdom.

tablish a distance from Judas because one is on the side of Jesus is to avoid the very function that Judas might still have in the continuing narrative about Jesus — the one in which humanity in general still partakes and in which it may be asked: Could this be you? This existential function of the figure of Judas is possible only when he is seen not merely as an objectification of evil, but as expressing a common human disposition, and one that could easily be triggered by our conception of our place, role, and identity in a community with others with whom we share important values — including "religious" ones.

Peter's Denial

At one point Peter shares with Judas not wanting to be identified with Jesus anymore. As with Judas, Jesus also foresees Peter's denial of him, and he nevertheless does not exclude him from community. Peter, on the other hand, tries to distance himself from the relationship with Jesus and the community of the disciples in this situation. Different from Judas, though, is the fact that Peter only denies Jesus when Jesus is already in real trouble. This attempt thus models another approach to the relationship with Jesus than the one we found in the analysis of Judas above: Peter is not willing to be recognized as one of Jesus' followers because he fears the negative consequences of this for himself. His concern for himself overshadows his relationship with Jesus and the community of the other disciples.

Peter's breakdown, triggered by the cock crowing, indicates that the identity he tried to maintain when confronted by the bystanders who recognized him as one of Jesus' followers is indeed impossible to uphold. Before the breakdown, however, the story indicates that he was willing to deny his relationship with Jesus three times and thus not just randomly. The repeated and emphasized denial suggests that the trouble Jesus faces also confronts Peter with an identity crisis: He seems unprepared for what is happening and undoubtedly had other expectations for Jesus' visit to Jerusalem than those now taking place in front of him. He is thus thrown into insecurity, and has to relate to something beyond the immediate situation in order to regain his determination and knowledge about where he belongs and what is his identity.

Like Judas, Peter also models an existential option: even those closest to Jesus might come to deny him, given the "right" circumstances. The fact that the New Testament speaks so openly about Peter's denial has without doubt to do with an acknowledgment of this fact. Peter, then, is just as much a divided identity, with differing and conflicting desires, as the rest of humankind. He lacks the very same wholeheartedness and love for God that Jesus said was necessary in order to keep the basic commandment of the law. Seen in this context, the story not only serves to avoid any kind of idealization of the first leaders of the church, it also points to the common possibility that denial is for everyone.

There is, however, one element in the story about Peter that merits further attention: the fact that the bystanders are perceived by him as dangerous. Why are they so perceived? Because he might be exposed by them to others who might be even more dangerous than they are. The possibility calls for understanding the history of Peter in a wider framework, a kind of play in which parts are handed out: potential victim, bystander, perpetrator. The question emerging from the narrative is this, then: What part does the reader play?

Perpetrators and Bystanders:
Collective Evil Reconsidered

In the present section, I will go more deeply into the work of Arne Johan Vetlesen on collective evildoing, because I think he can shed further light on some of the mechanisms at play in the trial and crucifixion of Jesus. This might also give us a chance to see that what is at play in the history of Jesus is not unique, but the manifestation of powers that are still very much at work. In this sense, the following might be read as making the story of Jesus' victimization and crucifixion an illustration of more general phenomena. While this certainly is partly the case, such an approach might also help us understand the specifics of the history of Jesus in light of this generic approach. Hence, again we need not see our analysis as privileging one mode of understanding over against another. Moreover, this might also help us see that the experiences reported in the Gospels belong to the very conditions of the present world as well.

The un-discussed — and taken-for-granted — assumption in the following is that *it was evil to sentence Jesus to death,* and should not have been done. His was an unjust and unjustified death. I underscore this here already because some forms of more or less popular theology tend to overlook or obscure this fact by different claims about how this death was a "necessary" part of God's plan to save the world from sin, or something that originated in God's own will in a manner that makes it possible to see what takes place as a mere extension of God fulfilling God's aims. Such interpretations of the trial and death of Jesus often appear as lacking consistency with convictions about God as a God of life and love, and render God as a kind of sadistic entity who is pleased by what takes place here, or at least is able to let what takes place be justified by other — and presumably higher — aims. Recent scholarship has to a large extent taken issue with these conceptions, but I will not be going into a detailed rehearsal of that criticism here.[1] That notwithstanding, I still hold that in order to provide a comprehensive and coherent *theological* interpretation of Jesus' death we need to establish this point first. Any attempts to see some "hidden goodies" in these events as they are in themselves easily make Christianity into a perverse celebration of suffering, unless we further qualify what is taking place here, how, and why.[2] This need not, then, imply a rejection of the assertion that Christ's death led to something good. But it was not the death in itself, but rather, what God *made* out of this death in terms of revealing possibilities for identity and new life that is important to theology, and makes this death important to interpret.

Vetlesen defines the act of doing evil as "to intentionally inflict pain and suffering on another human being, against her will, and causing serious and foreseeable harm to her" (p. 2). Given that we accept the above premise that what happened to Jesus was evil, and the definition given by Vetlesen as well, we can say that Jesus' death is not taking place as an expression of either God's or Jesus' original will. His pain and suffering are only expressions of his subjection to evil if they are *against his will*. If this is not acknowledged, the question emerges as to what extent these events are really evil. This question appears almost immediately against the backdrop of a tradition that reads what happens to Jesus in light of his prayer in Gethsemane, where he says "Abba, Father, for you all things are possible; remove this cup from me; yet, not what I want, but what you want." Here we are immediately in the center of the mystery of what takes place at Easter, and must ask if God actively wants, or just allows for, what takes place. If the former is the case, we can hardly interpret the death of Jesus as an expression of evil. If the latter is the case, and God only allows for the crucifixion to take place, we must find an explanation for what this will of God is that Jesus so obediently expresses his willingness to follow.

I take it that the only viable route for Christian theology is to continue to perceive what happened to Jesus as an expression of evil. This means that what happened to Jesus is an expression of his total devotion

---

1. A good overview is given in J. Denny Weaver, *The Nonviolent Atonement* (Grand Rapids: Eerdmans, 2001).

2. That history is full of examples of the opposite is no argument for the alternative: it is rather an indication of the necessity for stating this even more clearly.

and witness to God, a God calling for humanity to realize who God is, even by being willing to expose God's own Son and primary witness to death, if necessary. Jesus does not die because God wants his death, but because God has chosen to take the vulnerable path in revealing who God is. This vulnerable path implies the risk of God's witness being subjected to death.

A short consideration might help clarify this further: What would it say of God if Jesus withdrew from his mission? What would it say about Jesus? It would say about Jesus that he was able to go most of the way, but not all. Hence, he would also be a witness to God in a manner that suggested that God was worth following *to some extent.* Thereby he would compromise his ministry, because he had himself proclaimed that God is the one to love over and above *everything* else. By being willing to die, but not by *wanting* to die, Jesus expresses how he is in accordance with the message he preaches and practices throughout his whole ministry. Similarly, we can say of God that God is at work in the death of Christ. Not as its initiator, but as one who willingly accepts the consequences of being a God of love and life. Strangely enough, as we shall see later, God thereby is also revealed as a God of love and life.

Vetlesen's definition of evil thus also allows us to clarify in what respect we can see Jesus as *subjected* to evil in a manner that rules out both God and Jesus as *active subjects* in the events: Jesus is given over to "the powers of this world" in a way that finally means death, and God has nothing to *do with* these powers. By being subjected to, exposed by, and handed over to such powers Jesus also reveals them, as well as the final outcome of their rule, as death. His subject-position thus does not exclude that even in his *passivity* Jesus — like other passive humans — might serve as a revelation of what God is and is not.

The importance of underscoring both Jesus' and God's passivity at Easter is also important to make sure that the responsibility for what takes place is not in some way compromised: It is those who reject Jesus as the true witness of the kingdom of God that are the active subjects here, and they are responsible. However, just as with Judas and Peter, the Gospels suggest that this is a position that everyone could find themselves in. It is not only the Jews, the Pharisees, the Romans, or some other group who are responsible: it is all those who are not willing to follow the calling of God to the very end who — implicitly or explicitly — partake in the crucifixion of Jesus. They then sacrifice goodness, justice, and love for the sake of the short-term goals of personal complacency and security. This means that perpetrators and bystanders are not as different as one might think at first.

Vetlesen's definition of evil makes it a subcategory of the immoral. Hence it can be understood as "wrongdoing at its absolute worst" (p. 3). Not every immoral act is evil, but every evil act is immoral. His own aim is to understand acts of *collective* evildoing, and the desire to inflict evil upon others. He claims — and he gives an extensive argument for this claim — that such evildoing springs from a combination of character, situation, and structure (p. 2). Moreover, given the broad explanatory scope of his investigation, he claims that doing evil is not only based in some kind of ideology (or, for our part: theology), but that this ideological layer has to work together with psychological dispositions that resonate deeply in the subjects who perform such evil acts. In accordance with what we have already presented, this means also that individualizing approaches are insufficient to explain what takes place:

> Rather than collective evil resting on an uncoupling between the single individual's beliefs and desires, and the goals pursued on a macro-level by the large institutions in which individuals perform the actions required of them, such organized evil will often occur in a situation where these individual and institutional factors meet halfway; when they are allowed to merge, to work in tandem in the same direction. (pp. 50-51)

Within the context of the present work, there are two elements that need to be clarified in order to promote my argument further: First, I suggest that we see the trial and death of Jesus as the result of a collective act. As indicated already, the collective behind this act cannot be defined as specific groups: the Gospels suggest that almost everyone partakes in the handing over, the suggestion, the pressure, or the coercion that leads to his death. This also means that the narrative itself invites the reader to be alert to the fact that she could have been among those shouting "crucify him!" together with the others, due to the combination of character, situation, and structure. Hence the story should not be seen as suggesting that a specific group is to blame. Rather, it is a story in which all can see mirrored their own (possible, imagined) participation in what takes place. The undecidability of the answer to the question "Who killed Jesus?" in present and former scholarship points to the theologically relevant insight that no one is guilty due to his or her belonging to a specific group or having a specific position. It is exactly by attributing guilt or responsibility to a person due to his or her belonging to a specific group that makes atrocities such as genocide possible.[3] That should be avoided for moral reasons as well as for the theological reasons I have presented for relativizing family or group identities earlier in this book.

The other element in my present argument that needs further clarification is that although Vetlesen deals with instances of collective evildoing by one group against another, I also think his insights are valuable — and accordingly, applicable — to cases against individuals, like Jesus. Exactly because I hold that it is important for Christian theology to argue coherently that what happened to Jesus was an act of evil and immorality, I also argue that we must understand the mechanisms behind this event in such a perspective. Accordingly, we must go beyond the immediate *theological* interpretations that present themselves so easily when dealing with this topic, and ask if there is a *moral* lesson to be learned here before we proceed to a more theological interpretation. Such an approach might also open up insights of more general relevance, and prove insightful from a more general angle as well, and not only for theology.

Evil is located in an experiential and existential context, which makes it hard to detach from the possibilities of personal agency. In contrast to the seemingly impossible kingdom that Jesus preaches, evil appears as a very real possibility of human life. Vetlesen sees it as related to certain given, irremovable, and non-optional conditions of human life (cf. p. 10). These "givens" are thus necessary, but that does not imply that evil is necessary: it is a possibility. What then are these givens to which evil is related? Vetlesen lists these givens as dependency, vulnerability, mortality, the frailty of human relationships, and existential loneliness.

This list is very interesting from a Christological point of view, and for a double reason: first, throughout the Gospels, there are several events in which Jesus addresses people who are in one way or another suffering because of the way these givens manifest themselves in their own lives: Think of the *dependency* of the paralytic on his friends (Mark 2), the *vulnerability* of the woman suffering from hemorrhage (Mark 5), or the lepers who are marginalized or excluded from society (Mark 1); consider how *mortality* is expressing itself in the stories about the resuscitation of the

---

3. This is one of the underlying points in Vetlesen's book.

dead (Mark 5:21ff.), the *frailty of human relationships* as they are exhibited in the stories of Judas and Peter, or the *existential loneliness* of the Samaritan woman who has to go alone to the well (John 4). In all these instances, Jesus addresses the conditions and improves them, by recognizing the persons he meets as being more and something other than merely afflicted by how these conditions express themselves in their lives. Moreover, it might also, against this background, be justified to say that in the kingdom Jesus proclaims, these existential givens are recognized for what they are and taken into account. The community to which Jesus invites can safeguard human relationships, protect from being exposed to vulnerability, and compensate for existential loneliness. As for mortality, the kingdom is not a protection against it; but the message of Jesus implies that mortality is not a "given" that is the definitive element in determining human life.

The people Jesus heals and live with are thus also vivid reminders of these existential "givens." The disturbing character of these givens for those unable to recognize them, or who desire to ignore them, might be one of the reasons that people took offense at Jesus and his practicing of the kingdom. The givens as they were experienced and exhibited in the company of Jesus were, in a word, reminders of human *finitude*. Theologically speaking, to recognize that one is the image of God, and not oneself God, means acknowledging this finitude. The opposite is to reject finitude, and thereby also one's calling to be an image of God. Given that premise, we then are able to establish a possible connection between the rejection of the human vocation to be *imago Dei*, of human finitude, and evil. I underscore here that this is a *possible* and not a necessary connection, but it is nevertheless one worth pursuing further.

As indicated, Vetlesen sees a relation between the existential givens and evil. They do not *cause* evil, but they might be preconditions for it, in a very specific way. As they are indications of the boundaries and limits of human existence, evil appears as acts that try to negate the finitude expressed in them. Writes Vetlesen:

> Evil has much to do with this dimension of human existence — be it as the attempt to transcend, negate, or deny boundaries and limits, be it as a symptom of individuals' intolerance of existential givens as such — as in evildoing that is carried out in the form of a protest against such givens; recognizing their realness for others — in the form of the "weakness"-inducing vulnerability of one's victims — but denying

their realness for oneself. In this perspective, evildoing is about hurting others in order to get relief from one's own vulnerability, to gain a sense of mastery over it.[4]

The perspective suggested here adds a profound dimension to the interpretation of the antagonisms that express themselves in the narratives about Jesus: suddenly this is not only a struggle between a present-oriented and closing, control-directed attitude toward life versus a welcoming, open, other-directed way of living. Rather, it has to do with how one is related to very concrete conditions of living in a manner that might, given the right circumstances, also imply that one is acting evilly. The opposite side of Vetlesen's description is the implication that the acknowledgment and recognition of these basic conditions if human life make life better, and helps us to be more open to others, than does the neglect of them. Be this as it may, there is here an implication that we can now spell out clearly and in a way that needs no metaphysical framework in order to be understandable: what takes place in the Jesus-story is a revelation of the struggle between good and evil. *Evil appears now in a more precise manner as the very rejection of the conditions for created life.*

Vetlesen holds that our vulnerability and dependence *qua* human beings play an equally fundamental part in our wishing to do evil to others and in our own susceptibility to suffering evil as victims. When we inflict evil upon others, it is because we thereby get relief from our own vulnerability and gain a sense of mastery over it (p. 10). In other words, we do evil to others so that we do not have to face it as part of our own possibilities. Hence, evil appears as the opposite of good in a way that is structurally the exact opposite of what is expressed in the norm, "In everything do to others as you would have them do to you; for this is the law and the prophets" (Matt. 7:12). Evil is to do to others what you will not and cannot perceive as being done to yourself. By inflicting it on others, you attempt to avoid the perception you might have of your own vulnerability. Thus, to do evil is to create and sustain an illusion about who you yourself are. This illusion is possible to express metaphorically as the conception that you are as God — i.e., outside the limits that mortality, vulnerability, and fragility impose on you.

---

4. Cf. Arne Johan Vetlesen, *Evil and Human Agency: Understanding Collective Evildoing,* Cambridge Cultural Social Studies (Cambridge and New York: Cambridge University Press, 2005), p. 10. References in parentheses in the text are to this work until further notice.

Against this background, we then also have a tool for making explicit the extent to which Jesus is exposed to evil, and how others so expose him to it. Jesus, in his suffering and death, is exposed to a lack of human relations (his friends leave him, deny him, or betray him); he is totally exposed to — and thus dependent on — those who have captured him; his vulnerability is expressed in his punishment, as is finally his mortality. Moreover, the given of existential loneliness expresses itself in his cry at the cross, "My God, why have you forsaken me?" Jesus encountered and had to face the givens of human life, which implies that the given of existential loneliness is a part of human existence that Jesus had to share with the rest of humanity, and that even for him this could not be obliterated by his close relation to God. As we can then see, he is making manifest the real conditions of human life, and this partly explains why his death is probably perceived as shameful by the bystanders: he shows humans what they do not want to see in themselves as their own possibilities. But he thereby also — in a manner we shall dwell on more extensively later — shows that the wages of sin is death. Only, the sin causing this death is not his own. He reveals that humans who refuse to recognize any other human — including Jesus — as a witness to God's gifting activity with creation are acting on the side of death.

The other side of what Jesus is exposed to when punished and crucified is expressed accordingly in the way that the perpetrators are able to maintain their self-delusion by means of his very suffering and death: They need not see themselves *in this situation* as those who are to die; in this situation they are not the vulnerable, the fragile, the exposed, and the mortal. I underscore *in this situation,* as this delusion is only temporary, and might constantly be in need of new occasions of reiteration. To put it in a manner that anticipates our later discussion of Girard: As long as the mechanisms behind these events are not exposed or realized, they will continue to demand new sacrifices for the sake of upholding this delusion.

Envious Desire

Given that we are still working with the premise that what happens to Jesus on Good Friday is evil, we can now consider another approach to understanding this evil, namely, that of *envy.* Again, we are anticipating elements of our later discussion of Girard,[5] but here the approach is more psychological. Psychologist Melanie Klein considers envy as the desire to destroy what is perceived as good.[6] Envy is based "on the perceived fact that there exists outside the self something or someone that is good" (p. 124). Applied to the Jesus story this might be seen as calling for further explanation, as the reconstruction we made above might suggest that those who initiated his arrest and crucifixion saw him as a danger. There is, however, a difference between perceiving someone as a danger to what one holds valuable, and perceiving that person as evil. Given the validity of that distinction, people could hold Jesus to be good, and still seek for his destruction.

This approach might be in accordance with an understanding of evil as the willful destruction of the good. Evil is evil exactly because it destroys that which we can perceive as good. It is this relation between the act of destruction and the recognized goodness that makes it possible to speak of evil as evil. Unless this relation is maintained, the evil act might appear as "not so bad," as motivated by some or other good, or as something negotiable. However, what makes evil an evil is exactly its attempt to destroy the good. People become evil when they want to destroy that which is good. They are not evil in themselves, but only in relation to the good they seek to destroy.[7]

When Jesus appeared as good (which he undoubtedly did), he might also have triggered envy (cf. Matt. 27:18). This envy might in turn have led to the wish to destroy him. Vetlesen recounts Klein's position in a way that also makes visible the close connection between our analytic concepts of *desire* and *recognition*:

> In terms of logic, to envy someone implies (or, more accurately, presupposes) a recognition. The experience, however, entails that this other is someone who is something, or has something, or does something, that I myself am not, do not have, or have not done; and since I lack this, I do not want anybody else to have it either. In other words, envy involves the agent in a comparison with something or someone

---

5. More specifically: Girard's conception of mimetic desire. See below, pp. 253ff.

6. I still follow the research of Vetlesen on the psychological background of evil. The following is based on his work, *Evil and Human Agency*, pp. 124ff.

7. This is a different twist on the Hegelian point on how identity is always constituted in relation to how you recognize the other that you relate to, and yourself in relation to that.

that is perceived as different, with the result that the one who makes the comparison emerges as inferior, as lacking in some quality that is deemed valuable. (p. 124)

Hence, the very presence of goodness calls for recognition of my lack of it. The unwillingness to recognize myself as lacking goodness corresponds to my desire to destroy the goodness in/of the other. With the Other not present, I am able to set my own standards, and I still might be able to maintain some illusions I need to have about myself. Hence, the challenge of Jesus to his contemporaries might not have been only in challenging their basic institutions. It might just as much have been in his indirect revelation of their lack of goodness. It is important here to note that Jesus did not need to say this directly (although he most likely also had ways of expressing it like that): it is just as much in the positive disclosure of his own goodness in his practice as in the negative evaluation of hypocrisy in his preaching that he reveals this lack of goodness. This suggests a dialectic relationship between the presence of goodness and the recognition of its lack. Or to put it the other way around, in a way that might now be taken to be more than a mere tautology: the presence of evil is there due to the lack of goodness, or due to the desire resulting in the attempt to make goodness disappear.

Klein's approach to evil suggests that it emerges out of a recognized lack in the subject — the lack of goodness. This lack of goodness is something that is more easily inscribed in a person when he or she is not recognized — by others or herself — as good. Given the background of our description of the *imago Dei* as a basic recognition of human goodness and its internal relation to the good, we now have a chance to see the emergence of evil as due to *a profound lack of belief in oneself as good in the sense expressed by conceptions of* imago Dei *and* human dignity. The lack of trust in God's calling corresponds to a deep lack of trust in one's own goodness — a fact that in turn leads to destructive envy towards anyone who is perceived as having the goodness that I do not have myself.

Against this background, we need not see the envious person as one necessarily lacking goodness in the moral sense. It is more a question of his/her lack of ability to "build up a good object in the first place, to develop a sense that there is something within him that matches and so helps protect the goodness encountered in the outside world" (p. 126). This lack of affirmed goodness in oneself calls for three comments in order to elaborate this more extensively:

1. The envious person is insatiable in his or her desires due to a lack of an internalized perception of personal goodness. He or she needs an external object to focus on. But in envy desire is expressed negatively: envy is, as Vetlesen formulates it "the desire to destroy goodness *for its own sake,* because it is good; because, that is, the very existence of goodness outside the self is an intolerable insult, dealing a tremendous narcissistic blow to a self that is haunted by inferiority" (p. 126). Given our previous descriptions of desire, the desire expressed in envy is one that is trapped in lack and in the world of the self-contained subject, where the other as the third can never come fully to expression, and where the desire for the impossible expresses itself only in striving for the impossible satisfaction one strives for. Desire is here based on a lack of recognition of the object of desire as unattainable. It feeds on the illusion of the subject's ability to control, express, or even eradicate goodness from the world, although the subject is in these efforts also expressing negatively its own determination *by* goodness.

However, we need to see the desire at work in evil as something more and something other than just an opposite of morality. Vetlesen describes Kant's understanding of the propensity to do evil as making morality a servant to desire. Tacit here is of course a specific form of self-deception in which one can allow for pursuing self-interests even when they imply that one stop treating others as ends in themselves. Kant's description leads to a conflict between desire and true morality: "The result is that 'morality' is instrumentalized for, or by, the desires flowing from self-interest, so that what is 'good' to do and what enhances one's self-interest come to be but two sides of the same coin, thus denying the conflict between the two — going back as it does, in Kant, to the dualism that we are, namely between autonomy (freedom) and heteronomy (determinedness) — that essentially defines our predicament as human and moral agents" (p. 128). At this point Vetlesen suggests that Kant is not radical enough in his understanding of evil. Evil in its most radical forms need *not* be seen as flowing from a desire rooted in mere self-interest: "Evil is more than just the negation of the good or, more precisely (bearing Kant in mind), the attempt to make what is really morally bad look good so as to be able to do wrong with a good conscience" (p. 128). More radical than the negation of the good is the destruction of the good because it is good. That is what Klein points to in her combination of evil and envy. But Vetlesen suggests a further, even more radicalizing trait in evil: *Evil is even more present in forms of actions where there is no demonstrable spin-off for the evildoing agent.* When evil is done in a manner that makes it even harder to identify as an expression of selfish desire, it exhibits one of its most radical and dangerous forms. This is the form of evil justified ideologically, which we commented on above: here evil can appear and be recognized as evil, and thus as *opposite to* personal self-interest, and still be justified as something one must do in order to secure some form of higher aim to which one considers oneself subjected nevertheless.

The *theological* notion for this approach is *redemptive violence.* In his profound engagement with the passion story, S. Mark Heim sees this as the type of violence that the passion story tries to overcome, in spite of the fact that it is presented by some of those contributing to the death of Jesus as a means for saving the nation. In a generic statement about the way this type of violence plays its part in the passion, Heim writes:

> Redemptive violence — violence that claims to be for the good of many, to be sacred, to be the mysterious ground of human life itself — always purports to be the means for overcoming sin (removing pollution, punishing the transgressor who has brought disaster on the community). The sin it characteristically claims to overcome is the offense of the scapegoat, the crime the victim has committed. But in the passion account the sin in view is that of the persecutors. It is not the sin of the one that jeopardizes the many, but the sin of the many against the one. In the passion narratives redemptive violence stands forth plainly and unequivocally as itself the sin that needs to be overcome.[8]

Heim develops his insights from a Girardian perspective, which we will return to below. But here we notice that Vetlesen's approach also seems to be able to shed important light on the different elements implied in the condemnation and crucifixion of Jesus. Hence, theology and philosophy can here contribute to each other's perspectives.

2. When we ask what makes this lack of perceived goodness appear, the answer is easy to give from a psychological point of view: The lack of positive self-esteem is due to *the lack of unconditional recognition and acceptance.* When your personal identity constantly has to be affirmed and reaffirmed by your own ability to live up to the standards of the law, and when there is nothing behind or beyond the law in which you can root

8. S. Mark Heim, *Saved from Sacrifice: A Theology of the Cross* (Grand Rapids: Eerdmans, 2006), p. 196.

your identity, you remain trapped in the search for self-righteousness. The flipside of this striving is envy. Psychologically speaking, the unconditional recognition of the human as created in the image of God can only serve the liberation of desire when it is expressed within an unconditional framework. Such unconditional recognition is the basis for the individual's ability to recognize oneself as good, and hence, as someone who can identify with goodness outside of oneself instead of envying it. As Klein says, "full identification with a good object goes with a feeling of the self possessing goodness of its own."[9] In other words, a practice where the demands of the law are established as the ultimate condition for righteousness only captures the self in a position of lack. The law then serves the negative function where its positive character cannot become fully articulated. Given that this analysis holds, an opinion that sees Jesus' preaching as one opposed to Jewish law appears as misconstrued. Jesus reaffirms the importance of the law from the angle of something outside the demands of the law, something impossible for the subject to establish by her own agency. The impossibility of *becoming* the image of God or of *meriting* that designation is the very condition for its foundational character in a moral life marked by goodness and without envy.

3. Klein suggests that envy results from a specific form of narcissism. Against the background of what I wrote in the previous point, one can see Jesus' criticism of religious hypocrisy as one of the challenges to that form of narcissism. On the other hand, the only way out of this form of narcissism is by recognizing the illusory character of an identity in which your dignity is based on merit. Envy directed toward the destruction of goodness might in light of this be seen as a desperate expression of narcissism, in which one tries to hold on to one's picture of the world, and to oneself as the standard against which everyone and everything else has to be measured. Narcissism is, in its illusory forms, a psychological correspondent to the theological notion of *sin:* not as a deed, but as an attitude towards the world and self in which everything that counts is the self in its present form. It is exactly this form of life that Jesus breaks into, challenges, and tries to liberate us from.

These considerations taken together indicate that evil as envy is a phenomenon that can more precisely be described as *relational,* and even

---

9. Vetlesen, *Evil and Human Agency,* p. 126, following Melanie Klein, *Envy and Gratitude, and Other Works, 1946-1963* (New York: Free Press, 1984), p. 192.

more, as a negative expression of the triadic relationship we have developed previously. The two parties that the individual is internally related to, and which is expressed in his vocation to be what he is, an *imago Dei,* are both now denied: the calling of goodness and towards goodness in an act of disbelief in one's personal connectedness to goodness, and in the concrete eradication of the Other who represents the goodness I do not have. The desire of someone who is evil is the desire not to have to recognize one's own relation to the good by means of the perception of one's own lack of it, and also not to recognize anyone else as someone to whom one has to relate. The final consequence of this is the attempt to eradicate the other.

At one point in his study, Vetlesen compares envy with jealousy in a way that is relevant in the present context. He points to how jealousy, in contrast to envy, involves a triad. "Jealousy by definition involves a triad: aggression is directed against what is perceived as a threat from some other person against one's relationship with a loved or cherished object (person)" (p. 124). Envy involves making the world narrower, smaller, and more self-centered by excluding or ignoring the possible third part (who in my theological context might represent the law, for example). It is expressed in a relationship where only two parts exist, and the counterpart remaining there is perceived as a threat by the subject of envy:

> By contrast, in envy no triad is necessarily involved; nor is love or some relationship perceived as precious. Envy thematizes the elemental relationship between a person and the world. Initially, envy relies on a positive evaluation of some quality in the other, even though this recognition-based evaluation is not expressed, but stubbornly denied. (p. 124)

Let us here call attention again to how recognition implies a specific constitution of the identity and the subjectivity of both self and other. It is the recognition of what is valuable — but necessary to repress — in the other that makes me into an envious subject. It is also the very same recognition that puts the other in the situation where he has to be attacked by me, subjected to my intentions, deprived of the quality I cannot bear to see that he has instead of me. This clearly expresses the dyadic structure where envy manifests itself: I know that once I admit to being envious, I admit to a third, a standard, and communicate in a language that can also judge or assess the content of my envy as bad. Hence, what determines me (envy) is most "wisely" something I should keep to myself. Once I communicate my envy, I distance myself from it and deprive it of (some of) its powers. Only when the third is excluded as a way of mediating envy can it remain fully directed towards the other.

Against this background we can see the envy that Jesus provokes as emerging out of his recognized goodness. However, there is no explicit mention of envy in relation to his trial and crucifixion. That is not surprising given that envy is something difficult to admit having, because that would mean admitting to a lack, which could be shameful. However, the most important element in a possible reconstruction of what takes place here, from the angle of a theory that combines envy and evil, is *the total lack of language that expresses the other as the third.* When Jesus appears before the council, he opens a discourse in which the reality of God (as the third) is present, but this causes strong outrage (Mark 14:6off.). God is never voiced, never contemplated by the envious participant in this setting.

As Vetlesen points out, envy can express itself in many different practices, but need not necessarily imply murder: "The type of evil that most typically springs from envy entails devaluing, denigrating, and ridiculing the features in the other which arouse envy in the first place" (p. 124). Hence, Jesus is mocked as a king and a prophet. The progressive development of such measures has a specific aim: to show, finally, that the person subjected to them "has nothing positive, admirable, and worthwhile to show for himself or herself, in short, nothing that would merit the affirmation of others and so justify the existence of the otherness in question" (p. 125). The ultimate expression of this denigration in the trial of Jesus occurs when he is considered by the mob as someone less justified in his existence than Barabbas, who had been condemned for serious crimes. By asking for Barabbas to be freed, they thereby explicitly communicate that Jesus is less worthy than he is. This denigration denies Jesus his goodness in a manner that is unsurpassable. Hence, what takes place is not only a rejection of Jesus as a true witness to God, it is a rejection of his goodness. That this rejection has important theological overtones is expressed aptly in a quote Vetlesen offers from Melanie Klein:

> There are very pertinent psychological reasons why envy ranks among the seven "deadly sins." I would even suggest that it is unconsciously felt to be the greatest sin of all, because it spoils and harms the good

object which is the source of life. This view is consistent with the view described by Chaucer in *The Parson's Tale:* "It is certain that envy is the worst sin there is; for all other sins are sins only against one virtue, whereas envy is against all virtue and against all goodness."[10]

What I find here are some striking elements that might help us access the events so central to Christian faith, in a way that allows for identification with features and experiences common to all human beings. The risk in describing possible mechanisms behind the trial and crucifixion of Jesus along the lines of Vetlesen and Klein is that we may make the people actively involved in it, or the bystanders, more morally depraved than they might have been. Moreover, it is not my intention here to scapegoat anyone involved, but rather to point out that the mechanisms are such that they could be attributed to anyone, more or less.

Evil and Identity

Identity is as important as it is difficult. I suggested in the previous part of the book that there are some important identity issues to be addressed in and by the Jesus narrative. However, in the present context, discussing evil and rejection, the question of identity now takes another turn, and a more deadly one: Present-day politics suggest that identity may also be used in order to dispel, eradicate, or in other forms victimize people due to, because of, their identity — be it hereditary, ascribed, attributed, or what have you.

Identities are open. Even a theologically constituted identity that defines humans as created in the image of God is still to a large extent dependent on contextual and other interpretations in order to become meaningful. Moreover, as many theoreticians today hold, identity is also a project, and is part of the construction that humans make out of their own or others' lives. But instead of understanding identity as something resulting from the individual's own efforts of construction, I hold it to be important to see identity as something emerging from the interplay and interaction between the individual, the other, and the accessible cultural resources. It is the combination of these features that in the end makes up an identity.

10. Klein, *Envy and Gratitude,* here quoted from Vetlesen, *Evil and Human Agency,* p. 125.

Against this background identity is something that can be realized and articulated, but is still rooted in social forms and in a given recognition by the other(s).

A specific problem emerges from the fact that generic attributed identities may be used in order to repress others. Even though someone's identity can be that of a Jesus-follower, a Pharisee, or a Jew, none of these identity-descriptions hold *per se* specific reasons for treating individuals belonging to them in specific ways. No identity-description is exhaustive or unequivocal, says Vetlesen (p. 160), and for good reasons. Accordingly, a generic attribution of specific characteristics that call for a specific evaluation, treatment, or rejection of an individual is a major danger in the way we deal with identity. Identity is important, but focusing on identity can only have one valid moral purpose: to secure the freedom of the individual, and to make sure that she is able to express herself freely in a manner that allows for her to be a fully recognized member of the human community. To recognize that somebody belongs to a specific community does not say anything about his or her moral worth. A category of moral worth in individuals does not allow a hierarchy of human individuals. Rather, it calls for recognition of the fact that every human individual may be a carrier of multiple identities, and this recognition resists one-criterion identity marks, none of which jeopardize this worth. Vetlesen sees the normative implication of this as one by which every human is allowed to express this multiplicity freely and openly (p. 161). Only in this manner are we able to avoid using identity as a repressive or marginalizing tool against groups with whom we are not willing to identify.

What does our reconsideration of identity offer us in the present context? The answer is twofold: first of all, one can see Jesus' own practice as one in which tax-collectors and sinners were also recognized as something more: as people in need of repentance, as belonging to a community in which they could participate freely, and so on. Hence, to put it in modern and fashionable terms, Jesus' identity-politics was subversive and stood in clear contrast to a society divided according to clear ethnic, religious, moral, medical, and gender boundaries. His hospitality implies a rejection of the marginalization and division of the identity-politics of his day. We have already noted that this rejection meant that he felt free to engage with those who belonged to the more privileged groups as well.

Against this background we then, secondly, can interpret the trial and crucifixion of Jesus as a rejection of his attempt to subvert the identity-politics of his context, the very structure of which allowed for others to sustain their self-perception as better and more worthy than others who were marginalized in one way or another. This structure represents the attempt to maintain a way of organizing society according to features that give different people different moral and religious worth depending on how they are defined. When Jesus is crucified, we can see this type of politics as one that ultimately expresses itself in death: this is a way of dealing with differences that necessarily leads to the eradication of elements that are perceived to be threats to society. This does not, however, imply that there are no differences at work in the practice of Jesus. Jesus affirms two basic differences: First, between those who recognize him as God's witness and those who do not, and second, the difference between God and humans. The first difference is made in order to make clear that God is not automatically recognized in every type of pious practice, while the second is made to help people realize what it means to be the image of God. Both differentiations, however, are made in order to *liberate* people to recognize themselves and others as part of a possible community, and not in order to exclude anyone from community.

Bystanders

Most of the people witnessing Jesus' trial and death were not actively involved — they were what we have already called bystanders. Bystanders can, according to Vetlesen, not be considered neutral in any sense of the world. They often have important bearings on the quality of the evil in question (in terms of its intensity, extent, duration). He accordingly claims that the actions of third parties may be just as decisive for the outcome of events as the actions of direct perpetrators (p. 220). Hence there is only a thin line between bystanders and perpetrators. One of the main reasons he gives for this is that bystanders who decide to not intervene and/or remain "indifferent in the face of those victimized commit the same destruction of the moral foundation of the other" (p. 231). In this process the other becomes reified or categorized in a manner that makes him or her no longer unique, but only a member of a category, an expression of the same (Levinas).[11]

---

11. Vetlesen develops this argument in far more detail than I do here, especially with reference to Arendt and Tester.

Vetlesen argues that bystanders have moral obligations. These imply that one has to relate to and judge what happens in light of the law, and to act against what is violating it. In the Good Friday narrative, not only is Jesus rejected — be it in terms of his goodness, of who he represents and witnesses to, or his ways of rejecting identity-politics — but so is the *law* that he calls to. He is the other who is not recognized, but who constantly invokes the law for the sake of the other. By not acting, the perpetrator is given a message from the bystander: these acts can proceed. As Vetlesen aptly writes, "Knowing, yet still not acting, means granting acceptance to the action — if not wholesale moral acceptance, then pragmatic and factual acceptance in the sense that what is being done is allowed to be done without there being any action taken to help prevent it" (p. 237).

We can see two intertwined implications of this attitude. First, as the law is silenced in the cries of the mob, so are the foundations of a morality where everyone is regarded as having equal footing. The trial of Jesus reveals humanity's ability to totally neglect and ignore the call of the law, even when the victim of this practice is the one who claims to represent a generous and gifting God. The suspension of the law in the name of the law (which this must be taken to be, eventually) shows the impossibility of establishing justice by means of the law without living within a horizon of more than the individual and the law. It also confirms that the law can be used for purposes leading to death as well as for purposes leading to life. Hence, one is not only responsible to the law, but also to the use of the law, and for the context in which one chooses to understand and practice it.

Second, bystanders are accordingly called to action. By not acting, they comply. Vetlesen refers to Hannah Arendt, who says that to act is to make a new beginning in the world. It means to set something in motion that you cannot ultimately control. When you act against those who behave badly, however, you also run the risk of being subjected to repercussions. Hence, to be a bystander who does not act is to have more control, but it also makes you more responsible for what is bad. "Therefore, to realize one's potential as a human agent means to expose oneself to the role of sufferer, insofar as action is by definition to engage in something that is as unpredictable as it is irreversible" (p. 238). The implication of this is that the call to do good is difficult to fulfill when the law is suspended by others. This is so not only because you then risk changing the way that things go in a direction you cannot control, but also because you run the risk of being subjected to repercussions by others when you make the presence of possible goodness visible in this way. Accordingly you must realize your own vulnerability — possibly, in given situations, also your mortality. By not acting, you don't need to relate to and realize this in the same manner. It is interesting to see that what Jesus does when calling people into community is exactly the opposite of this lack of realization. He can compensate the negative effects of this realization by placing them within a situation where the people participating in the community safeguard each other. That is what is lacking for the individuals participating in the mob who would still be able to heed the call of justice.

We can now turn back to the denial of Peter once more. In light of what I have developed here, his denial can now be seen in another light. Peter's denial need not only be seen as a rejection of his community with Jesus. It may also, more positively, imply a rejection of the way in which the description as "Jesus-follower" is used by bystanders as a possible means for identifying and destroying him. This identification is, however, not something he can reject without also having to deny what he so far has had as his most important foundation for social and religious identity. His situation thereby reveals exactly what an evil and immoral use of identity-marks might do to you. By being forced to reject your identity, you not only have to reject a specific identity, but also those with whom that identity has been shared and shaped. This deprives you of your social world, and throws you into despair, darkness, and loneliness. The evil is thus unavoidable: either you can maintain your identity and risk that the mob uses it as a means for rejecting you; or you can reject your identity and risk losing your belonging to the community where you are rooted. Peter's was in this sense a deep predicament, which not only had to do with what could happen to him, but just as much with what kind of self-identity could be recognized by himself and others. The cost of rejecting being subjected to an identity-politics based on his most important identity-mark is that he rejects that very identity.

Jesus as a Scapegoat Preventing Violence?
Reflections on René Girard's Theory

Mimetic Desire and the Mechanisms Behind Scapegoating

"We can't say, 'Jesus died for us,' and mean it, unless we can locate the process that killed him in our own social history, and unless we can see other ones than Jesus who died for us in this sacrificial sense. It is Jesus' revelatory identification with the scapegoat that equips us to make this connection, that enables us to look into our own context and see those who may be in Jesus' place."[1] These words, by theologian S. Mark Heim, suggest that there is no metaphysical explanation for the death of Jesus. Moreover, they suggest that the death of Jesus — *qua* a sacrificial death — is not the unique thing about his crucifixion. Rather, it is the *who,* and not the how and why, that constitutes the uniqueness of this event. No one has made this more apparent in present scholarship than René Girard.

Recently, Girard's theory about the function of sacrifice in stabilizing, civilizing, and developing society has been much appropriated in theology in order to deal with the death of Jesus and find a way to interpret his crucifixion as something that also has meaning in societal terms.[2] Girard's the-

---

1. S. Mark Heim, *Saved from Sacrifice: A Theology of the Cross* (Grand Rapids: Eerdmans, 2006), p. 306.

2. The most extensive attempt to appropriate Girard for a constructive theology of the cross can be found in the book by Heim, mentioned in the previous note. Heim uses Girard to develop the main point of his book: that the passion accounts are not a rationalization of redemptive violence, but undermine such violence. This is then also the reason for the increasing discomfort with the cross itself, which he sees as emerging as an effect of the cross (p. 11). A critical and constructive engagement with Girard's work, and with the con-

ory can be read as a long footnote to the statement of Caiaphas reported in John 11:50, saying "You do not understand that it is better for you to have one man die for the people than to have the whole nation destroyed." Although we have already offered some interpretation of that saying, we may still interpret it from a different angle — though not one that excludes the insights of the previous one — when reading it in light of Girard. One of the main advantages of his theory in our context is that it allows for understanding what happens to Jesus not only as a unique event, but as an expression of mechanisms that are at work in many places. Hence, it connects to experiences and patterns common to humans everywhere.

In a generic statement Girard claims that "all religious rituals spring from the surrogate victim, and all the great institutions of mankind, both secular and religious, spring from ritual [. . .] It could hardly be otherwise, for the working basis of human thought, the process of 'symbolization,' is rooted in the surrogate victim."[3] Accordingly, it is possible to see something positive in what happens in processes of victimization. Bearing in mind our previous affirmation that what happened with Jesus was evil, we now have to ask: Was it not evil after all, or has this evil a positive outcome, that might make it possible to evaluate the crucifixion as more than a mere atrocity?

Girard holds that humans develop by imitating each other. The main reason for conflicts is that they, in this imitation, desire the same object. This *mimetic desire* is defined broadly, to explain a phenomenon that incorporates imitation, rivalry, and envy. *Desire* is here shaped after the model of the other; and due to the presence of the other and the expression of the other's desire becomes what it is.

> Rivalry does not arise because of the fortuitous convergence of two desires on a single object; rather, the subject desires the object because the rival desires it. In desiring an object the rival alerts the subject to the desirability of the object. The rival, then, serves as a model for the subject, not only in regard to such secondary matters as style and opinions but also, and more essentially, in regard to desires. (pp. 134f.)

---

ception of sacrifice in Christianity in general, can be found in Bernd Janowski and Michael Welker, eds., *Opfer: Theologische und Kulturelle Kontexte* (Frankfurt: Suhrkamp, 2000). One of the important insights of that book is that focusing on sacrifice and victims allows for a nuanced understanding of the complex patterns of power that work behind the scene in cultural formations that allow for sacrifice.

3. René Girard, *Violence and the Sacred* (London New York: Continuum 2005), p. 321.

Mimetic desire thus emerges not from the presence of the object desired, but from the presence of another's desire. Girard allows us to see here a different configuration of a triadic structure by which the individual becomes what she is: due to how she does or does not relate to the other and to the other's relation to the third. In the case of Jesus, his desire for the community of the kingdom was what made others desire it. However, the quality of their relation to this kingdom was dependent on whether they saw it as *an exclusive or an inclusive object:* one to be shared, or one to be a possession expressing privileges and a specific status. In the latter case, it ended up in a form of envy that could mean deadly rivalry.

Desire is always mediated through the other's (the rival's) desire. If there is no rival, there is no desire. Desire is not spontaneous, but infused by the presence of the other's desire, which is the model for the desire in the subject. Hence, the object of desire is not the origin of desire — it is the other's desire for the object that is the origin of desire in the subject. To see agency as something solely emerging from a self-contained subject, or expressions of desire as specific forms of moral or immoral acts, thus prohibits itself: In order to judge the desire in question, one has to evaluate it in its constitutive social context. Here is one of the telling indications of how a postmodern understanding of the subject as constituted and shaped by pre-subjective conditions can prove itself fruitful for interpreting what takes place in the events leading to Jesus' death.

The New Testament describes these mechanisms in the following way, according to Girard:

> Both Jesus and Satan are teachers of imitation and imitators themselves, imitators of God the Father. This means that human beings always imitate God, either through Jesus or through Satan. They seek God indirectly through the human models they imitate. When the model determines his imitator's desire through his own acquisitive desire, they both desire the same object. This is mimetic rivalry; once it is triggered, the two competing desires mutually keep reinforcing each other and violence is likely to erupt. Imitation must be intrinsically good, nevertheless, since Jesus recommends it. It will never lead us into temptation as long as we imitate him, Jesus, who, in turn, imitates God in a spirit of childish and innocent obedience.[4]

4. René Girard and James G. Williams, *The Girard Reader* (New York: Crossroad, 1996), p. 215.

The triadic relationship is manifested negatively in the violence generated by this process. Girard can even say that "violence is the process itself when two or more partners try to prevent one another from appropriating the object they all desire through physical or other means."[5] He holds that the struggle for the same object may thus end up in violence and murder if it is not controlled. It is in this connection that religion has played an important role — although an ambiguous one:

> Religion shelters us from violence just as violence seeks shelter in religion. If we fail to understand certain religious practices, it is not because we are outside their sphere of influence but because we are still to a very real extent enclosed within them. [. . .] As soon as the essential quality of transcendence — religious, humanistic or whatever — is lost, there are no longer any terms by which to define the legitimate form of violence and to recognize it among the multitude of illicit forms.[6]

If we understand the trial of Jesus against this background, the very same religion that he himself expressed was also the one that led to his death. As the expression of transcendence, this law contributed to a societal order that had to be maintained against the threat of chaos. When the people's leaders perceived this threat in Jesus, they saw it as necessary to get rid of him. It is interesting to note that Girard sees the threat that leads to what he calls a sacrificial crisis as something that emerges from the destruction of distinctions by which the society is ordered. In contrast to what I have developed in the previous chapter, such distinctions are seen by him as important in maintaining societal order. The sacrifice is an expression and affirmation of such distinctions, and thus, of order. From this perspective, then, the victimization of Jesus becomes necessary in order to secure the institutions of society.

> The hidden violence of the sacrificial crisis eventually succeeds in destroying distinctions, and this destruction in turn fuels the renewed violence. In short, it seems that anything that adversely affects the institution of sacrifice will ultimately pose a threat to the very basis of the community, to the principles on which its social harmony and equilibrium depend. (p. 52)

5. Girard and Williams, *The Girard Reader,* p. 9.
6. Girard, *Violence and the Sacred,* p. 25.

Given that this is the case, Girard can shed some light on the political function of the death of Jesus that also links this death to what we have identified as core elements in his practice: Jesus brings to an end cultural and human differences and distinctions as important for participating in community. As indicated, he thereby jeopardizes the political, cultural, and religious order. In order to reestablish this order, following Girard, one has to make a sacrifice that makes a difference, that exhibits a distinction between people. It is paradoxical and at the same time logical to reestablish this order by sacrificing the one who threatens the order in question.

On the other hand, as Girard shows, the death of Jesus is also the final exposure of the negative content of the sacrificial order on which the society is built. By exposing this order, Jesus shows that the society needs to be established on other principles.[7] However, as long as this is not recognized as a final revelation of a cruel and gruesome way of reestablishing order, but seen as only one of many instances of necessary evil, the mechanisms behind these events are not perceived as unnecessary, as contingent, but at best as something ambiguous, which calls for both disgust and veneration. Girard seems to have identified a major strand in the Christian relationship to the death of Jesus when he describes the ambiguity that sacrifices are met with along lines that pertain to all sacrifices in the history of human civilization:

> The scorn, hostility, and cruelty displayed toward the animal prior to the ritualistic slaughter are replaced upon its death by a show of ritualistic veneration. In bearing away into death the scourge of reciprocal violence, the victim has performed its assigned function. Henceforth the victim will incarnate violence in both its guises, beneficial and baneful; that is, it will personify the All-Powerful who rules from on high. Having been so flagrantly abused, it is only reasonable that the victim should be greatly honored — just as it was reasonable to banish Oedipus when he seemed the bearer of ill fortune and reasonable to honor him when his departure assured the community's well-being.

---

7. These insights can also be related to exclusive practices still prevailing within Christianity: one seems to assume that it is by upholding differences between the sexes that societal order can continue. Hence, it is necessary to exclude/silence/hide and make problematic those who are not witness to this order of difference, be it women living alone, women or men acting in other than the accepted gendered roles, or gays and lesbians living in partnership.

That adopting the former attitude assures the latter result seems to confirm the rationality of the plan, despite its contradictory appearance. (pp. 103f.)

Against this background, ritual and sacrifice not are only related, there seems to be an internal and necessary relationship between ritual, civilization, and sacrifice. Sacrifice in both symbolic and real forms is the means by which a society excludes itself from chaos. It is a collective action of the whole community (notice how this corresponds with the fact that there are no specific agents targeted as perpetrators to be blamed for the death of Jesus).[8] The sacrifice is the action by which this community "purifies itself of its own disorder through the unanimous immolation of a victim, but this can happen only at the paroxysm of the ritual crisis."[9] When this approach is related to the death of Jesus, it is important to ask if the chaos and threat of chaos is something he himself has initiated, or if he is an *innocent* scapegoat and sacrifice, i.e., one that cannot be blamed for the threatening chaos against which his society tries to protect itself. This is a question Girard, as far as I can see, does not address directly. He restricts himself to saying how the scapegoat must appear. Against that background, he claims that Jesus became the victim of "the scapegoat effect":

> By a scapegoat effect I mean that strange process through which two or more people are reconciled at the expense of a third party who appears guilty or responsible for whatever ails, disturbs, or frightens the scapegoaters. They feel relieved of their tensions and they coalesce into a more harmonious group. They now have a single purpose, which is to prevent the scapegoat from harming them, by expelling and destroying him.[10]

8. Cf. Girard, *Violence and the Sacred,* p. 8: "The victim is not a substitution for some particularly endangered individual, nor is it offered up to some individual of particularly bloodthirsty temperament. Rather, it is a substitute for all the members of the community, offered up by the members themselves. The sacrifice serves to protect the entire community from its own violence; it prompts the entire community to choose victims outside itself. The elements of dissension scattered throughout the community are drawn to the person of the sacrificial victim and eliminated, at least temporarily, by its sacrifice."

9. Girard and Williams, *The Girard Reader,* p. 11.

10. Girard and Williams, *The Girard Reader,* p. 12. Note here also the possible connection to the issue of securitization, mentioned in the previous chapter.

To establish someone who can serve as a scapegoat, one has to understand him as neither innocent nor impotent. Although Girard holds that he need not necessarily be perceived as a culprit, he must nevertheless appear to be likely responsible for the disorders and ailments of the community. In other words, he must appear as responsible for the crisis that has triggered the mechanism of scapegoating.[11] Within Girard's theoretical framework, this implies that Jesus was seen as a rival in terms of developing a specific social order. Given that we speak of a society where religious, political, and other dimensions of order remained mainly undifferentiated, this rivalry expressed itself in competing claims for the best way to live in the society and to organize it as a whole. That is, as far as I can see, the basic premise on which an application of Girard's theory can be seen as viable. The disorder emerges from a perception of Jesus' practice as attempting to establish a competing social order that would leave the former order both obsolete and religiously inferior. Hence, the goodness of this order might be perceived as a cause for envy as well.

This suggests that the victim is not perceived as a victim when made to function as scapegoat. Rather, he is depicted as "subversive of the communal order and as a threat to the well-being of the society. His continued presence is therefore undesirable and it must be destroyed or driven away by other gods, perhaps, or by the community itself."[12]

We note here that Girard says that the victim is *perceived* as subversive. This is not the same as saying that he is actually being subversive. But who is then to judge that? For the present study, we need not make a final decision about this issue. It suffices to say that Girard makes possible an interpretation where Jesus could *appear as a threat* — it is not necessary to conclude that he actually wanted to overthrow a social order to make him into a scapegoat. Girard himself, however, seems to hold that "Jesus is the direct, though involuntary, cause of the division and dissension that is stirred up by his message, by virtue of the fact that it meets with almost universal incomprehension."[13] By underscoring the involuntary effects of his actions, Girard thus seems to be in accordance with our previous interpretation of what happened to Jesus as evil, i.e., as something that took place against his will.

11. Girard and Williams, *The Girard Reader*, p. 15.
12. Girard and Williams, *The Girard Reader*, p. 15.
13. Girard and Williams, *The Girard Reader*, p. 180.

Girard on the Non-Sacrificial Death of Christ

Girard claims that there is nothing in the Gospels to suggest that the death of Jesus is a sacrifice, whatever definition (expiation, substitution, etc.) we may give for that sacrifice.[14] He is right in this, insofar as the Gospels are concerned. This does not exclude the fact that in other New Testament writings his death is interpreted as a sacrifice (e.g., Rom. 3:25; Heb. 9–11; 1 John 4:10). Moreover, he claims that from his perspective, "the sacrificial interpretation of the Passion must be criticized and exposed as a most enormous and paradoxical misunderstanding — and at the same time as something necessary — and as the most revealing indication of mankind's radical incapacity to understand its own violence, even when that violence is conveyed in the most explicit fashion."[15]

In such a context of misunderstanding, it becomes understandable why the rejection of Jesus took place. This rejection also implies a lack of ability to cope with the knowledge that Jesus reveals about how violence and scapegoating are at work in his society. His radical inclusiveness is his way of working against the violence at work in scapegoating, and his redirection of desire toward a God of goodness and gift is the alternative to the rivalry of mimetic desire, with its disastrous consequences for those who fail to win in that game. The message about the kingdom is also a message about a social order where mimetic desire is not at work. Girard says, in a lengthy passage:

> Refusing the Kingdom means refusing the knowledge that Jesus bears — refusing the knowledge of violence and all its works. In the eyes of those who reject it, this knowledge is ill-omened; it is the worst of all forms of violence. That is indeed how things must look from the perspective of the sacrificial community. Jesus appears as a destructive and subversive force, as a source of contamination that threatens the community. Indeed, to the extent that he is misunderstood he becomes just that. The way in which he preaches can only make him appear to be totally lacking in respect for the holiest of institutions, guilty of hubris and blasphemy, since he dares to rival God himself in the perfection of the Love that he never ceases to make manifest.[16]

14. Girard and Williams, *The Girard Reader,* p. 178.
15. Girard and Williams, *The Girard Reader,* p. 178.
16. Girard and Williams, *The Girard Reader,* p. 182. Cf. also the following: "Faithful to

The above quote is important from another angle than the one that Girard establishes: he makes clear that recognition plays a central role here — a role that we could almost call the source of ontological attribution: Depending upon how he is recognized, Jesus is given a status that makes him either a blasphemer and a rival of God, or his true witness. These different recognitions have ontological implications insofar as they serve to create and manifest different types of social order, types of order that eventually lead to either life or death for those involved. At the ontological level, Jesus' practice is counter to that of sacrifice. Hence, to understand his death as sacrifice seems, from Girard's point of view, to offer a real, but nevertheless inauthentic understanding of what takes place in his crucifixion.

For Girard, an authentic understanding of Christ's death cannot see it as sacrificial. "Jesus dies, not as a sacrifice, but in order that there may be no more sacrifices."[17] This is also a "no" to violence in all its forms, including the sacrificial. A concomitant recognition is one that sees God as nonviolent and as rejecting violence. Understanding Jesus' death as deliberately and originally willed by God becomes problematic, if not to say impossible, within this framework.[18] Girard rejects any assertion of a concealed element of violence which makes it necessary for God to have a sacrifice that requires the obedience of the Son. He sees this interpretation as an expression of *an economy of violence,* which is human and not divine, and which can, from the standpoint of the gospel, only be rooted in a projection of human violence onto God.[19]

Girard thus contributes to our understanding of the dichotomy between two different and opposite logics at work in the Jesus narrative. The logic of mimetic desire and sacrifice is opposed to a logic that rejects and discloses the other.[20] All of Jesus' actions are directed toward nonviolence,

---

the logic of sacrifice, those who have refused the invitation to the Kingdom are obliged to turn against Jesus. They can hardly fail to see in him the sworn enemy and corruptor of the very cultural order that they are vainly attempting to restore. This means that violence will find in Jesus the most perfect victim that can be imagined, the victim that, for every conceivable reason, violence has the most reasons to pick on. Yet at the same time, this victim is also the most innocent" (p. 182).

17. Girard and Williams, *The Girard Reader,* p. 184.

18. In this, Girard underpins recent feminist criticism of understanding Christ's death as atonement where God is the main agent. For an overview and further development of this, see J. Denny Weaver, *The Nonviolent Atonement* (Grand Rapids: Eerdmans, 2001).

19. Girard and Williams, *The Girard Reader,* p. 188.

20. Girard and Williams, *The Girard Reader,* p. 184.

and no more effective form of action could be imagined, according to Girard.[21] His death is the failure of this logic to see itself through in the world. However, this failure also has some potentially positive effects, which is the reason why Christ's death is celebrated as so important and decisive by his followers:

> The Christ of the Gospels dies against sacrifice, and through his death, he reveals its nature and origin by making sacrifice unworkable, at least in the long run, and bringing sacrificial culture to an end. The word "sacrifice" is not important in itself, but the singularity of the Passion is obscured if the same word is used for the Passion and for what takes place in sacrificial rituals.[22]

The crucifixion thus serves to reveal the sacrificial logic in a way that makes it unworkable. That is the claim of Girard. But this is a claim *in principle.* There are still more than enough examples of sacrifices made in order to prevent chaos from ruling, according to those who sacrifice. While this is being written, the people of Iraq are being sacrificed in an operation for the sake of securing an imagined stability.[23] This is even being done in a way that has partly been justified by reference to so-called Western (Christian) values. Accordingly, one has to ask if the revelation of the sacrificial logic has done more than making us able to detect that it is, under certain circumstances, still at work.

The question then arises: To what extent can we continue to talk about salvation in Christ — given that these structures are still at work? Girard attempts to develop something positively here by following two lines of reasoning, based on the true humanity and true divinity of Christ:

(1) As human beings are entrapped in a mimetic predicament, the revelatory act that saves them must be performed by the one who represents the unity of humanity and divinity. "Christ is the only agent who is capable of escaping from these structures and freeing us from their domi-

---

21. Girard and Williams, *The Girard Reader,* p. 180.

22. Girard and Williams, *The Girard Reader,* p. 18.

23. Other examples of recent origin can be found in Arne Johan Vetlesen, *Evil and Human Agency: Understanding Collective Evildoing,* Cambridge Cultural Social Studies (Cambridge and New York: Cambridge University Press, 2005), who also uses Girard to identify mechanisms behind present atrocities. He links Girard's contribution more extensively to psychological literature as well.

nance."[24] He must be human, because that is humanity's only chance of comprehending what happens within the structures of existence. "But this agent must also be God, for only God is able to subject himself to human desire and violence, overcome them, and show us the way to life."[25] Moreover, "This unprecedented task of revealing the truth about violence requires a man who is not obliged to violence for anything and does not think in terms of violence — someone who is capable of talking back to violence while remaining entirely untouched by it."[26]

(2) On the other hand, the divinity of Christ "is the full truth of the innocent victim." In order to express what happens to Christ, Girard has to establish a hiatus between the divine and the human that can explain the fate of Christ: His is "a truth which cannot abide in human culture, but must be inevitably expelled. The full disclosure of this truth can occur only in the moment it is being driven out." Hence, Girard is able to make visible that in the very event where Christ seems to suffer defeat, a crucial revelation takes place: "It is the Passion of Christ that is the key to revelation and it is the resurrection of Christ that confirms the work of God the Father rather than just another in the long line of victims transformed into gods by their lynchers."[27] What remains unclear here, though, is which works of God are confirmed in the resurrection. A likely interpretation, and one that is in accordance with the main lines of argument in the present work, is that what is confirmed is Christ's ministry as a whole, which discloses the "alternative logic." Any other understanding that limits the confirmation to only God's work *in the crucifixion,* is likely to make that event an expression of God's genuine will, separated from the context of Jesus' ministry as a whole.

The above suggests that it is the resurrection of Jesus that makes his contribution to the exposure of sacrificial logic unique. However, this is only partly the case. The uniqueness of Jesus is also related to the place he occupies in the world and what he makes of it. Moreover, this analysis suggests that the world in which Jesus lives cannot be completely ruled by violence, but that there are other powers already at work as well. Writes Girard:

24. René Girard, Jean-Michel Oughourlian, and Guy Lefort, *Things Hidden Since the Foundation of the World* (London: Athlone Press, 1987), p. 219.

25. Girard and Williams, *The Girard Reader,* p. 189.

26. Girard and Williams, *The Girard Reader,* p. 192.

27. Girard and Williams, *The Girard Reader,* p. 189.

It is impossible for such a human being to arise in a world completely ruled by violence and the myths based on violence. In order to understand that you cannot see and make visible the truth except by taking the place of the victim, you must already be occupying that place; yet to take that place, you must already be in possession of the truth. You cannot become aware of the truth unless you act in opposition to the laws of violence, and you cannot act in opposition to these laws unless you already grasp the truth. All mankind is caught within this vicious circle. For this reason the Gospels and the whole New Testament, together with the theologians of the first councils, proclaim that Christ is God not because he was crucified, but because he is God born of God from all eternity.[28]

One of the more interesting and valuable contributions of Girard's theory is that he makes it possible to affirm consistently that the God whom Jesus gives witness to is a God of life. There is no ambiguity in the picture of God emerging from Girard's interpretation of the death of Christ. Moreover, to "recognize Christ as God is to recognize him as the only being capable of rising above the violence that had, up to that point, absolutely transcended mankind [. . .] Christ is the only agent who is capable of escaping from these structures and freeing us from their dominance." On the other hand, the revelation of Christ assumes a paradoxical character here, as Girard claims that "a non-violent deity can signal his existence to mankind only by becoming driven out by violence — by demonstrating that he is not able to remain in the Kingdom of Violence."[29] We here note that this notion of God seems to be much in accordance with the conception we suggested in the previous part of the book, where we argued that God — under conditions to be defined more precisely — may be understood as vulnerable to the way human practice is shaping the conditions of this world. Where there is no actual witness to God as the God of life, God is in a certain sense not *positively* present as recognized, but only present as absence, as the experience of lack, suffering, and the desire for a different situation. The recognition of God here is thus a negative one, shaped by the desire for that which is different than the present.

Whereas the Council, according to John 11, was willing to sacrifice a specific other (Jesus) in order to save the nation, the very consequence of

---

28. Girard and Williams, *The Girard Reader*, p. 192.
29. Girard and Williams, *The Girard Reader*, p. 193.

Girard's theory implies that God is willing to be sacrificed for the sake of others. Hence, there is a more or less unthematized dichotomy between the willingness to sacrifice oneself and to sacrifice another in the story about the trial and death of Jesus. That Jesus is willing to let this happen has nothing to do with the fact that he thereby satisfies God's need for sacrifice. Rather, it is the outcome of the event, in the revelation of the deadly and empty structure of scapegoating that may be seen as his motivation for letting this happen to him. Hence, the crucifixion does not originate from God's need for sacrifice, but from God's will to overcome and abolish the institution of sacrifice. In the institution opposed, people are sacrificed on behalf of others, while Jesus as the true human who witnesses to the God of life and love is willing to be sacrificed himself in order for others not to be subject to the mechanisms of sacrifice anymore.

As indicated above, since violence still rules the world, and the aggressive victimization of the other in order to be(come) as God (to be the ruler of the world) is still a prevalent expression of sin, the logic of scapegoating can be detected on different sides of global conflicts. Every side is willing to sacrifice some of their own sons and daughters in order to establish the world order as they see it in their narcissistic vision. If Christ can reveal that the order shaped by this violence is something to be overcome by a new reign, a generous reign that recognizes the other and sees her/him as the unconditioned gift to my own existence and identity, this might be a way for the gospel to still prove relevant in the world. The message from Christ to the world would then be: Who do you love? Is your life, identity, desire expressing violence, or based on it? Girard's theory allows us to disclose the sacrificial logic as unchristian as well as inhuman.[30] He also calls for a more precise way of articulating what it means when one within the church speaks of Christ's necessary sacrifice. We must be clear as to what this means, and ask how such a conception can be articulated in a way that is in accordance with an understanding of God as the God of life and love.

---

30. In Heim's words: "To believe in the crucified one is to want no other victims. To depend on the blood of Jesus is to refuse to depend on the sacrificial blood of anyone else. It is to swear off scapegoats. Sacred violence promises to save us from retaliatory catastrophe. But what will save us from sacred violence? Only some event that may achieve once for all what sacred violence attempts by endless repetition." Heim, *Saved from Sacrifice: A Theology of the Cross*, p. 195.

Dalferth: Sacrifice as Non-Necessary

In his main contribution to Christology so far, Ingolf Dalferth indicates that even when the images of a sacrificial cult are used for developing patterns of understanding in both Paul and Mark (and are central in the letter to the Hebrews as well), their presence nevertheless need not imply that they are necessary, essential, or the most decisive way to develop an adequate understanding of the event of Jesus' death. One of the reasons for this is that we find already in the New Testament itself a clear tendency against a sacrificial cult, and this cannot be ignored.[31] Hence, Dalferth concludes that "We cannot speak of the *necessity* of having to understand Jesus' death as a sacrifice [Opfertod]."[32] Given the validity of this consideration we nevertheless have to ask what it means, or what one seeks to express, when one speaks about Jesus' death as sacrifice. The very use of such language suggests that there is something one seeks to express here that needs to be re-theologized within another framework in order to come to the fore in the present.

Dalferth holds that the images of sacrifice are not the only hermeneutical tools we have in order to articulate the salvific significance of the death and resurrection of Jesus. Moreover, he clearly understands that not every use of the concept of sacrifice is adequate. Adequacy, he claims, cannot be determined only from the angle of other ways of expressing the significance of his death, but must also be considered in light of how these ways of articulation relate to and function within the framework of those who confess him as savior. It is by making God's saving acts in Christ transparent that the adequacy of such conceptions is put to the test.[33] This is especially important in light of more repressive uses of the conception of self-sacrifice, which have caused feminist theologians to criticize the use of Christ's self-sacrifice as a model for human life and behavior.[34] Dalferth uses the latter argument as an indication of the necessity of having to formulate the salvific significance of the death of Christ in different ways:

31. Ingolf U. Dalferth, *Der Auferweckte Gekreuzigte: Zur Grammatik der Christologie* (Tübingen: Mohr Siebeck, 1994), p. 249.

32. Dalferth, *Der Auferweckte Gekreuzigte: Zur Grammatik der Christologie*, p. 293.

33. Dalferth, *Der Auferweckte Gekreuzigte: Zur Grammatik der Christologie*, p. 262.

34. See further on this below, pp. 278-88; and for a more extensive collection of such criticism, see Weaver, *The Nonviolent Atonement*, passim.

Persons live in concrete relationships, and have a history marked by experience and action that cannot be substituted for anyone else, and articulate this in their own language. The multiplicity of languages belongs to the essence of the Christian experience of salvation, and the non-reducible plurality of soteriological images and conceptions is the immediate consequence of this.[35]

Concluding this pattern of argumentation, Dalferth holds that it is what the category of sacrifice tries to express, and *not the category itself,* which is theologically important. The salvation it seeks to express is linked to *how God is revealed* in the very same event.[36]

God is determined by God's identification with Jesus, and this identification reveals God as the loving Father. Dalferth sees this identification as expressed in how God lets Jesus participate in the Spirit, in a way that allows for Jesus to partake in God's own identity. This participation can take place without God giving up God's identity or without Jesus giving up his humanity. Jesus thereby becomes a double identity, but what is just as important is that God is thereby revealed as having a differentiated identity. God can identify with something else only if there is something other than God, and this identification still allows for God to exist over against creation as its Other.[37] Writes Dalferth:

> God's self-identification with Jesus implies God's self-determination, in which God differentiates Godself so from Godself that God becomes one with an Other without ceasing to be different from him. God's self-identification with Jesus means that in this way God determines Godself in new ways by means of the cross of Jesus, by differentiating Godself from Godself, in order to integrate Jesus into God's own divine identity, without having to negate either the human and the creaturely character of Jesus, or God's own being as divinity and creator.[38]

---

35. Dalferth, *Der Auferweckte Gekreuzigte: Zur Grammatik der Christologie,* p. 266.

36. Cf. Dalferth, *Der Auferweckte Gekreuzigte: Zur Grammatik der Christologie,* p. 270. See for a further development of how God is positively revealed in Christ as sacrifice Kathryn Tanner's analysis of the same concept below, pp. 286-88.

37. Dalferth, *Der Auferweckte Gekreuzigte: Zur Grammatik der Christologie,* p. 279.

38. Dalferth, *Der Auferweckte Gekreuzigte: Zur Grammatik der Christologie,* pp. 279-80.

The quote makes clear that Dalferth — as I do — sees the main contribution of the cross of Christ as one revealing who God is, and thereby as revealing God's identity. This is not necessarily done by the notion of sacrifice. So although he offers a good discussion of the hermeneutical conditions for using the category of sacrifice in the case of Jesus,[39] in practice Dalferth is arguing for taking leave from that way of articulating the significance of Jesus' death. There are several reasons for this step. One is the deep ambiguity of the language of sacrifice in the New Testament: Jesus is the end of sacrifice both because he reveals that sacrifice is not necessary in order to restore the community between God and humans; and because he is the final and complete sacrifice.[40] These two ways of understanding his death as sacrifice seem to be in tension.

From a more hermeneutical angle then, Dalferth concludes that when we consider the use of the category of sacrifice in the New Testament, this category is used in order to show itself as obsolete (überholt). Hence, the category is used in order to exhibit its own *impossibility*. It deconstructs itself and its meaning when it is used in order to express the surplus expressed in the salvation in Jesus Christ.[41] This way of reasoning does not, however, preclude investigating other possibly valid concerns in our attempts to understand Jesus' death. To this task we now turn.

39. Dalferth, *Der Auferweckte Gekreuzigte: Zur Grammatik der Christologie*, pp. 296-300.

40. Dalferth, *Der Auferweckte Gekreuzigte: Zur Grammatik der Christologie*, p. 295.

41. Cf. Dalferth, *Der Auferweckte Gekreuzigte: Zur Grammatik der Christologie*, p. 299. Dalferth claims that this goes for the argumentation in the letter to the Hebrews as well: "Nicht die Erfüllung aller Erfordernisse des Kultopfers durch Jesus Christus, sondern die Ablösung des Opfers als kultischer Praxis und die Auflösung der Opfervorstellung als soteriologischer Kategorie ist die Pointe der paradoxalen Gleichsetzungs- und Übersteigerungsargumentation des Hebräerbriefs und der soteriologischen Umbesetzungsargumentation des Paulus" (p. 299).

Anselm's *Cur Deus Homo* and Beyond:
Escaping the Trap of Exchange and Violence

Anselm's *Cur Deus Homo* is among the most discussed treatises on the death of Jesus. In a remarkable effort to spell out a coherent doctrine regarding the necessity of both the incarnation and the death of Jesus, Anselm utilizes the social framework of the Middle Ages to give the doctrine of atonement a consistent articulation. The treatise is sometimes attacked — unjustifiably — as arguing that God is wrathful and demands some kind of sacrifice in order to be satisfied, and hence, as depicting a too-anthropomorphic understanding of God. That the picture he offers is anthropomorphic might be the case, but that this is due to the passions that God exhibits (such as wrath) is not clear from a careful reading of his treatise. Rather, it is due to the way Anselm develops the relationship between God and humans — his assumptions of a feudal society with its concepts of obligation and obedience, respect, honor, and satisfaction — that the accusation of anthropomorphism appears as justified. This very same framework is also what makes it so hard to appropriate his conceptions in the present world. That does not, however, mean that there is nothing valuable to be learned from his treatise.

A basic distinction for Anselm is that between punishment and satisfaction. The weight is clearly on the latter in Anselm, and this satisfaction is understood as something contributing to and reestablishing the honor of God, and as something giving God the vindication God deserves after his honor has been violated by the sins of humans. Hence the framework for interpreting the death of Jesus is not that he dies as a *punishment* for sin, but rather, that he dies in order to provide *satisfaction for sin*. If these two concepts are not kept separate, Anselm's way of reasoning becomes incomprehensible.

A major presupposition in Anselm is, accordingly, his relational understanding of sin: sin is to not render to God what is due.[1] By not being *willing* to do this, we violate the honor of God. The feudal framework allows Anselm to see humans as bound to give God honor, as God is the one who has given humans everything. Also here, then, God appears as giving. The righteousness of the will (comparable to what we have previously called the direction of desire) does works that are acceptable to God — and it is through such works that God is honored (cf. here the understanding also of functioning as *imago Dei* as the way in which God's glory is made apparent). The twist in Anselm, however, is that he turns this into a system of debt and exchange, once he claims that "Whoever does not pay to God this honor due Him dishonors Him and removes from Him what belongs to Him; and this removal, or this dishonoring, constitutes a sin. However, as long as he does not repay what he has stolen, he remains guilty."[2] This transformation of the relation into one that can be built upon a system of debt, guilt, and payment of satisfaction is what seems to corrupt the Anselmian way of understanding Christ's death.

This economic approach allows for Anselm to place humans in a situation of insolvable debt to God: Humans remain guilty of what they have taken (the honor of God), but they are not only obliged to repay what they have taken, they should also provide compensation. It is this surplus expressed in compensation of what is taken that Anselm defines as the satisfaction humans need to provide in order to restore the order of the universe and let God be recognized as God again.

There is an interesting element of recognition in this understanding of satisfaction that can be developed in other directions than those immediately present in his exposition. Anselm implicitly points to how the compensation implied includes recognition of the violated as someone who is justly due to have the offense committed against him recognized. By using the language of satisfaction in the way he does Anselm thus points to a *humane* and constructive application of the use of satisfaction. The "debt" is not one that can be paid off simply by "doing time" or similar punishments, as these would imply that there is only a relation between the law and the individual who performs the crime, but not with the one offended.

1. Anselm, Jasper Hopkins, and Herbert Richardson, *Why God Became Man: Cur Deus Homo* (Queenston, ON, Canada: E. Mellen Press, 1985), vol. 1, p. 11 (p. 67).
2. Anselm, Hopkins, and Richardson, *Why God Became Man* (pp. 67-68).

This constitutes another way of manifesting the constructive elements in the triadic approach to both Christology and anthropology that I have tried to develop in this book: On Anselm's account, humans do not only relate to the law, but also to the one offended. Or, in a different form: by allowing Christ to provide satisfaction, they not only recognize him and/or God as one who had to see God's good will violated, but also recognize the law and themselves as standing under the law.

The last point is one that actually is reflected in Anselm's discussion of why God cannot simply forgive out of mercy alone. Without going into all the reasons he offers for rejecting this, we here simply point to how the demand for some kind of punishment of and satisfaction for sin implies recognition of the fact that humans live under the law. If someone is forgiven out of mercy alone, that would imply that they are no longer under the law, and that they accordingly find themselves in a position that makes them privileged. This interpretation basically implies that the just and the unjust are treated as equals, which in turn implies that injustice is more privileged than justice.[3]

The basic premise in Anselm is that everything in creation owes the Creator honor. By sinning, humans are not in communion with God (like the angels). Satisfaction is necessary in order to have this communion restored. However, Anselm is clear about the fact that humans are not themselves in a situation where they can establish such a satisfaction because they already, prior to sinning, owe God everything. The demands for a satisfaction involving a surplus is thus something they cannot possibly meet. To put it short: *Satisfaction by humans is impossible.* This is even more of an impossibility when we consider the fact that the amount of the satisfaction that humans owe God, according to Anselmian reasoning, is larger than we can ever imagine ourselves able to *pay*.[4]

Anselm understands humans as indebted to God already before they become sinners, and this debt is due to what they have received from God. But sin makes the debt unpayable, and also adds the necessity of satisfaction. When we reconstruct his argument in this way, it becomes clear how much he is understanding the gifts of God within the very framework that Derrida and Tanner both oppose: Because this makes God's gifts something that created an obligation, and puts specific demands on humans.

---

3. Cf. Anselm, Hopkins, and Richardson, *Why God Became Man,* vol. 1, p. 12 (p. 69).

4. I put *pay* in italics here, for reasons to become clear further down.

This makes God's gift problematic as a gift — rather, it makes God's gifts seem as instruments by which the feudal lord ties his subjects to him and makes them dependent on him, in order for him to have his way with them and to establish himself as their master. This instrumentalizing and economizing of the gifts of creation then seem to crucially impair the function that Christ has for humans: he is not the one calling them to a community of freedom from merit and economic standards. Rather, the role he has in Anselm's framework reinforces how the relationship between God and humans must be understood in terms of economic exchange. As is well known, Christ is the one who, by the merit of his death for others, is able to provide satisfaction and to receive sinners as his companions in heaven. Humans, as sinners, are not able to provide even the smallest amount of satisfaction.

The main objection that can be raised against Anselm's understanding, from the interpretative angles we have provided, has accordingly to do with this *economization of atonement*. Given that Christ's death really provides a form of atonement (in the sense so well described when the word is divided so as to express the implication of his death as at-one-ment between God and humans), we have to ask if this is adequately described by seeing him as providing satisfaction. One of the main reasons for this question is that satisfaction (and ransom, which is sometimes also used as a metaphor for what Jesus provides by his death) is an economic term that is *external* in relation to the parts involved. This externalization of the process of satisfaction and atonement seems to render Christ's witness and ministry as being of little or no relevance to this process of atonement. Even worse, it becomes possible to see an implicit contradiction between the ministry of Jesus as we have reconstructed it and his death as satisfaction: His ministry opposes understanding relationships from the angles of merit and desert, while Anselm understands his death as something confirming such a way of framing the relationship between God and humans. As Christ thus becomes a *means* for providing satisfaction (admittedly, a unique means) the process of atonement is made something external rather than implying a real change of identity and recognition in the parties involved.[5]

5. For further discussion of how the cross involves a change of both recognition and identity, see below, in the next chapter. A concomitant critique of the external and instrumentalized understanding of satisfaction I offer here can be found in Vincent Brümmer, *Atonement, Christology and the Trinity: Making Sense of Christian Doctrine* (Aldershot, UK, and Burlington, VT: Ashgate, 2005), p. 76: "God does not love me for myself alone, but

The central aims of Anselm — to show why it was possible for God to become human, and why salvation is possible to achieve only by Christ — are both laudable. However, as indicated, this is done by developing a framework that seems to separate the ministry of Jesus from his death, and moreover makes his death the main purpose of the incarnation. When we add to this that there is hardly any mention in the New Testament of God's honor as something that humans violate, Anselm's reconstruction seems distorting.

Whereas Anselm is able to maintain the importance of understanding Christ as true human and true God, the framework within which this unity is developed for making salvation understandable is not only reductive and distorting, it is also not taking fully into account that what happened to Christ was *evil*. With his emphasis on how Jesus provides satisfaction, Anselm's conception is an easy target for criticisms like "Why is God demanding this in order to make satisfaction?" This makes God the main subject behind the death of Jesus, and one who deliberately wants his death, even though God wants it for a positive outcome. While we can see this as an expression of God's love and willingness to save humanity from the consequences of sin, it is very hard in the present world to understand why the death of Christ can have its ultimate meaning only within such a feudal framework.

Against a Girardian background, the primary criticism that can be made regarding Anselm is that it is wrong to assume that God became human only to die. Furthermore, Christ did not die as he did in order to cancel the punishment that humanity deserved by means of the infinitely undeserved suffering of his innocent divinity. Hence, to see the legal apparatus present at the crucifixion as there because God has a satisfaction case to prosecute and a punishment to enforce on humanity is totally wrong. Christ's task is to reveal the inhumanity of that machinery of false accusation and political and religious legitimacy, and to show the way sacred violence works. Anselm fails to establish this, and in doing so, he has made the cross a celebration of the sacrifice it was meant to overcome.[6]

---

merely for the obedience with which I render him honour. To put it crudely: God values my serving his honour more than he values me. For this reason, too, I am replaceable for God by anybody else who is able to satisfy his honour adequately. It does not matter to him whether it is I or Christ in my stead who does so, provided his honour is satisfied."

6. S. Mark Heim, *Saved from Sacrifice: A Theology of the Cross* (Grand Rapids: Eerdmans, 2006), p. 301.

Seen from critical distance, the strength in Anselm's conception is its ability to express the seriousness of sin and how it distorts relationships between God and humans. He is also able to maintain that the law has a positive character of goodness and justice, which makes it important to hold responsible those who are violating it. On the other hand, Anselm offers little in terms of understanding Christ's death as (vicarious) punishment, which is another important line of interpretation of his death. The vicarious element is tied to *satisfaction,* not to *poena.* It is even so that the one who is able to provide satisfaction is free from punishment. When Anselm limits his emphasis on poena in favor of satisfaction, this is a clear parallel to his emphasis on Christ as *actively* providing satisfaction more than *passively* suffering (poena). Thereby the death of Christ is not foremost understood as a vicarious punishment, but as a merit equivalent with the amount of human sin. Gunter Wenz claims that this makes the active character of his death as value or merit the most important. That Christ suffers under a burden of God's wrath and human guilt and sin is, on the other hand, not prominent in Anselm.[7]

Wenz also makes one more critical remark on Anselm's theory, and one that is important in order to see Christ's death as a double representation, which is a point we will return to later. He says that *de facto* it is only the human nature of Christ that is providing the means for satisfaction. Hence the necessity for God to become human was in order for God *as* human to provide this. Thereby the unity of God and humanity in Christ appears to be of limited importance. Writes Wenz:

> The *unio personalis* is in fact only allowed to have the function of establishing and multiplying infinitely the value of the human nature of Christ and the value of his salvific work. The redeeming act itself is fundamentally fulfilled by the human nature, i.e. the human will, of Christ.[8]

Given that this seems to put great emphasis on the humanity of Christ, we have to ask if this humanity can still be articulated and expressed in its

---

7. Gunther Wenz, *Geschichte der Versöhnungslehre in der Evangelischen Theologie der Neuzeit,* 2 vols., Münchener Monographien zur Historischen und Systematischen Theologie; Bd. 9, 11 (München: Chr. Kaiser Verlag, 1984), vol. 1, pp. 46-47. My translation.

8. Wenz, *Geschichte der Versöhnungslehre in der Evangelischen Theologie der Neuzeit,* vol. 1, p. 55.

unity with God in a way that makes what takes place at the cross understandable from the angle of both God and humanity. Hence, a question emerging from the discussion of Anselm is if there are other, and more suitable ways of interpreting the death of Christ in recent theology, and without having to utilize a feudal framework based on honor, vindication, and satisfaction.

J. D. Weaver: An Alternative to Anselm's Violence

An alternative to Anselm, which interprets him as one advocating a violent God, is J. D. Weaver's *The Nonviolent Atonement.* As the title suggests, the interest of Weaver is atonement, but one in which God is not understood as the initiating subject of what takes place in Jesus' death. The alternative Weaver spells out is called *Narrative Christus Victor,* and as indicated by the title, this position has much in common with Gustaf Aulen's position developed in his *Christus Victor.* Furthermore, Weaver shares my concern of relating the death of Jesus more closely to his ministry. Hence the "narrative" put in front of "Christus Victor": It is in light of the total narrative of Christ that he becomes the victorious. Whereas the polemical scope of Weaver's treatise is directed against satisfaction atonement, he sums up his own position as this:

> Narrative Christus Victor is a way of reading the entire history of God's people, with the life, death, and resurrection of Jesus as the culminating revelation of the reign of God in history, whereas the various versions of satisfaction atonement concern a legal construct or an abstract formula that functions outside of and apart from history. Seeing the long historical context of narrative Christus Victor underscores the extent to which satisfaction atonement is separated from ethical involvements and allows oppression [. . .] to continue without challenge.[9]

As the quote itself witnesses to, Weaver's argument is very much shaped by his opposition to Anselm. But he directs his critique mostly against the conception of God that he claims Anselm has to assume. He sees Anselm as arguing that "God saves via divinely sanctioned or divinely willed violence"; and this is the result of a construction in which "the divine econ-

9. J. Denny Weaver, *The Nonviolent Atonement* (Grand Rapids: Eerdmans, 2001).

omy has a need for a death penalty to balance the sin of humankind as the basis for restoring justice."[10] Although he might be justified in questioning the image of God derived from Anselm's argument, it is nevertheless not the case that the divine economy he describes is construed in this way. The apparent reason for this is that it conflates satisfaction and poena, thereby making it seem that God is like an American government official with an errand to perform and death penalties to execute. As I have shown, there seems to be little or no element of penalty (poena) in Anselm. The emphasis is on satisfaction.

This notwithstanding, it is hard not to sympathize with the positive reconstruction that Weaver offers, and that paints another and more consistent picture of God and what the kingdom of God means. His reconstruction is also much in accordance with what I have developed in previous sections.

> Jesus' mission was not to die but to witness to the reign of God. Jesus died not via divinely instigated violence but at the hands of those who represented the powers opposed to the reign of God. Rather than cooperating with divinely sanctioned violence, Jesus countered the violence of the powers. And as he submitted to the evil of the violent powers rather than meet it on its own terms, he made visible the fact that the rule of God does not depend on violence. The God revealed by Jesus, and the rule of God revealed by Jesus, do not respond to violence with violence. They respond to violence with its opposite.[11]

Weaver is able to hold together an understanding of God as nonviolent with an understanding of atonement seen as a result of the totality of Jesus' ministry. Moreover, he underscores that human participation in the salvation provided has to do with whom or what we identify: We have to identify with sin. He thereby follows the already suggested approach expressed in the statement that "it could have been me who participated as an agent or a bystander in the trial and death of Jesus." Hence, Weaver sees the importance of recognition, and the challenge of developing a specific recognition of oneself in order to participate in the salvation that Jesus opens up. By stressing that we are enslaved by the very same powers as those that killed Jesus, and as siding with those who might also have op-

---

10. Weaver, *The Nonviolent Atonement*, p. 74.
11. Weaver, *The Nonviolent Atonement*, p. 74.

posed the reign of God,[12] he underscores how a Christian — who believes that Jesus died *for* him/her, has to develop a multilayered identity. In a quote that also (again) expresses his distance from Anselm, he writes:

> To confess to being a "sinner" is not merely an abstract concept involving a debt owed to the divine honor. Being a sinner means to acknowledge our identification with those who killed Jesus and our bondage to the powers that enslaved them. Every human being, by virtue of what human society is, participates in and is in bondage to those powers and is therefore implicated in the killing of Jesus.[13]

Weaver holds our identification with the powers that killed Jesus to be a precondition for understanding what it possibly could mean that he died "for us." The cost of the death of Christ was in order to make God's rule visible, he claims, and as such, he can also say that it was a "vicarious sacrifice," i.e., something he did in order to achieve something for us. However, as should be apparent by now, "vicarious sacrifice is not a payment to God nor a payment to a plan established by God nor a scheme to punish Jesus instead of punishing us."[14] Rather, it means that there is a negative revelation taking place, in which "the full character of the powers that enslave sinful humankind and that oppose the rule of God" become visible to us.[15]

There are some elements in need of further development after having presented Weaver's approach. First, one has to ask if it is sufficient to say that Christ's salvific work on the cross is captured in how he reveals our enslavement to sin and calls us to repent from it. As will be apparent in a later chapter, I hold as necessary that we are not only able to identify with

---

12. Weaver, *The Nonviolent Atonement*, p. 75. Cf. for this also Rowan Williams's apt comment about the function of the Eucharist, both past and present: "Those who eat at Jesus' table are his betrayers, then as now; yet from the death and hell to which our betrayal condemns him, he returns to break his bread with us as before. [. . .] We do not eucharistically remember a distant meal in Jerusalem, nor even a distant death: we are made 'present to ourselves' as people complicit in the betrayal and death of Jesus and yet still called and accepted, still 'companions' of Christ in the strict sense — those who break bread with him." Williams, *Resurrection: Interpreting the Easter Gospel* (Cleveland: Pilgrim Press, 2002), p. 34. Note how this also makes the Eucharist an instance for mutual recognition of different layers of identity.

13. Weaver, *The Nonviolent Atonement*.

14. Weaver, *The Nonviolent Atonement*.

15. Weaver, *The Nonviolent Atonement*, p. 76.

sin, but also to identify Christ as both God's representative and our representative; and the latter is important in order for us to identify with him as the one we should have been. Thereby we can also recognize his recognition of us as God's images.

Second, in need of further clarifications are the interrelated expressions "for us" and "vicarious." One way that recommends itself for achieving this is to look more carefully into Kathryn Tanner's work on this subject.

Kathryn Tanner on the Link Between Incarnation, Cross, and Sacrifice

K. Tanner claims that serious attention to the question of incarnation is a fruitful approach to understanding the significance of the cross for human salvation. She holds that by starting from the incarnation, one might be able to overcome some of the criticisms that feminist and womanist theologies have leveled against classic theories of atonement — criticisms that are very much echoed in the book by J. D. Weaver just analyzed.

Tanner distinguishes between several different "models" in her discussion of the atonement. In order to clarify how her position appears, we can list them briefly here:

- The moral example/moral influence model, which sees Jesus' dying for us as the manifestation of God's self-sacrificial love, and thus as an example of imitation or a power enkindling a similar love in us;
- The Christus Victor model, which we have already partly discussed in connection with Weaver above, who emphasizes how God on the cross is engaged in a decisive battle with the forces of sin and death;
- The vicarious satisfaction model of Anselm;
- The model of penal substitution, which emphasizes how Jesus is obediently fulfilling the law and/or suffering the punishment due to violators of the law. Thereby he fulfills the terms of the law and exempts sinners from the penalties otherwise owed;
- The happy exchange model, in which Christ takes our sins and puts them to death, while we can put on Christ's righteousness through our faith and thereby find acceptance before God.[16]

16. Kathryn Tanner, "Incarnation, Cross and Sacrifice: A Feminist-Inspired Reapprai-

Anyone who looks more closely into the content of these models will see that they differ in ways that make them hard to combine. They differ on who is *responsible* for the crucifixion, on who is *changed* through what happens, on the question of *how* things are changed, and on the understanding of the situation in general. Tanner stresses as specifically unappealing the one-sidedness in the picture of God that many of these models express, and she rightly underscores the validity of some of the criticism that has been brought forward against the different models:

> God in the moral example or influence model seems a sentimental patsy, without righteous anger or horrified concern for the destructive and wayward effects of sin on human life. On the vicarious satisfaction model, God appears more concerned about slights to God's own dignity than the sufferings of a death-filled world. Here and in the penal substitution model, God seems straitjacketed in the expression of loving concern by a rigid law or penal code of God's own construction. In many cases, one suspects God derives pleasure or satisfaction from death and suffering. Feminist worries about the cross as a model for abuse are perfectly continuous with the last concern, which hardly seems to me objectionably novel or outlandish in its basic form.[17]

Tanner also concurs with the criticism I have already stated against some of these models as ignoring other elements in the Gospel story, and thus making major dimensions of Jesus' life virtually without importance to what happens on the cross. A major flaw in the models of moral influence and vicarious satisfaction is the lack of importance given to the resurrection, while the incarnation appears as unnecessary from the point of view of the penal substitution model. The most important criticism Tanner launches is that none of these models seem to consider Jesus' public ministry as important, and this is a point underscored by recent feminist and womanist theologians.[18]

---

sal," *Anglican Theological Review* 86, no. 1 (2004): 36f. Cf. for a similar overview, Ted Peters, "Six Ways of Salvation: How Does Jesus Save?" *Dialog* 45, no. 3 (2006).

17. Tanner, "Incarnation, Cross and Sacrifice: A Feminist-Inspired Reappraisal," p. 37.

18. Tanner, "Incarnation, Cross and Sacrifice: A Feminist-Inspired Reappraisal," p. 38. Cf. also for this Weaver, *The Nonviolent Atonement.* Weaver's writing seems to be based on many of the same concerns, and accordingly even launches the notion "narrative" in his argument for the Christus Victor model.

The critique Tanner refers to is well worth repeating, as it consistently articulates the attempt we are making in the present book to link Jesus' public ministry and his death: The lines of the argument take two distinct forms. (1) Jesus' ministry is what gave rise to the opposition that led to his death, and (2) One should stay on the course in one's dedication to the mission of God despite the costs in suffering and death to oneself that are likely to be incurred in a world marked by sin.[19] While we have so far emphasized (1) in our study, (2) is one that should not be ignored, and even less so as there are distinct warnings in the Gospels about the fact that suffering and death are a likely outcome for anyone who is a disciple or witness. However, the second line, which we could easily describe as a version of the concerns of the moral model, needs to be developed further in order to make clear that it is a specific mission that Jesus' life is dedicated to. Not everything is worth dying for, and not every kind of dedication may appear as commendable. Hence there must be a *substantial link between the mission and the death of Jesus.*

This presence of a substantial link is, however, jeopardized by the flipside of the very same argument: As Tanner sees it, Jesus' death can be seen as an impediment to his mission, and not a positive culmination of it. The rejection and death of Jesus are accordingly things that block his mission more than expressing its content. From this angle, then, she says, "it would presumably have been better — a sign of the kingdom come — if the suffering and crucifixion of Jesus had never happened."[20] From this account alone, then, the death of Jesus appears as unnecessary, contingent, and is not at all a sign of God's master plan, but only of what happens to witnesses to goodness and community in a world where sin rules and where challenges to a world ordered around economical exchange and merit are not welcome.

Tanner holds the above model (2) as being compatible with models of atonement from the Reformation, where Christ is subjected to the death of sinners, and his death is brought about by those who reject God's witness. However, she also thinks that this model is in need of supplement, and the means for such a supplement she finds in a specific understanding of the incarnation. Tanner sees in the incarnation the inner heart of atone-

---

19. Tanner, "Incarnation, Cross and Sacrifice: A Feminist-Inspired Reappraisal," p. 38.

20. Tanner, "Incarnation, Cross and Sacrifice: A Feminist-Inspired Reappraisal," p. 39.

ment, as this is the condition of possibility for union with God in and through Christ. As such, it replaces models of vicarious satisfaction or penal substitution, and confirms important features in both the Christus Victor and the happy exchange models at the same time, but without all of their problems. In the Christus Victor model, Tanner claims, the incarnation is the very means by which the fight against the destructive powers is waged and won.[21] Understood as the Word's assumption of humanity, it is in virtue of this assumption that humanity is saved: "first the humanity of Christ himself, and then through him that of every other human being, one with him."[22] In a manner that resembles the old Church Fathers and apparently is much inspired by them, she sums it up thus:

> The humanity of Christ (and united with Christ our humanity) is purified, healed and elevated — saved from sin and its effects (anxiety, fear, conflict and death) — as a consequence of the very incarnation through which the life-giving powers of God's own nature are brought to bear on human life in the predicament of sin. Humanity is taken to the Word in the incarnation in order to receive from the Word what saves it.[23]

When Tanner combines this idea of incarnation with the happy exchange model, she is able to disconnect the latter from the idea of penal substitution. The happy exchange model then becomes one in which the atonement is "just a case of the saving communication of idioms that the incarnation brings about."[24] The exchange accordingly becomes one in which the life-enhancing powers and properties of the Word receive the alien properties of humanity in a way that saves humanity from sin and death.[25]

Since we have put much emphasis on criticizing models of exchange previously, we may now ask if there are any reasons for applying the same kind of criticism to the happy exchange model. There seems to be none: this

21. Tanner, "Incarnation, Cross and Sacrifice: A Feminist-Inspired Reappraisal," p. 41.
22. Tanner, "Incarnation, Cross and Sacrifice: A Feminist-Inspired Reappraisal," p. 41.
23. Tanner, "Incarnation, Cross and Sacrifice: A Feminist-Inspired Reappraisal," p. 41.
24. That atonement implies communication can also be well expressed from quite another, and possibly non-metaphysical, angle: G. Bader writes: "Wer unversöhnt ist, redet nicht. Sprachliche Kommunikation ist an sich bereits Versöhnung." See Günter Bader, *Symbolik des Todes Jesu, Hermeneutische Untersuchungen zur Theologie,* 25 (Tübingen: Mohr Siebeck, 1988), p. 89.
25. Tanner, "Incarnation, Cross and Sacrifice: A Feminist-Inspired Reappraisal," p. 41.

is a kind of non-economic exchange, where both parties are involved initially with each other, and not only by external means. This involvement means also a profound recognition of who the other is, and what this exchange means to him — be it either Jesus or the human. Moreover, the exchange implies an increase of life, and even more distribution of life, whereas what humans have to give away is not inflicting them with a loss; rather, they give away the sin and the consequences of sin that contribute to loss in life.

Against the backdrop of our continuous emphasis on the community that Jesus realizes as part of his ministry, we can now see how this conception is in accordance with Tanner's position: atonement (at-one-ment) is happening in all the instances where humanity is at one with the divine in Jesus, be it on the cross or elsewhere in his ministry.[26] One obvious gain of this approach is that this does not render God's work, as it appears in the forensic framework, as something that comes too late to save Jesus.

At this point, Tanner identifies as problematic how legal or contractual terms function in the understanding of the causal connections between what happens on the cross and God's saving acts:

> What happens on the cross does not evoke what God does to save, in any strong sense. Those saving acts flow to the humanity of Christ in virtue of an already present community with that humanity — the strongest possible community in which what is the Word's becomes humanity's own — a community that holds prior to the meeting of any conditions and which in its intimacy obviates the need to meet them.[27]

What is the connection between the cross and salvation against this background? At this point Tanner echoes the Church Fathers by saying that the Word must become one with a life that suffers under the forces of sin and death in order to reach humanity. That Jesus is obedient to death in order to be exalted means that and only that, and not that his exaltation and resurrection are a reward for his obedience and humiliation. Jesus' death is then a precondition for salvation in the same way as being sick is a precondition for going to the doctor, and not similar to how one has to repent in one way or another in order to be forgiven or return to the community.[28]

---

26. Cf. Tanner, "Incarnation, Cross and Sacrifice: A Feminist-Inspired Reappraisal," p. 43.

27. Tanner, "Incarnation, Cross and Sacrifice: A Feminist-Inspired Reappraisal," p. 43.

28. Tanner, "Incarnation, Cross and Sacrifice: A Feminist-Inspired Reappraisal," p. 44.

We are now at a point to consider what Tanner's exploration of the phrase "Christ died for us" might mean. This "for us" formula has more to do with our benefits, rather than being an expression of legal conditions. This allows for a positive understanding that can emphasize that Jesus does what he does, including suffering humiliation and death, on our behalf. He does this so that we will no longer have to live in a world that is affected by sin and death. He can do this because of the kinship between the Word and humanity manifest in the incarnation.[29] At the same time, this positive understanding also gives Tanner the chance to distance herself from an understanding of the cross that emphasizes how Jesus is standing before the law and is our substitute in the prosecution of our case. She says, "Jesus does not represent us, stand in for us, primarily by taking on the position of guilty, death-deserving persons before the law. That, once again, is not what 'died for us' necessarily implies."[30]

At this point I partly agree with Tanner, and in part I disagree. The reasons are the following: I agree insofar as she emphasizes the necessity of

---

29. Tanner, "Incarnation, Cross and Sacrifice: A Feminist-Inspired Reappraisal," p. 44.

30. Tanner, "Incarnation, Cross and Sacrifice: A Feminist-Inspired Reappraisal," p. 44. There is, however, a different way of understanding substitution here, namely, that of Levinas. In the essay "To Which Question Is 'Substitution' the Answer?," in *The Cambridge Companion to Levinas,* ed. Simon Critchley and Robert Bernasconi (Cambridge: Cambridge University Press 2002), p. 239, Robert Bernasconi indicates this by developing Levinas's ideas in a way that makes it possible to see the persecuted Christ as the one taking responsibility for even those who persecute him: "The 'for' of 'one-for-the-other' of substitution signals a surplus of responsibility that extends even to those one does not know, including people of the past and the future. Substitution is not the psychological event of pity or compassion, but a putting oneself in the place of the other by taking responsibility for their responsibilities. Because substitution is my responsibility for everyone else, including their responsibility, the relation is asymmetrical: 'No one can substitute himself for me, who substitutes myself for all' [. . .]. Hence the trope of the-one-for-the-other is contradictory [. . .]. My responsibility for the responsibility of the other constitutes that 'one degree of responsibility more' [. . .], a 'surplus of responsibility' [. . .]. Against the traditional notion of responsibility Levinas can claim that I am for the other without having chosen or acted: 'Without ever having done anything, I have always been under accusation: I am persecuted.'" Cf. also Jacques Derrida, *The Gift of Death, Religion and Postmodernism* (Chicago: University of Chicago Press, 1995), pp. 48, 51. Against this background, the death of Christ is in a double sense a revelation of the responsibility of humans. They are responsible for his death, and they are responsible for this never to happen again. As one can see, this is an interpretation that goes hand in hand with the one Girard offers, cf. above.

relating the incarnation more extensively to all that happens in Christ's life, and in her affirmation of the happy exchange model as one that might express important and vital aspects. I also agree with her that the expression "for us" does not necessarily mean that he takes the position of those that deserve death before the law. But that need not be the only way in which Christ stands in our place with regard to the law:

Christ is in the place of everybody who rejects God and thereby the law. He is in this place undeserved and due to injustice done to him. He is in their place due to the fact that it is not he, but those rejecting him who should be facing the consequences of death by rejecting the God of life. As we shall see more extensively developed in the next chapter, rejection of God means death because it means separation from the God of life. Those who part from God become the servants of death. Moreover, it is in their practice that the law also becomes an instrument for death. Jesus is subjected to the law as an instrument of death. He is in our place insofar as his death expresses what the final outcome is for anyone who is, as Weaver suggested, able to identify with those who crucified him. In siding with these perpetrators, we are those who ultimately must face death. But instead he takes our place. Hence there is a mix-up of roles in the crucifixion: those who ultimately will have to face death due to their rejection of the God of life and God's witness are free, while the witness himself dies. The happy exchange thus has a root in a specific reading of the history itself, and is not only the result of a theological reading that does not take the historical circumstances into account. In its utmost consequence, this means that Christ suffers due to the sins of others: his death is both a result of others' sin, and *because of the concrete sin of rejection itself.* In his death, he suffers the consequences of what it means to be subjected to sin and injustice. But in contrast to everyone who can identify themselves as perpetrators or bystanders to his crucifixion, he is innocent. I think it is important to be aware of this possibility for understanding what it means that he died "for us." He thereby exposes the consequences of using the law as a tool for securitization. Again, the unity of the Word with Humanity is important here, as Tanner underscores: As a human, Christ is suffering that which is the fate of humans separated from God — but since he is not separated from, but in full unity with God, his suffering is also possible to become something more than an expression of love and obedience; it can be the expression of what happens to the human who is united with God when God is rejected. This negative element in the crucifixion thus allows for two meanings of "for us": (1) on our behalf, to our benefit, and (2) because of us and our rejection of God (due to misjudging Jesus as not being the representative of God).

As for the criticism voiced by feminist/womanist theologians, Tanner's approach apparently meets their concerns. Her theology depicts God as working in and with Christ, unswervingly for our good, and in a manner that puts no value on death or suffering and no ultimate value on self-sacrifice for the good. Instead, God is depicted as a God of gift-giving abundance struggling against the forces of sin and death, in the incarnational solidarity with us. There is something saving implied in the cross, "but there is nothing saving about suffering, death or victimhood, in and of themselves. All these elements are things that humanity needs to be saved from. Similarly, Jesus' *obedience* should be thought of as a result of the saving force of incarnation and not as the condition for salvation."[31]

At this point we can insert a reflection that might be taken as confirming the above position: It is possible to understand the death of Jesus as a sacrifice that humans offered to God in order to restore the honor of God, and that, due to their misconception, they accordingly thought had been offended. But God rejects this sacrifice, and thereby God makes clear that Jesus is a *victim* of a perverse logic of sacrifice that God does not support. (The resurrection is the event that reveals this rejection on God's side.) Instead, God makes Jesus a representative of those who believe that he was truly the one he said: he represented the unrepresented, those who suffered unjustly, and could only do so by being a representative in the sense of making God present. Along such lines, the death of Jesus could be conceived of as a sacrifice in the Girardian sense, revealed (in the resurrection) as a victimization of someone subjected to a logic where grace has no place.

A valuable element in Tanner's proposal is the way she tries to reconstruct the possible conditions for understanding Christ's death as a sacrifice. In order to understand her correctly, we have to restate from the outset that Christ's death is not something that is done in order to perform a sacrifice; but as this evil happens, it can also be interpreted as a sacrifice, or rather, his death can be seen as having a sacrificial quality. This interpretation demands that we do not see sacrifice first and foremost in modern

31. Tanner, "Incarnation, Cross and Sacrifice: A Feminist-Inspired Reappraisal," p. 47.

terms and apart from the non-cultic sphere. Sacrifice does not mean — in the context from which it is originally derived for use in the New Testament — some kind of self-renunciation for which one can only be sorrowful. Rather, the cultic sacrifices of Israel are events where one either celebrates or ends in joyous communion. Especially important is that this joyous communion is between God and humans. Hence, the point in sacrificing is not to give up something, but to return to God what is God's as an appropriate act of thanksgiving. All the sacrificial rites of Israel should, according to this reading, be understood in light of a community where the joy of God's presence is the presupposition and the end of the celebration meal.[32]

Tanner holds that forensic understandings of atonement distort this understanding of sacrifice, and acutely so when the sacrifice is understood as propitiatory. Aptly, she points to how there is no legal connotation of the sacrificial act as a satisfaction or penalty. Hence the point of sacrificial rites is to "wipe away the fault in ways that a God already desirous of communion with us institutes."[33] It is not to change God from wrath to mercy, an understanding that would again involve God in some kind of exchange economy where the gifts of God would be dependent upon the merits or deserts of humanity:

> Benefits do not come back to the offerer because the conditions of something like a contract have been fulfilled but because the rite trades on God's unbroken faithfulness to a decision to be with those engaged in temple service. Propitiation is not the reason why the rite wipes away sin; no real explanation indeed is offered. God simply wants to reinstate God's people to full communion with God and that is what God tells God's people to do in such cases.[34]

---

32. Tanner, "Incarnation, Cross and Sacrifice: A Feminist-Inspired Reappraisal," pp. 50-51. Against this background one can also read the words at the institution of the Last Supper as indicating that "these are my contributions to the fellowship and community," thereby concretely expressing both hospitality and forgiveness (at the meal and thereafter), and as an occasion for manifesting communion more than an anticipation of self-renunciation taking place at the cross.

33. Tanner, "Incarnation, Cross and Sacrifice: A Feminist-Inspired Reappraisal," p. 49.

34. Tanner, "Incarnation, Cross and Sacrifice: A Feminist-Inspired Reappraisal," p. 49.

As becomes clear, the conditions on which Tanner establishes her understanding of Christ's death as a sacrifice do not make it possible to identify his death as a result of a demand in an contractually based exchange. Rather, it is God's way of making peace. According to this understanding, it is not death in itself that is at the center of what happens at the cross, even when it is identified or recognized as a sacrifice. It is a sacrifice in the way it establishes and maintains a community between God and humans.[35] Although she does not state it explicitly, a connotation of Tanner's understanding of Christ's death as a sacrifice is that sacrifice cannot be the *main* element in understanding the cross and death of Jesus. Rather, "sacrifice" is to be understood metaphorically. This provides us with a background against which one can also be clear about in which sense the cross is *not* to be understood a sacrifice. In this connection Tanner actually points to how the New Testament construction of Christ's death as a sacrifice might disrupt the common connotations that are at play in cult as well as in language:

> The political execution of a beaten and scourged subversive on a polluted site outside the gates is not anything close to the sacrifice of an animal without blemish in the temple at the hand of a priest. Sacrificial language is obviously being applied to something that is not a cultic sacrifice in order to throw some novel interpretative light on the cross. But this means that the differences from ordinary sacrifice should also be salient.[36]

In light of her understanding of incarnation, Tanner can accordingly see the sacrifice of the cross as a rite performed by God, and not by human beings. God does this for us and our salvation, and the sacrifice is therefore not directed to God but from God to us. This is what God gives to us. *As a sacrificial act, the whole act is God's, since God is both the sacrificing and the one sacrificed.*[37]

However, this immediately calls for further clarification, because this interpretation implies that there is something double taking place in the cross of Christ. On the one hand, his death is a result of evil, something

35. Tanner, "Incarnation, Cross and Sacrifice: A Feminist-Inspired Reappraisal," p. 51.
36. Tanner, "Incarnation, Cross and Sacrifice: A Feminist-Inspired Reappraisal," p. 52.
37. Tanner, "Incarnation, Cross and Sacrifice: A Feminist-Inspired Reappraisal," pp. 52-53.

not wanted by him, and something in which he is passive, given over to the hands of those who destroy him. As such, he is a subjected subject, one who goes where his dedication to the cause leads him. On the other hand, and on the presupposition of the previous, God turns Christ's crucifixion into a sacrifice, where he *by the very means of the death of Christ still invites to celebrate this community — now a costly one — with God.* Here, God is the subject, and one who refuses to be bound by regular rites of sacrifice. Instead, God makes the most lowly and debased into a sacrifice that is an offer of community. Again, God appears as one who never, even when rejected and put to death, stops offering community. God continues to play God's own game, even when humans try to restrict, narrow, and dissolve all the conditions on which God's offering of community can express itself. The multilayered identity of Christ as true human and true God is then also expressed in the way he is both a *sacrifice* (offered by God as Godself) and a *victim* (rejected). To keep these two understandings of sacrifice apart is of crucial importance.[38]

Salvation as Finding One's Place: C. Gestrich

The German systematic theologian Christoph Gestrich develops an important interpretation of *salvation* in his seminal study of what it means to stand in vicariously for an other as a substitute (Stellvertretung). Although basically oriented towards a Trinitarian theology, his investigation opens up levels of understanding relevant for a post-metaphysical Christology as well. Gestrich suggests that salvation in Christ means *the overcoming of the human state of being lost.* This state of being lost is related to the fact that you have no place in the world anymore.[39] As becomes immediately clear, Gestrich's conception is easy to relate to the formerly developed understanding of humans as lacking a point of orientation. Moreover, if we see human identity as something lacking important coordinates when not relating to the Other as the third, and to God and the law as the basis for this relation, this deepens the understanding of what it is to be lost in more re-

38. For further elaborations of this, see Christof Gestrich, *Christentum und Stellvertretung: Religionsphilosophische Untersuchungen zum Heilsverständnis und zur Grundlegung der Theologie* (Tübingen: Mohr Siebeck, 2001).

39. Gestrich, *Christentum und Stellvertretung,* p. 12.

lational ways as well. The conception can thereby be explicitly related to the understanding of God as the "point of orientation" we developed in Part I, where we presented Dalferth's understanding of God as an index-word: When God is lost as a point of orientation, the human itself is lost. To be lost is to not have a place in the world where you can find or orient yourself anymore.

Gestrich develops in detail a phenomenological framework for this understanding of what it is to be lost, and we can here only give a brief summary of the most relevant points he offers. One who is lost is no longer where he or she belongs. On the other hand, when you lose something you search for it (if you consider it worthwhile). Moreover, in order to not lose something, you need to protect it. A human who belongs somewhere also belongs to or is related to someone. All this makes sense in the God–Self–Other triadic relationship we have developed. When a human is no longer recognized by others as being created in the image of God, he or she is marginalized and made invisible — she is lost. God, on the other hand, constantly searches for those who are lost, and tries to protect humans from being lost (cf. the parables of Jesus about being lost and found). We have seen Jesus as the primary revealer of that feature in God. The basic recognition of a human being, then, is that he or she belongs with God, and as long as this recognition is made, he or she is not lost. Then you cannot witness to anything.

Although we cannot demand a place in life, says Gestrich, we become — I might say, are given — such a place when we are spoken to and answer. By being included in a discourse we are not only made response-able and given a place so that we are not lost; this discourse also contributes to our protection. The first initiator of this discourse is God, who calls us to be responsible to God — for the neighbor.[40]

As indicated: to be lost is to have no place to be, it is to have no one speaking to you and making you responsible. When I have lost my place, one way of finding it is to turn around (repent); another is to be found by someone else. What Jesus does is to overcome the condition of being lost for those who are excluded and marginalized, and to make visible the fact that God's calling is for them as well as for those who already seem to have found their place. As indicated above, to be given a place is a gift, and it is a

---

40. Gestrich, *Christentum und Stellvertretung*, p. 12. Cf. for this also Oliver's conception of the response-ability in witnessing.

gift given by a relationship to somebody else. The loss for those who are excluded is that their place as well as their relationship with others is lacking. Thereby, it seems as they are not being recognized by anyone as either response-able (Kelly Oliver's term) or as someone with a specific place and standing within the community. Jesus' inclusive practice says: "Here is your place — this is where you have a position; this is where you belong." The kingdom of God is about being found, and about being given a place.

When we speak of humans the question becomes acute: Who is looking for a human who is no longer where she belongs? It is at this point that the idea of being a substitute shows its relevance for how Gestrich understands salvation. Christ is my substitute in being lost — he expresses the utmost state of being lost when he is where he should not be — on the cross.

That someone takes my place means that someone else keeps my place open, makes it possible for me to have a place when I have lost it or when I am not present in it.[41] When someone keeps my place open, he or she represents me. Speaking Christologically, if Christ represents me, it means that he keeps my place open, stands in for me, when I am lost from God.

However, the basic representation that *humans* are called to take care of is the one in which they represent *God*. This immediately raises the question if God *can* be represented, and the answer to that is, not only in Gestrich, but also from our previous considerations, "Yes." However, Gestrich underscores that it is *not Christians, as Christians, who represent God*, but God is represented by all human as humans, since all humans are created in the image of God.[42]

Gestrich differentiates between processes of representation and processes of substitution, and applies this distinction to his understanding of Christ as taking part in both. As he sees it, representation makes it possible for someone *with* power to be present in a distant or foreign place, while the substitute makes it possible for someone who does *not* have the powers to be present in his or her own place in order not to lose it. This does not exclude the fact that the two functions may also be intertwined in several respects, because the place you have and who you are might be seen as two different elements that belong together.[43] In this manner, it becomes possi-

---

41. Gestrich, *Christentum und Stellvertretung*, pp. 12-13.
42. Gestrich, *Christentum und Stellvertretung*, p. 65.
43. Gestrich, *Christentum und Stellvertretung*, pp. 235-36.

ble to have a differentiated understanding of Christ as *representing God* (making God's powers present) and as a *substitute for humans* (standing in for those who are lost and with no powers to keep their place).

As our task in the present is to clarify what it means that Jesus is both representing God and someone who substitutes for humans, we need to focus on the three different ways in which Gestrich holds that this substitution (Stellvertretung) must be differentiated. When one is substituting one *does* something, *is* something, and is *placed* somewhere specific.[44] This differentiation makes it possible to ask *what Jesus does,* and *what he is* as a substitute, and also *where he is.* Gestrich offers the following answers to these questions:[45]

a) Jesus' *exclusive* substitution consists in the fact that he suffers something with the aim that other humans should be liberated from the same kind of suffering. His condition of being lost on the cross is something that no one else should need to suffer. This is also a substitution and sacrifice in which we have nothing in common with him — this is his offering for us, not ours for others. He does here provide us with the means for obliterating every kind of sacrifice in the Girardian sense. However, to state, as Gestrich does, that this is something that Jesus *does* should not preclude us from maintaining that he is not the active subject in this. Rather, Jesus is a passive subject, one to whom this is done, or one who does this because he is subjected to the sacrificial powers of others, which then determine him. His sacrifice is — in this connection — not something that can be understood as an *act* in the strict sense of the word.

b) The *inclusive* substitution of Jesus is linked to his being an image of God and thereby a truly human being. Jesus is not blurring the distinction between Creator and creature. Rather, he is a human that recognizes and knows God, and thereby is able to have a true relationship with God. Simultaneously, he is one with whom other humans can identify themselves, as he is himself also one who identifies with other humans.

c) *Where* does Jesus stand? In answering this question, Gestrich speaks

---

44. Gestrich, *Christentum und Stellvertretung*, p. 224.

45. For this and the following, see Gestrich, *Christentum und Stellvertretung*, pp. 389-90.

of a *prospective* substitution: Jesus stands where we are not yet, but where we are to be and what we are to become. He stands at the place of our not-yet-realized self, our identity to come. He stands where the antagonisms and divisions of our identity have been overcome.

To see Jesus as standing in this place implies recognizing our future identity in him. That this identity is something other than our present one is especially crucial in terms of *sin*. *Sin is what makes us different from him.* What does Jesus then do with our sins? It is claimed — for good reasons — that it is a position both immoral and illusionary to say that Jesus "takes our sins away" when substituting for us (referring to Isaiah 53). Gestrich, accordingly, sees this position to be a misinterpretation, and he refers here to the important work by the Old Testament scholar B. Janowski.[46] Jesus does not make humans free from their responsibilities, but *in* their responsibilities. In the very situation where persons have to face that they are falling short of their responsibilities and that their guilt is too large, Jesus "stands in" for them in a way that makes it possible for them to distance themselves from their past. He reveals that they are the images of God. This "standing in" implies that he recognizes them as persons being more than what their past determines them to be. He thereby also makes it possible for them and others to recognize them as something else and something more: His presence there for us suggests that there is a surplus in our very being that transcends what is given with our past and with our failed responsibilities. Against this background, Gestrich can also formulate the implications of forgiveness:

> *To forgive sins is not to cleanse away debt, but is a change of place by means of the power of faith.* Not so, that what makes the human who did something wrong free is that she does not have to suffer the consequences of that wrongdoing, but only this, that she is not any longer bound by her wrong desire and the victimizing consequences of it.[47]

The above quote is important because Gestrich explicitly addresses how humans who are not able to distance themselves from their past by understanding themselves (or being understood by others) as anything

---

46. See Bernd Janowski and Michael Welker, eds., *Opfer: Theologische und Kulturelle Kontexte* (Frankfurt: Suhrkamp, 2000).

47. Gestrich, *Christentum und Stellvertretung*, p. 436.

more than their past merits, are captured in a desire fully determined by the past (and by the desire to overcome it, get rid of it). They thereby become victims of the past (even their own pasts), instead of being liberated from it. Faith, on the other hand, liberates by directing desires towards that which you are not and cannot have by yourself. To be forgiven is thus to be offered a new way of relating to yourself, in which the past is something that does not determine your existence in its totality. Forgiveness redirects desire.

The question is then, of course, *what* does the cross, and the crucifixion of Christ, contribute to this situation? How does it make it possible to establish this kind of liberating distance? Gestrich himself suggests the answer to this question when he indicates that it implies a change in position or place. If Christ is in my place (as a substitute), it means that he is where I *cannot be,* as I am something else and more than this. Since I have not myself the powers to be in the place of the condemned, I can see Christ as the one who holds that place for me — not in order for me to take it, but in order for me to be elsewhere.

Moreover, Christ is, according to Gestrich's conception, both representative and substitute: he is God's representative as the one who places himself in the place of the sinner (which he himself nevertheless is not) and he is my substitute insofar as he takes the place I am not able to hold. He takes responsibility for my lack of being responsible. As such, he holds the place open until I can be responsible — and then I, due to this renewed responsibility, can be in a different place than where he is (on the cross). Then I can stand before God and have the identity given with Christ, who recognizes me as more than what I am responsible for.

As we can see, Gestrich's conception builds on the premise that humans are in need of a place. What this place is might be understood literally, but it can also be understood metaphorically: we need to find our place in order to orient ourselves. As we have hinted, God is the ultimate point of orientation in life, and when God gets lost, our place and orientation get lost — we get lost. Hence, a person's basic desire is one for a place, a position, somewhere to belong. This desire is both for something in our world and for something beyond the present world. As indicated, human desire is desire for that which is still not the case (the impossible) — but which can nevertheless shape our perception of the world here and now.

Gestrich also tries to see Christ's intercession as similar to intervention, i.e., as something taking place in order to disrupt and reorient, especially where a catastrophe is threatening. Against such an interpretative background, Jesus' mission was an intervention in human history. We can assume, Gestrich claims, that it not only took place in order to let our souls reach their final destination, but also in order to link Godself to the further development and history of the world. Understanding why God became a human being partaking in human history is possible from the point of view of God's intention to change the course of history, so that as many people as possible could experience a renewed relationship with God.[48] Important in this connection is the fact that Gestrich sees the corresponding faith in God as an intercession based on the recognition that human righteousness is God's gift. Emerging from this righteousness is then in turn a relationship to other humans that recognizes *them* as parts of God's creation. Those who partake in this community are called into a way of life where they intervene for the sake of other and represent them.[49]

48. Gestrich, *Christentum und Stellvertretung,* pp. 444f.

49. Gestrich's own text here suggests that this might have different implications also for the society in which Christians live, and that these intercessions or interventions cannot be seen as something only related to a spiritual realm. It is also a praxis that may have ecumenical consequences.

The Crucifixion as Realization of Identity:
The Gift of Recognition and Representation

Doctrines of atonement all have one thing in common, one presupposition upon which they are founded: They presuppose the mutual recognition of oneself and the other as parties both in opposition to, but still as belonging to each other, and as basically directed towards the other. Without such recognition there can be no process of atonement. In other words: there can be no atonement unless there is established a mutual recognition of the elements of identity that are crucial for maintaining community. This calls for a further reflection on how recognition is internal to and provides a basis for atonement. That is the purpose of the present chapter.

The Scandalous Gift: The Cross

Against the background of the previous chapters in this part of the book, it is an obvious scandal to present the cross as a gift. We have underscored that what happened to Jesus was the result of evil. Although we have also indicated that there was a close identification between Jesus and God, there is still a long way to go before we can argue that the cross is a gift.

The main parts of the present chapter go back to a previously published article, but are here worked over in order to make visible the links to the different strands of this study. See Jan-Olav Henriksen, "The Crucifixion as Realisation of Identity: The Gift of Recognition and Representation," *Modern Theology* 22, no. 2 (2006).

How can it be a gift when it is an instrument of torture and pain, a means for the destruction of everything that is good in human life?

Presenting the cross in such a way also seems to place many demands on the receiver of this gift. First and foremost, it places her in a very strange position, pressing upon her a perspective foreign to how she commonly and otherwise understands herself. Receiving the cross as a gift is to affirm a kind of identity that is fundamentally at odds with what most people immediately feel they need, deserve, and desire. Presented with the cross as a gift, one has to ask oneself: Who am I to receive this gift? What does the offering of this gift say about me — and about the one who presents it to me? Indeed, the cross as a gift not only throws into question the identity of the receiver and the giver, it also reconfigures the relationship between them. To the extent that this relationship is determinate for their identity, the crucifixion on the cross can also be seen as a place where the identity of both giver and recipient is realized in a specific form. That is the main thesis of this section, and one that will help us see the cross as a gift where nothing is demanded in order to receive it as a gift of identity, but where everything is nevertheless demanded in terms of being willing to give up our preconceptions of who we are.

In order to understand the cross and crucifixion[1] of Christ as a gift, there is a need for developing a broad understanding of not only myself and the giver (God, or Christ), but also of the gift itself: What makes the cross a gift (without having to sublate or suspend its character as a scandal) when it is presented to me as something I should "receive" for my own good? Various "theories" of atonement, some of which we have already discussed, have provided different answers to that question during the course of history. But the task here is not to offer a new version of such doctrines;[2] rather, my task is to present a possible understanding of the

---

1. In the following I distinguish between the cross as the place and the symbol on the one hand, and the crucifixion as an act Christ is subjected to on the other. It is as an act that the crucifixion is important for the manifestation of identity. As I will argue, it is the way one relates to that very act that makes it possible (or not) to see the cross itself as gift.

2. This should not be taken to indicate that the present chapter does not have any bearings whatsoever on other attempts to formulate such doctrines. But they will not be discussed extensively, although some of the relevance of the present discussion for them will be mentioned in the last section of the chapter, below. For a survey and discussion of positions, cf. Gunther Wenz, *Geschichte der Versöhnungslehre in der Evangelischen Theologie der Neuzeit*, bd. 9, 11 (München: Chr. Kaiser Verlag, 1984). A discussion of more recent contribu-

cross as a gift from a perspective shaped more by recent theories of recognition and representation. In doing so, I draw on the material already presented in Part I, and explicate it further.

It is my contention that *how one relates to* the crucifixion is inseparable from identity and self-understanding. In Lutheran theology, this cross-shaped identity is characteristically understood to be an expression of either law or gospel. For the one who understands herself as a sinner, the cross is gospel (inasmuch as she sees the promise of salvation in Christ as the one representing her on the cross). On the other hand, for anyone who refuses to recognize his representative as the one hanging on the cross, the cross is law (inasmuch as the cross expresses God's judgment of the sinner who, on the basis of the deadly use of the law, rejects God's representative). It is not clear, however, on what conditions the cross can express this type of judgment, but given the suggestions already made in the previous chapter, it can be taken as something the individual brings upon herself as a consequence of rejecting community with God. In that sense, the cross expresses a consequence not realized by the one who rejects, and a judgment that is God's only insofar as God draws the conclusion that this person will not take part in life. Christ on the cross thus represents those judging him to his death.

Realizing that the cross can be a gift requires, on the other hand, a relationship with God that is positive, affirming, and recognizing. But that is only the start. In the present chapter, I want to explore constructive conditions connected to what happens when we relate to the cross, and under what conditions we can understand it as a gift. My basic thesis is that the cross can be understood as a gift only in light of the logic of a complex structure of *identity-in-relationship-as-recognition*. I thereby try to further develop the relational concerns that so far have been expressed mostly in terms of recognition.

Recognizing the cross as a gift implies a recognition on our part that

---

tions can be found in J. Denny Weaver, *The Nonviolent Atonement* (Grand Rapids: Eerdmans, 2001), which I have already mentioned. A contribution relevant to much of what is developed here, but from other angles, is Dorothee Sölle, *Stellvertretung: Ein Kapitel Theologie nach dem "Tode Gottes,"* um ein Nachwort erw. Neuaufl. ed. (Stuttgart: Kreuz, 1982). [ET, *Christ the Representative: An Essay in Theology after the Death of God* (Philadelphia: Fortress Press, 1967]. However, I try to formulate the following in a way that can offer a constructive alternative to Sölle, be it in contradiction as well as in confirmation of what she wrote in the work mentioned above.

God is at work — and, moreover, God is at work in the event of the cross for us — in some mysterious way. But precisely what kind of recognition is this? And what bearing, moreover, does that recognition have on our understanding of *how* it is that God is at work in the cross? It becomes urgent to answer such questions, especially on the basis of the self-identification of God with Christ.

Recognition has a double meaning in English, which is relevant in this context, a double meaning that is not so apparent in the German Anerkennung. For me to recognize someone is to be able to identify that person as one whom I already know or of whom I have a prior grasp. Recognizing my friend from a long distance, for instance, would not be possible unless — in some sense or another — I already had previous knowledge of him, and enjoyed a friendship with him. My recognition in this context places him in a distinct relationship to me in a way that is different from the way I relate to all others present in the crowd. This recognition, one might say, makes my friend "present to me"; he signifies something for me that no one else in the crowd does in the same manner. The impact of his presence-for-me is there even though he is not present in the sense of being physically proximate to me: there can still be a great spatial distance — and many other people — between us. But my recognition nevertheless makes him signify something special, and this significance is present to me in that recognition.[3]

A second dimension of recognition becomes apparent on the basis of the first. This second dimension has to do with seeing a person as someone who is special or important for me. And thus this type of recognition also concerns how I understand myself as obliged to respect him or treat him in a certain manner.

By recognizing someone in this second sense of the term, I affirmatively express the respect I give him or her. This recognition is one of positive acknowledgment. To acknowledge someone, then, is to recognize him or her affirmatively; but there is also a sense in which recognition can be granted

---

3. For different understandings of recognition, and the importance of differentiating between them, see Paul Ricoeur, *The Course of Recognition* (Cambridge, MA: Harvard University Press, 2005), esp. pp. 6-16, and Patchen Markell, *Bound by Recognition* (Princeton: Princeton University Press, 2003). Among other differentiations, Markell discusses the difference between cognitive and constructive modes of recognition on pp. 39ff., in a way related to what I do here. As the task of his work is not close to what I discuss here, I will only use his work briefly in the following.

even while withholding respect — in which case our recognition of that person is to recognize that person as unworthy of our acknowledgment. The latter therefore involves a kind of negative recognition. The notion of negative recognition thus helps us account for those situations where we recognize someone even though we are not willing to respect him or her.

But recognition is even more complex and multifaceted; it is a wider phenomenon than simply recognition-as-acknowledgment. For prior to both the positive and negative expressions of recognition-as-possible-acknowledgment is the recognition of the other in a more basic sense: as someone who is related to me, to my life, in such a way that the question of possible acknowledgment or not becomes relevant in the first place. And it is on this level that we come close to the kind of recognition that is in view when considering how it is that God is at work on the cross.

One can relate to the cross in a historical or sociological sense as an instrument of torture. One can recognize it, in other words, as the means by which people were executed. Viewed thus, the cross is neither a gift nor a scandal — it is simply present for us in a mode that does not immediately or necessarily open up to such interpretations. This can be taken as a truism, but it needs to be repeated. For as the layers of theological understanding invested in the presence of the cross easily make us forget what it is, a reconstruction of the understanding of the cross needs first of all to state the plain fact that a cross is to be recognized as a mechanism of torture and execution before we can understand it in any other way. As such it is one cross among many. It is only when we talk about God and the cross — and when the possibility of recognizing God at work emerges — that the cross as a place for the realization of identity becomes apparent. God is thus the constitutive agent in letting the cross become something more and other than an instrument of torture. This is how, theologically, the cross becomes transformed into a gift.

The constitutive participation of God in making the cross a gift should not be swiftly by-passed. The turn in the relationship between God and the world that makes the cross a gift *builds* on the cross as a means of death: the cross makes apparent and manifest that death is the end of all human life. The cross makes death appear; it makes death as our outcome evident for everyone to recognize, believer and non-believer alike. Seeing death as the end of human life made present through the cross is something that every human being is able to perceive, even those who do not see God as involved in what happens on or with the cross of Jesus.

However, when one recognizes God as involved, this recognition is not only of God, but also of the cross as a means for God's work. How, then, is God related to the manifestation of finitude and sin present on the cross?

Seeing the cross as an event in which God is involved, and seeing what happens on the cross as an act by God for us, presupposes a faith that can acknowledge this cross as more than a manifestation of sin, death, or human finitude.[4] It is through a recognition shaped by the reception in faith that one sees the cross as a manifestation of human identity on different levels, the identity of the human as sinner as well as a person to whom a new identity is offered in Christ. How the cross serves as such a means for the realization of human identity on different levels will occupy us in what follows.

Recognition in Hegel: Relevant for Staurology?

As we have seen already, for Hegel recognition is a complex phenomenon. It involves two aspects, one from the perspective of the giver of recognition, and the other from the perspective of those who receive recognition. The reciprocal relationship that constitutes the phenomenon of recognition opens up a dynamic understanding of identity (or identities), by which the individual is what he or she is only by partaking in a relationship, and this relationship is then what contributes the concrete manifestation of her identity.[5] In the conflict-shaped understanding of the master/slave, this identification of oneself and the other is negatively expressed: I am not what the other is, and the otherness of the other is what makes him my master/slave. However, this negativity need not be understood as negative, but can also be seen as a chance for me to recognize my own positive limitations compared with others. That is what takes place when humans understand themselves as created in the image of God. Although it can be stated negatively, as "I am, as a created human being, not God, and God is

---

4. Cf. the distinctions offered by Wenz, *Geschichte der Versöhnungslehre in der Evangelischen Theologie der Neuzeit*, vol. 2, p. 476, who insists on the necessity of differentiating between death and finitude because it otherwise would mean that death belongs to the destiny of the human being.

5. Cf. Georg Wilhelm Friedrich Hegel, *Phänomenologie des Geistes* (Leipzig: Felix Meiner, 1921), pp. 127ff. [ET: *Phenomenology of Spirit*, trans. Arnold V. Miller and J. N. Findlay (Oxford: Clarendon Press, 1977)].

not human" this is an affirmative, and need not be taken as a negative statement. The very relationship between the parties is thus what constitutes and makes it possible to explicate the complex identity of the two. Without this relationship, which builds on and is constituted by mutual recognition(s), the parties are, as said, *nothing,* and they have no significance for each other whatsoever. Robert R. Williams writes aptly on how Hegel employs these insights:

> [T]he double significations of the concept of recognition are rooted in the self-repulsing subjectivity that is the opposite of itself, that is, at once itself and the opposite determination of itself. Recognition implies that subjectivity is intersubjectivity, and intersubjectivity introduces additional possibilities of double signification, which Hegel plays on in the course of his analysis. Double signification in turn creates possibilities for dramatic reversals in "self-understanding" on the various levels of recognition.[6]

There are two matters in Williams's remark that I want to highlight. First, Hegel's relational approach to human subjectivity can and should also be taken as support for the understanding that no human being is what she is only in and of herself. This is also true from a theological point of view. Human identity is relationally constituted, which means that there is no such thing as a given, static, and once-and-for-all-granted identity. Moreover, the identity we have, we initially receive as a gift emerging from the very relationships that bind us to others in the world. When we try to speak of the cross as a gift against this background, this gift cannot be explicated as gift, or say, given, when we do not understand ourselves as committed to relationships with others in the world. As I have tried to develop throughout this study, this is what our community with Christ discloses: understanding ourselves as living in a community of mutual recognition with all other humans created in the image of God. Pursuing this Hegelian approach further, we can see how identity *and* difference are at play here. Citing Hegel, Mark C. Taylor writes:

> The self-relation that is supposed to establish self-identity is actually pure difference. Within the dyadic structure of opposition, identity

6. Robert R. Williams, *Hegel's Ethics of Recognition* (Berkeley: University of California Press, 1997), p. 52.

appears to be "difference that is identical with itself. But difference is only identical with itself insofar as it is not identity, but absolute non-identity. But non-identity is absolute insofar as it contains nothing of its other but only itself, that is, insofar as it is absolute identity with itself. Identity, therefore, is *in its own self* absolute non-identity." Difference from other turns out to be a relation to other that negates simple self-relation and "infects" pure self-identity.[7]

If one interprets the death of Jesus in light of the above, what does this say about the identity of God as the God of life? It says that the death of Jesus was the final inscription of God as the God of life in the history of Jesus. That by relating to death, subjecting himself to death, Jesus relates himself to this negativity of death in a way that reveals him as its opposite, this difference: God emerges as the giver of life. God's identity is established by the relation to the difference of death, which God is not. But the relation of Jesus to death also reveals that beyond this difference, and beyond the identity in difference of Jesus and death, is a God who is more than Jesus and more than death, who is life even when life is subjected to death. Because God, in the death of Jesus, reveals what it is to live in love; it might even mean that you have to die instead of holding on to life. Hence, not only Jesus' identity as the constant and coherent witness/image of God/love is revealed when Jesus dies, but also, the one he testifies to — the one he is related to in an identity as difference-and-communion — is revealed as God. God is revealed as present and absent, as beyond, not graspable, moreover still one to be grasped by the identity of his witness. God thus still can be identified by the acts and circumstances in which Jesus is involved, as within this but still in difference, and hence, God's identity manifests itself as established in this world in the manner identity is always established: through difference. The point here is that even though God is present in the acts and preaching of Jesus, God is revealed even more when Jesus is identified by Jesus' relation to what is opposite of his life, namely death.

We are now able to explicate the outcome of our analysis so far in this book in the following manner: *Before and apart from the nexus of relations that constitute the self, the very word "I" remains empty of content; it is*

---

7. Mark C. Taylor, *Erring: A Postmodern a/Theology* (Chicago: University of Chicago Press, 1984), p. 109.

a mere placeholder for a name, and for an identity that is to come. "I" in rela-
tion to Christ is the index-name for the one who desires being given his or her
place by and in relation to the index-word "God." The establishment of that
identity, moreover, is indebted to the ways I am able to see myself thanks to
how others (as the third) recognize me, and how I develop and relate myself to them in acceptance of, opposition to, or confrontation with that offered recognition. Hence, human self-identity is possible by virtue of the
very web of relationships in which we are invariably embedded and participate; these relationships make us what we are and who we are. Our lives
are relational through and through, and the world to which we relate is a
world in which God is at work. If we are to discern how God works in the
world, then it is crucial that we gain some understanding of the ways that
God recognizes us through and by others, and how, in turn, we recognize
God in our ordinary lives in the world.

The central theological question (and its corollary) might be put
thus: How does God recognize us and how do we recognize ourselves on
the basis of God's prior recognition? The conditions for answering this
fundamental question are of course related to whether or not we recognize
God as God — as our main point of orientation. Hence we determine our
own identity to a certain extent, but this identity is not something acquired
egocentrically — i.e., on an individual, subjectively shaped basis — but always and only within the intersubjective play that expresses itself as a God-
human relationship. That, at least, would be a theological reading of what
Williams denotes above as the "double signification" that creates dramatic
possibilities of reversals in self-understanding.

My claim — and here is where I wish to advance Williams's point in
an overtly theological manner — is that *these dramatic possibilities of rever-*
sals in self-understanding arise fully when the cross is presented as a gift. A gift
is a social phenomenon, implying a context of understanding and patterns
of meaning that are not given in what I referred to above as a more immediate way of recognition. The gift implies an overcoming of the naturalness
and immediacy that characterizes human life, and involves a dimension of
freedom. It makes possible a self-understanding that transcends the identity given by what is present in oneself as an isolated individual. Williams
offers a quotation from Hegel that illustrates this aptly:

> Men must want to rediscover themselves in one another. However, this
> will [to recognition] cannot arise so long as they are confined to im-

mediacy and naturalness [Natürlichkeit], for it is precisely these that cut them off from one another and prevent them from being free in regard to one another. [...] Thus freedom has to be struggled for; merely to assert that one is free is not enough.[8]

Protestant theology has a long tradition of presenting the cross as a challenge that brings humans out of their "natural state" as sinners in order to receive "salvation" (a new identity and recognition). The proclamation of the cross as something that relates to and determines the identity of the human is exactly what can shape the conditions for overcoming immediacy and present the human with new possibilities of recognition of both God and self. This recognition is not something that is only tangentially linked to the human's own life: it meets and corresponds to the very fact that we are what we are by virtue of our relation to others. In order to become who we are, and gain our freedom, we need to relate to the recognition of others. That is why our desire "drives self-consciousness beyond its mere parochial interests and subjective certainty in search of objective confirmation and legitimation in another's recognition. This 'need' is better characterized as a desire for the other."[9]

The foregoing analysis is far from adequate on the theological plane. For when God presents us with the gift of the cross, he is not answering to our desire. On the contrary, he contradicts this desire — and in so doing both affirms and transforms it. The cross is not what we want as the answer to our desire for recognition, nor is the cross something we can understand as the immediately given result of our strivings for identity. Playing on the distinction — offered by Richard Kearney — of the difference between onto-theological desire (implying a lack) and eschatological desire (for the impossible),[10] one can say that the cross, exactly because it is a contradiction of "natural" human desires based on deficiency or lack, can appear as a scandal.

In light of human onto-theological desire that tries to make God into something (i.e., some *thing*) that can confirm my narcissistic needs and my

---

8. Williams, *Hegel's Ethics of Recognition*, p. 76, quoting Hegel, *Enzyklopaedie*, § 431, Zusatz.

9. Williams, *Hegel's Ethics of Recognition*, p. 76.

10. Richard Kearney, "Desire for God," in *God, the Gift and Post-Modernism*, ed. John D. Caputo and Michael J. Scanlon (Bloomington: Indiana University Press 1999), pp. 112ff.

yearning to be someone (read: struggle for self-justification and self-righteousness), the cross offered to me scandalously implies that I must give up my present identity as well as the kind of desire through which it expresses itself: The cross exposes my life as a sinner centering around myself. By demanding that I relinquish my "natural" desires, the cross also simultaneously transforms my desire into something that strives for the impossible; namely, a fulfilled identity in the present. *This non-present identity is what is offered via the cross as a gift.*

The challenge of the cross is precisely this: it confounds our "natural" self-chosen identity and presents us instead with the kind of identity that we would not want to desire. Indeed, what becomes sublated or suspended by the cross is the desire to gain my own, self-chosen identity in the recognition of the other, insofar as the cross presents me with the negation of my own previous, egocentrically constructed identity. This confounding of my egocentric, self-chosen identity expresses itself spontaneously in the exclamation, "This is not where or who I wish to be, nor is it the identity I desire!" Moreover, insofar as the cross is presented as a gift, and only as such can it be received, am I able to recognize how my identity is predicated on the fact that I am not there — it is my non-presence on the cross (negativity) that constitutes the very possibility of God offering it as the basis for the identity I receive from God in God's offering of this cross as a gift. This, then, is the nature of the gift as the answer to the desire for the impossible — that which we cannot expect or demand, let alone make ourselves deserve. Hence, the cross is a paradoxical example of an answer to eschatological desire — the desire for the impossible, that which transcends every expression of sameness, surpasses every expectation, every pre-given condition or merit.

I have already hinted that Hegel helps us more than just understand the common or basic patterns involved in recognition as such; his analysis also offers categories for elaborating a theological understanding of the cross. One such category is freedom, which in Hegel's view is a corollary of recognition. In relation to the passages mentioned above, freedom both arises out of recognition and is something to be struggled for. From what has been said so far, we can see this freedom as involving at least four dimensions:

- Freedom as the overcoming of the immediacy given with a non-substantial identity that does not relate to God — or, affirmatively stated: as the substantial life-form given with an identity-in-relation to one who recognizes me (God).

- Freedom as the overcoming of the onto-theologically constituted desire for identity.
- Freedom as the possibility of recognizing myself as not present on the cross and thus as the receiver of a new identity in a positive relationship with God by virtue of being absent from the cross (more on this below).
- Freedom as the offering of an identity that is still open, but nevertheless dependent on a certain relationship — a unity — with God.

Williams, in his treatise on Hegel, elaborates on the relationship between freedom and the ethical in the mutual reciprocal recognition offered to one another by the parties in question — in this case, master and slave. Whereas Williams's intent is to show how such patterns of mutual reciprocal recognition open up to the ethical in a very substantial mode, my interest now is to suggest that the "religious" could just as easily substitute for the "ethical." Indeed, the virtue of that substitution is that it would allow us to identify another element that is only tacit here:

> Freedom involves a mutual reciprocal union with the other in which the other comes to count for something. "The other has to count within my existence [Dasein] as well." When the other comes to count for me, then the threshold of the ethical [read: religious] is crossed; recognition is the medium in which and through which ethical [read: religious] life is constituted.[11]

It is when God "count[s] within my existence," i.e., counts for me, that my religious life in a positive manner, as positive religious subjectivity, begins. This does not imply that I have not hitherto had any life with God. However, it is in the recognition of the gift God has offered, already before I could affirmatively recognize him (cf. Rom. 5:8, 10), that my religious life awakens as a quest to appropriate the freedom implied in this gift. Human freedom is consequently not such as would maintain a self in a state independent from others, but one that is based exactly on a relationship with a specific and concrete other (Christ as the representative of God, cf. below).

---

11. Williams, *Hegel's Ethics of Recognition*, pp. 76-77.

The cross offers one of the possibilities for establishing such a relationship with God.[12]

However, in order to establish and partake in this relationship humans must overcome the immediacy of a mere "neutral" perception of the cross as a cross and begin to recognize it as a (possible) positive gift from God. These possibilities still present themselves in a double manner when this happens. Presented with the gift, we can receive it and enter into a relationship with God according to the terms offered. On the other hand, we can reject the gift and establish for ourselves a specific and distinct kind of negative freedom, in and by which we say that the cross is not something on which I want to base my identity. Either way the cross functions as an occasion for the realization of identity. In the latter case, freedom and unity are not achieved; but freedom presents itself in a separation that is not able to recognize God as God, i.e., as one worthy of our adoration and devotion. This is what Hegel would probably call abstract or negative freedom.

Positive freedom, on the other hand, is predicated upon recognition of me by God. Moreover, it is something God offers as gift. Nevertheless, God's gifting cannot be expected or demanded — it is given freely; it grows spontaneously out of the very relationship in which it is presented. As a gift, this recognition can be received, but the reception is not only a reception of the gift (I receive an identity, myself, as I am in relation to you, in your eyes), but this reception is in turn also itself a recognition of the one who recognizes, the one who is the giver of the gift of recognition. Hence, to receive the cross as a gift implies the reception of God into my life — as the basis of my identity.

Against this background, the cross implies far more than recognition of God as the giver; it also entails a complex self-relation that so far has not been explicated: a relation that implies seeing both oneself and God as being represented on the cross. This type of double representation needs further development.[13]

---

12. As indicated throughout the present book, this is not the only possible way to construe this. The Gospels are full of examples of other instances, where the proclamation of the kingdom of God and the practices related to that proclamation are opened up to similar relationships.

13. I am of course not the only one who develops ideas about such a double representation. Cf. for a parallel but still different account, Graham Ward, *Christ and Culture: Challenges in Contemporary Theology* (Oxford: Blackwell Publishing, 2005), pp. 44f.

From Recognition to Representation

So far I have discussed the significance of the cross (as a signifier of a multiply-constituted identity) without entering much into the discussion of *who* is hanging on the cross. For the present argument, I cannot come to terms with this question without referring back to the issue of representation. We have already met the notion in different contexts, both in dealing with the understanding of the human being as *imago Dei* and also in dealing with Hermann Deuser's suggestion that incarnation may be formulated as semiotic representation.

My proposal is that Christ on the cross can be presented to humans as a gift that realizes human identity precisely because he is the true image of God and as such, he is also God's gift of Godself to humans (as the incarnated God). This proposal is made in order to clarify some of the anthropological presuppositions concerning soteriology without having its content immediately subsumed under conceptions emerging from a "high Christology."[14]

By fulfilling the task of living as the image of God, humans make manifest two key realities: (1) that they — in faith — recognize God as God, and (2) that they recognize God's recognition of themselves as those who can make God manifest in the world as love, mercy, and care for all that is.[15] Human life as *imago Dei* is consequently a life in freedom — in faith, hope, and love[16] — based upon both the recognition of God's recognition of us, and upon God's determination of us as representatives of God. However, it also presupposes that humans realize that they are not themselves God (i.e., recognition of *difference* serves as a basis of identity), and that they actually destroy the purpose of human life if they live as if they themselves were God, the ultimate source and end of all things. God is not human — and the human is not God. This positive-negative relationship and recognition

14. This should not be taken to indicate that the present reflections are opposed to or in some way try to contradict such ways of doing Christology. Rather my endeavor here is to show that some of the themes dealt with in Christology can also be articulated by means of a more philosophical approach.

15. This is more extensively elaborated in Jan-Olav Henriksen, *Imago Dei: Den Teologiske Konstruksjonen av Menneskets Identitet* (Oslo: Gyldendal, 2003).

16. Note that the notion of freedom here is a substantial one as suggested above: freedom is related to the fulfillment of the substantial relationship with God, and not a kind of neutral detachment from relationship and commitments.

is a precondition for both the fullness of human life (as a life representing God) and, moreover, for the fulfillment of the purpose and will of God.

Leaving aside for the moment the fact that this is not always the actual case, there are two points that should be noted in relation to this basic determination of human life in Christian theology. First, to understand oneself as *imago Dei* means, as indicated, to see that I am not God, and God is not me. My identity, in other words, is in both what I am — and in what I am not. Hence there is an element of affirmation and negation in this basic self-understanding — and as we shall see below, the very same double character is relevant when it comes to how I understand Christ as *my* representative on the cross.

Second, understanding oneself as *imago Dei* also means that God is simultaneously both present and absent. The very existence of someone as *imago Dei* presupposes that God makes his presence manifest in spite of his actual absence. How is this absence then to be understood? I suggest it is to be understood as an absence that makes it possible for humans to partake in the positive functions of God, since God allows humans to fulfill and realize the positive potential of human existence exactly by not keeping all this for Godself. Hence, God's absence is paradoxically also a means of making present the possibilities of fulfilling God's purposes for freedom in human life. In other words, God's positive will for human freedom, love, and faith is manifestly expressed through his absence, which is at the same time, functionally, a presence in the human as the *imago Dei*.

Representation by someone consequently involves both absence and presence, as we have seen in our analysis of Gestrich above. The one represented is absent, but, as absent, he or she can still be present by and through the representative, who has *her* identity determined precisely by means of the absence of the one she is representing.

Theologically, the designation of the human being as the image of God covers all of humanity, including Christ. As for Christ, he is able to represent humanity on the cross only because he also partakes in this designation or destiny. At the same time, Christ maintains and contributes to a specific trait that is important for my identity, as well as for my understanding of God, and these are mutually interlinked. Christ proclaims that the God he represents is a God who is still coming, still under way (im Kommen[17]).

---

17. Cf. Eberhard Jüngel, *The Doctrine of the Trinity: God's Being Is in Becoming* (Grand Rapids: Eerdmans, 1976).

Hence, the identity of this God is in some sense open, despite the fact that he is truly and fully represented in Christ. Moreover, this also implies that my identity, as far as it must be seen as dependent upon my relationship to God, is still open, undecided, floating, not fulfilled. The absence of God thus also manifests the absence of my own fulfilled identity. Thus, God's absence also keeps open and living my *desire for identity,* for becoming someone, for being fully recognized in God's presence.

God's absent presence or present absence is important also in another respect. By this mode of existence in the world (as represented), God remains controversial; God's actual existence remains open, questionable (this is so also because we, as God's representatives, often corrupt the mode in which God could be present by and through our way of life). Thus, God cannot be grasped, but remains elusive, impossible to contain or control conceptually. Hence, representation plays on the combination of the presence and absence of the one represented in order to secure the freedom of the one represented. God is more than what we can represent and thus make present. All language about God — and to God — involves this important reservation.

The most profound expression of how humans must live with the unfulfilled certainty of desire for God we find in Jesus' words on the cross: "My God, my God, why hast thou forsaken me?" (Matt. 27:46). Here the absent God is invoked in a language that presupposes that God is present. God's presence is the only condition that makes the utterance meaningful. Simultaneously, the actual experience is that God is not represented in what happens there: God cannot be recognized on the cross and involved in Jesus' actual fate as a life-giving and loving power.

Now, Christ's despair can be interpreted as a result of the fact that he lived in faith, as the one who actually fulfilled his task of being *Imago Dei.* Hence, his fate is not what he deserved, and not what he rightly expected. However, when Paul interprets Christ as the true *Imago Dei,* it is not only because he is seen by Paul as the true representative of God. That would leave his fate even more undeserved. But Paul also interprets the cross of Jesus in light of how Christ represents *humanity,* and makes it clear that Jesus Christ can represent humanity only because he is righteous (Rom. 5:18). He is the one who represents and manifests the alternative life to our sinful fate as humans (Adam).

Hence, in Paul we can already see the shape of an understanding of Christ as a bearer of a double representation: as the one who represents both God and humans. Christ represents God as the true human, and he represents the human as the one who is convicted for being a false witness to (representative of) God — as a blasphemer.[18]

How then can I see myself as represented on the cross by Christ, who is truly what I am not? He can represent me only due to my absence — the fact that I am not the one convicted. I am possibly convicted, but he is the one actually convicted. He can be recognized as the one who represents me there, on the cross, in my absence — but only if I accept being represented by him.[19] This, however, also implies that I have to see myself in a specific way — namely, as one *who stands in need of being represented*, one who is a sinner, one who deserves to be convicted for blasphemy, since I have not lived as a true *imago Dei* but have rather tried to be or become God in my own life. Hence, because I am the one who does not live up to my destiny as the image of God, I am the negative reason for Christ hanging on the cross (insofar as I am part of humanity's rejection of him as the true witness to God). However, I am also the positive reason for him hanging there, because, as the true image, he loves me in a way that unites me with him in a recognition that allows him to be my substitute — and he can take that place only because he is the righteous one and thereby represents my own true destiny. Hence, I can recognize myself as represented by him. That is his gift of love to me.

Ontologically, I could never represent Christ in a similar manner. And we need not assume some kind of high Christology to make this affirmation. The fact that I could never represent Christ in the way that he represents me on the cross arises for another reason. He is more than I am; he is more "up to what it means to be human" than I am. Hence, for me to represent him in the same way as he represents me on the cross would amount to nothing less than a mockery.[20] But for him to represent me

---

18. It is against this background that the section in 2 Corinthians 5:14-21 about atonement and reconciliation can take on a clear meaning for the present. Further, on the conviction of Jesus as a blasphemer, see Raymond Edward Brown, *The Death of the Messiah: From Gethsemane to the Grave: A Commentary on the Passion Narratives in the Four Gospels*, 1st ed., The Anchor Bible Reference Library (New York: Doubleday, 1994), esp. pp. 520-47.

19. Note that this formulation still makes it possible to say, in more doctrinal language, that Christ died for all — including Judas. However, such formulations are not capable of expressing sufficiently the relationship between recognition and representation.

20. This does not exclude the idea presented in the New Testament that those who believe in Christ in some sense also take part in his suffering. Such matters seem to be sug-

would imply not only recognition of who he is and who I am in distinction from him (asymmetrically), it would also imply a realization of what we have in common (as sharers in the same destiny of *imago Dei*). The latter introduces an element of symmetry in the relation as well, which is important for my identity in relation to him. It is this symmetry that links us, while it is the asymmetry in faith, hope, and love (righteousness) that allows for the representation (and the substitution, if you like) to only go one way.

Jacques Derrida (who in *The Gift of Death* discusses related issues) writes aptly on these matters, without basing it on an explicit Christology, and in a way that is also very much in accordance with the understanding of the gift, as we have discussed it previously:

> On what condition does goodness exist beyond all calculation? On the condition that goodness forget itself, that the movement be a movement of the gift that renounces itself, hence a movement of infinite love. Only infinite love can renounce itself and, in order to become finite, become incarnated in order to love the other, to love the other as a finite other. This gift of infinite love comes from someone and is addressed to someone; responsibility demands irreplaceable singularity. Yet only death or rather the apprehension of death can give this irreplaceability, and it is only on the basis of it that one can speak of a responsible subject, of the soul as conscience of self, of myself, etc. [. . .][21]

Derrida thus points to how death, love, responsibility, and the Good become intertwined in the constitution of the identity of the mortal individual. The mortal who emerges from the singularity manifest in death is one who by the presence of death is called to relate to goodness and love. By partaking in the infinity of God's goodness and love, the finite individual is nevertheless also giving a content to her identity. This is so even

---

gested, for example, in passages like Romans 6, 2 Corinthians 5:20, and Colossians 1:24. However, it is important to note that all such cases where humans are thought of as representing Christ are based on the prior acknowledgment of Christ as our representative on the cross, and hence, as the one who has offered as a gift the identity that makes the latter representation possible.

21. Jacques Derrida, *The Gift of Death, Religion and Postmodernism* (Chicago: University of Chicago Press, 1995), pp. 50f.

though it is still not shaped concretely how and what this identity will be in the concrete situation in which the individual lives. That is up to her own responsibility:

> But the mortal thus deduced is someone whose very responsibility requires that he concern himself not only with an objective Good but also with a gift of infinite love, a goodness that is forgetful of itself. There is thus a structural disproportion or dissymmetry between the finite and responsible mortal on the one hand and the goodness of the infinite gift on the other hand.[22]

I will not here elaborate on how Derrida also develops this "structural disproportion or dissymmetry" by way of the theme of guilt — but he does that as well.[23] The important point here is that he spells out how the confrontation with a good rooted in the infinite transforms the subject who receives this good in an apprehension of her own irreplaceable singularity — and that this good by means of being rooted in the infinite is a gift that contributes to — indeed, is constitutive of — the realization of my identity.

Moreover, it should be noted that this is an expression of asymmetry we often find elaborated in the historically based framework of understanding where Christology is typically pursued. But Derrida's remarks show us that the content of Christology in this respect need not be something totally alien to structures analyzed by philosophy.[24] At the same time, the quotation above also underscores how the gift of identity must

---

22. Derrida, *The Gift of Death*, p. 51.

23. A point often neglected in conceptions that try to develop a positive relationship between God and humans out of the fact that Christ removes our guilt is that a relationship established upon the foundation of guilt is never advantageous for anyone involved. Guilt cannot give rise to authentic love. See for more on this Vincent W. Wynne, "Abraham's Gift: A Psychoanalytic Christology," *JAAR* 73, no. 3 (2005): esp. 760-63. Hence, it is necessary to develop the relationship between God and humans in a manner that makes all questions of guilt secondary, and as something developed out of a positively articulated and nonconditional community.

24. Thereby, this approach presupposes the conviction expressed in the initial part of this book that matters central to Christology benefit from being analyzed by means of philosophical theory. Such theory can clarify how matters of Christology are linked to other, common structures of our world, and should not only be understood exclusively in terms of their inherent theological logic and theological context.

have its source in the infinite, and this infinite can be read as the instance that keeps the future of human identity open. This reading presupposes that it is possible to read the philosophical concept of infinity in Derrida as a correlate to that which we call God.[25] The very fact that God can sustain us as finite beings and still keep us open to his future is the best theological argument for this possibility.

Death as a Conclusio and Abandonment

No matter what we do, what interpretations we provide, what new chances for identity are given us, the future cannot be kept open forever. Death is facing us. The most paradoxical element in the crucifixion is that my death confronts me there as something offered to me. By receiving it as a gift *pro me,* I receive life from the source of all life. This is only possible if I can recognize the death of Christ as *my* death — as the death that I should be facing given the fact that I have not lived in a righteous relationship with God, who is this source. The cross allows for me to focus on the Other (Jesus) as the third in the relationship with God, and thereby to recognize my predicament.

John Milbank has recently articulated an interpretation of the death of Jesus that offers a fruitful point of departure in relation to how the cross and death of Christ serve as a point that manifests my identity.[26] Transcending a mere Bultmannian understanding of the cross as a vehicle through which I have to face my own death, Milbank elaborates on how the death of Jesus is related to the fact that no one truly and honestly wants to relate to (read: recognize) him. Consequently, Jesus is handed over from the one to the other in a way that signifies no (positive) form of recognition or willingness to relate (affirmatively) to him. Summing up the impression from the Gospel narratives, Milbank writes:

25. For a development of the relationship between the concept of infinity and God, as this underlies the present argument, cf. F. LeRon Shults, *Reforming the Doctrine of God,* (Grand Rapids: Eerdmans, 2005), §§ 2, 5 and 9.1 (God and Causality), where he shows how the link between the two makes it possible to address God's immanence as well as his transcendence, thereby expressing how this topic is also intimately related to the present discussion of God's presence and absence.

26. John Milbank, *Being Reconciled: Ontology and Pardon,* Radical Orthodoxy Series (London and New York: Routledge, 2003).

The only consistent thread in these narratives is that Christ was constantly handed over, or abandoned to another party. Judas betrayed his presence; the disciples deserted him; the Sanhedrin gave him up to Pilate; Pilate in turn to Herod; Herod back to Pilate; Pilate again to the mob who finally gave him over to a Roman execution, which somehow, improperly, they co-opted. Even in his death, Jesus was still being handed back and forth, as if no one actually killed him, but he died from neglect and lack of his own living space.[27]

We can see here how Milbank's description echoes Gestrich's description of what it is to be lost: to lack a place. Moreover, by this constant handing over, those who hand over also say that they do not want to have anything to do with this man. He is not part of their world, not recognized as part of a relationship with God (as the other being the third). Christ is not our business. He is an outsider. Hence, leave him to someone else. It is this lack of relation to a specific context that makes the death of this human being a manifestation of my identity.

Eberhard Jüngel has pointed out that death is the lack of all relations.[28] From such a perspective, there is no recognition, no possibility of representation. Christ's way to death is marked by the other's unwillingness to relate. In it, he is excluded from humanity, because no one, as Wolfhart Pannenberg aptly points out, can stand to have another human being claim that he/she represents God. No human can bear to see another human as someone who identifies himself with God. Hence, it is this claim that provokes the antagonists of Jesus to have him crucified[29] — be it just as much in terms of handing over, leaving responsibility to someone else, as actively and whole-heartedly partaking. In this lack of responsibility and recognition, God — as the one calling to relationship, responsibility, and recognition of the other — finds no place. This death is thus a negative closure off from all that Jesus himself has represented in his life. Hence Milbank is correct when he states:

---

27. Milbank, *Being Reconciled: Ontology and Pardon*, p. 82.

28. Eberhard Jüngel, *Death, the Riddle and the Mystery* (Philadelphia: Westminster Press, 1975).

29. Wolfhart Pannenberg, *Systematische Theologie*, vol. 2 (Göttingen: Vandenhoeck & Ruprecht, 1988), p. 480 [ET: *Systematic Theology*, vol. 2, trans. Geoffrey W. Bromiley (Grand Rapids: Eerdmans, 1994)].

He died as three times excluded: by the Jewish law of its tribal nation; by the Roman universal law of empire; by the democratic will of the mob. In the whole summed-up history of human polity — the tribe, the universal absolute state, the democratic consensus — God found no place. He was shuttled back and forth, with an undercurrent of indifference, as though not really dangerous, between their respective rules. He became *homo sacer* cast outside the camp, abandoned on all sides, so that in the end he died almost accidentally. He died the death of all of us — since he died the death that proves and exemplifies sovereignty in its arbitrariness.[30]

Can Christ *represent* me in my death? The answer is "yes," and by now we are also able to determine more precisely what it means to be represented in one's death: It means that Christ holds my place open, and is present in death for me. I still have to die myself, but he can represent me in my loneliness — my lack of recognizing relations, my lack of being affirmed by anyone for what I am and what I have done wrong. As I still have to die, his representation does not exclude my own participation in death. On the other hand, exactly because he represents me, my death is more than my own. Loneliness is in one, existential sense overcome. The consolation, if one can call it that, is that even in my death I have not lost the relation with him, when I can believe that he was in death *for me*.

Thus, if Christ takes my place, represents me, it is not in a manner that spares me the experience of my own death. Rather, it implies that those who recognize him as their representative, by being related to him (and thus not alone in death), are also related to the new life in the resurrection that becomes apparent after the death of Jesus.[31] On the other hand, it also implies that the one who does not recognize Christ as his representative in death and consequently rejects him, cannot and will not receive his cross as gift.[32] Thus the fate of the one who does not recognize the cross as the conclusion of his/her own sinful life in opposition to God be-

---

30. Milbank, *Being Reconciled: Ontology and Pardon,* pp. 96f.

31. Cf. Pannenberg, *Systematische Theologie,* vol. 2, p. 471.

32. Again, note a point similar to the one made above about what this says and does not say concerning those who never knew Christ. I speak here only of those who were confronted with the cross as a possibility for the realization of their identity. This does not exclude the possibility that God could constitute this identity in other ways, but to enter into that discussion is beyond the scope of the present work.

comes evident. Without a representative we have to face death as this final conclusion, since death in some way or another implies that we are separated from the source of life (God). Thus, here the cross only appears as a symbol in which finitude and death are conflated, with no possibility of being differentiated.

What is happening on the cross is, moreover, severely reduced if it is only interpreted as an event between the Godhead (Father) and Jesus. It is a complex triadic relational event, in which the human being is involved as the one who rejects God and God's representative (by "handing him over") as well as the one who recognizes God by recognizing his representative, thereby establishing herself in a double identity as a sinner and a Christian by virtue of how she interprets the absence of herself on the cross.[33] On the other hand, if one does not admit that God is present on the cross, or claims that it has nothing to do with God, or that it is not his gift, then one also does not face or encounter God here. Theologically speaking, this lack, or failure of recognition, constitutes the judgment under which humans who do not believe submit themselves.

The delusion of the sinner is thus rendered transparent by the fact that she is unable to recognize the possibilities for a new identity offered by God on the cross. It is my absence on the cross that constitutes the basis of my identity both as a Christian and as a sinner. This absence of mine — in the presence of my representative on the cross — manifests my new identity as a Christian, i.e., my new life in community with God and others who have received a similar identity.

Implications and Consequences

What I have argued so far points in a direction that corroborates Wolfhart Pannenberg's insight: namely, that one has to guard against reading all that the scriptures say about Christ as dying "for us" in ways that reduce his death exclusively to an expiatory function.[34] To be sure, some passages nevertheless have to be read in such a manner, as Pannenberg himself ad-

---

33. I think it is possible to see this point also against the backdrop of Girard's work, especially in how he shows that the crucifixion can be read as a way of both unmasking the mechanisms of victimization and overcoming them.

34. Pannenberg, *Systematische Theologie,* vol. 2, p. 463.

mits. In the New Testament, both expiation and covenant are implied as frameworks for understanding the sacrifice that Christ presents for us. But in light of our previous discussion, we have seen (especially in Tanner) that this sacrifice is not one that God demands, but rather one that God offers in order to celebrate community.

What I have done in the above is to try to spell out conditions that are logically as well as substantially prior to the conceptions and interpretations offered in different "models of atonement," and elements that can serve as their background. (For example, the notion of covenant implies recognition precisely in a form elaborated above.) One should also note that I have not been arguing for an understanding of the cross of Christ as vicarious suffering demanded by God. Nor have I understood the cross as a condition for forgiveness.[35] Moreover, I have not developed the presentation above in a way that lends itself to understanding the cross in terms of satisfaction, as we find in Anselm. However, one could argue with Luther, when he speaks of new life in faith (as acceptance, reception of unmerited grace), that this new life nonetheless includes forgiveness, the reception of the Holy Spirit, and all that humanity needs in order to fulfill its destiny as image of God. My intention here rather has been to draw attention to and argue for a basic paradigm of recognition and representation that is prior to these matters — and even prior to the new identity constituted by faith.

One distinct advantage of this basic paradigm is the way in which it exposes the absurdity of the position that sees faith as its own source. God is the initiator and source of this constitution of identity. Faith arises out of what happens in the human experience of being confronted with the gift

35. This in contrast to Milbank, who designs all his Christologically based elaborations on a specific understanding of forgiveness. See Milbank, *Being Reconciled: Ontology and Pardon*, pp. 60ff. Thereby the question surfaces: Is forgiveness given priority to the question of identity? This is clearly seen in Milbank's summary on Aquinas: "Rather, the occasion for incarnation is God's free will to redeem according to his goodness, and hence the occasion for incarnation is the offer of forgiveness — although in the sense already described of an offering of the possibility of reconciliation with God and other human beings" (p. 66). The question is whether this doesn't also give priority to questions of morality over questions of ontological identity — contrary to Milbank's own intentions. I nevertheless agree when he states: "So if forgiveness is a reality, then it seems that it is somehow not subordinate to ontology, or rather that being is now shown in time as forgiveness and finality and as revisable via narrative. Here, therefore, finite ontology does not yield to, but nonetheless coincides with, eschatology" (p. 71).

from God, and it thereby transfigures the cross from being a possible scandal and a mere instrument of torture, into a gift of life and new identity.

Who is hanging on the cross? Why is he hanging there? These have been the basic questions for any Christology since the event itself. Finally, as a way of concluding, I will offer a reading that tries to reconstruct the event and its potential meaning on the basis of resources given in the contemporary, theoretical approaches I have sketched in this chapter. The intention of my reading, to state an obvious point, is not to render all other historical approaches or interpretations obsolete, although it should be clear that the foregoing discussion does not favor Anselm's approach by suggesting that the whole meaning of the cross is that it offers us a gift of satisfaction. Rather, it is an attempt to develop old insights in a current framework of thought, so as to make clear that in this central event of Christian faith there are matters that allow Christology to shed light on basic phenomena important to ordinary human life. This is an attempt to make the cross-as-gift meaningful without limiting or reducing our language merely to language of atonement or expiation. The cross is not an expiation that God inflicts upon the unjust; it is about humans who demand an unjust punishment for God's true representative. Several other important, constructive insights offer themselves as well:

1. We have seen that sin is not first and foremost to act against specific commandments, but expresses itself in the neglect of the first commandment: Thou shall not have other gods. Hence, the primordial character of sin is better described as either (a) to make something else one's god (including oneself, other humans, other desires, to put trust in one's own achievements or merits), or (b) to worship a different god than the one true God. This different god is one who basically confirms the already given identity of the human as a sufficient condition for a true relationship with God (fulfilling onto-theological desire), and hence, one that does not challenge the already existing identity of the human in order to change it or make it become more true by means of the achievement of another identity represented in Christ and his work. Against this backdrop, human identity marked by sin is constituted by the human as relating first and foremost to him/herself, and not to the gifts of God, when it comes to the determination of one's religious status. It keeps the human locked in a self-centered relationship that is not able to see the other (Christ, God) as someone who is anything other than a means for the confirmation of the previously established and already existing self-relation. Hence one is un-

able to transcend the already given identity by receiving something else through the recognition of the Other. (Note the double direction in the phrase "through the recognition of the Other.")

2. To live in a relation of faith to God as the Other (also: as different from me, but still recognized and acknowledged by me) liberates me to realize, express, and articulate an identity that is authentically my own, but my own as given by the recognition by the Other (God). This relationship is marked by devotion and trust. The one who lives in and by faith lives on the basis of other sources than the ones present in one's own self-reliant identity (insofar as that identity manifests itself outside the relation of faith). Living in and by faith is also to recognize and acknowledge the other in whom one believes as someone other than, and not merely an extension of, oneself. Hence, faith also recognizes difference and acknowledges the asymmetry between God and the human being.

3. As the representative of God, Jesus proclaims a specific message about who and what God is: He is a God for everyone, a God that offers gifts of community to all, a God who lets it rain on just and unjust, good and bad alike. This God is generous and graceful, merciful and engaged in every individual, no matter his or her status (cf. Luke 14:15ff.).

4. This message of Jesus can be met with trust or unbelief. The one who does not accept it indirectly finds the judgment of Jesus as a blasphemer a just one, and thereby he/she also sides, tacitly or overtly, with those who crucified him. The one who accepts his message identifies with it and with him, and recognizes him as the one who in faith and devotion lives by and from faith in God, and loves the world and his crucifiers, just as God does.

5. The recognition of the message of Jesus is also the recognition of myself as dependent on the gifts and the mercy of God. However, it is simultaneously a negative recognition of what I am not. I am not the one who is willing to give up my life in love in the same manner; I am, rather, one who is seeking my own way instead of seeking God. Hence, in practice, I am the blasphemer.

6. When the presence of God manifests itself in faith, Jesus appears in a twofold manner as my representative on the cross. The cross reveals to me that I am the sinner who should rightly have been hanging there because my way of life as a sinner leads to death. This situation consequently implies that I recognize (a) that this is where I should have been, since in my life marked by sin I have lived in a way that did not recognize God as

God, and (b) that it is Jesus who manifests and expresses fully what is the truly human way of living, when he in love for his fellow human beings remains faithful unto death to his own message about who God is.

We see here clearly how it is God who, through Jesus, is the initiator of the change of self-understanding and identity. Hence Jesus remains faithful to the belief in God expressed in his message, despite all the negative, personal consequences resulting from such fidelity. This faithfulness manifests how he is actually at one with the God he proclaims, and thus that he really represents this proclaimed God when in love and faithfulness he offers his life as a gift in order that this message may be truly expressed through and by all that he is and does. As his death is a gift that manifests a life lived in unity with the God he proclaims, it must be understood as his freely chosen way of giving human beings the chance of being represented there by him. At the same time, his gift of himself all the way to the cross proclaims that this message itself is worth dying for. *The crucifixion is, for the crucified, the highest possible way of expressing trust in God. Nothing can tempt him away from this trust. Indeed, any alternative allegiance would imply that his trust is in something other than the God he proclaimed.*[36]

7. Consequently, faith can recognize in Christ on the cross the gift of love, since here I am represented before God by Christ, who is there for me, instead of me (who, as a sinner refusing life with God, faces death as a natural conclusion of this refusal). But the cross is also — from this perspective — necessarily the place where God is re-presented for me in Christ as the only One in whom it is worth putting one's trust, even unto death. This is the conception of God we get from the scene of the cross.[37]

8. The ontological significance of the cross is that it makes it possible for humans to relate to an instance in history where God manifests himself as both righteous and loving. By seeing Christ as my representative, I claim that his righteousness is my righteousness, and that he is living and dying in a manner identical to the life and death that I myself was destined to: a life in faith and love towards God.

---

36. One could also argue that to give in to such a temptation would be to give in to an onto-theological desire instead of trusting that which on the basis of the present seems *impossible,* namely the fulfillment of the eschatological desire, i.e., to desire that which seems most impossible when having to face death.

37. I am speaking here of refusal in a sense that should be distinguished from the failure to accept the message, which is something different, and involves the lack of possibilities for even establishing acceptance or refusal.

9. However, it is still possible to see the cross as expiation for blasphemy. Blasphemy is serious because it means that God is misrepresented, and hence, that people do not see God as God is. This could have fatal consequences, because it could imply that people do not relate to the God who is self-offering love, but to one who demands a sacrifice of human works. Christ is falsely accused of this misrepresentation; hence the one who rejects God and tells lies about God is subjected to death, as God (as he proclaims God) is rejected as the source of life. His is a punishment for (instead of) us, as far as we are the ones who deserved it. As sinners we have made the basis of our lives something other than God's recognition of us as his images, and in refusing his self-offering for us we have consequently rejected (read: negatively recognized) him.

10. This being the case, the cross is a vicarious suffering for the consequences of sin, which is the reason why it is sometimes also understood as a punishment that bears within itself the very consequences of being separated from God as the source of life. However, if the metaphor "punishment" is aptly used here, it must mean that this is something self-inflicted. Anything else would imply that the trial and condemnation of Christ be seen as an expression of justice. Against this background, I can recognize the cross as representing the identity that I myself should have had, given that I have not believed in God. Here the absence of God manifests itself in a twofold manner. For the believer this absence can still be seen as an expression of *God as life-giver represented as embodied in the one who hangs on the cross.* For the non-believer, the cross manifests what the absence of God means for the one who closes him/herself off from God. He/she is left alone, left to the outcome of a life that inevitably is based on something other than its true source. Ultimately, that outcome means death. The death of the unbeliever is thus represented by Christ on the cross. However, there is no positive eschatological dimension implied in this death — since Christ is not recognized as God's representative, which means that anything new with respect to the non-believer's already given identity is foreclosed, cut off. The unbeliever thus remains forever alone with him/herself.

11. Thus, at the cross it becomes manifest that God is one who takes all human beings with equal seriousness in his judgment. For those who believe, the cross appears as a promise and a gift: a gospel. For those who do not believe, the cross is a sign of the judgment confronting everyone who blasphemes God by not believing in him and by not recognizing his

recognition of them as the very grounds of their identity.[38] At this point it should be noted that the cross makes the identity of the Christian emerge as a more complex realization of what the human being is, since it is only the Christian that is able to recognize him/herself as both the sinner and the image of God. This recognition is possible, on this account, only by relating to Christ the representative as the one who dies in the place of sinners and the one who is the true image of God.

12. The understanding that Christ dies in the place of sinners thus points in the direction of the traditional understanding of the cross as a vicarious expiation for me — that is, for those who recognize that it is taking place for their sakes. The recognition of this being the case is at the same time also the presupposition for reconciliation, as God, by offering himself and his love in this manner, offers the human being a chance to transcend him/herself and his/her already given identity in order to live in a faith that grasps the gift that Jesus offers by giving his life as a sacrifice for us. I am what I am as a Christian because of my absence on the cross: it is my nonbeing there and my representation there by another that makes my identity what it is. I am defined by where I am not and by what Christ is for me and instead of me. My absence on the cross is compensated by Christ's presence there, and this is a compensation that offers me freedom from the final death as separation from God as the source of life. It is also what makes it possible for God to differentiate between finitude and death in my life. Because I receive my finite life as a gift from God, its finiteness is not terminated, brought to an end, but is maintained because I recognize the difference between the infinite God and myself by living in faith (cf. how we have seen that to live as *imago Dei* implies recognizing your own finitude). This way of reasoning then seems to be coherent with the positive understanding of sacrifice as celebration of community developed by Tanner. Such a community can only be celebrated when there is an actual recognition of the gifts being presented and the community they seek to establish.

13. As a true human being and as true God, Jesus can be our vicarious representative. Had he himself been a sinner, he would not have been able to do what he now does for the sake of others — in which case his crucifixion would be his, for him, due to him. Now, however, it can be for our sake.

---

38. Note how this can be related back to our discussion of the parable of the last judgment.

In this regard, Jesus acts as the true *Imago Dei* insofar as he makes evident and manifests the love and faithfulness towards creation that God has shown since the beginning of the world. Hence, all of his life can be a gift for others; it is not something that he needs to keep for himself, but something that he freely offers and gives for our benefit, although in so doing it does not benefit *him* in any way whatsoever. However, being one with God, who is love, he cannot do otherwise, not as a result of external force, but by virtue of internal desire.[39] From this perspective the cross can be seen as expressing Jesus' generous love towards those he is called to represent: both God and other humans.

14. The cross reveals that the one who does not live with God ultimately faces death. However, because it is Jesus who is hanging on the cross, and not us, the cross also reveals that God wants to eliminate our sin and overcome its consequences. At the same time, the cross contributes to the development of an understanding of what it means to live as a representative of God in this world marked by sin: he/she will have to face the consequences of sin and rejection of God by him/herself risking rejection, persecution, spite, and death. In this sense, the one who suffers the death on the cross carries the burden and consequences of sin in a twofold manner. On the one hand, he dies as a consequence of sinful humans and their antipathy and decision against God, but, on the other, he also dies for the sake of the very same humans. It is fruitful to elaborate both of these elements in light of the idea of Christ as the representative of humans on the cross.

15. Accordingly, the cross is the locus where the true God and the true Human can be identified and become identical: The true God is the God who suffers injustice in order to win back what he has created in love. This is a God who sacrifices *and* offers everything in order to win humanity back. The true human being is the one who lives in faith and devotion to this God, thereby also bearing the consequences of being handed over to sinful humans who do not recognize him as the true representative of the true God.

16. Hence a salvific faith is one that at its heart embraces the conviction that on this cross hangs the one who takes my place, the one who is there instead of me. No other human has been a true representative of the true God; no other has been the *imago Dei* in the same fulfilled manner.

---

39. For this point I am indebted to Niels Henrik Gregersen.

How Christ is the *imago Dei* reveals itself in the way he is the one who suffers for my sins — and for the sins of the world. This revelation is rooted in his own proclamation of who God is, and this revelation of God makes it possible for faith to recognize the gift of his cross and to see him as my representative. Believing that Jesus dies on the cross for me *(pro me)* is nothing other than stating that he is God's true representative, who, by suffering the death I should have suffered as a blasphemer, offers me the gift of life. God is the God of Life. God overcomes death by exposing himself to death.

17. This establishes the link between the works and proclamation of Jesus (paradigmatically stated in "Go home — your faith has saved you" [Mark 5:34; Luke 7:50]) and his death (for our blasphemous sins, as he was convicted as a blasphemer). Already before the death of Jesus there were people who believed that he was God's representative, and recognized him as such. In his death this recognition of his claim to be this person becomes manifest for all: those who believe in him as well as those who reject this claim. However, it is because he thereby also represents us as the true image of God, lives and dies for us, that we can live with him.

18. Believing in Jesus hanging on the cross for me as a gift for me, and believing in God, are accordingly two sides of the same coin. We believe in Jesus as God's representative, and we can see his death on the cross also as our representative. He is the one taking our place, freeing us from what we have not been (the fulfilled *imago Dei*) by affirming how we can have an identity in what we are by not being on the cross, but being there by and through our representative. At the same time, this implies that I recognize in his being on the cross my own calling to be *imago Dei,* living in faith, hope, and love.

From a doctrinal point of view, the foregoing can be summed up as follows: As true God and true human being Jesus Christ is the only one that can represent God for humanity and humanity for God. This double determination of the identity of Christ is the reason why he is the only one who can establish a true relationship between humans and God (atonement), which installs humans as being what they are meant to be: images of God. In this sense, the cross of Christ serves as a realization of the identity of God as savior, as well as of humans as sinners that are called by the savior to receive their renewed identity as believers in the God whom they themselves are called to represent in the world.

How, then, does the present proposal differ from a traditional subjective interpretation of the atonement? The ontological notion of representation is here developed as a presupposition for the recognition, which is the main element in the interpretation we find, for example, in Abelard.[40] Also, there is a vicarious element present here, inasmuch as Christ suffers a real punishment as a consequence of sins. He is the victim of the sins of others, namely those who crucify him. Their main sin is that they are rejecting him and thereby, implicitly, the one he represents, i.e., God. Hence, he suffers the consequences that rightly belong to those who separate themselves from God. However, the punishment should not be seen as an expression of a God full of vengeance, but rather as what humanity brings on itself when turning away from God as the source of life.[41] The denial of the source of life paradoxically presents itself as a judgment in order to secure his honor and glory. Thus it becomes apparent how the fatal misunderstanding of God on our part is turned into a construction by which humans can actually maintain a distance from him, but present this distance in religious clothing as a way of acting in accordance with his will.

40. In Milbank, *Being Reconciled: Ontology and Pardon,* p. 100, he states: "Hence the divine answer to the original human refusal of his gift is not to demand sacrifice — of which he has no need — but to go on giving in and through our refusals of the gift, to the point where these refusals are overcome. Christ's abandonment offers no compensation to God, but when we most abandon the divine donation it surpasses itself, and appears more than ever, raising us up into the eternal gift-exchange of the Trinity." What is missing here is the fact that Christ offers himself as a gift in the mode of sacrifice — not because God demands it (as in Anselm), but rather because this presents a possibility for humans to have a new identity, in which they have to admit that God is God, that they are God's images, that they are sinners, and that Christ in spite of this is the representative of both God's will and human destiny.

41. The issue here is not that of punishment. But there are still some matters that should be mentioned in order to suggest an alternative background for seeing Christ's death as punishment. It is a punishment for sins, yes. But this is a punishment that is typically designed by humans in order to exclude those who cannot be integrated into the community by subscribing to (a) the commonly accepted standards, or (b) the standards of those who are in power with regard to what is acceptable God-talk. From this perspective, then, the punishment of Christ is not something God wants; rather, it is something that he allows for Christ — as God's representative — to be subjected to in order to include himself in the group of those who are excluded by others who in this instance falsely consider themselves as representatives of God. The presupposition behind this interpretation is how Christ himself proclaims the open and inclusive community given with the kingdom of God as opposed to the religiously dividing practices of his contemporaries.

What is here developed is thus a combination of an inclusive inter-pretation of the cross (it is given for all) and an exclusive interpretation (in the sense that it can only by given as a gift by one and only one). However, this exclusive interpretation is not totalitarian, since the fact that Christ represents me is not something that is forced upon me; it is not something I have to recognize. Christ's substitution for me is not something that nec-essarily contradicts my independence and leaves me alone with my own subjectivity in a way that is irrelevant for what is happening in the cross. At the same time, one has to say that what he does offer is a new basis for my subjectivity as self-relation and God-relation. Thus, subjectivity proceeds by way of an identity based on a gift. Hence the cross of Christ becomes a gift of recognition and representation of myself as more than an agent, and in so doing contributes to the realization of my identity.

Epilogue to Part III:
Identity Issues Revisited

Hanging on the cross, waiting for death, Jesus is alone. But he is also in the same place as many other humans, who eventually have to face the existential loneliness of death, without consolation. The question is: How can this man, who is just one of history's many victims of injustice and exclusion, be seen as one with whom others who suffer can identify? How can there be hope in this? The truth is: there can be no hope, unless something else happens. On the other hand, despite lack of hope, there might still be something implied in this event that reveals something about the world of the victims:

1. The cross of Christ — as the cross of one who undeniably follows the path of goodness and righteousness — reveals that the consequence of following this path might be deadly. Opposition, injustice, and repressive powers may still have the upper hand in the end. In this respect, the cross reveals that living with integrity and in full commitment to justice has risks. These risks, however, appear worth taking when we consider the alternatives:

a) To give up one's commitment to the good and to justice and community is to give up the very basis on which identity is founded. This goes for Jesus as well as for any other victim of injustice. What one then gives up is basically oneself. A breakdown in commitment is a breakdown in personal integrity that destroys the world and the relation to God as the point of orientation from which witness was given and life was led.

b) To give up the commitment then also means that the witness to justice and goodness in the world is silenced. Thereby, the powers that oppress the voice of goodness win a larger victory than the one presumably won by putting Jesus (or any other witness of goodness) to death.

2. When Jesus suffers a death of injustice, he reveals that others who are suffering the same type of death need not see their death as a result of their own failure, as a result of what is deserved. Rather, Jesus' death reveals that the death of those struggling for justice is a result of the opposition to goodness and justice. Hence, he opens up to a self-recognition in which the victim can see herself as "on God's side" — i.e., as being in the same place as God was when God was human. Her desires are directed toward an object worth pursuing. The underlying point here is that the failure is neither God's nor that of those struggling for justice. As Jesus manifests the "solidarity" of God with the victims, his "being in the same place or position as the victims" also indicates that God's cause is vulnerable, and that God's justice and goodness might become the victim of the sin that is present in God's own creation. Moreover, goodness and justice are vulnerable, not triumphant. Victims who experience this vulnerability need not see their fate as one they are alone in suffering, because Jesus, on the cross, reveals that the very same happened to him who most truly represented the source of goodness and justice.[1]

3. The death of Christ is also a final expression of *God's incarnational commitment*. Death is not contributing to the sanctification of either Christ or any other who suffers from injustice. However, as Tanner suggests, death is itself being transferred to God on the cross, "in and through the already given fact of God's assumption of mortal flesh." God can side with us this completely, and not even death is foreign to God — thanks to the incarnation and the death of Christ.[2] This does not in any way give death a positive contribution to God's salvific plan, but it makes clear that no part of human existence is such that we can say of it: "This is a place where God is not; this is a place where God cannot, in one way or another, be witnessed."

1. This is an issue crucial to liberation theology. See for extensive discussion of these issues Sturla J. Stålsett, *The Crucified and the Crucified: A Study in the Liberation Christology of Jon Sobrino* (Bern and New York: Peter Lang, 2003).

2. Kathryn Tanner, "Incarnation, Cross and Sacrifice: A Feminist-Inspired Reappraisal," *Anglican Theological Review* 86, no. 1 (2004): 53-54.

4. When God is identified with Christ, and Christ is seen as God's foremost representative, this means that the true king is in a different place than the kings of this world. Jesus' reordering of worldly orders is also a deconstruction of what is perceived as true kingship: True kingship is directed toward others, opening up to others, creating community, solidarity, and justice. This might look quite different from the glorious kings and emperors of this world. In this respect, Jesus' death might be taken as the ultimate deconstruction of the legitimacy of a kingship in which rule means oppression. As we suggested at the start of Part II, his whole ministry can be seen as one where repressive and exclusive uses of power are questioned and opposed. That this deconstruction is one of the elements related to his trial and crucifixion is most vividly expressed in two texts about Jesus' trial and crucifixion that more or less directly address issues concerning his identity, John 19:19ff. and Mark 15:39.

Both these texts can be read as either ironic, as simple matter-of-fact statements, or as having some kind of deeper theological significance. This multi-layered content thus in itself suggests that the question of identity is not easily given a closure. The reason for taking these texts up for a short analysis here is, of course, that they have a specific contribution to make in order to frame our understanding of the deconstruction of kingship that takes place, and thereby also to make problematic two highly important names that are bearers of identity.

John 19:19ff. reports a discussion between Pilate and the Jews, which is very interesting from the point of view of recognition:

> Pilate also had an inscription written and put on the cross. It read, "Jesus of Nazareth, the King of the Jews." Many of the Jews read this inscription, because the place where Jesus was crucified was near the city; and it was written in Hebrew, in Latin, and in Greek. Then the chief priests of the Jews said to Pilate, "Do not write, 'The King of the Jews,' but, 'This man said, I am King of the Jews.'" Pilate answered, "What I have written I have written."

Let us consider the different possibilities that this discussion suggests, apart from the very fact that it contributes to the overall perception that the trial and death of Jesus is reported as one in which issues of identity are repeatedly taken up for discussion.

Pilate may have put the inscription on the cross for different reasons:

- Stating the fact that Jesus should be recognized as the King of the Jews — thereby positively acknowledging Jesus as something more than his accusers took him to be.
- Stating that by being King of the Jews, Jesus was without power, and this is what happens to anyone who threatens the emperor — hence an exhibition of Jesus' powerlessness and the powers of the Roman Empire.
- Concomitant to the previous: stating that the King of the Jews (which basically is God and no one else) is here manifest as powerless. Then the inscription is mocking, a cruel joke.[3]
- Stating Jesus' title as King in order to make an ironic and/or mocking statement.

Apart from making an apparent tension between those who were responsible for the death of Jesus, the narrator's inclusion of Pilate's refusal to alter the inscription makes another point: Pilate did not want to state as the basis for Jesus' crucifixion something more or different than just the claim to be King of the Jews. On the other hand, those who wanted to alter the inscription could have had theological as well as political reasons for doing so:

- A political reason would be to make visible that Jesus was not recognized as a king of the Jews, and that his crucifixion accordingly was not something that had import on Jewish self-perception, as in "This is what happened to our king." Rather, by insisting on an alteration, this is done in order to make it possible to distance oneself even more from Jesus — since he would then not be recognized in a manner that allowed for him to have a legitimate standing or relationship with those who wanted him convicted.
- The theological reason would be to underscore the possible accusa-

---

3. This is the interpretation offered in John D. Caputo, *The Weakness of God: A Theology of the Event,* Indiana Series in the Philosophy of Religion (Bloomington: Indiana University Press, 2006), p. 15. He writes: "But there is something deeply true about this bitter Roman irony that backfires on such brutality and is visited on Roman power itself. The kingdom that Jesus called for was a kingdom ironically, one that was itself mocking the business-as-usual of the powers that be, one in which a divine madness reigned, even as it was, from the point of view of the Roman Empire, of the brutality of the world, simple foolishness, outright stupidity."

tion of blasphemy, in which a claim to be the king, and thus to be chosen by God, was rejected explicitly.

Read in every possible way, the present discussion finds no final closure, although the inscription is kept intact. However, the discussion exhibits that the Jews, to whom Jesus belongs, rejected him for reasons different from those of the political powers. An interesting twist, and one to consider, is that this discussion also serves to indicate that Jesus' national significance is rejected (he is not recognized by the Jews as in any way a king of the Jews), while the universal significance of him being recognized as such is indicated by the fact that his (assumed) claim to kingship is stated in all the global languages of his times. Hence, Pilate's inscription tacitly recognizes Jesus' kingship. Jesus, however, due to this kingship being crucified, reveals a different possibility for kingship than does Pilate: His is to the end a kingdom related to devotion and goodness, and not — as Pilate, the representative of the emperor — one of repression, exclusion, and death.

By this report, John contributes to the biblical construction of Jesus' identity as the king disturbing all conceptions of kingship. Both by birth and death, Jesus is recognized as a king by foreigners; but this recognition has nothing whatsoever to do with his earthly powers, his glorified social status, or his wealth. It has solely to do with the God to whom throughout his whole life he is a witness: The God who is in solidarity with the oppressed, outcast, and marginalized.

It is thus apt to conclude these reflections by looking at Mark 15:39: where the centurion who was nearby as Jesus died, after his death said, "Truly this man was God's Son!" The obvious and instantly arising question to that expression is, "How can he say that?"

The first answer to that question would be in line with one of the possible interpretations of Pilate's inscription above: it is ironically meant. Thus, it says that "God is without power; this is really not a man worth recognizing. If he is truly God's son, why then this utterly repulsive and disgraceful death?" This is not the most likely interpretation, at least not from the point of view of the evangelist, who presumably wanted the centurion, as a foreigner, to say something about the positive identity of Christ being recognized.

Even more so, as the man who testifies to this is indeed a foreigner, one not presumed to know the God to whom Jesus is then related. The narrative construction here suggests that even beyond or behind the crucifixion there was a kind of tacit awareness of something more, a surplus to the situation, which was not articulated or coming to the fore in what took place. This surplus causes the witness,[4] but there is no more reasons given for this than the impact which Jesus' death itself must have made on him.

Consider, however, how this witness can be one of generic attribution, or one of unique attribution. Generically attributed, the loss of a human to death makes it apparent what he or she has been, and how the riches of his or her life and presence are now suddenly lost. In the realization of this loss, one can express this type of recognition. This approach is, however, not very likely in the situation where the man bearing witness is a foreigner in more than one respect: he represents a power different from and opposed to Jesus (like Pilate), but he also, like Pilate, belongs to another type of religious community. Moreover, his ethnic and cultural background is that of a foreigner as well. *Despite all these differences, his witness to the identity of Jesus is the last thing reported about the identity of Jesus.* It suggests something about the unique identity of Christ: even from a distance, even across differences, even in the disgraceful circumstances of death, it can be recognized that this human is related to God in a specific manner. *As the Son of God, Jesus is what God is like when God is a human.*[5]

---

4. Cf. here Oliver's concept of witnessing, as presented in Part I, pp. 58-59.

5. Cf. Jürgen Moltmann, *The Crucified God: The Cross of Christ as the Foundation and Criticism of Christian Theology* (London: SCM, 1974) [U.S. ed. (New York: Harper & Row, 1974), p. 211]: "When the crucified Jesus is called the 'image of the invisible God,' the meaning is that this is God, and God is like this. God is not greater than he is in this humiliation. God is not more glorious than he is in this self-surrender. God is not more powerful than he is in this helplessness. God is not more divine than he is in this humanity."

PART IV

RESURRECTION AND INCARNATION AS GIFT

The Impossible Impossible:
Resurrection from Other Angles

Resurrection? Seriously? It is impossible. The impossible is indeed impossible. Nothing in our present life attests to such phenomena. At best, the resurrection seems to be an expression of somebody's wish for the good to continue, for the good events never to stop, or for the story to have a happy ending despite its apparently disgraceful and catastrophic outcome. The resurrection is not something that can be linked to our present world, emerging from present conditions of experience, or probable within reasonable horizons of expectation.[1]

In a way, that seems to be exactly the point about resurrection: when we see it in light of what happened on Good Friday, the resurrection is the total opposite, that for which all conditions of possibility are eradicated by the death of Jesus. Jesus manifested the powers of life, but when he was himself dead, these manifestations were no longer possible. Hence, the resurrection appears as the impossible (adjective) impossible (noun) — that which is not impossible only from our ordinary point of view or a Derridaean one (as with some of the other things taking place in the presence of Jesus), but the impossible impossible — given that Jesus as dead is no longer someone we can consider as a condition of possibility for the impossible. The death of Jesus makes the impossible totally impossible.

But: The alternative to the reality witnessed in the proclamation of

---

1. Cf. Rowan Williams, *Resurrection: Interpreting the Easter Gospel* (Cleveland: Pilgrim Press, 2002), p. 88: "[N]othing which occurred on Easter Day or after was anticipated. We read of fear, grief, doubt, ecstatic joy, but not of a simple sense of prophecy fulfilled." Hence, the element of dissociation with the past on the side of the disciples is one of the main obstacles when they are attempting to understand what happens.

the resurrection is not that we live in a reality where God is dead, but perhaps, to state it differently from Nietzsche, that in our reality *death is God,* i.e., that death is the reality which in the end determines the outcome of human life, and lets life and goodness come to an end. Is death God? No, says those who talk ambiguously, metaphorically, blurrily about resurrection: Death is not God, and the resurrection is spoken of in order to make manifest that life overflows even death when it is bound in the love that gives beyond justice, beyond merit, beyond possibilities as we usually see them.[2]

As the resurrection appears to us as impossible and not linked in any way to our present conditions of life, it appears as something that — if it takes place at all — appears as a *gift. The resurrection is the impossible gift.* It is something coming out of nothing, not conditioned positively by anything in the world, but breaking into this world, providing a focus, a new and radical point of orientation. In this sense, the resurrection can be interpreted from all the angles I have used in this book in order to reconstruct important and tacit strands in the story about Jesus: Resurrection has to do with gift as well as desire, with recognition as well as points of orientation.

1. As a *gift,* the resurrection appears as unexpected and unconditioned by any of the present circumstances. This unconditional character is reflected in the fact that the New Testament never says anything about *how* the resurrection took place, or *what* really happened. The statements only say *that* this happened, or report of what happened *after* the event. The event itself is never reported. Moreover, there are no agents bringing it about, no one who has to do something in order for it to happen. The resurrection is a mere event, but we do not know (and probably, we *cannot* know) what it really is. From a theological point of view, I take the elusive and indefinite character of resurrection as a token of its character of gift: unconditionally given, but when given, providing us with a new point of orientation.

The unconditional character of resurrection also suggests that it expresses a *surplus* over against what are the present conditions of the world. The notion of surplus allows us to see it as something that expresses an excess compared to what can be determined from experience. This excess is in some ways anticipated in how the gifts of life are expressing themselves

---

2. Cf. Mark C. Taylor, *Erring: A Postmodern a/Theology* (Chicago: University of Chicago Press, 1984), passim.

as surplus in Jesus' life before Easter, but in the resurrection this excess is more radical, as there is no continuation here in a way similar to, for example, that between the presentation of bread, and the full baskets after the meal in the feeding miracles. The continuation between before and after Easter implies a reconfiguration of the very manifestation of the life of Jesus, as he is not present in the same way as before, according to the reports about his resurrection. There is something more to him, a surplus, a difference, *and we have no way to say what is the change, the difference, and how exactly he is present and presenting himself in this new way.* I take this lack of possibilities for pinning down the newness in the new as a way of expressing both the excessive surplus this reality reveals compared to the one in which we now live, but also as something underscoring the gift-character, which implies that this new gift of resurrection-presence is not something that can be possessed — it is something that has to be given over and over again — it remains a gift in giving, something still to come, not yet fully to be.[3]

2. As *a point of orientation,* the resurrection maintains that God, as the power of life, is still working in the world, and that this world is not to be conceived as if death has the last word. This interpretation does not imply that death has *no* word, *no* impact, and that resurrection is a consolation that lets us ignore the horrors of death, or a way for those believing in it to have their narcissistic dreams about eternal life fulfilled. But as a point of orientation, resurrection opens up a new perspective of the world: the world has a future that is not determined finally by death. Hence, the existential dimension of the resurrection is that it allows for us to be liberated from the closed horizon which death imposes on us in such a way that this horizon appears as the only and final one. Instead, by stating "Resurrection!," there is a witness to something more, something other than what is present. The radical otherness of resurrection also implies that it is not just a continuation of the best of the present — it signals something *different.* No matter how we understand it, the New Testament witness sees the resurrection of Jesus as something more than resuscitation. It is a reversal of the powers of death, so that these powers are no longer in control. Moreover, the resurrection means that Christ is alive, and that he will never die again (unlike those the New Testament reports that he resuscitated).

---

3. This is a point of view that has important implications for how to evaluate attempts to "secure" the historicity of the resurrection of Christ. See below.

In his book on resurrection Rowan Williams indicates that to speak of the resurrection of Jesus is also to speak of one's own humanity as healed, renewed, and restored. As this means to be "re-centered in God," the problems when we talk about this — and about the resurrection — is the problem of describing where one stands and who one is.[4] In other words, it is a question of where you orient yourself. Hence, he points to how in the resurrection we are faced both with the problems related to recognition and those related to points of orientation. This opens up to the recognition of yourself in the presence of Jesus:

> You cannot see your own face, except in a mirror; you cannot describe with satisfactory completeness and objectivity the new life of grace except by looking at the resurrection of Jesus. But "the risen Jesus" only has clear content in relation to the life of grace as experienced now [. . .]. Jesus' risen-ness and our risen-ness are visible only obliquely, in relation to each other. And this means that they are really uttered and manifested only in a speech that belongs directly within that relationship, a speech that is an intrinsic part of the process of discovering myself, and the human future overall, in the presence of Jesus.[5]

In this manner, Williams suggest that resurrection can have meaning only as a way of interpreting present experiences of grace (and gift). Apart from this, as a question about the mere historicity, it easily becomes empty. Thereby he also indicates one of the points I suggested from the outset of this book: that theology must help to interpret or to open up to new experiences. In this respect, the conception of the resurrection opens up to understanding present experiences of grace as something pointing towards the gifts of the future. However, as Williams himself points to, this way of understanding resurrection theologically might easily lead to understanding "resurrection" simply as a metaphor for grace, or triumph over adversity, etc. The theological challenge is to relate this to the actual execution of a supposed rebel or blasphemer. In other words — the theological challenge is to relate the recognition of oneself and the hopeful future to the fate of Jesus as a point of orientation.

3. If we determine the resurrection along the lines of gift, this has profound implications for how it relates to *human desire*. Initially, resur-

---

4. Williams, *Resurrection: Interpreting the Easter Gospel,* p. 111.
5. Williams, *Resurrection: Interpreting the Easter Gospel,* p. 111.

rection seems to be the utmost expression of *ontological desire,* i.e., a desire for continuation of the present, a fulfillment of the narcissistic dream of lack of suffering and of the restraints of finitude. A central theological task must be to avoid a reconstruction that approaches the conception of resurrection in a way that enhances such conceptions. The most obvious argument for avoiding such an approach is that resurrection is then nothing other than an expression of the individual's egotistic wishes. Ontological desire like this closes or narrows the horizon of the individual, and leaves out the perspective of the other. It also construes resurrection as something that the individual can possess as his or her own, something that is an internal quality to a specific type of life rather than a way of relating to and experiencing the world of God and others.

Against this negative background, the conception of resurrection is one that can be construed as an object of *eschatological desire* — i.e., as the object of a desire that knows, acknowledges, and recognizes the object's impossible character in terms of being determined by, emerging from, or conditioned by, anything in the present world. As eschatological desire is a desire shaped and formed by the presence of the impossible, i.e., by God, this means that human desire for resurrection implies a desire for community, for justice, and for the Other, including God. One does not desire resurrection for oneself, but for the other: in this sense, the hope of resurrection is also a hope for the vindication and justification of those who suffer unjustly. Hence, desire for resurrection is a desire for the continuation of the story that began in the life of Christ. Unless the desire for resurrection is shaped in this way, it easily becomes another expression of the individual's wishful thinking for herself.[6]

The resurrection can, however, also be seen as an expression of *God's desire* to save and heal the world. To understand it as an expression of such desire is consonant with understanding God as love. God has no desire to leave creation to the powers of death.

---

6. This description allows for a more positive content of the desire positively related to resurrection than the one Williams develops, when he links desire to lack and to the recognition of incompletion. However, in the end, he comes to a conclusion that fits aptly with that of giving up the control and possession of self and world, and thus as a good expression of eschatological desire: "There is a fundamental level at which I have to say, almost nonsensically, that I do not and cannot know what I want." This is a lack that allows for being changed, for openness to the unknown, for being put into question by what happens. Cf. Williams, *Resurrection: Interpreting the Easter Gospel,* p. 77.

4. The *concrete* experience of recognition is something that seems very hard to come to, given the New Testament witness. Everybody has problems seeing Jesus as Jesus, or as the risen: The wanderers to Emmaus (on whom more below), Mary at the empty tomb, the disciples thinking the resurrected is a ghost, etc. This lack of ability to concretely recognize Jesus suggests that something might be different — despite the fact that when they finally recognize him, they can recognize him as *Jesus*. This strange composition of continuity and difference, which we cannot grasp and have no means of resolving or explaining, I suggest that we interpret along the same lines as we interpreted the impossibility above. This is suggesting that the continuity between our present world and the reality to which Jesus belongs is one that cannot be determined on the basis of the conditions of the present world. Thereby, in a sense, it cannot be determined at all, but only stated, suggested, indicated, postulated. If we were to determine this presence as something to be defined by the present conditions, it would mean an attempt to define and possess the reality we are talking about, instead of letting it be an event to come, to expect, to be open for, and understood as something that really breaks in, surprises, alters, and cannot be anticipated.

Given that Christ is the full and true *Imago Dei,* in whom we can recognize ourselves, the face he now has, which is hard to recognize, is in a way also something we can understand as a calling: not only to recognize him as our future, but also to recognize him as the future of every face we meet.

Moreover, we can then see the resurrection as an event that provides us with specific chances for recognition of identity: God can be recognized as both one who has power over death and who can raise Christ from the dead. Thereby, God also recognizes and vindicates the life of Christ, and puts right what was unjust in his death. God's raising Christ from the dead *is God's witness to Christ,* recognizing Jesus' witness to God as true (cf. Rom. 1:4). This, in turn, makes it possible to relate to and recognize Jesus not only as the Son of God, but also as the one whose witness is confirmed by God. As Rowan Williams aptly writes:

> [. . .] We tell the story of Jesus as the record of a life which not only embodied gift, meaning and freedom in a unique and definitive way, but also was crowned by a strange and elusive event which declared this life not to be over. This human life is declared to be God's, to belong

with God; that is, it is shown to share in the radical creative energy that generates all things. Thus its meaningfulness is not restricted by historical circumstance.[7]

In addition to this way of understanding the relationship between God and Christ, it is clear that the New Testament sees the resurrected Christ as the firstborn of a new creation, in which the divisions of this world are no longer. This world is present in Christ as Christ is present in this world; but it is also absent, still underway, to the extent that the risen Christ is not possible to experience in this world. There is still something ungraspable about this event, and about the claim of his resurrection, that makes it hard to place the claims about the resurrection in the realm of being. At this point, it thus seems fitting to employ the distinction of Jean-Luc Marion, and see the resurrection in light of the distinction he makes between gift and being.

7. Williams, *Resurrection: Interpreting the Easter Gospel*, p. 43.

Resurrection Faith, Recognition, and Gift: Marion

In a small work where he deliberates on the possibilities of grasping the resurrection, Jean-Luc Marion[1] develops a hermeneutic of resurrection that is both consonant with and deepens the perspectives on resurrection that I have already presented above. Marion develops his argument against an understanding of faith that sees faith as compensation for lack of clarity and faulty intuition. Such an understanding of faith makes it possible to believe what I cannot otherwise hold as true.[2] For good reasons, Marion takes issue with this position, because it makes the individual the one who accepts or rejects the existence of God and the truth of Christ. Moreover, it is a blasphemous position, according to him, as it makes God and Christ either impotent in terms of fulfilling the revelation, or makes them perverse judges who by masking themselves expose humans to unbelief and condemn them to faith without reason. Instead of seeing faith as a compensation of what can be established by intuition, Marion suggests that "we should believe not in order to recapture a lack in intuition, but rather to confront its excess in relation to a deficiency of statements and a dearth of concepts" (p. 146). This approach, as one can see, allows for us to understand the resurrection as impossible not in the sense of being an ontological impossibility, but first and foremost as a conceptual and epistemological impossibility. The resurrection presents us with an intuition that is so

---

1. Jean-Luc Marion, "'They Recognized Him; and He Became Invisible to Them,'" *Modern Theology* 18, no. 2 (2002). References in parentheses in the following are to this text until further notice.

2. Cf. Marion, "'They Recognized Him; and He Became Invisible to Them,'" p. 145.

excessive it cannot be expressed or developed by means of our usual conceptual tools. Marion is no doubt right in pointing this out, and I think this position suggests some of the reasons for what is conceived as the impossibility of resurrection. It is precisely because it is conceived as an ontological impossibility that it presents us with an intuition that contains a surplus in comparison with what can be conceptually stated.

Marion employs the same method as I did above in discussing Peter and Judas, when he sees the two men on the road to Emmaus as our counterparts. He formulates the similarity between them and us with relation to what happened at Easter thus:

> Like us, it is thus not the intuition of facts that they lack, but rather the intelligence (the concepts), as do we, today: well do they know, as do we, with scientific certainty, that Jesus died, and that one does not come back from the dead; we can deplore this fact, especially in this case, but in the end that's how it is; we must stay reasonable and not lose our heads. They stick by this evidence no less than do we, to the point of no longer envisaging that the question might even be worth discussing. (p. 147)

By talking about his death without understanding, the disciples are also kept from recognizing Jesus when he enters their company and speaks with them. Marion holds that this lack of recognition was not due to any lack in their perception or intuitions. The reason for their lack of recognition is due to their lack of *imagination:* they cannot even *imagine* that it is him (p. 147). All their preconceptions and ways of understanding what has happened are saturated with the conception of the impossibility of the resurrection, and imply that they "see" the resurrection as exactly that: as the impossible. Hence, the story is about *the lack of recognition.* Or, as Marion says aptly: the events "leave them petrified within a matrix of irrefutable prejudices" (p. 147), a situation in which they are given intuitions their concepts are unable to catch.

Marion uses the notion of intuition here, and with good reasons: intuitions are *given us* and are, as he says, phenomena of excess or surplus, i.e., they contain more than can be contained in concepts, and they are also passively constituted, while conceptually based understanding demands an active effort of cognition and re-cognition. What the disciples on the way to Emmaus lack, however, is an understanding of the events that took place, even the event of resurrection, which they have heard reported, but not comprehended, as events of gifting. They have a perception of the history, but no perception of the events taking place as events of a gift: "Why do they not understand? Because they do not recompose the significations from the starting point of the Passion as revelation of the charity of God, and thus also of the Resurrection as the fulfillment of this very charity" (p. 148). By combining intuition and an openness for gift and charity with the history that Jesus retells them, they could have gained access to the significance of the events. But as the story makes clear, this is not the case.

Marion consequently argues that the lack of recognition is due to lack of concepts by which they can make sense of the intuitions. There is no lack in *revelation*, but only in the travelers' (i.e., our) ability to deal with the intuitions that revelation gives rise to. In this way Marion safeguards the reality of the revelation and the phenomenon of the resurrected, but at the same time he is giving account for how and why this impossible phenomenon seems impossible. The solution to the tension between concept and intuition is given with the teaching of Christ, which gradually — by means of the scriptures — allows for a different reading of the reality in which they find themselves — or, with my words — for a different interpretation of the reality they experience. "By allowing themselves to be taught by Christ, they finally experience that the concept at last matches the intuition" (p. 149). By being open to receive this teaching,

> they ask to receive his *logos*, his interpretation of what has happened in the intuition and which they have nevertheless neither seen, nor caught, nor understood. They at last ask him *his* meaning, *his* concept, *his* interpretation of the public, yet unintelligible to spectators, intuition of Easter. (p. 150)

I think Marion is saying something of great importance here, not only for the interpretation of the story in Luke, but even more so concerning the conditions of resurrection faith: This faith cannot be the result of any deduction based in present conceptions, but must — as the event itself — be conceived as a gift. As he construes what takes place among the disciples on the way to Emmaus, all that happens in order to change their perspective is a gift: They are given the intuition with which they cannot cope; they are given by Christ the concept that finally makes them realize the significance of the events and recognize Jesus. He becomes visible to them by including them in a meal that manifests community, and where he (again) shares the gifts of God with them. Moreover, this gift allows them to see their place in the world differently, and to orient themselves anew. The stranger, who, as long as he is not recognized as Jesus remains an Other, allows them to see and perceive the story differently. The difference is manifested because they cannot fit what he says into an already anticipated pattern of sameness. Their openness to difference is made possible by the way the stranger appears to them.

This means that the capability of understanding the resurrection as resurrection is something that itself must be given and/or revealed. However, this revelation is not abstract, but concrete and personal, and a chance for recognizing both oneself and God. In his interpretation of the story about Mary and the open grave, Rowan Williams points to how the chances for remembering oneself and God are both linked to the utterance of the name of Mary:

> Mary is offered her name, her identity, the name which specifies her as the person with a particular story. And in this context, the utterance of the name re-establishes a relation of trust and recognition: Mary suddenly sees the stranger as the one who has in the past called her by name, accepted and affirmed her identity. Prior to this, it is not simply the Lord's body that has been carried away — it is the Lord who has loved and affirmed Mary, and so, in a sense, it is Mary herself who has been "carried away."[3]

Mary's story exemplifies the necessity for establishing a conceptual framework of gift in order to cope with the event of resurrection. It also points to the lack of immediate access to this phenomenon. Marion actually points to how difficult it is to establish some kind of objective status that allows for the resurrection to appear — and even more to appear as an event in the history of God with God's people. The interpretation of the scriptures that Jesus reportedly offers in order to explain what has happened is only one

---

3. Rowan Williams, *Resurrection: Interpreting the Easter Gospel* (Cleveland: Pilgrim Press, 2002), pp. 38f. As Williams indicates later, this process of remembering and recognition must be seen as a saving process, in which the disciples' identities are recovered in a way that overcomes the trauma of Good Friday and allows them to recognize themselves as related to the resurrected Christ. In this sense, their memories of the past are reshaped and given a direction for a new and different future.

among many possible approaches to the event. It is, however, the only one that has proved solid enough to persist through history — at least among those understandings of this event that did not render it impossible in the sense of *rejectable*. In this sense, the recognition that Jesus opens up to is also a recognition of what is at stake in this history.

Returning then to the initial point about what faith can contribute in terms of understanding the events of resurrection, from Marion's point of view it becomes clear that resurrection can *only* be understood from the point of view of faith. This does not mean that resurrection cannot take place outside of faith, but it means that resurrection as a phenomenon cannot appear as phenomenon without faith. Faith is what makes us *see* what is at stake:

> What we lack in order to believe is quite simply one with what we lack in order to see. Faith does not compensate, either here or anywhere else, for a defect of visibility: on the contrary, it allows reception of the intelligence of the phenomenon and the strength to bear the glare of its brilliance. Faith does not manage the deficit of evidence — it alone renders the gaze apt to see the excess of the pre-eminent saturated phenomenon, the Revelation. (p. 150)[4]

The problem that emerges from this way of understanding the phenomenological conditions for understanding the resurrection is linked to the fact that this can be read as faith being the requisite for the content of faith. However, at this point I think we are well served by considering how the very language that we share also allows us to shape perspectives and points of orientation that indicate different possibilities of understanding. Despite the fact that you need a specific faith in order to understand the resurrection as resurrection, you can nevertheless contemplate that possibility already by listening to, and being provided with, a particular understanding that someone else shares with you and offers you. By entertaining such a possibility, you can either come to the conclusion that you understand the resurrection as a resurrection, or you can conclude

---

4. For a different, but still in many ways parallel account of the same, cf. Sarah Coakley, "'Not with the Eye Only': The Resurrection, Epistemology and Gender," *Reflections* 5 (2002). Coakley also points to how the language of the resurrection destabilizes and subverts common forms of understanding the world, and opens up to a whole new way of "picturing" the world.

that there is something here that you are not able to see as significant, or that it is something that you do not see as a phenomenon altogether. But when you believe, you believe in something that is there, something that is not constituted by your concepts, but *given to you in intuitions and concepts, as a gift, an event presenting itself.*

Seeing the revelation as *a saturated phenomenon,* as Marion does, allows for this phenomenon to be richer than what can be conceptually articulated, but without having to take recourse to apophatic mysticism. Rather, it allows for several different and explorative ways of understanding the revelatory event in question. We can illustrate this by providing two different ways of understanding the elusiveness of Jesus at the end of the Emmaus story:

Marion sees the disappearance of Jesus as an indication that the issue is not, from now on, to see Jesus, but to *show him,* "to make it so that all receive the significations that allow them to see that which the intuition offers, without rendering it manifest again" (p. 151). Also, he says, such a saturated phenomenon cannot be touched, nor even contemplated in this world, which does not have the space to contain the significations that could have been written.[5] He does not, however, in the context of the article develop this point further, but the last point underscores that this is a phenomenon allowing for a multitude of interpretations.

"A theology of the risen Jesus will always be, to a greater or lesser degree, a negative theology, obliged to confess its conceptual and imaginative poverty — as is any theology which takes seriously the truth that God is not a determinate object in the world," writes Rowan Williams.[6] My own suggestion would be, accordingly, that the elusiveness of Jesus not only underscores his presence in the world as an unconditional event of gifting, but even more, it also suggests that Jesus cannot be possessed by or taken captive by the forces of this world. His resurrection existence as a pure gift — for him and for us — allows for our desire to be directed towards something we realize cannot be fully present, but nevertheless can be represented in the world: the community of Jesus with others who believe in the reality he represented. The presence of Jesus is represented — in its absence — by the community of believers who by this belief not only keep

5. Marion, "'They Recognized Him; and He Became Invisible to Them,'" p. 152, with reference to John 21:25.

6. Williams, *Resurrection: Interpreting the Easter Gospel,* p. 84.

the memory of him present, but also, by keeping this memory present, keep the future that his life and resurrection promised open to faith and future experience.[7]

On the Inconclusiveness of Historical Evidence

Present discussions of the resurrection still seem to revolve around questions of historicity and plausibility, on the one hand, and questions of theological significance, on the other.[8] Given the impossibility with which I have already indicated that one can label the conception of the resurrection, this is not surprising. As there is no way to finally secure that Jesus did rise from the dead, is it possible to still make a case out of *this* fact? The fact that we cannot establish the resurrection *as a fact* needs to be affirmed by everyone wanting to address the issue of resurrection. The fact that there is no established fact is the only fact that can be certified. But that is, of course, not all there is to say.

7. This is not so only for present believers, but for the first ones as well. As Rowan Williams puts it, "The preaching of Jesus crucified and raised occurs in a specific human context in which Jesus and his death are available in the public memory. This man and his way of living and dying, this man rather than any other, is exalted, approved and vindicated." *Resurrection: Interpreting the Easter Gospel,* p. 20.

8. Recent or still important contributions that are also open to the more problematic elements in the event of resurrection include: Gavin D'Costa, *Resurrection Reconsidered* (Oxford, UK, and Rockport, MA: Oneworld Publications, 1996); Wolfhart Pannenberg, *Grundfragen Systematischer Theologie,* vol. 2 (Göttingen: Vandenhoeck & Ruprecht, 1980); and Ted Peters, Robert J. Russell, and Michael Welker, *Resurrection: Theological and Scientific Assessments* (Grand Rapids: Eerdmans, 2002). Among the more apologetic we find G. Habermas, whose several publications all contribute in different forms to the attempt at making the resurrection historically plausible. See, for example, Gary R. Habermas, *The Resurrection of Jesus* (Lanham, MD: University Press of America, 1984); Gary R. Habermas, *The Risen Jesus & Future Hope* (Lanham, MD: Rowman & Littlefield, 2003); Gary R. Habermas, Antony Flew, and John Ankerberg, *Resurrected?: An Atheist and Theist Dialogue* (Lanham, MD: Rowman & Littlefield, 2005); Gary R. Habermas, Antony Flew, and Terry L. Miethe, *Did Jesus Rise from the Dead?: The Resurrection Debate,* 1st ed. (San Francisco: Harper & Row, 1987). He nevertheless fails to make plausible *what* resurrection is, in a way that settles the debate about how to understand it. See also N. T. Wright, *The Resurrection of the Son of God,* 1st North American ed., Christian Origins and the Question of God, vol. 3 (Minneapolis: Fortress Press, 2003), and the critical discussion of his work in Michael Welker, "Wright on the Resurrection," *Scottish Journal of Theology* 60 (2007): 458-75.

This point should, first and foremost, not be seen as trying to avoid making claims about the historicity of the resurrection. From a logical point of view, there is no point in speaking about resurrection unless there is some type of historical reason for it. Nevertheless, my point is that one should be open to the fact that although there is considerable emphasis on the resurrection in the New Testament, these facts are disputed and disputable — and that there might even be theological reasons why this is the case. The fact of the disputable fact is a fact that also those in favor of the resurrection should recognize.

Pannenberg and others who — rightly, I hold — argue that the future must be seen as determining the present, allow us to approach this problem in a more fruitful manner. Given that the contingencies of what happens cannot be predicated on the basis of the past, the future seems to hold more than what we can determine. Moreover, as the future holds this surplus, we cannot possibly be expected to have a concept that can contain all that this future implies. The fact of the disputed fact of the resurrection is based on what has happened in the past, and how this has so far shaped our perception of what can be the case. On the other hand, the future is no longer a future, something underway, but something in our possession, if we can establish the resurrection as a fact among others. That would imply that the future reality witnessed by the resurrection is already present and in our conceptual possession. In a strict sense, that would rule out the possibility for the very contingency with which it is now characterized, and which makes it so elusive to us.

So far, however, this argument is epistemological — it relates to our ability to comprehend what takes place in the resurrection. However, that we in principle have to be open to future contingencies and events that we cannot predict is in itself no argument for claiming that such things that we cannot predict do in fact happen. Even if we — ontologically — state that the future is open and cannot be determined based only on past and present events, this is different from saying that the future is something that entails resurrection as one of its possibilities. In the introduction to the present section (Part IV), where I wrote about the resurrection as the impossible impossible, this is what I had in mind: the resurrection seems to be one of the impossibilities of the world, and not one of the possibilities. At this point, I think that Pannenberg and others who try to secure the plausibility of the resurrection based on the conception of contingency and an open future are making their case too easily.

The theological reason for putting forward this type of argument is that I think Christian theology needs to realize that the resurrection is not something we can possibly build a case for in terms of present, generic conditions of arguing. In the literature dealing with the possibility or impossibility of resurrection we see two approaches: one starting with the generic conditions, the other with the actual belief in the veracity of the resurrection of Jesus as the event on which to base further argument for its reality.[9] A combination of the two can also be observed. None of these approaches would have been entertained, however, had it not been that we are facing the actual claim that Jesus did rise from the dead. This implies a claim about something taking place in human history, but the event is nevertheless something that we also lack adequate means to determine as part of that history. There are many hard tasks to face, going along with that claim:

- We have the *conceptual* impossibility: a dead human does not come to life again. What exactly does resurrection then mean? At best, we can see the concept as a metaphor for a new way of living in the presence of God, but it is a metaphor that has little *explanatory* value. Its value lies in the way it opens up to the saturated phenomena that the disciples experience. But it seems difficult, indeed, impossible, to define clearly the concept of resurrection. Accordingly, I would suggest that we see it as a *metaphor* that allows us to see and experience the world differently, and to orient us in the world from other conditions than those given before Easter. Resurrection is in the fullest sense reality as gift.[10]

9. I think this is basic to arguments of people as different as G. Habermas, W. Pannenberg, and W. L. Craig, to mention a few of the most discussed figures in recent literature.

10. Cf. for this also, the way that M. Bockmuehl defines the function of resurrection as a metaphor: "The resurrection, in other words, is indeed a metaphor, as is often said — but its function is quite the opposite of conventional metaphors. From Plato's cave to Lewis's Narnia, ordinary religious metaphors tend to employ the literal and familiar to speak (however truthfully) of an otherworldly reality. The New Testament witness to the resurrection of Jesus, by contrast, redescribes earth in terms of heaven and history in terms of eschatology. For the early Christians, this marks the place in which God's world irreversibly invades the world of violence and corruption, planting here the flag of redemption. Heaven is no longer a metaphor of earthly bliss, or the world to come a pleasant postscript to mortality. Instead, Easter morning claims the redeemed cosmos as a metaphor of heaven, and

- Then we have the *ontological* impossibility, which is given with the predictions we can make on the basis of the past. This impossibility is, however, *in principle* softened by pointing to how the future is open and to the importance of being open to future contingencies and the newness of events. Nevertheless, when we speak of the resurrection, we speak of something that might be considered outside the scope of even future contingencies: it is something that seems so ontologically impossible, it is hard to argue that *this event* (which we are only able to speak about metaphorically) could possibly take place at all. In this respect, the resurrection equates with a square circle: it operates on other premises than does the rest of this world (as the post-Easter reports also indicate).
- We also have the *historical* improbability, on which most of those opposed to the historical claims about Jesus' resurrection base their reasoning.[11]

In the previous part of this book, I spoke about the necessity for interpreting the death of Jesus in order to establish a foundation for why this death must be remembered. The reports about resurrection visions present us with a different kind of task: here it is not primarily a question about interpreting a historical event, but a question of being at all able to understand the reports in such a manner that it can appear as an event that is important for the understanding of our own future.

The logical structure of everything that the resurrection reports open up to is that the resurrection reality — so far — belongs uniquely to Jesus. No one else has a part in this reality in the same manner. But the reports nevertheless seem to be written in order to provide more than a foundation for the memory of this uniqueness. Rather, they are attempts

---

transforms mortal life into the vestibule of paradise. The resurrection here constitutes the defining historical, moral and ecological reality that is the 'new creation.'" "Resurrection," in Markus N. A. Bockmuehl, *The Cambridge Companion to Jesus*, Cambridge Companions to Religion (Cambridge and New York: Cambridge University Press), p. 117.

11. For the most recent critical discussion, see Robert M. Price and Jeffery Jay Lowder, *The Empty Tomb: Jesus Beyond the Grave* (Amherst, NY: Prometheus Books, 2005). In New Testament scholarship, we have positions questioning this probability, for example in M. D. Goulder, *Incarnation and Myth: The Debate Continued* (Grand Rapids: Eerdmans, 1979) and Gerd Lüdemann, *The Resurrection of Jesus: History, Experience, Theology*, 1st British ed. (London: SCM Press, 1994).

to inscribe in our world a foundation for understanding a possible (and from other angles impossible) future for ourselves as part of the community that Jesus was the beginning of. These stories provide reasons for conceiving that Jesus can be with his followers also in the future, and as something more than a memory. How can that be?

The stories contribute to the consciousness about *where* we are — they contribute to establishing a point of orientation. They show in different ways that we are part of the community of Jesus, and at the same time that we are still different from him. This maintaining of unity in difference is important to orient ourselves not only to the past, but also to the promised gifts of the future. As indicated, these gifts cannot be understood as something for individual possession, but only as realizable in the presence of the community which we recognize ourselves as participating in by faith.[12]

The critical function of that identity is that it allows for us to not totalize the present world, and to confront it with a consciousness of what happens as something that is still not fully captured by the powers of death. According to the above, resurrection must be seen as the ultimate gift that still only exists as a promise for us — but a promise that is nevertheless anticipated by the proclamation of Christ's resurrection. As a gift — indeed a gift of life — it also establishes a contrast between a gifting way of living, and ways of living that lead to death. This gift of life reveals that God is not letting the world surrender to the powers of death, and that God wants to expose these powers as not mighty enough to have the last word. These powers are by the very instance of resurrection exposed as those that shall *not* be in the end, and as those that destruct both the gifts of life and life as a condition for gifting.[13]

12. Peter's case is illuminating here: After his denial of Jesus, his past demands that he recognize himself as a betrayer, but his meeting with Jesus after the resurrection *heals* that memory and makes it possible for him to recognize himself from another point of view, from another orientation. The whole story of John 21 is about how Jesus' recognition of him and his love allows a future to be opened for him that is not determined by his ruined past.

13. In this sense, the memory of Jesus' resurrection provides a critical tool for evaluating the present. Williams, *Resurrection: Interpreting the Easter Gospel*, p. 25, points with regard to this to J. B. Metz's understanding of memory as "the means by which reason [can] become practical as freedom." Metz "refers to Marcuse's linking of memory with imagination, both being a means for the critical understanding of the present, 'a way of mediation that can momentarily at least break through the omnipresent power of the given facts.' When the power of given present facts is challenged as we come to see the present situation

By establishing this contrast between what is (the end of life in death) and what is to be (the life in community with God and others), hope is founded. Moreover, this allows for living in the world with freedom based on the knowledge that a different world is possible, and that God is the one who ultimately not only supports this world, but will also bring it to its realization. Christian hope is a hope for the impossible, because ultimately, only that which is impossible is worth hoping for.

As indicated, it is not without importance that this hope for the impossible is based on *Christ's* resurrection. He was the one who suffered injustice, and who also claimed to be a witness to the kingdom of God. In the resurrection, not only is his claim vindicated, but his unjust suffering is also a sign that unjust suffering is not the end for those who suffer it. In this way, the resurrection is the reason for hope and for proclaiming that those who hunger and thirst for righteousness are blessed, because they will be filled (Matt. 5:9). They need not think that death is their final defeat. This does not mean, however, that they should console themselves with the injustice they suffer, but rather that they should struggle against it in light of the final, eschatological vindication of their cause.

The social and ethical dimensions of the resurrection indicated here are developed further in Rowan Williams's treatise on the resurrection, where he sees the transformation of the world as more than a mere change in attitude: It provides us with a point of orientation from which we can see the world as gift, as something to be given, and as the call to give. This, he says, has a "straightforwardly material dimension" as oppression and violence; the chains of destructiveness that occur socially, economically, and quite simply physically, always occur in connection with the possession of the world's resources. Williams sees it as a way of dealing with the world "that locks Christ out, and constitutes a denial of Christ's Lordship: it is a sign of unbelief in the resurrection. When convertedness is embodied in a transforming of economic relationships, material reality will have become charged with the life of Christ risen: the world will be revealed as his."[14]

Without trying to make it an argument *for* resurrection in the strict

---

as the issue of contingent processes and choices, we gain resources for new decision, and openness to new stages of process. We learn to act and to hope. Memory, at this level, can be the ground of hope, and there is no authentic hope without memory." Williams's reference to Metz is taken from Johannes Baptist Metz, *Faith in History and Society: Toward a Practical Fundamental Theology* (New York: Seabury Press, 1980), pp. 193-95.

14. Williams, *Resurrection: Interpreting the Easter Gospel*, p. 103.

sense, it is worth considering the alternative here as well. Had Jesus not been resurrected, this would have meant that even the one who gave his life fully to God and to other humans in order to proclaim the kingdom of God, in the end had to see himself defeated by the powers of death. That would not only have meant that his own proclamation was a failure, but also that the God he witnessed to was not the one Jesus claimed God to be. In that sense it is possible to see Jesus' resurrection not only as a consequence of his bearing a truthful witness to the true God. It is also possible to see that his resurrection allows for others to recognize him as the one in whom one can trust, when it comes to how God relates to our future, when we in faith, hope, and love struggle for community, justice, and the distribution of the gifts of God. The alternative is to conclude that Jesus' witness was false, and that those who struggle in faith, hope, and love for a just world might sometimes succeed, and sometimes fail. That is of course an option to be considered, but it is an option that is hard to make coherent with the affirmation that God is the God of life.

Concluding then, that although this last line of reasoning is not an argument for the reality of the resurrection, it is nevertheless an argument for the fact that the resurrection — if it took place — is in full accordance with the confession that God is the creator and sustainer of life and human community. In this way, we can also see the resurrection as a confirmation of Christ's identity as a witness to the God of life.

The Paulinian Core Argument — a Discussion

The preceding argument can also be read as a meditation on the following. In his first letter to the Corinthians, Paul makes some strong statements about the centrality of the resurrection for the belief of the Christian community. Paul's argument implies a clear rejection of a position that tries to found the belief in Jesus only in the past — rather, he indicates that unless Christian belief is a belief in the future, it is no good:

> If there is no resurrection of the dead, then Christ has not been raised; and if Christ has not been raised, then our proclamation has been in vain and your faith has been in vain. We are even found to be misrepresenting God, because we testified of God that he raised Christ — whom he did not raise if it is true that the dead are not raised. For if

the dead are not raised, then Christ has not been raised. If Christ has not been raised, your faith is futile and you are still in your sins. (1 Cor. 15:13ff.)

The striking openness with which Paul presents his line of reasoning is worth considering: He argues that for our faith in Christ to not be futile, belief in the resurrection is necessary. His argument can — critically — be read in two ways:

- The resurrection is the condition for a faith that is not futile. Hence, the resurrection is the warrant for faith and the condition for its possibility. In other words: The impossible (resurrection) is the condition for the possibility of faith. This, in turn, means that faith is always a faith in the impossible, in that which is beyond control and rational argument — but which still need not be totally irrational.
- Those who believe must continue believing in the resurrection in order to not be proved wrong or admit to failure. Respectively, in order to not have to recognize themselves as "still being in their sins" the affirmation of the resurrection is necessary.

While the first of these angles is the one usually taken, and one we need not discuss much further here, the second also merits some consideration. A *Nietzschean* twist on this second line of interpretation would be that it is better to believe in nothing (i.e., the impossible, the resurrection) than to not believe at all. As long as one believes, one is directed towards something, life is expressing itself, and desire is oriented toward an aim. Hence, belief (even if belief in something Nietzsche would regard as nothing) is a way of experiencing oneself as alive and active. However, to reject the resurrection would be to admit that the desire directed toward that which is projected into resurrection is empty, void, and nil. A Nietzschean twist such as the one suggested here then seems to indicate that there is a kind of psychological pressure, once having stated belief in the resurrection, to continue to do so. Anything else would be to admit failure, and to give up the possibility for experiencing oneself as alive and engaged in something that could contribute to positive self-recognition.

The Nietzschean twist of that argument only holds, however, if the resurrection faith is a faith that primarily has to do with *me:* because only then does it become necessary for me to believe, because faith is about *me* and *my* possibilities. However, as Paul argues, the resurrection faith has first and foremost to do with how we perceive of God — and of Jesus. The belief in resurrection is a way of specifying that we believe in a God that ultimately will let life, justice, and community reign — for others — instead of death. The hope in this God is thus not a hope for us and for our petty desires, but for the world. The frankness of the Pauline way of reasoning suggests this. Paul admits openly that one must consider that there exists the possibility that the dead are not resurrected. But his concern is not primarily that this makes our faith futile (although he also admits that, of course), but rather, that this makes witnessing to God a *misrepresentation*. I would argue that his concern about misrepresentation is the core of the Pauline argument: If Christ has not been raised from the dead by God — then God is different, God is other than the believers in Christ have assumed. Hence, again it all comes down to the very question with which we have dealt throughout this book: Who is God? or, to put it otherwise: If the story about Jesus does end at Golgotha, then the story about the God Jesus proclaimed and practiced also ends there.

The aim of the above reflections is to make clear that the confession of the resurrection of Christ is always part of a very risky enterprise: all is at stake with this confession, and the confessor must be aware of the risk exactly because of this. Attempts to make the resurrection a less risky affair will always be an attempt to trivialize the phenomenon of the resurrection into something that can be controlled and possessed, while the Pauline argument suggests that resurrection is what finally binds Christ and God together in a reality that is gift, not possession, future, not full presence, promise, not yet fully realized.

The risky business of resurrection faith is one that is underscored by the somewhat inconclusive and elusive stories about the resurrection in the New Testament. The empty tomb is itself not an argument for resurrection. The apparently (at least initially) unrecognizable Jesus in the appearances before the disciples also indicates that there is no immediate access to a secure conviction about the risen Lord. As it seems impossible to develop a clear statement about Jesus' whereabouts after the resurrection, the difficulties are even more present.[15] But these uncertainties do not pro-

---

15. G. Lüdemann, in William Lane Craig et al., *Jesus' Resurrection: Fact or Figment?: A Debate Between William Lane Craig and Gerd Lüdemann* (Downers Grove, IL: InterVarsity Press, 2000), pp. 40f., observes that the question "Where did he go afterwards?" is impossible

vide us with clear arguments *against* the resurrection, either. One can claim that the very same approach that tries to establish a secure historical foundation for the resurrection also expresses itself negatively in the struggle for the opposite: in both instances a conviction is expressed that this is a reality we can more or less sufficiently access, control, or determine the content of. But given that the resurrection is the example *par excellence* of what Marion and others call the saturated phenomenon, this argument is hardly convincing. Hence, a more or less positivistic approach to the resurrection seems to not only fail to describe what characterizes that phenomenon, but also seems to deviate from Paul's admission that such faith involves risk. Paul openly admits to the fact that we will have problems with that which seem impossible. To pretend otherwise would be to ignore the fact that the resurrection cannot be firmly established as a historical truth among others.

Before we conclude this section, one more element needs to be addressed: Paul claims that resurrection means bodily resurrection. In this he sides with Luke. Luke's report of Jesus as eating, and about the empty tomb, secure resurrection faith from two important challenges: the empty tomb is important in order to establish that there is some kind of *continuity* between the risen Christ and the pre-Easter Jesus, while the eating is important in order to avoid understanding the appearances of Jesus as those of a ghost. According to ancient understanding, ghosts were not able to eat and drink.[16] In both instances, *the body* is of utmost importance, because the body makes it possible to situate the risen Christ in time and space, but also to recognize him as risen. However, the body is also understood as something that has changed. How can this narrative trait be explained? From an exegetical point of view, it can be reasoned as Eckstein does in his treatment of resurrection in Luke:

> And if the "physical" existence of the earthly Jesus is not characterized
> negatively, but is in the context of the Old Testament-Jewish theology

---

to answer, and uses this to argue against resurrection faith. However, as Pannenberg indicates in *Grundfragen Systematischer Theologie*, pp. 167f., the vagueness of the New Testament in dealing with such questions cannot in itself be taken to provide reasons for rejecting the resurrection.

16. Further on these points, see Hans-Joachim Eckstein, "Bodily Resurrection in Luke," in *Resurrection: Theological and Scientific Assessments*, ed. Robert John Russell, Ted Peters, and Michael Welker (Grand Rapids: Eerdmans, 2002), esp. pp. 118ff.

of creation connoted altogether positively, then for Luke as well as for the other New Testament witnesses it goes without saying that God at Jesus' redemption does not leave the soma, the mortal body, to the reign of death but transforms him physically.[17]

There is a tacit element in Eckstein's reasoning here that needs to be highlighted: Jesus — as a true human — has the same mortal body as the rest of humanity. That he was an embodied being was part of the fullness of incarnation (for more on the incarnation see the next chapter). To be participating fully in the community with the God of life implies that this mortal body must — in some non-definable way — be transformed. It is nevertheless still a body (in Paul's words: a *soma pneumatikon*), but a body different from the one we have now.[18]

This point illuminates the possibility for Christians to recognize in themselves a future that means and implies a concrete, embodied difference: Resurrection is not only about being in full community with God and others, or being fully able to receive the gifts of God: it is also to be given the bodily preconditions for this fullness, which implies that resurrection is manifesting a reality that exceeds the present also in bodily terms, and that the fullness of this reality implies a surplus over against what is currently present in the creation of God.

17. Eckstein, "Bodily Resurrection in Luke," p. 123.
18. Further on a Christology of the body, see Ola Sigurdson, *Himmelska kroppar* [Heavenly bodies] (Gothenburg: Glänta, 2006).

Resurrection as Manifestation
of Incarnation: Dalferth

The preceding chapters of this part have been developed partly in order to provide a backdrop for the dogmatically relevant construction of the relation between resurrection and incarnation. Resurrection and incarnation are, as indicated, closely tied together, although it also has to be maintained, as indicated above, that the resurrection implies a surplus in terms of being compared to what is manifested in the pre-Easter bodily incarnation of the Word as Jesus from Nazareth.

Among the most heated debates in modern Christology is the one that took place after the publication of the volume edited by John Hick about the incarnation.[1] Dalferth[2] claims that almost everything is — and remains — unclear in the debate about this book: when it asks if the incarnation is a myth or a truth, it is not clear what any of the terms — incarnation, myth, or truth — mean in this context (p. 6). In the following, I will present his more constructive responses to this volume, without going into detail about his more critical remarks. In general, however, his evaluation of this collection of essays is that it demands a more nuanced approach than the authors provide.

Dalferth suggests that we distinguish between different elements in our discussion of the incarnation. If it is not clear which dimension is be-

1. *The Myth of God Incarnate* (1977). Recently reissued as John Hick, *The Metaphor of God Incarnate,* 2nd ed. (London: SCM Press, 2005).
2. Ingolf U. Dalferth, *Der Auferweckte Gekreuzigte: Zur Grammatik der Christologie* (Tübingen: Mohr Siebeck, 1994). References in parentheses in the text are to this book until further notice.

ing discussed in approaching the incarnation, obscurity remains (pp. 9-10). He describes the different dimensions as follows:

- The event of incarnation,
- Conceptions of incarnation,
- Confessions of incarnation,
- Doctrine of incarnation, and
- Theories of incarnation.

Moreover, he identifies two mutually excluding theses that seem to be at the forefront of the discussion: Is the event of incarnation the basic theme of Christological articulations, or is the incarnation only one, and one mistaken, way of expressing the *theme* of Christology (p. 11)?

Dalferth identifies the main problem with Hick's critical approach in his identification of the historical human being Jesus from Nazareth before Easter as the sole referent of Christological formulations. This approach, he holds, implies a theological under-determination, because it goes astray at a very decisive point: It misses the *confessional* element (p. 21). Dalferth holds that it is necessary for the logical structuring of Christological formulations to see them as attempts to express something about the resurrected crucified. Hence, the formulations try to say something more than merely making statements about the identity of the pre-Easter Jesus. Dalferth consequently argues that the resurrection implies that we are dealing with something that exceeds what can be grasped as the pre-Easter reality of Jesus: The resurrection provides us with a surplus compared to what was at hand before. Hence, he says, the main theme in any *confession* about Jesus Christ is not his historical reality as such, but his existence as the one whom God rose from the dead (p. 24).

Against this background, Dalferth formulates "the grammatical" conditions of Christology in a way that holds together resurrection, cross, God, and world. The connection between these different instances is one that is determinative for the identity of all, and in this sense, one can say that the Jesus story is not only a story about Jesus' identity, but also a story about the identity of God and the world:

> So is resurrection to be interpreted with regard to the cross, the cross with regard to God, and God in the light of the preaching of Jesus, and God's actions in cross and resurrection with regard to us and our

world. This is the direction of an argumentation in Christology and Christian theology that is in accordance with a Christian confession of faith. (p. 27)

Christian faith is first and foremost a confession of the life-giving power of God in the resurrection of Christ, according to Dalferth. Hence most important is the confession that Jesus is the first whom God has risen from the dead, and not *who* one confesses that Jesus is. It is the resurrection by God that allows us to see the witness he gave to God as final, irreversible, and unsurpassable (p. 28). Due to this understanding, Dalferth holds as important that the way one allows for Jesus to be the theme of Christological confession allows for more than one mode of thematization. He argues that just as we have to differentiate between theme and content, and between theme and the formulation of the theme, the foundation for all reasoning about the resurrection must be that Jesus is the first one to be raised by God (p. 31). How one then formulates the content, the background, and the horizon of this event may vary, but prior to all these ways of formulating the content is the event itself, which is the basis and object of Christian faith.

In a way that may seem surprising due to the way we have developed the previous chapters of this book, Dalferth thus argues that the resurrection is the primary determination of the theme of Christological confessions. It is not the incarnation. He sees the doctrines of incarnation as both historic and epistemic secondary interpretations of the primary determination of the resurrection (pp. 30f.). Hence, everything that the Christological confessions say about Christ in terms of incarnation is dependent on the fact of the resurrection. The resurrection becomes, so to say, the axis of Christology. If this breaks, there is not much point in anything else we can say about the historical person Jesus from Nazareth, including the incarnation.

There are several important implications of this way of arguing, and Dalferth himself presents some of them. Before I proceed with presenting his conclusions, it is important to notice that by giving the resurrection such a crucial place in the theme of Christology, he is underscoring the possible failure as well as the extreme incoherence that every type of theology risks that does not take its point of departure in this event. This is not an argument for the resurrection as such, but it is an argument for the centrality of the resurrection (which has to be distinguished clearly from the first). Hence, at the center of the Christian confession to Jesus as the savior of the world is an event that cannot be established as a fact — but which, as we have indicated, we can only approach as a gift and a promise.

The most important result of this way of reasoning for Dalferth himself is that it allows him to see incarnation Christology as unnecessary: it is not the primary element in the confession of Jesus. Instead of bringing the central element of Christology to its expression, it contributes to the interpretation of the life of Jesus in light of his resurrection, and contributes in different ways to the explication of the importance of that event. These Christologies are results of efforts to comprehend the work God did in resurrecting Christ. They are not the work of God, but interpreting the works of God. On the other hand, the resurrection is to be seen as the event that precedes our interpretative work, and which we come to too late in order to grasp fully. Hence, we also need a plurality of different ways to access the life and death and resurrection of Christ. No content of a confession is able to exhaust the theme of the confession or to take the place of that which is referred to with the name Jesus Christ — including the confession to him as the Son of God. This is so because this confession as well does not give a conceptual clarification of the Christological thematic, but instead, refers us back to the resurrected Jesus, and thereby also to the eschatological actions of God for our salvation. These actions are the basis that transcends every attempt of interpretation and, as such, is the basis of Christian faith (p. 31).

Dalferth thus makes a move that identifies the singular reality of the resurrection as the only indispensable foundation of belief in Jesus as the true witness to God, and at the same time, he allows for — even sees the necessity for — a plurality of different ways of explicating the content that has been possible to develop given the event of the resurrection. While he underscores that formulations about the resurrection of Christ cannot be interpreted simply as reflective formulations (Reflektionsaussagen), he also holds that such formulations imply propositions and claims about a reality (Realitätsaussagen, pp. 55-57).

The axis function of the resurrection reveals itself in more than being a point of departure for reflections and confessional formulations. It reveals itself also as the final means by which identity is sufficiently revealed to become liberating for all the parties involved. Dalferth develops the establishment of Jesus' identity along the following lines, which also allows for us to see the close relationship between God and Jesus that incarnation theology tries to explicate.

We can start by asking "Who is it that God raised from the dead?" The answer would be "It is the crucified Jesus from Nazareth." This answer then allows for another question of identity: "Who is Jesus from Nazareth?" Here the answer turns back in the form "It is the one whom God raised from the dead." This answer then provokes the third and final form of the question: "Who is the one who was crucified and resurrected?" The answer to this final question is now opening the soteriological horizon in which we can find a way of recognizing ourselves: "He is the one with whom God has identified Godself irrevocably for our sake. He is the Christ, the Lord, the Son of God" (cf. p. 86).

The resurrection as the axis of Christology thereby reveals itself as the axis of Christian theology in general. When we contemplate on how the being of Christ for us is founded in a divine reality, the Trinitarian way of reasoning presents itself as the conclusion to this story (cf. p. 159). And in Dalferth, it is obvious that the precondition of his work is the result of the Trinitarian discussion and its final formulation. Without this, he would not be able to lay out how the relation and the different schemas of understanding Christ from the point of view of resurrection can be explicated. I point to this here, as this is an indication that the Trinitarian language — which is not the theme of the present book — nevertheless might be founded in and contribute to having new experiences related to Jesus from Nazareth. Trinitarian language is not to be rendered obsolete, but can open up to a concrete and contemporary understanding of the reality that is revealed in Jesus Christ. The argument for how this is the case must, however, be carried out in another context than that of the present book.

Conclusion:
Resurrection as the Symbol
for a Reopened Future

We are unable to explicate fully what "resurrection" is, but we have indicated that it is a *saturated phenomenon,* or a *phenomenon of surplus,* as other phenomena we have dealt with in this book: forgiveness, hospitality, gift, recognition, openness, joy, health, community and belonging, the externality of desire and the hope for justice. Moreover, resurrection is a symbol for a future that contains a surplus compared to the conditions of the present world. That this surplus is linked to the good of this world, as manifested in the life and death of Jesus, provides us with a hope for goodness and justice. It supplies us with a point of orientation that allows humans to recognize themselves as loved and not lost to the powers of this world.

From a Christological point of view (that is still linked to our experience), we can have an established hope, which helps us recognize how history goes on in a way that is not determined by death, but by the God of life, who sent God's Son for us. God is a gifting God, and as the infinite source of all gifts, God becomes apparent (revealed) in and by God's gifts.[1]

---

1. Robyn Horner, *Rethinking God as Gift: Marion, Derrida, and the Limits of Phenomenology,* Perspectives in Continental Philosophy, No. 19 (New York: Fordham University Press, 2001), underscores the web I have constructed here between God, gift, self, other, and desire, when she says that "It is my argument that the question of God and the question of the gift come from the same aporetic space, that it is not only possible to think God as gift, but highly appropriate to do so. I maintain this on the basis of an approach to the gift by way of and beyond phenomenology [. . .]. It seems to me that the Christian belief that God gives Godself in relationship with persons, freely and generously, must be characterized by the same condition of impossibility. If God gives Godself without condition, then we will not be

This God is life and sustains life, and confronts death as that which means destruction of the life and the goodness of God's creation. In this sense, the mission of Jesus is also a mission that is in consonance with God's love for creation. However, as indicated, the resurrection implies a surplus compared to that of creation, as death is no more. Jesus — as the first who bears a true, ultimate, and unsurpassable witness to God as life and community — is the first to take part in the community of the new creation and thus to realize it. The point of confessing the resurrection is not to look backwards to the events surrounding his death, but to recognize him as the one who is living — and who is manifesting the future of all creation. Resurrection implies a future in which God's life, justice, and goodness rule. In the future of God, there is no competing economy that leads to exclusion and injustice.[2] Resurrection to life is gift. Everything is gift.

---

able to identify that gift as such: it will never be present. The relationship must rest on a freedom that risks the possibility of misunderstanding or rejection, or else it will not be a relationship of love but one opening onto coercion. Further, the gift will never be returned, not only because there could never be sufficient return, but because there will be no return address. Any God-gift will disseminate in desire, as Levinas (in conversation with Derrida) might say, not for God but for the undesirable par excellence, my neighbor. Not every gift (is) God, but it seems that God is only to be thought starting from the gift, which places us in agreement with Marion in orientation [. . .]" (pp. 246-47).

2. One implication of this book is that salvation has a social dimension, and that present-day capitalism, which is organized around merit, possession, and exchange, lacks the ability to recognize this dimension. As long as this is the case, Christian faith will be at odds with the political and economic system expressed in totalitarian economics. This is not to say that Christianity favors a specific economic system, but it nevertheless has a vision about the reality of human life in the presence of God that will make it critical of any exclusion of the other from the gifts of God. If one reads this book without getting that message, I have failed in saying what I wanted to say. If the message gets through, it is not mine, but the message of the Other who appears as the third in the triangle where we are present before God.

Bibliography

Albertson, David. "On 'The Gift' in Tanner's Theology: A Patristic Parable," *Modern Theology* 21, no. 1 (2005): 107-18.

Anselm, Jasper Hopkins, and Herbert Richardson. *Why God Became Man: Cur Deus Homo.* Queenston, ON, Canada: E. Mellen Press, 1985.

Augustine, and R. P. H. Green. *Augustine: De Doctrina Christiana,* Oxford Early Christian Texts. Oxford and New York: Clarendon Press, 1995.

Bader, Günter. *Symbolik des Todes Jesu, Hermeneutische Untersuchungen zur Theologie, 25.* Tübingen: Mohr Siebeck, 1988.

Bernasconi, Robert. "To Which Question Is 'Substitution' the Answer?" In *The Cambridge Companion to Levinas,* edited by Simon Critchley and Robert Bernasconi, pp. 234-51. Cambridge: Cambridge University Press, 2002.

Best, Thomas F., Martin Robra, and World Council of Churches. *Ecclesiology and Ethics: Ecumenical Engagement, Moral Formation and the Nature of the Church.* Geneva: WCC Publications, 1997.

Billings, J. Todd. "John Milbank's Theology of the 'Gift' and Calvin's Theology of Grace: A Critical Comparison," *Modern Theology* 21, no. 1 (2005): 87-105.

Bockmuehl, Markus N. A. *The Cambridge Companion to Jesus,* Cambridge Companions to Religion. Cambridge and New York: Cambridge University Press, 2001.

Borg, Marcus J. *Jesus: Uncovering the Life, Teachings, and Relevance of a Religious Revolutionary,* 1st ed. San Francisco: HarperSanFrancisco, 2006.

Brown, Raymond Edward. *The Death of the Messiah: From Gethsemane to the Grave: A Commentary on the Passion Narratives in the Four Gospels,* 1st ed. The Anchor Bible Reference Library. New York: Doubleday, 1994.

Brümmer, Vincent. *Atonement, Christology and the Trinity: Making Sense of Christian Doctrine.* Aldershot, UK, and Burlington, VT: Ashgate, 2005.

Capps, Donald. *Jesus: A Psychological Biography.* St. Louis: Chalice Press, 2000.

Caputo, John D. *On Religion: Thinking in Action.* London and New York: Routledge, 2001.

————. *The Prayers and Tears of Jacques Derrida: Religion Without Religion,* Indiana Series in the Philosophy of Religion. Bloomington: Indiana University Press, 1997.

————. *The Weakness of God: A Theology of the Event,* Indiana Series in the Philosophy of Religion. Bloomington: Indiana University Press, 2006.

Caputo, John D., and Michael J. Scanlon. *God, the Gift, and Postmodernism,* Indiana Series in the Philosophy of Religion. Bloomington: Indiana University Press, 1999.

Caputo, John D., Mark Dooley, and Michael J. Scanlon, eds. *Questioning God,* Indiana Series in the Philosophy of Religion. Bloomington: Indiana University Press, 2001.

Coakley, Sarah. "'Not with the Eye Only': The Resurrection, Epistemology and Gender," *Reflections* 5 (2002): 24-57.

Craig, William Lane, Gerd Lüdemann, Paul Copan, and Ronald K. Tacelli. *Jesus' Resurrection: Fact or Figment? A Debate Between William Lane Craig & Gerd Lüdemann.* Downers Grove, IL: InterVarsity Press, 2000.

D'Costa, Gavin. *Resurrection Reconsidered.* Oxford, UK, and Rockport, MA: Oneworld Publications, 1996.

Dalferth, Ingolf U. *Der Auferweckte Gekreuzigte: Zur Grammatik der Christologie.* Tübingen: Mohr Siebeck, 1994.

————. *Die Wirklichkeit des Möglichen: Hermeneutische Religionsphilosophie.* Tübingen: Mohr Siebeck, 2003.

————. "Umsonst. Vom Schenken, Geben und Bekommen," *Studia Theologica* 60, no. 2 (2005).

Derrida, Jacques. *The Gift of Death, Religion and Postmodernism.* Chicago: University of Chicago Press, 1995.

————. *Given Time: 1. Counterfeit Money.* Chicago: University of Chicago Press, 1992.

Derrida, Jacques, and Gil Anidjar. *Acts of Religion.* New York: Routledge, 2002.

Deuser, Hermann. "Inkarnation und Repräsentation," *Theologische Literaturzeitung* 124, no. 4 (1999): 356-70.

Ebeling, Hans, ed. *Subjektivität und Selbsterhaltung. Beiträge zur Diagnose der Moderne.* Frankfurt: Suhrkamp, 1976.

Eckstein, Hans-Joachim. "Bodily Resurrection in Luke." In *Resurrection: Theological and Scientific Assessments,* edited by Robert John Russell, Ted Peters, and Michael Welker, pp. 115-23. Grand Rapids: Eerdmans, 2002.

Gestrich, Christof. *Christentum und Stellvertretung: Religionsphilosophische Untersuchungen zum Heilsverständnis und zur Grundlegung der Theologie.* Tübingen: Mohr Siebeck, 2001.

——. *The Return of Splendor in the World: The Christian Doctrine of Sin and Forgiveness.* Grand Rapids: Eerdmans, 1997.

Girard, René. *Violence and the Sacred.* London and New York: Continuum, 2005.

Girard, René, Jean-Michel Oughourlian, and Guy Lefort. *Things Hidden Since the Foundation of the World.* London: Athlone Press, 1987.

Girard, René, and James G. Williams. *The Girard Reader.* New York: Crossroad, 1996.

Goulder, M. D. *Incarnation and Myth: The Debate Continued.* Grand Rapids: Eerdmans, 1979.

Greene, Colin J. D. *Christology in Cultural Perspective: Marking Out the Horizons.* Grand Rapids: Eerdmans, 2004.

Gregersen, Niels Henrik, and Jens Holger Schjørring. *Fragmenter af et Spejl: Bidrag til Dogmatikken,* 1. opl. ed. Frederiksberg, Denmark: Forlaget Anis, 1992.

Grenholm, Cristina. *Moderskap och Kärlek: Schabloner och Tankeutrymme i Feministteologisk Livsåskådningsreflektion: Cristina Grenholm.* Stockholm: Nya Doxa, 2005.

Habermas, Gary R. *The Resurrection of Jesus.* Lanham, MD: University Press of America, 1984.

——. *The Risen Jesus & Future Hope.* Lanham, MD: Rowman & Littlefield, 2003.

Habermas, Gary R., Antony Flew, and John Ankerberg. *Resurrected?: An Atheist and Theist Dialogue.* Lanham, MD: Rowman & Littlefield, 2005.

Habermas, Gary R., Antony Flew, and Terry L. Miethe. *Did Jesus Rise from the Dead?: The Resurrection Debate,* 1st ed. San Francisco: Harper & Row, 1987.

Hauerwas, Stanley. *A Community of Character: Toward a Constructive Christian Social Ethic.* Notre Dame: University of Notre Dame Press, 1981.

Hegel, Georg Wilhelm Friedrich Hegel. *Phänomenologie des Geistes.* Leipzig: Felix Meiner, 1921. ET: *Phenomenology of Spirit,* translated by Arnold V. Miller and J. N. Findlay. Oxford: Clarendon Press, 1977.

Heim, S. Mark. *Saved from Sacrifice: A Theology of the Cross.* Grand Rapids: Eerdmans, 2006.

Hemming, Laurence Paul. *Heidegger's Atheism: The Refusal of a Theological Voice.* Notre Dame: University of Notre Dame Press, 2002.

Henriksen, Jan-Olav. "The Crucifixion as Realisation of Identity: The Gift of Recognition and Representation," *Modern Theology* 22, no. 2 (2006): 197-220.

——. *Grobunn for Moral: Om Å Være Moralsk Subjekt i en Postmoderne Kultur.* Kristiansand: Høyskoleforlaget, 1997.

——. "Guds Rike og Etikken — Uten Sammenheng? Linjer til en Systematisk-Teologisk Rekonstruksjon," *Tidsskrift for Teologi og Kirke* 69, no. 1 (1998): 47-63.

——. *Imago Dei: Den Teologiske Konstruksjonen av Menneskets Identitet.* Oslo: Gyldendal, 2003.

Henriksen, Jan-Olav, ed. *Friedrich Nietzsche. Filosofi og Samfunn.* Kristiansand: Høyskoleforlaget, 1999.

Hick, John. *The Metaphor of God Incarnate,* 2nd ed. London: SCM Press, 2005.

Honneth, Axel. *The Struggle for Recognition: The Moral Grammar of Social Conflicts.* Cambridge: Polity Press, 1995.

Horner, Robyn. *Jean-Luc Marion: A Theo-Logical Introduction.* Burlington, VT: Ashgate, 2005.

————. *Rethinking God as Gift: Marion, Derrida, and the Limits of Phenomenology,* 1st ed., Perspectives in Continental Philosophy, No. 19. New York: Fordham University Press, 2001.

Janowski, Bernd, and Michael Welker, eds. *Opfer: Theologische und Kulturelle Kontexte.* Frankfurt: Suhrkamp, 2000.

Jeanrond, Werner. "På Väg Mot en Kristologi i Dag." In *Jesustolkningar i Dag. Tio Teologer om Kristologi,* pp. 235-62. Stockholm: Verbum, 1995.

Jensen, David Hadley. *In the Company of Others: A Dialogical Christology.* Cleveland: Pilgrim Press, 2001.

Jones, James William. *Religion and Psychology in Transition: Psychoanalysis, Feminism, and Theology.* New Haven: Yale University Press, 1996.

Jüngel, Eberhard. *Death, the Riddle and the Mystery.* Philadelphia: Westminster Press, 1975.

————. *The Doctrine of the Trinity: God's Being Is in Becoming.* Grand Rapids: Eerdmans, 1976.

Kaposy, Chris. "'Analytic' Reading, 'Continental' Text: The Case of Derrida's 'on Forgiveness,'" *International Journal of Philosophical Studies* 13, no. 2 (2005): 203-26.

Kazen, Thomas. *Jesus and Purity Halakhah: Was Jesus Indifferent to Impurity?,* Coniectanea Biblica. New Testament Series, 38. Stockholm: Almquist & Wiksell, 2002.

Kearney, Richard. "Desire for God." In *God, the Gift and Post-Modernism,* edited by John D. Caputo and Michael J. Scanlon. Bloomington: Indiana University Press 1999.

————. *The God Who May Be: A Hermeneutics of Religion,* Indiana Series in the Philosophy of Religion. Bloomington: Indiana University Press, 2001.

————. *On Paul Ricoeur: The Owl of Minerva, Transcending Boundaries in Theology and Philosophy.* Aldershot, UK: Ashgate, 2004.

Kierkegaard, Søren, Howard Vincent Hong, and Edna Hatlestad Hong. *Philosophical Fragments, Johannes Climacus.* Princeton: Princeton University Press, 1985.

Klein, Melanie. *Envy and Gratitude, and Other Works, 1946-1963,* Free Press ed. New York: Free Press, 1984.

Koch, Traugott. *Jesus von Nazareth, der Mensch Gottes.* Tübingen: Mohr Siebeck, 2004.

Kosky, Jeffrey L. *Levinas and the Philosophy of Religion,* Indiana Series in the Philosophy of Religion. Bloomington: Indiana University Press, 2001.

Kristeva, Julia. *Desire in Language: A Semiotic Approach to Literature and Art.* New York: Columbia University Press, 1980.

Kristeva, Julia, and Toril Moi. *The Kristeva Reader.* New York: Columbia University Press, 1986.

Kvalbein, H. "The Kingdom of God in the Ethics of Jesus," *Studia Theologica* 51 (1997).

Layman, Charles S. *The Shape of the Good: Christian Reflections on the Foundations of Ethics,* Library of Religious Philosophy, vol. 7. Notre Dame: University of Notre Dame Press, 1991.

Levinas, Emmanuel. *Totality and Infinity: An Essay on Exteriority.* Pittsburgh: Duquesne University Press, 1969.

Lowe, Walter. "Christ and Salvation." In *The Cambridge Companion to Postmodern Theology,* edited by Kevin J. Vanhoozer, pp. 235-51. Cambridge: Cambridge University Press, 2003.

Lüdemann, Gerd. *The Resurrection of Jesus: History, Experience, Theology,* 1st British ed. London: SCM Press, 1994.

MacIntyre, Alasdair. *Dependent Rational Animals: Why Human Beings Need the Virtues.* Chicago: Open Court, 1999.

Macquarrie, John. *Christology Revisited.* London: SCM Press, 1998.

———. *Jesus Christ in Modern Thought.* London and Philadelphia: SCM Press and Trinity Press International, 1990.

Marion, Jean-Luc. *God Without Being: Hors-Texte, Religion and Postmodernism.* Chicago: University of Chicago Press, 1991.

———. "'They Recognized Him; and He Became Invisible to Them,'" *Modern Theology* 18, no. 2 (2002): 145-52.

Markell, Patchen. *Bound by Recognition.* Princeton: Princeton University Press, 2003.

Mauss, Marcel. *The Gift: The Form and Reason for Exchange in Archaic Societies.* London: Routledge, 1990.

McFadyen, Alistair I. *The Call to Personhood: A Christian Theory of the Individual in Social Relationships.* Cambridge and New York: Cambridge University Press, 1990.

Metz, Johannes Baptist. *Faith in History and Society: Toward a Practical Fundamental Theology.* New York: Seabury Press, 1980.

Milbank, John. *Being Reconciled: Ontology and Pardon,* Radical Orthodoxy Series. London; New York: Routledge, 2003.

Moltmann, Jürgen. *The Crucified God: The Cross of Christ as the Foundation and Criticism of Christian Theology.* London: SCM, 1974.

———. *The Crucified God: The Cross of Christ as the Foundation and Criticism of Christian Theology,* 1st U.S. ed. New York: Harper & Row, 1974.

Moore, Sebastian. *Jesus the Liberator of Desire.* New York: Crossroad, 1989.

Nietzsche, Friedrich, Giorgio Colli, and Mazzino Montinari. *Sämtliche Werke: Kritische Studienausgabe.* Berlin and New York: De Gruyter, 1988.

Nolan, Albert. *Jesus Before Christianity.* Cape Town: David Philip, 1986.

Odell-Scott, David W. *A Post-Patriarchal Christology,* American Academy of Religion Academy Series, No. 78. Atlanta: Scholars Press, 1991.

Oliver, Kelly. *Witnessing: Beyond Recognition.* Minneapolis: University of Minnesota Press, 2001.

Pannenberg, Wolfhart. "Christologie und Theologie." In *Grundfragen Systematischer Theologie. Gesammelte Aufsätze.* Göttingen: Vandenhoeck & Ruprecht, 1980.

―――. *Ethik und Ekklesiologie: Gesammelte Aufsätze,* 1. Aufl. ed. Göttingen: Vandenhoeck & Ruprecht, 1977.

―――. *Grundfragen Systematischer Theologie,* vol. 2. Göttingen: Vandenhoeck & Ruprecht, 1980.

―――. *Grundlagen der Ethik: Philosophisch-Theologische Perspektiven.* Göttingen: Vandenhoeck & Ruprecht, 1996.

―――. *Jesus — God and Man,* new ed. SCM Classics. London: SCM, 2002.

―――. *Systematische Theologie,* 3 vols. Göttingen: Vandenhoeck & Ruprecht, 1988.

Peters, Ted. "Six Ways of Salvation: How Does Jesus Save?" *Dialog* 45, no. 3 (2006): 223-35.

Peters, Ted, Robert J. Russell, and Michael Welker. *Resurrection: Theological and Scientific Assessments.* Grand Rapids: Eerdmans, 2002.

Price, Robert M., and Jeffery Jay Lowder. *The Empty Tomb: Jesus Beyond the Grave.* Amherst, NY: Prometheus Books, 2005.

Rayment-Pickard, Hugh. *Impossible God: Derrida's Theology, Transcending Boundaries in Philosophy and Theology.* Aldershot, UK, and Burlington, VT: Ashgate, 2003.

Ricoeur, Paul. *The Course of Recognition.* Cambridge, MA: Harvard University Press, 2005.

―――. *Figuring the Sacred: Religion, Narrative, and Imagination.* Translated by David Pellauer. Minneapolis: Augsburg Fortress, 1995.

―――. *Oneself as Another.* Chicago: University of Chicago Press, 1992.

Saarinen, Risto. *God and the Gift: An Ecumenical Theology of Giving,* Unitas Books. Collegeville, MN: Liturgical Press, 2005.

Sandnes, Karl Olav. *A New Family: Conversion and Ecclesiology in the Early Church with Cross-Cultural Comparisons.* Bern and New York: P. Lang, 1994.

Schäfer, Rolf. "Glaube und Werke nach Luther," *Luther* 58 (1987).

Schillebeeckx, Edward. *Jesus: An Experiment in Christology.* New York: Seabury Press, 1979.

Schleiermacher, Friedrich, Hugh Ross Mackintosh, and James Stuart Stewart. *The Christian Faith*, 2 vols. New York: Harper & Row, 1963.

Schrijvers, Joeri. "Ontotheological Turnings? Marion, Lacoste and Levinas on the Decentring of Modern Subjectivity," *Modern Theology* 22 (2006).

Sherwood, Yvonne, and Kevin Hart. *Derrida and Religion: Other Testaments*. New York: Routledge, 2005.

Shults, F. LeRon. *Reforming the Doctrine of God*. Grand Rapids: Eerdmans, 2005.

Sigurdson, Ola. *Himmelska kropper* [Heavenly bodies]. Gothenburg: Glänta, 2006.

Smith, James K. A. "The Call as Gift: The Subject's Donation in Marion and Levinas." In *The Hermeneutics of Charity: Interpretation, Selfhood, and Postmodern Faith*, edited by James K. A. Smith and Henry Isaac Venema, pp. 217-27. Grand Rapids: Brazos Press, 2004.

Sölle, Dorothee. *Stellvertretung: Ein Kapitel Theologie Nach Dem "Tode Gottes."* Um ein Nachwort erw. Neuaufl. ed. Stuttgart: Kreuz, 1982.

Stålsett, Sturla J. *The Crucified and the Crucified: A Study in the Liberation Christology of Jon Sobrino*. Bern and New York: Peter Lang, 2003.

Svenungsson, Jayne. *Guds Återkomst: En Studie av Gudsbegreppet inom Postmodern Filosofi, Logos Pathos; Nr. 3*. Göteborg: Glänta produktion, 2004.

Tanner, Kathryn. *Economy of Grace*. Minneapolis: Fortress Press, 2005.

―――. "Incarnation, Cross and Sacrifice: A Feminist-Inspired Reappraisal," *Anglican Theological Review* 86, no. 1 (2004): 35-56.

―――. *Jesus, Humanity and the Trinity: A Brief Systematic Theology*, Scottish Journal of Theology. Current Issues in Theology. Edinburgh: T. & T. Clark, 2001.

Taylor, Mark C. *Erring: A Postmodern a/Theology*. Chicago: University of Chicago Press, 1984.

Tillich, Paul. *Systematic Theology*, vol. 1. London: SCM, 1978.

Van Huyssteen, J. Wentzel. *Alone in the World?: Human Uniqueness in Science and Theology*, The Gifford Lectures, 2004. Grand Rapids: Eerdmans, 2006.

Vanhoozer, Kevin J. "Theology and the Condition of Postmodernity." In *The Cambridge Companion to Postmodern Theology*, edited by Kevin J. Vanhoozer, pp. 3-25. Cambridge: Cambridge University Press, 2003.

Verhey, Allen. "Science at the End of Life: Contributions and Limitations," *Princeton Seminary Bulletin* (2007): 18.

Vetlesen, Arne Johan. *Evil and Human Agency: Understanding Collective Evildoing*, Cambridge Cultural Social Studies. Cambridge and New York: Cambridge University Press, 2005.

Vries, Hent de. *Philosophy and the Turn to Religion*. Baltimore: Johns Hopkins University Press, 1999.

Wainwright, Elaine. "The Gospel of Matthew." In *Searching the Scriptures: A Feminist Commentary*, edited by Elisabeth Schüssler Fiorenza. London: SCM Press, 1995.

Ward, Graham. *Christ and Culture: Challenges in Contemporary Theology.* Oxford: Blackwell Publishing, 2005.

Weaver, J. Denny. *The Nonviolent Atonement.* Grand Rapids: Eerdmans, 2001.

Webb, Stephen H. *The Gifting God: A Trinitarian Ethics of Excess.* New York: Oxford University Press, 1996.

Welker, Michael. "Wright on the Resurrection," *Scottish Journal of Theology* 60 (2007): 458-75.

Wenz, Gunther. "Die Zehn Gebote Als Grundlage Christlicher Ethik: Zur Auslegung Der Ersten Hauptstücks in Luthers Katechismen," *Zeitschrift für Theologie und Kirche* 89 (1992).

―――. *Geschichte der Versöhnungslehre in der Evangelischen Theologie der Neuzeit,* 2 vols., Münchener Monographien zur Historischen und Systematischen Theologie, bd. 9, 11. München: Chr. Kaiser Verlag, 1984.

Westphal, Merold. *Overcoming Onto-Theology: Toward a Postmodern Christian Faith,* 1st ed., Perspectives in Continental Philosophy, No. 21. New York: Fordham University Press, 2001.

Williams, Robert R. *Hegel's Ethics of Recognition.* Berkeley: University of California Press, 1997.

Williams, Rowan. *Christ on Trial: How the Gospel Unsettles Our Judgement.* Grand Rapids: Zondervan, 2002.

―――. *Lost Icons: Reflections on Cultural Bereavement.* Edinburgh: T. & T. Clark, 2000.

―――. *Resurrection: Interpreting the Easter Gospel,* new and rev. ed. Cleveland: Pilgrim Press, 2002.

World Council of Churches. Commission on Faith and Order. *Church and World: The Unity of the Church and the Renewal of Human Community: A Faith and Order Study Document, Faith and Order Paper,* No. 151. Geneva: WCC Publications, 1990.

Wright, N. T. *Jesus and the Victory of God: Christian Origins and the Question of God,* vol. 2. London: SPCK, 1996.

―――. *The Resurrection of the Son of God,* 1st North American ed., Christian Origins and the Question of God, vol. 3. Minneapolis: Fortress Press, 2003.

Wynne, Vincent W. "Abraham's Gift: A Psychoanalytic Christology," *JAAR* 73, no. 3 (2005): 759-80.

Zizek, Slavoj. *On Belief: Thinking in Action.* London and New York: Routledge, 2001.

Index of Names

Index of Subjects

Atonement, 269-77; economization of, 272; models of, 278-79; nonviolent, 275-77

Body: maternal, 81; resurrected, 359-60
Bystanders, 231, 236, 240, 248

Christ: as dead for us, 283-84; as Imago Dei, 95-98, 134, 206, 229; as incarnated, 26, 110, 329; as judge, 188-95; as positive sacrifice (in Tanner), 286-87; as victim, 285
Christus Victor, 281
Church, 161-73. *See also* Community of Jesus
Community of Jesus, 32, 45-46, 52-53, 76, 85-95, 147, 152-56, 158, 176, 195, 205, 230, 290
Cross as gift, 295-300

Death of Christ, 314-17; Girard on, 260-65; implications of, 320-27
Desire, 27-38 and *passim;* "closing" desire, 32, 304; envious desire, 240-48; eschatological desire, 29-32, 304; mimetic desire, 253-59; onto-theological desire, 304, 319

Evil, 248-52

Excess. *See* Surplus

Family, 76, 80, 85-88, 90, 191
Forgiveness, 149-54, 176

Generosity, 6, 9, 34, 49, 120, 140, 143, 145, 150, 178-80
Gift, 39-54, and *passim*
God: as basis for Jesus' identity, 85-88; as a God of community, 205, 224; as object of desire, 125-40; as point of orientation or starting point, 21-22, 90-91; as word, 15-22, 25-26, 114
God's relation to creation, 24

Identity, 73-95; crucifixion and, 295-327; and evil, 248-52
Identity issues, 11-42, 330-33
Imagination, lack of, 345
Imago Dei, 95-98, 106-9; as witness, 108, 122
Impossible/impossibility, 2, 29-31, 123; of gift, 47; of God, 109, 124; of resurrection, 337, 344-45
Incarnation and resurrection, 361-65

Kingdom of God. *See* Church; Community of God